P9-AGS-776

*f*P

SEASON OF THE WITCH

Enchantment, Terror, and Deliverance
in the City of Love

DAVID TALBOT

FREE PRESS

New York   London   Toronto   Sydney   New Delhi

Free Press
A Division of Simon & Schuster, Inc.
1230 Avenue of the Americas
New York, NY 10020

First Free Press hardcover edition May 2012

FREE PRESS and colophon are trademarks of Simon & Schuster, Inc.

For information about special discounts for bulk purchases, please contact Simon & Schuster Special Sales at 1-866-506-1949 or *business@simonandschuster.com*.

The Simon & Schuster Speakers Bureau can bring authors to your live event. For more information or to book an event, contact the Simon & Schuster Speakers Bureau at 1-866-248-3049 or visit our website at *www.simonspeakers.com*.

Manufactured in the United States of America

1   3   5   7   9   10   8   6   4   2

Library of Congress Cataloging-in-Publication Data

Talbot, David
Season of the witch : enchantment, terror, and deliverance in the city of love / David Talbot. — 1st Free Press hardcover ed.
p. cm.
1. San Francisco (Calif.)—Social conditions—20th century. 2. San Francisco (Calif.)—History—20th century. 3. San Francisco (Calif.)—Biography. 4. San Francisco (Calif.)—Social life and customs—20th century. 5. City and town life—California—San Francisco—History—20th century. 6. Culture conflict—California—San Francisco—History—20th century. 7. Social problems—California—San Francisco—History—20th century. 8. Social change—California—San Francisco—History—20th century. 9. Political culture—California—San Francisco—History—20th century. 10. Countercul-ture—California—San Francisco—History—20th century. I. Title.

HN80.S4T35 2012

306.09794'610904—dc23   2011032082

ISBN 978-1-4391-0821-5
ISBN 978-1-4391-2787-2 (ebook)

To Camille, who helped me finally and fully love San Francisco, while I was falling in love with her. And to the entire Peri family, the Italian-Irish-Greek clan that brought the city's history to life for me. And to my sons, Joseph and Nathaniel, who are making their own San Francisco history.

ACKNOWLEDGMENTS

Books are feats of enterprise as well as creativity. As always, I was mightily assisted in this endeavor by my work partner, Karen Croft, who brainstormed editorial strategies, managed the project's finances, arranged difficult interviews, helped me go spelunking through library caverns, read early drafts of the manuscript, and performed numerous other essential tasks.

Public libraries, like all institutions by and for the people in America these days, are endangered treasures. I relied enormously in my research on the dedicated and deeply informed staff of the San Francisco Public Library's History Center. Library archivist Susan Goldstein and her staff have a hidden empire of San Francisco history at their fingertips, and they bring it to life each day for numerous scholars and curious citizens. The serene and well-run History Center, on the sixth floor of the San Francisco Public Library's main branch, is the critical first stop for anyone trying to get a feel for this city's kaleidoscopic past.

The most vital way of touching this past, of course, is by speaking with the men and women who lived it. I am grateful to the more than 120 people who shared their stories with me, reliving the traumas and triumphs and the jaw-dropping wildness that was San Francisco.

For the chapters on Jim Jones and Jonestown, I am particularly indebted to Fielding McGehee III and the Jonestown Institute research project sponsored by the Department of Religious Studies at San Diego State University, as well as to the California Historical Society, the repository for the important and extensive files known as the Peoples Temple collection.

I was inspired throughout my toil by the energetic interest of my two sons, Joe and Nat, who kept wanting to know more, and more, about the unique city of their birth. Joe also helped with interview transcriptions, and with his usual pointed questions about his father's views and assumptions. I was also able to draw on the sharp editorial skills of my wife, Camille Peri, whose instincts are always true. My brother-in-law Don Peri—a collector of San Francisco memorabilia and also an eyewitness to some of the events chronicled here—was generous with his research materials and insights. And my brother Stephen Talbot and sister Margaret Talbot—fellow Talbot Players and sparkling siblings—were, as usual, sources of encouragement and wisdom.

Martha Levin and Dominick Anfuso of the Free Press have been the allies that every writer yearns for, but too seldom finds, in the book world. As the publishing industry goes through its convulsions, the Free Press has been a trustworthy partner for me on two books. I deeply appreciated working with talented editors Martin Beiser and Alessandra Bastagli, as well as publicity director Carisa Hays and her staff.

My fellow lover of ink and paper, Kelly Frankeny, brought her fine eye and hand to the book cover design, as she did on my previous book, *Brothers*.

Finally, my agent, Sloan Harris at International Creative Management, has always been a tough and astute defender of my forever-embattled realm.

CONTENTS

"It's the freedom of the city that keeps it alive."

—Geoffrey West, physicist

AUTHOR'S NOTE

I WAS BORN AND RAISED in Los Angeles, but even when I was growing up, I knew that I belonged in San Francisco. My father, Lyle Talbot, was a Hollywood actor, but he too loved San Francisco. In the early 1930s, while working for Warner Bros., he costarred with Bette Davis in *Fog over Frisco,* a snappy thriller about high-society types who fall into the violent grip of the underworld. The film brought my father on location to San Francisco, and he returned often to the city for business and pleasure. Years later, he regaled me and my brother and sisters with colorful stories about lavish parties at the Sheraton Palace Hotel; intimate soirees at a Nob Hill apartment where a female Chinese-American doctor raised money for the flying aces who were resisting Japan's invasion of China; and drinking escapades with Marion Davies, the fun-loving mistress of William Randolph Hearst. His tales conjured a city that was far more atmospheric and cosmopolitan than the sun-bleached Los Angeles suburb where I grew up.

During the 1960s, my father brought us to San Francisco when he performed in long runs at the Geary Theater, the city's grand old lady of pleasure. Setting out from the St. Francis Hotel in the middle of downtown, my siblings and I would trek the wind-whipped hills, wander through Chinatown and North Beach, and take the ferryboat to Sausalito. I knew—listening to some older, long-haired teenagers dressed like Moroccan tribesmen, as they played guitars and flutes in a Sausalito square—that I would make San Francisco my home one day. By then, San Francisco had come to stand for something far different than it had for my father; it was my generation's wild shore of freedom. The city held layers of allure for me that descended deeply through time.

By the time I moved to San Francisco in the 1970s, the city was at war with itself, beset by grisly crime and political violence. My city of peace and love and music, and my father's city of evening dress elegance, was being obliterated by a daily barrage of gruesome headlines. In the end, San Francisco not only survived this bloody turmoil, it emerged as a beacon of enlightenment and experimentation for the entire world.

As the years went by, San Francisco became not only my city but also my way of life. From the time I was a boy, I wanted to live in a place like my father's theater world, a magic box filled with lavishly made-up women, extravagant gay men, and other larger-than-life characters. I wanted a world that could encompass all worlds. I found something close to it in this soft-lit city in the ocean mists. I found myself here, got married here, raised my two sons here, started my own version of a theater company here—an eccentric web magazine called *Salon* that could have been born only in San Francisco, city of outcasts.

And now it's time to repay the debt. This is my love letter to San Francisco. But if it's a valentine, it's a bloody valentine, filled with the raw truth as well as the glory about the city that has been my home for more than three decades now. The story I'm about to tell is an epic one, filled with personalities and events. But in the end, this is what it is all about. It's the story of a city that changed itself, and then changed the world.

INTRODUCTION

S AN FRANCISCO WAS BUILT on a dare. The city was tossed up overnight on the shimmying, heaving, mischievous crust of the Pacific
rim. A gold rush city of fortune seekers, gamblers, desperadoes and the
flesh-peddling circus that caters to such men, San Francisco defied the
laws of nature. It was a wide-open town, its thighs splayed wantonly for
every vice damned in the Bible and more than a few that were left out.
San Francisco was the Last Chance Saloon for outcasts from every corner of the globe. If the earth didn't swallow them first, hell soon enough
would.

Great cities have usually been founded by wealthy burghers and
craftsmen—their spires and monuments a testament to the holiness of
the work ethic. But San Francisco high society was a devil's dinner party,
a rogue's crew of robber barons, saloon keepers, and shrewd harlots.
When the town's painted ladies went to the theater, gentlemen would
rise until they were seated. By 1866, there were thirty-one saloons for
every place of worship.

After the great earthquake struck in 1906, a wandering Pentecostal preacher who found himself among San Francisco's smoking ruins
inevitably declared the disaster God's vengeance on Sodom. In the emotional aftershocks of the catastrophe, the Holy Roller's hellfire preaching attracted a flock of dazed souls. But the size of his congregation was
dwarfed by the crowds that thronged the last theater left standing in the
city, where San Franciscans lustily cheered their beloved burlesques.

San Francisco's Barbary Coast district—with its black-stocking bars,
live sex shows, and opium dens—rose again from the earthquake's

ashes. And well into the new century—long before Las Vegas assured tourists that it knew how to keep their secrets—San Francisco aggressively marketed its libertine image. During the Prohibition era, the local board of supervisors passed legislation forbidding San Francisco police from enforcing the dry law. Drag queen shows were written up in the tourist guides alongside the ferryboat rides and Fisherman's Wharf dining spots.

By the 1930s, however, another San Francisco emerged: Catholic, working class, family oriented. The Church's influence could be felt throughout the town, particularly in city hall and the police department, where an old-boy's network of Irish Catholic—and later Italian Catholic—officials held sway.

Catholic San Francisco had its own wild heart: tough stevedores and cable car operators who fought bloody battles for labor rights; and immigrant kids who learned to love Puccini and Dante, and collected nickels for the Irish Volunteers back home. These working-class heroes eventually turned San Francisco into a pro-labor, arts-loving stronghold of the Democratic Party.

But as the Catholic hierarchy solidified its control of the city during and after World War II, it imposed a traditional social order on San Francisco, driving the city's Barbary outlaws underground. For years, the two San Franciscos waged a clandestine civil war. Gays and lesbians would be swept up in midnight police raids on bars. (Dykes had to wear at least one article of women's clothing—usually lacy panties—to avoid arrest.) Mixed-race couples were quietly blocked by real estate covenants from renting apartments in the city. Only occasionally did the city's culture war erupt onto the front pages of the metro newspapers—as it did in 1957 when poet Lawrence Ferlinghetti, owner of City Lights Books, was put on trial for publishing "Howl," Allen Ginsberg's declaration of war on the American Moloch, and the opening salvo in the 1960s' epic struggle for cultural freedom.

A decade later, San Francisco's culture war was in full fury, as the city absorbed a wave of runaway children—refugees from America's broken family—and transformed itself overnight into the capital of the 1960s counterculture. In the 1970s, San Francisco was overrun by another army of American runaways, as it became the Emerald City of gay liberation.

No other American city has undergone such an earth-shaking cultural shift in such a short span. Today San Francisco is seen as the "Left Coast City"—the wild, frontier outpost of the American Dream. Conservatives have declared war on "San Francisco values" and are bitterly fighting to stop the spread of those values. But long before the culture war went nationwide, San Francisco was torn apart by its own uncivil war. San Francisco values did not come into the world with flowers in their hair; they were born howling, in blood and strife. It took years of frantic and often violent conflict—including political assassinations, riots, bombings, kidnappings, serial race murders, antigay street mayhem, the biggest mass suicide in history, and a panic-inducing epidemic—before San Francisco finally made peace with itself and its new identity.

In the end, San Francisco healed itself by learning how to take care of its sick and dying. And it came together to celebrate itself with the help of an unlikely football dynasty and a team that mirrored the city's eccentric personality.

San Francisco's battles are no longer with itself but with the outside world, as it exports the European-style social ideas that drive Republican leaders and Fox News commentators into a frenzy: gay marriage, medical marijuana, universal health care, immigrant sanctuary, "living" minimum wage, bicycle-friendly streets, stricter environmental and consumer regulations. Conservatives see these San Francisco values as examples of social engineering gone mad. But in San Francisco, they're seen as the bedrock of a decent society, one that is based on a live-and-let-live tolerance, shared sense of humanity, and openness to change.

One of San Francisco's more flowery laureates anointed it "the cool gray city of love." But the people who cling to its hills and hollows and know its mercurial temperament—the sudden juggernaut of sea fog and wind that can shroud the sun and chill the soul—recognize San Francisco as a rougher beast. The people who radically changed San Francisco in the 1960s and 1970s—and thus, the world—have been ridiculed and trivialized for so long that we've forgotten who they really were. But it took a frontier breed of men and women to conquer a town like San Francisco—a town that was still more Dashiell Hammett than Oz. Ginsberg called them "seekers," which gives them their due. This is the story of their quest, and how they triumphed over the machinery of night.

SEASON OF THE WITCH

PROLOGUE

Wild Irish Rogues

San Francisco, June 1932

THE CITY WAS in a frenzy. Frank Egan—the once popular public defender, a man widely considered to be a future mayor—was on the run, accused of hiring two ex-cons to murder a fifty-nine-year-old widow named Jessie Hughes.

Before he disappeared, Egan emotionally insisted on his innocence. "Mrs. Hughes has been like a mother to me," he tearfully told reporters. But it did not look good for the public defender. He was the widow's executor, as well as the beneficiary of both her will and several insurance policies—and before her murder, she had been shrilly accusing him of looting her finances. When one of the ex-cons confessed his role in the brutal murder, naming the public defender as the mastermind, Egan decided to pull a vanishing act.

By the time he made himself scarce, Egan was San Francisco's most notorious criminal, even though he had yet to be formally charged with a crime. The newspapers were filled with grisly details about the widow's murder. The two ex-cons, one of whom bore a striking resemblance to George Raft and the other to Humphrey Bogart, had talked their way into the unfortunate Mrs. Hughes's Lakewood Drive home, knocked her out with several blows to the jaw, lugged her into her basement garage, put her under the wheel of a blue Lincoln sedan once owned by a gangster, and crushed the life out of her by running the heavy car back and forth over her body. Then they drove a couple blocks away and dumped the lifeless woman in the gutter, hoping she'd be mistaken for a hit-and-run victim.

The local papers also indicated that Mrs. Hughes was not Egan's only victim, that he had made a racket of bilking lonely and aging women out of their nest eggs. One of these sad victims—referred to as "a little hunchback" in the press—had fallen into Egan's clutches through the unsavory auspices of a female spiritualist, who recognized an easy mark when she saw one. Another victim was lured away from her loving husband by the George Raft look-alike accomplice, who was masquerading at the time as a debonair dancing instructor. While the woman's husband was away on business, the distraught man later recounted, his wife went "dance mad" and fell into a life of dissolution. She ended up in a gloomy Tenderloin flat, where she was kept in a permanent state of inebriation while Egan raided her savings and otherwise exploited her fallen condition. Finally, her husband charged, she was dispatched altogether with a poison powder by yet another sordid partner of Egan's—a thoroughly corrupt surgeon named Dr. Nathan S. Housman who made a living by patching up bullet-riddled hoodlums when not running criminal errands for Egan.

Hammett would have blushed to create villains as florid as Egan and his henchmen. Fortunately for Egan, he was represented by a lawyer who was well on his way to becoming a San Francisco legend: Vincent Hallinan, a brawling young Irishman with thick, wavy hair and the battered good looks of a prizefighter. Hallinan was a rising thirty-four-year-old defense attorney when he took the Egan case. He was also a confirmed bachelor and notorious ladies' man, having sloughed off his Jesuit schooling and, in his words, "the daffy theology of the Roman Catholic Church" and "embraced a pagan hedonism."

But young Vince Hallinan seemed to have finally met his match with his current romantic partner: a twenty-year-old, green-eyed, half-Irish, half-Genovese beauty named Vivian Moore. They were a true-life Nick and Nora—a young, stylish, dazzling couple who consorted with mugs and crooks and were always one step ahead of the cops.

If Hallinan drew a bad hand with Egan, those were the breaks of the game. He never bothered to ask Egan if he was guilty. A criminal lawyer can't concern himself "with the guilt or innocence of a client," he would say years later, looking back on the notorious case. "He can't. The whole thing is a racket. The prosecution puts on its case not for justice but for conviction, and you put on yours only to acquit. If you are unwilling to do all that is possible to obtain your client's acquittal, you are allowing a vicious system to grind him up, and you have no business on the defense side of the court. And you won't be there very long, either."

Later in his life, Hallinan would put his formidable courtroom skills at the service of labor leaders, Cold War dissidents, civil rights activists, and antiwar protesters. The legal victories that he and his colleagues won helped create a new San Francisco, and a new America. But there were few heroes in his life in those days. Hallinan learned his rough trade in the slimy trenches of the San Francisco courts—where the defendants were often morally depraved, and the cops and prosecutors were something worse.

Now Hallinan's biggest challenge was to bring Frank Egan safely to jail before he could commit suicide—an outcome that the newspapers were loudly suggesting the cops preferred so that the public defender couldn't make good on his threat to "blow the lid off the police department." What did Egan have on the notoriously crooked San Francisco Police Department? Hallinan didn't know. But he knew he had to find a way to safely convey Egan to the authorities—with a crowd of reporters to witness his surrender.

Each day that Egan remained at large, the city grew more frantic. The wanted man was last seen in a car with Hallinan and the lawyer's "more than attractive girlfriend," as the *San Francisco Chronicle* called Viv, while the trio drove away from Hallinan's summer cottage on Emerald Lake, south of the city. So now cops and sheriffs were combing the hills in San Mateo, and even dragging the lake. One wild rumor had Egan taking off from the lake in an amphibian plane to the open sea, where a speedboat whooshed him to a rum ship outside the twelve-mile limit.

How could the SFPD have let Egan slip through its fingers? The press smelled a rat. "What is the matter with the city's police department?" the *Chronicle* demanded to know in a front-page editorial.

"Here is a man indicted for one of the most appalling murders in the city's history . . . and the police did not even have their eye on him."

Mayor Angelo Rossi, who had ascended to his city hall suite courtesy of the all-powerful Irish political machine, knew he had to tread lightly with Police Chief William Quinn and his boys if he wanted to keep his job. But at long last, even Rossi's patience wore thin. While reporters listened outside his door, the mayor bellowed over the phone at Quinn that he wanted Egan in custody, and he wanted him now. Later, an agitated Rossi threatened to "clean house" at the police department if there was any more bungling.

With the flame turned high under his ass, the police chief knew he could no longer wait for Egan to turn up stiff—he had to go find him. And Quinn knew exactly where to look first: Vince Hallinan's various habitats. After secreting his client away in a safe place while he figured out a strategy, Hallinan drove to his house, where he was immediately greeted by four burly plainclothes cops. The top dog flashed his badge.

"We have orders to take you down to headquarters."

Hallinan was unfazed. He knew the dance. "Do you have a warrant?"

"No."

"Then you're not taking me anywhere."

The detective looked stymied. "Do you mind if we go in and call the chief on your phone?"

Hallinan normally got along with Quinn, who was an easygoing sort of man for a cop. But when Vince got on the phone with him, the chief sounded hysterical. "Listen, Hallinan, this town's in an uproar!" Quinn shouted. "You get Egan here right now, or I'm going to charge you with complicity in the murder of Jessie Hughes!"

Vince Hallinan was not the type who was easily intimidated. He grew up in a miserably poor family. Back in the old country, his father Patrick belonged to the Irish Invincibles, the terrorist fringe of the Irish Republican Brotherhood. After assassinating the agent of a rent-gouging landlord, Patrick was forced to flee to America—and to a lifetime of regrets and raw deals. Young Vince had been attracted to the law not only by the money but also as a way to fight bullies without using your fists—though he never forswore that more direct method of dealing with thugs, even if they wore three-piece suits. Hallinan took on poor Irish clients who were being evicted from their homes or had been maimed in streetcar accidents, whether or not a big payday seemed likely. And along the way, he stood up to brutal cops, corrupt court officials, ruthless corporate executives—even the powerful Catholic Church, which he always resented for robbing him and other Irish-Americans of their childhood with mysticism and fear.

So Quinn didn't scare him. Speaking firmly into the phone, Hallinan informed the chief that Frank Egan would appear only if he were indicted. Until then, if the police interfered with Hallinan in any way, he would sue them for false arrest. "You'd better simmer down and realize that you're an officer of the law, and stop letting your office be run by the newspapers," the young lawyer lectured the spluttering chief. Then he handed the phone back to the detective.

After a few minutes of "Yeahs" and "Uh-huhs," the detective hung up and turned to Hallinan.

"The chief says that you don't have to come down to headquarters . . . but we're going to stay right here with you, and we're not supposed to let you out of our sight until Egan comes in and surrenders."

"Make yourselves at home," Hallinan replied graciously. "I'll cook us up a pot of coffee."

Then Hallinan walked into the kitchen—and promptly went out the back door. He climbed over the fence into the alley, hurried to the home of a friend, and borrowed his car.

Hallinan was free, but he was in a jam. He wanted to arrange for Egan's well-publicized surrender—which he knew would not only be safer for his client but also look better in court. To do that, he needed to communicate with Egan. But with half the city's police force now looking for Hallinan, whose face had been splashed across the front pages for weeks, that wouldn't be easy. He had to find a messenger—and the first person who came to mind was his free-spirited girlfriend.

During their brief romance, Vivian Moore had already made a strong impression on Hallinan with her adventurous—some might call it reckless—exploits. The product of a broken marriage, and shuttled as a girl from one unpredictable home to another in her mother's sprawling family, Viv learned early on to take care of herself. One day she terrified Vince by plunging into the icy surf in Monterey Bay and swimming halfway to the Orient. "When she made it back to shore, I didn't know whether to slap her or kiss her."

Hallinan hated to bring his young lover into the Egan mess. But when he laid out the proposition to her, she immediately agreed to act as the go-between with his notorious client. "Of course, I was delighted," Viv recalled later. "Such excitement, and everything about the case all over the front pages!"

Soon after Vivian returned to her apartment on Fourteenth Avenue, however, the doorbell rang, and when she opened the door, two flatfoots barged inside.

"We're here to see Vincent Hallinan," growled one, a gruff old gray bear named Sergeant Mike Desmond.

"He isn't here," she shot back.

"Well, he will be," retorted Desmond. "You're his girl. He'll turn up."

Vivian sat down and began reading a book. She knew she had to think fast. Suddenly she stood up and walked across the room.

The bulky Desmond jumped up and got in her way.

She played the one card she had—the only one that would work on a tough Mick like Desmond. "I suppose that a person might be permitted to go to the bathroom," she said archly, looking the cop dead in the eye.

Desmond blushed as crimson as a cardinal's robe. "All right," he stammered, "but I'll have to stand right outside that bedroom door. I'm not supposed to let you out of my sight."

Shutting the bathroom door behind her, Vivian opened the window and shimmied through it feetfirst. Her apartment was on the second floor, and she needed to grope for the water pipe on the side of the building, but she finally grabbed on to it and slid down like a fireman to the landing below. After descending the stairs to the backyard, she took off her shoes, tipped over three large flowerpots, and stood on top of the rocky platform so that she could climb over the fence. Now she was on a sidewalk to the rear of her building, and the wild and sheltering canopy of Golden Gate Park beckoned to her, just blocks away. She sprinted for it, taking a secret path into its thick foliage that she had known from childhood.

Viv was supposed to rendezvous with Vince at the Great Highway, on the ocean end of the park, about two miles away. She had no money for a cab, so she took off on foot for her destination as the first cold gusts of afternoon began blowing in from the Pacific. Ten or fifteen minutes later, she heard the wails of police sirens, and she dropped to the ground and crawled inside the prickly shrubbery along the path, waiting there until they faded. Then she got up, brushed herself off, and headed west again.

By the time she reached Vince's car, parked near the beach, Viv was as flushed and wild eyed as an animal that had outrun a hunting party. Vince was flabbergasted. "I'm sorry I put you in this position," he told her.

She waved off his concern. "Listen," she said, still a little breathless, "I love it! Where's the message and where do I take it?"

After Viv delivered Vince's message to the strange, sallow-faced Egan at his hideout, the young couple lay low. They drove out to the country for the rest of the afternoon, and in the early evening they returned to the city and ducked inside a movie palace. The whole city was looking for them, but they were snuggled together in the theater's dark cocoon, watching a movie. At intermission, the orchestra leader turned around and cracked, "Is Frank Egan or Vincent Hallinan in the house?" The audience broke into laughter, and Vince and Viv laughed too.

It was around this time that Vincent Hallinan, bachelor for life, realized that he was going to spend the rest of his life with this woman. It had taken him awhile to arrive at this conclusion. But Viv had known all along that "the Mastodon," as she liked to call him, would finally be brought down. She knew from the moment she met him, with his blue, blue eyes and crooked smile, that this was the man who would fulfill her girlhood dream—the man who would be the father of her six children, all boys.

But before they could begin work on their brood, Vince and Viv had to navigate the mucky shoals of the Egan case. When they returned to their respective homes that night after the movies, their living rooms were occupied by armies of shotgun-wielding men in blue, who served each of them with a grand jury subpoena. When she showed up for her court appearance, Vivian, already a press sweetheart, was greeted with a fireworks of flashbulbs by the newshounds. Sweeping into the grand jury room in a jaunty flapper's cap, silky striped blouse, hip-hugging skirt, fur-lined jacket, and tight black leather gloves, Viv quickly seduced the dour-faced grand jurors. "Miss Moore told her version of [Egan's escape] fully to the jurors, who succumbed as one man to her charms and kept her in the grand jury room three-quarters of an hour—not that they thought she could give them any more information of value, but because she is such a delightful girl to talk to," the *Chronicle* reported the next day.

As for Vince, his "charms did not prove so effective," the newspaper dryly recounted, as one by one, the tough lawyer batted away the grand jury's questions and was quickly dismissed.

Soon after, the wild saga of Egan's flight finally came to an end, when Hallinan staged the public defender's surrender. Accompanied by a swarm of reporters, Egan strolled into the Golden Gate Park station and breezily greeted the cops behind the desk, a number of whom he had pounded the beat with back in his youth. "Good morning, boys."

"Good morning, Frank. How do you like our new jail?"

"I'd like to take a look at it," Egan replied—and he was given an extended opportunity to do just that.

The Egan trial enthralled San Francisco for several weeks more. Crowds jostled in the predawn damp and chill before the hall of justice opened to grab seats in the courtroom, where they marveled at Hallinan's unique blend of flowery and combative oratory. The details of the crime that emerged during the trial only darkened Egan's already villainous portrait. One of the ex-cons testified that all he got from Egan for carrying out his vile murder plan was a new hat; the public defender had threatened him with a return trip to San Quentin State Prison if he didn't comply. What sort of man offers a hat for a woman's life, the ex-con's teary mother asked? And all of San Francisco wondered the same. Only an attorney with the pugilistic artistry of Vincent Hallinan could have kept Egan from the gas chamber.

In the end, Frank Egan got life. By the time he slithered off to the penitentiary, Egan was such a reviled character that the press also turned its fury on his skillful young attorney for mounting such an aggressive defense. But the city's outrage soon found a new target: the SFPD. No sooner had Egan been convicted than a top police official confessed to the press that the cops knew in advance about Egan's murder plan but had done nothing to stop it. For months, the police department had been monitoring the phone calls between Egan and his accomplice, the nefarious Dr. Housman—which explained why the police seemed so certain of Egan's guilt from the very beginning.

Why didn't the cops rescue poor Jessie Hughes from a violent end? Their explanations seemed weak and slippery, and quickly raised new suspicions about the city's murky police bureaucracy. Was the brass somehow involved in Egan's criminal enterprise? Or were they sitting on evidence of his dark plots so they could blackmail him and secretly control the public defender's office?

The police bombshell confirmed what Hallinan knew all along: San Francisco justice was a contradiction in terms. The municipal corridors were awash in graft and vice. And the cops were some of the biggest offenders of all. The SFPD liked to boast that gangsters could never get a foothold in San Francisco, unlike mob-ridden cities such as New York, Chicago, and Philadelphia. "Good reason: the cops do their own 'protecting' in San Francisco and keep the payoffs in the family," Hallinan was quick to explain.

These unvarnished opinions didn't win Vince friends on the force. Nor did his combative courtroom style make him a beloved figure in the judges' chambers. If a defendant was to enjoy any rights at all in a judicial system as deeply putrid as San Francisco's, his lawyer had to be willing to wade in with both fists. But this style of rough justice had its costs.

Judges were in the habit of jailing Hallinan for disrespect. When one jurist asked the pugnacious lawyer if he meant to show contempt for his court, Vince replied, "No, Your Honor, I'm trying to conceal it."

Hallinan was particularly contemptuous of the judge who presided over the Egan trial, an aging courtroom despot with an obvious bias for the prosecution. The judge made sure that Hallinan would pay for his defiance.

Shortly after the Egan trial concluded, Vince finally embraced the inevitable and proposed to Viv. But as the young couple prepared to drive off on their honeymoon, a meaty paw suddenly reached into Hallinan's car and turned off the ignition. The paw, and the gruff voice, belonged to the old bear, Sergeant Desmond.

"Sorry, Vince, we have a warrant for your arrest, and we're taking you in."

"Listen, Mike," pleaded the bridegroom, "we're going on our honeymoon. Can't you hold it up for a week?"

"We held it up for a week already," growled Desmond. "We have positive orders to bring you up today."

"All right," Hallinan sighed. "Viv, this is Detective Sergeant Desmond."

The old bear looked at the young woman who some weeks earlier had slipped his grasp and bowed deeply. "I have had the pleasure."

Now Vivian Hallinan stood on the sidewalk in front of her mother's apartment as her freshly minted husband was hustled into a squad car. She was twenty years old and full of self-confidence. She had thrown herself into her new life with this "wild Irish rogue" with the same reckless abandon that she had plunged into the choppy surf of Monterey Bay. "Yet, as I stood there and watched the dark blue patrol car vanish down the street, a feeling of panic gripped me. Maybe I had bargained for more than I could handle."

In the years to come, all San Francisco would be seized by the same feeling, as the city leaped into the thrashing unknown.

DESPITE HIS PRINCIPLED OPPOSITION to married life, Vince turned out to be an enthusiastic father, energetically applying himself to the physical, intellectual, and moral development of his six children—all boys, just as Vivian had always dreamed. The most important piece of fatherly wisdom he imparted to his sons boiled down to, "Question everything in life."

"I'll always give you the best advice I can, but make up your own minds," the courtroom lion told his boys. "No matter how firmly I believe something, it might be one hundred percent false; everything I know may be wrong."

Hallinan further enforced this independent spirit in his offspring by teaching them all to box, swim, dive, ride horseback, and play a maniacal style of football and rugby at a tender age. Each boy was given a prizefighter's nickname—Butch, Kayo, Tuffy, Dynamite, Flash, Dangerous—in hopes that he would live up to their tough monikers.

It must have occurred on a frequent basis to Hallinan that he had created a monster, or rather six of them. Visitors to the Hallinan home were often shocked to hear the old lion roaring at the top of his lungs at one of his wild cubs. But the thunderous paternal blasts never seemed to faze their intended target, who would shrug, "All right, all right, don't blow your top."

Fortunately, Vivian turned out to be a resilient parent, weathering the crises of motherhood six times over—including a broken skull (Kayo) and a life-threatening case of polio (Butch). Somehow she also found time to teach herself the real estate game. Vivian proved to have the sharp business acumen associated with her Genovese ancestors. Her dazzling beauty didn't hurt, either. "She was just gorgeous. She would sit on the bankers' laps, and she would get the deals," her firstborn son, Patrick (Butch), would recall. By the time her growing brood was in knee pants, she had amassed a small empire of downtown apartment buildings, making the family rich in the process.

Despite the family's new prosperity, Vivian also became increasingly active in left-wing causes during the Cold War years, when they were least fashionable. And she dragged Vince along with her into the maelstrom of radical politics, away from his Democratic party-line comfort zone, where he had been content to throw his vote to "any Irishmen who were on the ballot." After the death of President Franklin Delano Roosevelt, the country seemed to take a sharp wrong turn toward empire expansion and militarism, and with six boys coming of age, Vivian wasn't about to let them die on some bleak, radioactive battleground.

It was the Harry Bridges trial that really turned Vince's head around. Bridges was an undereducated, beak-nosed Aussie immigrant who electrified San Francisco, and the entire West Coast, by organizing the city's deeply abused longshoremen. In 1934, when he shut down the San Francisco port—and along with it, the entire city—Bridges earned the undying hatred of the big business elite. One corporate conclave met in a boardroom to discuss hiring a hit man to get rid of the troublesome labor leader, but voted narrowly against it. Bridges's corporate enemies lobbied feverishly to have him deported as a radical subversive. In 1945 the Supreme Court ruled that Bridges was not a Communist and therefore should not be deported. But this only momentarily stymied the anti-Bridges conspirators. By 1949, Bridges was again on trial, facing federal perjury charges for denying he was a Communist—and Vince Hallinan was defending him.

Hallinan convinced Bridges that this time he had to take the offense. They would put the US government on trial for persecuting a genuine hero of American labor. Hallinan's aggressive strategy succeeded in exposing the parade of government witnesses as a scurrilous pack of conmen and liars. And he made the federal prosecutor—a fellow Irishman named F. Joseph "Jiggs" Donohue who struck him as the sort of slick traitor that his father, Patrick, would have assassinated back in the old country—a special target of his tart rhetoric. "He tells how he has been sent here as a special attorney for the United States government," Hallinan told the court, "and I submit, Your Honor, that I have not seen such inferior qualities better rewarded since Caligula made a consul of his horse and Charles II knighted a beefsteak."

But Hallinan misjudged the country's strange mood, and the clammy atmosphere of Cold War fear and obedience. The jury convicted Bridges—and the judge cited Hallinan for contempt and immediately dispatched him to the federal penitentiary on McNeil Island, in the cold waters of Puget Sound.

These were dark days for America, a scoundrel time when a man could be put on trial for his labor activism, or jailed for defending the wrong client. The Hallinan family—blessed with good fortune and everything America offered—was now banished to the shadows. Red paint was splashed on the gateposts at their Marin County estate, and a hammer and sickle scrawled on their driveway. The older boys, now teenagers, were jumped by thugs who screamed "Commie son of a bitch!" as they beat them.

A group of marines, just back from Korea, recognized sixteen-year-old Patrick Hallinan at a Marin drive-in and felt it was their patriotic duty to assault him savagely. Patrick fought back, but by the time they were through with him, several of his bones were broken, and the bone of his right arm flapped through his flesh. The Marin County district attorney apologetically told Vivian that he wouldn't be able to bring charges against Patrick's assailants. No jury in the county would rule in favor of a Hallinan, he explained.

When Vince returned home from McNeil Island, he made sure that his family's tormentors would think twice before going after his boys again. He renewed their boxing lessons, in earnest this time, bringing in professional boxers to hone his sons' martial arts technique in the family's basement gym. The Hallinans became accomplished fighters, especially second-born Terence (Kayo), who would emerge as a middleweight contender in the 1960 Olympic trials. Boxing also took young Terry Hallinan out of his sheltered Marin life and introduced him to San Francisco's rowdy nightlife. When not teaching him to bob and weave and jab, Terry's coach, Tommy Egan, a West Coast pro-circuit mug who had grown up on the tough streets of San Francisco's Potrero Hill, would take him to hooker bars in the Mission district and teach him to drink.

Vivian had qualms about teaching the boys how to solve their problems with their fists. It seemed a violation of the family's pro-peace principles. But Vince was adamant. "The chief trouble with liberals," he told her, "is that they hope to accomplish everything by talk."

The Hallinans' fearsome boxing regimen succeeded in deterring bullies, who soon found out that they themselves would end up bloodied on the ground if they challenged the brothers. If the world was against the Hallinans, now they had a way to fight back. Terry, in particular, became a tempest. His dad would be in and out of prison during the 1950s, and he was full of adolescent rage. With his growing physical prowess, Terry began striking out at the world, even when it wasn't necessary. By age seventeen, he was made a ward of Marin Juvenile Court after he ran three taunting coastguardsmen off the road and beat up all of them.

ONE NIGHT, THE VIOLENCE swirling around the Hallinans reached a new level of terror when three drunken men, including one of the marines who had beaten Patrick at the drive-in years earlier, broke into the Ross mansion and tried to rape Vivian. She was home alone—Vince was in New York, and the boys were out celebrating graduation night— when she heard the front door open. Thinking that Vince had come home early, she ran out of her bedroom, shouting, "Vin, Vin!" One of the men jumped out from the shadows and grabbed her, while the others tore off her nightgown. Vivian stood naked in front of them, her mind racing.

She had just been operated on for uterine cancer, and the incision was still red raw. Pointing to her wound, she said, "Look, boys, this scar here is from cancer, and cancer is contagious. You don't want to get cancer. You're young boys." To her amazement, they seemed to believe her.

The drunken men stood there, trying to gather their thoughts. "Why don't you go downstairs," she told them, "and help yourselves to some liquor?" They hesitated. Vivian was still stripped bare, and in middle age she was still a striking woman. But finally they left her bedroom.

She locked the door, dashed for the telephone, and began to call the police. But one of the men was listening at the door, and he kicked it open before the call went through.

Now the men were determined to go through with their plan. They tore the mattresses off Vivian's bed and lay them in the back of their pickup truck, and they dragged her downstairs. But Vivian kept talking to them. She kept it up for forty-five minutes. Finally, miraculously, they decided to leave her unmolested, though they would attack two other less fortunate women that night.

Patrick was camping in the Sierras when he heard on the TV news that the marine who had assaulted him was now a suspect in the attempted rape of his mother. "I got a .38, and I went to kill the bastard. I didn't even go home," he later recalled. But by the time Patrick got to Marin, the marine was in police custody. He eventually was sentenced to just one year in jail.

Outcasts and targets in their own community, the Hallinans refused to give in and withdraw from public life. Vince and Viv redoubled their political efforts, joining civil rights campaigns and enlisting in the Progressive Party, the anti–Cold War coalition started by Henry A. Wallace, FDR's onetime vice president. To the shock and horror of their neighbors in the smugly prosperous and Republican enclave of Ross, the Hallinans frequently threw house parties for their growing circle of subversive friends, including blacklisted Hollywood filmmakers, labor leaders, peace activists, and black leaders high on the FBI watch list such as Paul Robeson and W. E. B. DuBois. The Hallinans' Olympic-size swimming pool was often a churning froth of children of all races.

When Wallace gave in to the mounting Cold War hysteria and left the Progressive Party, Vince allowed himself to be drafted as the party's presidential candidate in 1952. The Progressives selected Charlotta Bass, an African-American newspaperwoman, as his running mate— the first time a black, let alone a woman, had run for vice president in America. Hallinan and Bass crisscrossed the country, calling for an end to the Korean War, denouncing the rise of McCarthyism as "the open face of fascism in American political life," and demanding a halt to racial injustice.

Hallinan turned out to be an effective campaigner, but the media largely blacked him out, halls canceled his speaking engagements, and apartheid laws in some parts of the country (including the nation's capital) even prevented the mixed-race ticket from dining together in the same restaurant. On election night, Hallinan and Bass scraped together only 140,000 votes.

If Hallinan couldn't get the media's attention, he certainly got the FBI's. J. Edgar Hoover, the bureau's Grand Inquisitor, put him on the list for "custodial detention" in the event of a national "emergency"— a Kafkaesque measure authorized by the controversial McCarran Act, also known as the Internal Security Act of 1950. Hoover's secret policemen tapped the Hallinans' phones, opened their mail, revoked their passports, and followed their comings and goings. The FBI couldn't determine which one—Vince or Viv—was more vile. Their union "was a case of one warped personality marrying another," concluded one report in the couple's security file.

The year after the presidential race, the government decided it couldn't wait for a national emergency. Hallinan was again sent to McNeil Island, this time on flimsy tax evasion charges. This latest blow nearly broke the family. While he was gone, the IRS brought them to the brink of financial ruin by putting a lien on their property and income. "We were all proud as punch that Vin was in jail for principle, but our strength was gone," remembered Patrick. "We needed a father. My brothers were going through puberty and learning to be men, and he was gone. The burden fell on my mother."

Prison didn't slow down Vince. He used his jail time to lead a movement to desegregate McNeil Island, in accordance with President Dwight Eisenhower's executive order. He sat with black prisoners in the dining room to make his point, and after desegregation allowed them to mingle, he pushed his black friends to sit with other white inmates.

WHEN VINCE FINALLY RETURNED home in 1956, the family's momentum was restored. He and Viv plunged back into political activities. By the end of the fifties, it seemed the Bay Area was mellowing toward their family.

The Hallinans were convinced a new day was arriving in May 1960, when the House Un-American Activities Committee came to San Francisco—and was quickly run out of town. HUAC was an aging but still pernicious tool of the Cold War inquisition. The congressional panel would show up in cities across the country, like a diabolical traveling circus, and subpoena suspected subversives. If a witness did not comply with the committee and betray friends and associates, his life could be ruined instantly. HUAC left behind a trail of job terminations, broken families and friendships, and even suicides. But not this time.

The committee, which came to San Francisco City Hall to turn the public school system upside down in search of disloyal teachers, was greeted by a flock of student protesters, still wearing the crew cuts and sport coats of the fifties, including Patrick and Terry Hallinan. While the Hallinans' parents looked on, the protesters noisily picketed the HUAC hearings. The young demonstrators were finally driven out of the building's Beaux Arts rotunda by police, who flushed them down a flight of marble steps with roaring fire hoses. Vince, now age sixty-two, couldn't help himself: when he saw cops fall upon a student with their clubs, he intervened and got manhandled himself.

The city hall melee was a turning point. Unable to create its normal atmosphere of cringing supplication, HUAC fled San Francisco and soon faded into history. "We said, 'No way, not this time.' And HUAC stopped," said Terry.

It was no longer just the Hallinans against the world—not in San Francisco. The demonstrations for a new society spread throughout the city during the early 1960s. And while the Hallinans were often leading or participating in them, hundreds of others now joined them. Civil rights protests broke out all along the city's exclusive Auto Row on Van Ness Boulevard, at the elegant Sheraton Palace Hotel, and at the more plebeian Mel's Diner, where blacks could never find jobs. Led by Vivian, the pack of Hallinan boys all began sitting in.

During one rowdy demonstration outside an auto showroom, SFPD chief Thomas J. Cahill—a ruddy-faced, blue-eyed peace officer who still had the brogue of his native County Kilkenny—watched in amazement as the elegantly dressed Marin matron was hauled away by his men. What was the world coming to? While Vivian was being loaded into the paddy wagon, Vince, struggling to maintain his reserve as the protesters' lawyer, rooted hoarsely on the sidelines for his wife. "Attagirl, Vivian!

If all the Irish stuck together like they used to, we could still run San Francisco!"

In fact, the Irish still did run San Francisco, but Cahill got the point. To militants like Vince Hallinan, he was a sellout.

By 1967, San Francisco's year of love, the old Irish Catholic order was holding on by its fingertips. Tom Cahill was in charge of the police department, Jack Shelley occupied the mayor's office, and Judge Raymond O'Connor was responsible for juvenile justice—a key position in the bulwark against the youthful army that was besieging San Francisco.

But because of the Hallinan family—and the growing number of activists and young lawyers who had been caught up in their brawling enterprise—the seeds had been sown in San Francisco. It all came back to the Hallinans.

PART ONE

ENCHANTMENT

Listen, my friends . . .

I

SATURDAY AFTERNOON

M ICHAEL STEPANIAN LOOKED up from the blood and muck of his rugby game at a dazzling vision in the sky. A parachutist came drifting slowly through the wisps of fog over Golden Gate Park, his billowing, paisley chute aglow in the afternoon's soft winter light. The skydiver landed in the midst of a sprawling festival that was being held at the opposite end of the Polo Field, and the crowd instantly swallowed him.

Stepanian was a tough young Armenian-American from New York who had recently graduated from Stanford Law School and was now working in Vincent Hallinan's legendary law office. On weekends, Stepanian played rugby for the Olympic Club, the same athletic organization where old man Hallinan played rugby and football and boxed, long after men his age were supposed to quit. All through the afternoon, as the Olympic Club rolled to lopsided 23–3 victory over visiting Oregon State University, the burly rugby players snarled at the long-locked festivalgoers whenever they trespassed on their side of the field. But Stepanian, intrigued by the waves of music and good cheer, strolled over to the festival after the game and wandered around in his battle-torn jersey and muddy cleats. "I looked like I was from a different planet, but nobody seemed to give a shit. The sun was shining, the kids were beautiful, the music was magic. That was the beginning of my education."

It was the Human Be-In, the January 14, 1967, celebration that was billed as a coming together of every tribe in the new, emerging America: from legendary beats, to Berkeley radicals, to the San Francisco love generation. "For ten years a new nation has grown inside the robot flesh of the old," proclaimed the event's starry-eyed press release. "The night of bruted fear of the American eagle-beast-body is over. Hang your fear at the door and join the future. If you do not believe, please wipe your eyes and see."

Years later, some would call this event the true—if belated—beginning of the sixties. More than twenty thousand people poured into the Polo Field that sun-dappled Saturday, on the wild west side of Golden Gate Park, where a swaying curtain of eucalyptus and Monterey pine trees shielded the tribal gathering from the raw ocean winds. Onstage, Allen Ginsberg—wearing white Indian pyjamas and garlands of beads and flowers—looked out over the vast human dynamo that he had helped ignite and turned to his friend, Lawrence Ferlinghetti: "What if we're wrong?"

It was a typical Ginsberg remark, and its whimsy and self-doubt reflected the better angels of the growing counterculture movement. The radical Berkeley component among the Be-In organizers, led by antiwar leader Jerry Rubin, was more certain about things. They sought to enlist the crowd in their political mission. But San Francisco's more ethereal ethos prevailed that day.

The leading icons of the emerging counterculture were all gathered onstage: Ginsberg, Ferlinghetti, and fellow poet-shaman Gary Snyder; psychedelic carnival barker Timothy Leary; the Grateful Dead, Jefferson Airplane, Janis Joplin and Big Brother and the Holding Company. But the more enlightened among them knew that the crowd itself was the center stage—no one was really listening to the speakers and singers.

The Jefferson Airplane's Paul Kantner—San Francisco homeboy, and a shrewd product of Bay Area Catholic schools—got it. "The difference between San Francisco and Berkeley was that Berkeley complained about a lot of things. Rather than complaining about things, we San Franciscans formed an alternative reality to live in. And for some reason, we got away with it. San Francisco became somewhere you did things rather than protesting about them. We knew we didn't have to speechify about what we should and shouldn't do. We just *did*."

The Airplane's "White Rabbit" and "Somebody to Love" would soon become part of the cultural revolution's soundtrack and make the band world-famous. But Kantner knew at heart they would always be a Haight-Ashbury house band, just like the Dead. He later memorialized the Be-In festival in song: "Saturday afternoon / Yellow clouds rising in the noon / Acid, incense, and balloons."

Young people sprawled on the grass, playing pennywhistles, harmonicas, guitars, and flutes. Naked toddlers chased their shadows in the sun. Only two mounted policemen patrolled the grounds; one came trotting through the crowd on his horse, cradling a small child in his arms. The loudspeaker announced, "A lost child has been delivered to the stage and is now being cared for by the Hell's Angels." It was a time when that made sense.

As the sun slipped into the Pacific, Ginsberg blew on a conch shell and beckoned everyone to turn to the west and watch the final sparks of daylight. Then he asked everyone to clean up the trash, so that they would leave the Polo Field—which he and Snyder had blessed at the beginning of the festival—just as they found it. Ginsberg, a cross between holy man and Jewish mother, was precisely the beneficent figure that the infant movement needed.

Rev. Edward "Larry" Beggs, a thirty-four-year-old Congregational youth minister who had come to the Be-In out of curiosity with his wife, Nina, was surprised to see the people all around him do as Ginsberg suggested. "Because I had seen how my fellow Americans could trash out even a sacred space like Yosemite National Park," he recalled, "I was amazed to see the people around me picking up not only their own discarded items but other people's paper cups, bottle caps, orange peels, and cigarette butts. The entire Polo Field, where thousands had sat and munched longer than a baseball double-header, was now restored to its pristine green."

The tousle-haired, bespectacled Beggs—who looked like one of John Kennedy's young Peace Corps volunteers—felt like Bob Dylan's Mr. Jones: he knew something was happening here, but didn't know what it was. Within a few months, the quiet lives of Ed and Nina Beggs would be turned upside down. Ed would be jailed for running a teenage shelter, the nation's first haven for the growing swarm of boys and girls who were fleeing homes seemingly everywhere in America. And Nina would find herself on the witness stand, testifying for the defense in the obscenity trial of Lenore Kandel, an erotic poet who roared around town on the back of a motorcycle driven by her lover, a ruggedly beautiful Hell's Angel known as Sweet William.

Kandel—a curvy, sloe-eyed, olive-skinned goddess who wore her hair in Pocahontas braids—set off a tempest when she published *The Love Book*. Her poetry collection was an orgasmic celebration of carnal love, filled with rising cocks, honeycomb cunts, and "thick sweet juices running wild." Kandel made a strong impression onstage at the Human Be-In, reading her passion poems from a clipboard and then tearing off each one as she finished, crumpling it in her fist, and tossing it into the crowd. But it wasn't until a few months later, when copies of *The Love Book* were confiscated at a Haight Street bookstore by San Francisco police, that she became another infamous counterculture name. Kandel's obscenity trial would become one of Catholic San Francisco's last stands against the onrushing cultural revolution.

On the witness stand, Nina Beggs made a strong impression for the defense. She was no dark-banged folksinger type; she was a pretty, blond, pageboy-coiffed clergyman's wife. But she too found salvation in Kandel's ecstatic poetry. Nina testified that she had devoured *The Love Book* in one gulp at the Psychedelic Shop, after dining with her husband at a nearby Haight-Ashbury restaurant. After finishing the poetry in the bookstore, she turned to her husband and urged him to read it. "This is the way it is for a woman," she told Ed. "This is what making love does for me." Then, speaking in a slow, clear voice, Nina shared her joy with the packed courtroom. "The oceanic" sexual feeling expressed in *The Love Book*, she said, is "one of the greatest proofs you have of your connection with God."

THE HUMAN BE-IN WAS the beginning of the story for thousands of people, many of whom would go on to take primary roles in San Francisco's revolution. In the crowd that day were Margo St. James, a big-hearted cocktail waitress and occasional hooker who would later found the prostitute rights movement; Stewart Brand, an army veteran and aspiring artist who jumped on Ken Kesey's bus and later launched the *Whole Earth Catalog* and linked the counterculture to the digital future;

Peter Coyote, cofounder of the Diggers, the "heavy hippie" anarchists who turned San Francisco into one big stage for their radical theater.

And there was Michael Stepanian, in his rugby battle gear. It was Stepanian who would defend dozens of Be-In celebrants when they were rounded up by police later that evening on Haight Street. He would go on to represent the Grateful Dead when their Haight-Ashbury house was raided by the drug squad, and cartoonist Robert Crumb when he was charged with obscenity. Like *The Love Book* trial, these legal battles would help widen the circle of light in San Francisco.

"When we started out, the city was antiblack, antigay, antiwoman. It was a very uptight Irish Catholic city," said Brian Rohan, Stepanian's legal sidekick and another brawling protégé of Vincent Hallinan. "We took on the cops, city hall, the Catholic Church. Vince Hallinan taught us never to be afraid of bullies."

By taking on the bullies, the new forces of freedom began to liberate San Francisco, neighborhood by neighborhood. They began with the Haight-Ashbury.

2

DEAD MEN DANCING

I N THE MID-1960S, San Francisco was still a city of tribal villages. The Castro district and the Noe Valley neighborhood were working-class Irish, though the Irish in the adjacent Mission district were giving way to Latino immigrants. The Fillmore section still clung to its reputation as the Harlem of the West, though the redevelopers' wrecking ball was reducing its former glory block by block. The Italians in North Beach lived in uneasy proximity to Chinatown. At one time, the Chinese could cross over Broadway—the boulevard that divided the two communities—only at their own peril.

The cultural revolution first came to North Beach, where cheap saloons and fleabag hotels and old Barbary Coast bohemianism beckoned the beats in the 1950s. Ferlinghetti was among the first. He was a World War II navy veteran and an aspiring poet and painter when he disembarked at the ferry building in 1951, wandering into North Beach with his sea bag slung over his shoulder. "It was a small city, nestled into the hills," he recalled. "All the buildings were white, there were no skyscrapers. It felt Mediterranean. It was beautiful."

A couple of years later, Ferlinghetti opened up City Lights Books with partner Peter Martin, son of the assassinated anarchist Carlo Tresca. Italian garbage truck drivers would roar up to the curb and run inside to buy the anarchist newspapers that the store got directly from Italy. It was a cramped one-room establishment in those days; they didn't even own the basement, which is where the Chinese New Year Parade's endless, red and gold dragon was tucked away the other 364 days of the year. But City Lights became a beacon to the poets, wanderers, and angel-headed hipsters who were making their way to San Francisco. You could browse forever, and nobody would bother you. It was here that Ferlinghetti first met Ginsberg, who entered the store one day trailed by his usual crowd of young men, looking more like a horn-rimmed Columbia University intellectual than the wild Whitman of Cold War America. Ginsberg would pound out "Howl" on his typewriter a few blocks away in his railroad apartment at 1010 Montgomery Street.

North Beach's Little Italy coexisted happily with the beat underground and the new folk and jazz clubs, topless bars, and gay caverns that began popping up in the neighborhood. But it was not North Beach where counterculture history would be made in the 1960s. It was across town in the Haight-Ashbury, a neighborhood of once ornate Victorian "painted ladies" that had seen better days. By the early sixties, the old Irish and Russian neighborhood had become so dilapidated that, like the Fillmore district, it was slated for demolition, to make room for a freeway extension along the Panhandle—the strip of greenery that led to Golden Gate Park. But the Haight was now populated by a feisty mix that included black home owners who had already been pushed out of one neighborhood, the Fillmore; artists and bohemians squeezed out of North Beach by tourists and rising rents; gays, who appreciated the neighborhood's live-and-let-live atmosphere; and San Francisco State College students, who desperately needed the cheap living quarters they found in the neighborhood's subdivided Victorian flats. San Francisco State was the launch pad for many of the young civil rights activists who headed to the Deep South each summer—including Terry Hallinan—and they came back to San Francisco a battle-hardened corps. The Haight's residents knew how to fight city hall. This time the redevelopment agency's bulldozers were stopped.

THE HAIGHT WAS NOW safe to become a haven for the young, broke, and visionary. Among them was a beautiful, dark-haired elementary school-teacher named Marilyn Harris, who moved into a Victorian flat on Ashbury Street in the summer of 1965. Two years earlier, Harris had walked out on her marriage to an Arizona lawyer and hopped on a Greyhound bus to San Francisco. She knew she belonged there ever since she and her husband had visited the city in 1960, taking in slashing comedy acts like Lenny Bruce, Mort Sahl, and Dick Gregory at the hungry i and other North Beach clubs and reveling in the city's breezy sense of freedom.

"Oh my God, this is where I'm supposed to live," Marilyn excitedly told her husband. Would he start over with her in San Francisco?

"Ah, no," he replied.

She arrived alone at the Greyhound station in downtown San Francisco, with $10 in her purse. She walked to a nearby motel and phoned her parents in New Jersey, asking them for enough money to start her new life, but they refused. So she walked into a Bank of America office. Based on her word that she was lining up a job as an elementary schoolteacher, the bank extended her a $400 loan. This is when the bank was still a local institution, and its corporate culture still held traces of its founder, Amadeo Pietro Giannini, who began the bank in a North Beach saloon and became known for extending loans to working people and not just high rollers.

The Haight was still just a scruffy, fog-bound neighborhood when Marilyn moved there, with Russian bakeries where you could buy piroshkis. But the fairy dust was already floating overhead. The year after she settled in the Haight, a young band called the Grateful Dead moved into a big Victorian across the street at 710 Ashbury. Janis Joplin rambled around the neighborhood in her scarves and boas, swigging from a bottle of Ripple with her bandmates, and Marilyn would bump into her at Peggy Caserta's clothes store on Haight. They all became friends. Nobody was a celebrity in those days. The neighborhood thought it owned the bands. Everyone took care of one another.

Marilyn was careful about whom she slept with, even in those less discriminating days. But at one point, she took up with a Hell's Angel, one of the Haight's irresistible bad boys, who gave her the clap. She didn't want to go to her ob-gyn, who had made her feel creepy the last time she saw him. So she went to the city VD clinic. It was 1967. Everyone was making love with everyone. And Marilyn knew at least thirty of the young people sitting in the waiting room's rows of pews. "Phil Lesh from the Dead was there. When I walked in, everyone just burst out laughing."

In the crush of patients, the city clinic was not taking the time to thoroughly sterilize needles, so Marilyn's blood sample that day was taken with a dirty needle. She came down with hepatitis C and became so sick that her doctor wanted to put her in the hospital. But she didn't want to go. Instead she went home, collapsed into bed, and phoned the Dead house and told Ron "Pigpen" McKernan, her closest friend in the band.

Pigpen might have looked like a greasy, badass biker, but he had a heart of gold. He tacked a signup sheet on Marilyn's front door, and various members of the band and its entourage would take turns bringing her meals and caring for her. Some nights Pigpen slept on her couch. She would wake up from a feverish nap, and there at the foot of her bed would be Pigpen or Lesh or Jerry Garcia, a couple of Hell's Angels, and the principal from her elementary school, all chatting amiably and watching over her like Auntie Em, Uncle Henry, and the farmhands hovering over Dorothy.

"The Dead were special," she later said. "They had a real devotion to friendship and care." She would soon have occasion to repay their generosity.

It took nearly three weeks for Marilyn to feel strong enough to get up from bed. One afternoon in October 1967, she was sitting in a wing chair in her third-floor bay window, soaking up the sun, when she saw a small army of grim-looking men sweep into the Dead house. The neighborhood knew the band as the sweetest of its minstrels, always plugging in and playing for free down on the Panhandle. But to the state and city drug agents who raided the band's Ashbury Street house that day, the thirteen-room Victorian was the center of a sinister narcotics ring. Boyish and spacey Bob Weir, who was meditating in the attic as the narcs invaded the house, and Pigpen were both dragged off to the hall of justice—though, as it happened, they were the nonsmokers in the band. As she saw the musicians and members of their extended family being escorted into unmarked police cars, Marilyn suddenly spotted Garcia and his girlfriend, Mountain Girl, ambling up the street carrying bags of groceries, unaware of the fate that awaited them. She leaned out her window and yelled to them, "I'm so glad you got my groceries. Come up *right now*!" Garcia and Mountain Girl immediately understood. They weren't arrested that day.

Michael Stepanian and Brian Rohan rushed to bail out Pigpen, Weir, and the others. By day, the two young lawyers worked in Vincent Hallinan's law office on Franklin Street. In the evenings, they toiled downstairs in the Dead house, doing free legal work for the Haight runaways, draft dodgers, and pot smokers who were constantly being snared in police dragnets. Stepanian and Rohan called their street practice the Haight-Ashbury Legal Organization (HALO), and it was kept afloat by benefit concerts, courtesy of the Dead and its friends. Now the band needed its own charity.

At the hall of justice, one of the narcs was dancing a victory jig. "I got 'em, I got 'em!" he taunted his prisoners, even though the task force had netted only a pound of marijuana and a little hashish.

After Stepanian sprang his clients, it was his turn to roar. Hallinan had taught his young colleagues to take the offensive, particularly in cases of police overkill, and the rugby bruiser now did exactly that. The Grateful Dead bust was a case of selective police enforcement, Stepanian told the press: "The Dead live in the Haight-Ashbury. If they lived on Russian Hill, they wouldn't be busted. If they lived on Pacific Heights, no officer would go near the house."

The next day, the band and its lawyers continued to take the offensive, holding a press conference to condemn marijuana laws as "seriously out of touch with reality," in the words of the Dead's press statement. To his young fans, Jerry Garcia, the band's spiritual leader, was Captain Trips. But he was no hippie dandelion. He was raised in the tough Outer Mission by his grandmother, a no-bullshit organizer for the local Laundry Workers Union. His free-spirited mother ran a bar near the Embarcadero, where young Jerry was regaled by hard-drinking sailors and longshoremen with tales of labor leader Harry Bridges and other working-class heroes. When city officials and cops growled about the long-haired outsiders who were turning the city upside down, Garcia thought they were talking out of their asses. His family had been here since the gold rush—Irish and Swedish and Spanish pioneers. San Francisco was as much his city as anyone else's. And Garcia, like the others in the Haight who were plugged into the city's electric current, knew that San Francisco was about to burst from its chrysalis.

———————

IN THE EARLY MONTHS of 1967, after the Human Be-In, the national media spread the message: San Francisco was the open-armed mecca of the new consciousness. And young people from all over the world were planning to arrive in time for the resplendent Summer of Love that year. It was the residents of the "little village of Haight-Ashbury," as Marilyn called it, who were the most concerned about the coming transformation. They were the ones who would bear its brunt, with swarms of homeless kids on the streets and only the city's angry, strained police force poised to handle them, or, perhaps, manhandle them. As the summer approached, the Haight dispatched a delegation—including neighborhood activists, head shop merchants, concerned clergymen, and physicians—to city hall to ask for help. Marilyn was among them. "I always got included in these things because I was respectable; I was a schoolteacher." The delegation was granted an audience with Mayor Shelley.

Another neighborhood group met with Police Chief Cahill. The chief, a big, thin-lipped man with a crown of closely cropped red curls, was known as a tough but fair cop. Cahill made a point of addressing school assemblies and youth groups. He wanted to feel in touch with the next generation. Now he listened patiently as two Haight store owners described how LSD had blown open their doors of perception. One of the merchants felt certain that Chief Cahill was "turning on" while they talked with him. That might not have been an accurate reading, but the top cop clearly did want to understand. "You're sort of the Love Generation, aren't you?" Cahill asked.

In the end, however, nothing came from the meetings with Shelley and Cahill. "All they did for the neighborhood was teargas us," Marilyn said. "You'd go down to shop on Haight Street, and suddenly some kids would go flying past you chased by cops, and you'd be choking on gas."

The old Irish Catholic brotherhood was not willing to cede control of its city. San Francisco was still a town of blue-collar family values, its public life ordered largely around the Church. People still identified themselves not by which college they attended but by their parochial schools: St. Ignatius High School, the breeding ground of the city's legal and political elites, or Sacred Heart, the funnel for the upwardly mobile children of the city's working class. As traditional San Francisco braced for the youth invasion, the city's guardians rushed to close its gates.

3

THE WALLED CITY

Mayor John Francis "Jack" Shelley was a true son of Irish San Francisco. Growing up in the Mission, Shelley would be shoved into a chair at the kitchen table by his father, Dennis—a longshoreman from County Cork—and told the way of the world. Nobody wanted to hire the Irish when he first came to America, Dennis told his son. To be Irish was to fight for every scrap, every ounce of dignity. "Jack," said the old man, in his thick brogue, "the day you forget where you came from, you won't belong where you are."

Shelley broke into politics through the labor movement, where he rose to become president of the San Francisco Labor Council and then the California State Federation of Labor. After serving a couple terms in the state legislature, he was elected to Congress in 1949, becoming friends with fellow Irishman Jack Kennedy. Shelley was not a skirt chaser, but he enjoyed his drink, and he loved the sea. The two young Democrats would go sailing on Shelley's thirty-eighty-foot Chris-Craft cruiser.

As he rose in politics, Shelley did not forget where he came from. He remembered his labor friends, and even during the height of the Cold War, he refused to join the rest of the San Francisco Labor Council in condemning Harry Bridges for his "subversive" beliefs. He was an early supporter of the civil rights movement, rising on the floor of Congress to denounce all discrimination based on race and religion, and linking the sufferings of black families to those of his Irish forebears.

Shelley loved Congress and life in Washington, even more after JFK moved into the White House in 1961. But Kennedy's election had unleashed new forces in San Francisco, and in 1963, Phil Burton, a rising Young Turk in the city's Democratic Party, maneuvered Shelley into vacating his congressional seat, which Burton coveted, and running for mayor. In November—shortly before the assassination of his good friend, the president—Shelley won the San Francisco mayoral election over conservative businessman Harold Dobbs.

Shelley was only fifty-eight when he took office. But with his sloped shoulders, receding white hair, horn-rim glasses, gray suits, and homburg, he seemed like a man from the past. He reacted with exasperated dudgeon when his first crisis exploded: a controversy over his decision to eliminate birth control funding from the city's public health budget. Planned Parenthood officials accused him of bending to pressure from his friends in the Catholic hierarchy, which Shelley heatedly denied. But, in truth, he ran all major issues by San Francisco archbishop Joseph McGucken—especially ones like this, on which the Church had strong doctrinal positions. Jack Shelley was typical of the old San Francisco breed. When it came to labor and civil rights, he was a man of progress. When it came to family and moral issues, he was a son of the Church.

The crises came fast and thick. The city was hit by a wave of social disruptions, including a strike by nurses at San Francisco General, the big public hospital, and a series of bawdy trials involving the owners of topless bars in North Beach. In September 1966 the city's simmering racial tensions erupted in Bayview–Hunters Point, the black ghetto that white San Franciscans saw only when they took backstreets to Giants baseball games at Candlestick Park. When a white cop shot and killed a black teenager, the city's first riot since World War II broke out, forcing Shelley to declare a state of emergency for six days.

Then things got weird. In March 1967 an unemployed circus clown was arrested for calling the FBI and threatening to kill the mayor. The police swept into Shelley's home, placing him and his family under around-the-clock surveillance. For Shelley, who had deeply felt the assassination in Dallas, it was history repeating itself as farce. He begged the press not to make a circus of the story. "It's creating havoc in my home, and it may give some other screwball ideas."

By the time the hippie revolution began shaking San Francisco, Shelley felt that he no longer recognized the city where he had grown up. A cartoon in the *Chronicle* showed a cranky Shelley telling a beaded and bell-bottomed young couple, "Stay off the grass—both kinds!" He kept coming down with colds and bronchial infections, and his drinking got more serious. Shelley was forced to defend his liquor habit in the press, insisting that he had cut out his "noontime belt." One friend explained to the *San Francisco Examiner* that the Shelley drinking stories only cropped up because "after three drinks his voice gets loud and he tends to slur his words"—which did little to reassure the public.

As the Summer of Love inexorably approached, like a Pacific tsunami, Shelley lacked the energy or imagination to figure out how San Francisco could absorb the enormous shock to its psyche and infrastructure. He was being talked about as a one-term mayor. The only reason that Shelley might hang on, speculated one newspaper article, was because the mayor—who supported a wife and two kids on his $38,000 salary—was "broke and he needs the job."

To solve the growing youth crisis, Shelley simply turned to his friend Tom Cahill and the San Francisco Police Department.

CAHILL WAS A FELLOW son of Eire who had emigrated to the United States on his own at the age of nineteen. The two men came of age together in San Francisco's blue-collar South of the Slot. While Shelley was leading the bakery drivers union, the broad-shouldered Cahill was hefting one-hundred-pound blocks of ice and representing the Ice Wagon Drivers' Union. After joining the San Francisco police force in 1942, Cahill made a name for himself as an expert on the Mafia, and after being loaned out as an investigator to Tennessee senator Estes Kefauver's organized crime committee, he quickly rose through the SFPD ranks. He became chief in 1958, and he prided himself on being a modern lawman with a grasp of crime's underlying social causes. But Cahill was the product of a strong Catholic upbringing in rural Ireland. "I grew up respecting the authority of my parents, and I had the wisdom of our parish priest, Father Carrigan, to guide me—and these teachings have stayed to this day," Cahill told an Irish journal early in his term as chief. And though he made an effort to understand the 1960s generation, the truth is he never could really fathom it.

Cahill bemoaned society's changing mores: "The swift kick in the buttocks by the old Irish policeman in the old days immediately becomes a violation of civil rights today." If cops were held in check, Cahill warned, juvenile problems would continue to increase. He urged fathers to use the rod on their children—and their wives.

Now, in the spring of 1967, Tom Cahill was facing the nightmare he had long predicted: an invasion of unruly children from all over the country, the progeny of America's failing family structure. And he made clear that he would greet them with the rod.

Alerted by the Diggers to the looming specter of homeless hordes on the San Francisco streets, some Protestant clergymen urged the city to allow camping in Golden Gate Park. But Chief Cahill would hear none of that. The laws would not be modified to accommodate youthful vagabonds, not on his watch. There would be no tents in any park after nightfall, and no playing of musical instruments. The radio was urging America's children to flock to San Francisco with garlands in their hair. But Cahill's message was blunt: Stay home or face "possible arrest and even injury."

"Law, order, and health regulations must prevail," the chief declared.

But the village of Haight-Ashbury knew that young people in Iowa, Texas, and Ohio were not listening to San Francisco police officials. They were listening to the music—and the music was telling them to fly "Translove Airways" and "Jefferson Airplane" nonstop, as Donovan sang, to San Francisco.

As the summer approached, it became increasingly clear to the people of the Haight that city hall would not help them. There would be no municipal resources for the new city about to be built on the old: no teenage shelters, food and clothing donations, health-care assistance, family mediation, or drug counseling. The Haight would have to do it all on its own.

4

THE FREE CITY

With San Francisco's city government abandoning its obligations, a haphazard collection of clergymen, philanthropists, and activists tried to fill the void. But none of these do-gooders did it with the flair and imagination of a troupe of political provocateurs known as the Diggers. Taking their name from a group of agrarian radicals in Oliver Cromwell's England who seized vacant land and tilled it for the poor, the Diggers created a variety of services for the army of young castaways that began pouring into the Haight, including food giveaways in the Panhandle, a network of crash pads, free clothing stores, street theater, and "ticketless" concerts in the park. But the Diggers were not simply a hippie Salvation Army, they were psychic inciters with much wilder ambitions. They wanted to liberate San Francisco's consciousness. Imagine a life, urged the Diggers, that was not bought and sold in eight-hour increments but was your own. Imagine a life where everything was free: food, music, love, but most important, you.

With the Diggers, it was not about the free food and clothes, it was about the *act* of giving away the free food and clothes. So they not only served their nutritious whole wheat bread and turkey stew to vagabonds in the park, they organized a "feed-in" at city hall, handing out picnic plates of spaghetti and meat sauce to municipal employees and even trying to serve Mayor Shelley in his office. The Diggers made sure the press got the point: their city hall action was meant to "affirm responsibility." They were simply doing what the city government should be. What do you want city hall to do? reporters asked the Diggers that day. "Eat," they replied. The menu for tomorrow would be fried rice.

Everything the Diggers did was a provocation. "You can't steal here," they told baffled shoplifters in their Free Store, "because everything is free. You can have the whole fucking store if you feel like it." The Diggers organized a bizarre procession in the Haight to celebrate the "death of money," with a group of masked mourners—made up to look like the animal gods in Egyptian funerary art—holding high a coffin stuffed with bills and coins. On another occasion, they set up an elegant dining table, including crystal glasses, linen, and champagne, on the side of a freeway during rush hour and invited the speeding commuters to take a break from their madly regimented lives and enjoy some downtime.

The Diggers did not see the Summer of Love as a catastrophe but as a welcome opportunity to free minds—not only those of San Franciscans but also of the estimated seventy-five thousand young Americans who were crowding into the Haight-Ashbury that season. "Our city has become the momentary focus of a worldwide spiritual awakening," read one Diggers street sheet. "The reasons for this do not matter. It is a gift from God which we may take, nourish and treasure . . . Recall that Saint Francis of Assisi is the patron saint of the city of San Francisco, and that therefore Saint Francis is the patron saint of the Summer of Love."

The Diggers' street manifestos were among the earliest and most passionate expressions of what would later be called San Francisco values. The leaflets' "free" ethos—which challenged the public to think of food, shelter, health care, and even entertainment as fundamental human rights, not commodities—began to shape the consciousness of the emerging new San Francisco. Decades later, echoes of the Diggers philosophy could still be heard in web mantras such as "Information wants to be free" and other slogans of the digital age.

The Diggers published a steady flow of such street communiqués, greeting San Francisco's young visitors with a barrage of news, advice, poetry, and philosophy on their street pole newsletters. Some of the Diggers street literature offered concrete legal counsel, such as the best way to be arrested if you fell into the hands of the police: "Don't resist . . . go limp . . . shout out your name while being dumped in the wagon so that bystanders can alert the bondsman." Some lit up the readers' day with flares of erotic poetry, like one by Haight homeboy Richard Brautigan, who became a counterculture literary sensation with his 1967 novel *Trout Fishing in America*. ("Pissing a few moments ago / I looked down at my penis affectionately / Knowing it has been inside / you twice today makes me / feel beautiful.") And some bemoaned the growing strains between white hippies and black residents of the Haight and Fillmore districts. "The spades, dear my brothers, are our spiritual fathers," explained a communiqué titled "Two-page Racial Rap." "They turned us on. They gave us jazz & grass & rock & roll, in the early beat days they provided a community for us, from the beginning they were our brothers deeper than blood, & now we & they don't like each other. If it weren't for the spades, we would all have short hair, neat suits, glazed eyes, steady jobs, and gastric ulcers, all be dying of unnamable frustration."

Diggers put everyone on notice. The hip merchants who were changing the face of Haight Street with their emporia of incense, beads, chimes, rolling papers, posters, LPs, and underground comics were "prettified monsters of moneylust"; radicals like Jerry Rubin and Abbie Hoffman (who took to calling himself a Digger) were "creep commies" on power trips; and counterculture gurus like Timothy Leary, who had lured America's children to San Francisco and then abandoned them to their own devices, were psychedelic charlatans.

"Have you been raped?" read one savage street sheet titled "Uncle Tim'$ Children." "Take acid and everything'll be groovy. Are you ill? Take acid and find inner health. Are you cold, sleeping in doorways at night? Take acid & discover your own inner warmth. Are you hungry? Take acid & transcend these mundane needs. You can't afford acid? Pardon me, I think I hear somebody calling me."

The Diggers attacked the commodification of hippie mantras like love and peace. "Love, by all means, but love People, not money." When a group of promoters calling themselves the Love Conspiracy Commune (who were rumored to be Mob connected) staged a "First Annual Love Circus" at the Winterland Ballroom, the old cavernous skating rink turned rock arena, the Diggers couldn't resist commenting on the absurdity of it all. The provocateurs greeted the show with picket signs reading, "Suckers buy what lovers get for free," and handed out broadsides declaring, "It's yours. You want to dance—dance in the street. You don't need to buy it back."

The Grateful Dead, the neighborhood's most beloved minstrels, were the headliners that night. And the band's manager—a red-diaper baby and University of California at Berkeley dropout named Danny Rifkin— took the irony even higher by getting into an argument with Digger Peter Coyote, spluttering at one point, "Money is sacred!" Which no doubt sounded as weird to Rifkin, son of a Communist printer, as it did to Coyote, son of a Wall Street stockbroker and later a well-known actor.

Reacting against the celebrity mania that was already infecting the counterculture, the Diggers tried to cloak themselves in anonymity. The media wanted photogenic spokesmen. But the Diggers led them in circles. When two eager magazine journalists showed up separately at the Free Store—one from *Time,* the other from *Life*—looking for the group's Mr. Big to interview, the Diggers convinced each reporter that the other one was the Diggers' mysterious leader.

"Beware of leaders, heroes, organizers: watch that stuff," the Diggers warned in one street sheet titled "Sheep? Baa." "Any man who wants to lead you is The Man. Think: why would anyone *want* to lead *me* . . . Fuck leaders."

BUT DESPITE THEIR ANARCHIC rejection of leaders and "structure freaks," the Diggers were, in fact, led by a cabal of handsome, charismatic rogues. They had met in the San Francisco Mime Troupe, the radical street theater group, and they knew how to command a stage. They called themselves "life actors." Emmett Grogan was a former Brooklyn Irish choirboy turned junkie and hustler. With his chiseled features, wavy red-brown hair, gold ear stud, and street swagger, he knew his effect on men and women alike, and he used it all the way. Peter Berg, the only one who actually had read all the anarchist and situationist literature underlying the Diggers philosophy, had a glowering intelligence that didn't let people off the hook. A transplanted "nigger-loving New York Jew" who had grown up in Florida, Berg liked to call himself a "heavy hippie." Now San Francisco was his stage, and revolution was his theater piece. And Peter Coyote, who had grown up Peter Cohon in New York, was a Grinnell College graduate with lanky, leading-man good looks and a rampant lust for women, adventure, and *the new*.

Both Peters were a little in love with Grogan. Everybody was. "Emmett was one of the most charismatic people I ever met—and I'm used to charismatic people," Berg said. "He really had it. He played dangerous, but he was a little bit sociopathic toward other people. He even stole stuff from me."

While the Diggers' men staged the spectacles that built the group's reputation, the Diggers' women did the grunt work that kept it all going. The women were the ones who woke up at five in the morning, got the old truck running, stole or charmed meat and vegetables from grocers, cooked up the hearty stews, lugged the steaming food out to the Panhandle in massive steel milk containers, and ladled it out to the hungry flocks.

Meanwhile, the Diggers' bad boys were becoming Haight-Ashbury stars. With their charisma and street cred, Grogan and his mates could amble easily from one scene to the next. They hung out with Hell's Angels and rock stars, the Black Panthers and Hollywood actors. Grogan and Coyote began spending time with Janis Joplin, in San Francisco and New York. They took her to clubs to see jazz and blues legends whom she had never heard. Coyote and Joplin became occasional bedmates in each other's passing parade of lovers, as well as dope partners. She liked Grogan and Coyote because to them she was just Janis, not a rock 'n' roll queen. "The money people, the managers, were pushing and pulling on her, and her psyche couldn't tolerate it," Coyote said. "Janis was not an icon. She was sad. She was confused and used and fucked over. She was an ugly girl with bad skin that came out of backwater Port Arthur with this gift, and she flayed herself to death in front of a crowd."

While hanging out with rock stars, the Diggers made fun of them. The rock star, they sneered, "is a man who can sing about the evils of the world while margining profits into war economies and maintaining his comfort on a consumer level of luxury." But the Diggers had their own growing contradictions, and they couldn't maintain them for long. In the summer of 1967—at the height of their fame, with people all over claiming to be Diggers—the group gave away its last worldly possession: its name. By the time the Summer of Love was over, the Diggers leaders had all drifted off to country communes, celebrity entourages, hard drugs, the Hell's Angels, or all the above.

"The Diggers were not very good at [running] institutions," Coyote said. The day-to-day assembly line of feeding and clothing people soon "got to be a drag. It's not like you were doing it because you felt sorry for poor people or something. It was a challenge: could you feed fifteen hundred people, or five hundred people?"

But as the Diggers dispersed, their "free" virus spread. Now San Francisco had free poetry readings, free concerts, free legal aid, free medical clinics, free shelters. And the city's next wave of "life actors" proved more adept at running institutions than the Diggers.

5

THE LOST CHILDREN
OF WINDY FEET

AFTER EDWARD BEGGS and his wife, Nina, experienced the "Bethlehem miracle" of a new world being born at the Human Be-In, the reverend began feeling like a prisoner of his own life. None of his daily routine measured up to the skyrocket splendor and purpose of that afternoon in the park. The youth minister enjoyed his rambling conversations with teenage worshippers at First Congregational Church in San Mateo. But the elders at his suburban church were growing concerned about the frank subject matter of those discussions, which included sex, drugs, and adolescents' rights. Even his habit of wearing corduroy coats and driving around in a red sports car began to annoy the church board. Beggs, in turn, felt the church was on "life support" and was increasingly irrelevant to young people.

Churches throughout the Bay Area were grappling with the upheavals of the sixties. Glide Memorial, a venerable Methodist church in San Francisco's seedy Tenderloin, had been taken over by a group of young clerical reformers who took down the cross and turned the church over to community free-for-alls like the Diggers' Invisible Circus, which featured billowing clouds of dope, a pulsating light show, belly dancers, and writhing naked bodies in the basement game room. Meanwhile, clerical San Francisco renegades like James Pike, the Episcopal bishop of California, compared the passion of Christ to the revolutionary struggles of the Vietcong and the martyrdom of Martin Luther King, denounced antihomosexuality laws, and challenged church orthodoxy so flagrantly that his fellow bishops charged him with heresy.

Pike was an electrifying figure to young clergymen like Beggs. He made religion seem urgently personal as well as political. And he turned his private agonies into public dramas. When his twenty-two-year-old son, James Jr.—distraught over his growing realization that he was gay— blew his head off with a rifle in a New York hotel room, Pike claimed he communicated with him during a séance that was televised in Toronto. Fellow church leaders expressed outrage, but Pike boldly defended himself. "If Christ was resurrected, then we are all resurrected. If Christ talked to his disciples after his death, then why can't we do the same?"

In this febrile environment, no minister with Edward Beggs's restless spirit could sit in suburban stupor for long. When Beggs heard that Glide Church was establishing a shelter for the growing teenage runaway population in San Francisco, he knew this was his pastoral calling. He left his life in the church and became the founding director of Huckleberry House. The name was Beggs's idea; his homage to American literature's most famous young runaway. Beggs saw Huck Finn as a "revolutionary" who hit the road with his black friend Jim rather than bow to the cultural values of the day, just like the young people pouring into San Francisco. When Huck decided, "All right, then, I'll *go* to hell," rather than condemn Jim to a life of slavery, Beggs believed it was one of the great moral epiphanies in the American odyssey. Had Huck and Jim been living in 1960s America, he surmised, they would have kept heading west, directly for the Haight-Ashbury.

Emmett Grogan thought Huckleberry House "was as lame as its name," calling it a "nice, mild, safe, responsible way for the church to become involved in 'hippiedom.'" The Diggers made an effort to take care of the boys and girls washing up on the shores of the Haight. "The city was telling all these kids—our age, a lot of them younger—to get lost," Coyote recalled. "And our feeling was that they were our kids. You know? This was America; these were our kids."

But the Diggers were never very good at housing children on the run. The communal havens in the Haight where the Diggers tried to stash runaways were nervous about sheltering the kids because they knew it increased their risk of being raided by the cops. Running away from home was a crime in 1967 if you were a teenager, and every agency— from Travelers Aid to the YMCA—and every individual, including family friends and schoolteachers, was legally obligated to turn over runaways to the police.

But Huckleberry House was something new. It was founded on the idea that runaways were family problems, not police problems. And if the kids refused to let Huckleberry House contact their parents, the shelter would not hand them over to the cops. They had the right to keep running. Grogan might sneer at Huckleberry's fresh-scrubbed piety, but in the end, Beggs and company had more guts and staying power than the Diggers. At the very first Huckleberry House meeting, Beggs and his staff discussed how to raise bail money in case they were dragged off to jail. They were right to be concerned. The police were constantly hovering around the Huckleberry House shelter, which was housed in a two-story brown Victorian at One Broderick Street, a few blocks from the tumult of Haight-Ashbury.

In the early 1960s, running away from home was depicted as a quaint American rite of passage. A 1964 article in the *New York Times Magazine* titled "Why They Run Away from Home" was illustrated with a picture of a boy toting an overstuffed bag peering longingly into the kitchen, as his mother—oblivious to his brief fling with freedom—cooks a delicious dinner. But by 1967, running away had become a more deeply disturbing cultural phenomenon. For one thing, girls were doing it, not just boys. And kids were not just hitting the road for a day or two and quickly returning home. They were running *somewhere*: into a mysterious new world that baffled and terrified their parents.

THE UNDERGROUND RAILROAD OFTEN led to San Francisco. And the local press was filled with stories of frantic mothers and fathers trying to track down their missing children on the streets of the city. In January, shortly before the Human Be-In, the *Chronicle* began running a series under the blaring headline "Runaway Girls: Life with the Hippies." The newspaper followed the trail of fifteen-year-old Diana Phipps, a "pretty, slender blonde" who had vanished from her suburban home into the shadowy "Beatnik society."

The desperation of America's families was fully displayed on the Huckleberry House bulletin board, which was papered with pleading letters and photos of missing teens. "Dad promises to ease up. You can trust Aunt Lou," read one. "Until there is some contact with my daughter, my life will be miserable," read another. Some seemed certain to drive the runaways even deeper into their new world: "Rick Hoyfeld—you have received your draft notice. You've been reclassified 1-A. Contact your mother."

Beggs would try to reunite runaways with their parents, offering to hold family counseling sessions at Huckleberry House. He wasn't interested in "demonizing" fathers and mothers, "because ultimately the kids were going to go back home." But first he had to grapple with parental rage—by the time they walked in the shelter's front door, the fathers in particular were often ready to blow. "I'd disarm the son of a bitch right there," Beggs recalled, "and I'd say to him, 'I'd like to compliment you on raising a son who has the courage to oppose you, because you're one intimidating person.' I'd tear the rug out from under his ass. And pretty soon the father is telling the kid his frustrations, and the kid is explaining why he wants to keep his hair long. And by the end of the session, the father might be saying, 'You know, our relationship is more important to me than your hair.'"

But the roots of family agony were sometimes so deep and twisted that Beggs had no chance of making it right. He heard it all: abusive fathers, alcoholic mothers, suicidal children; tendrils of incest and other worms of corruption that had thoroughly rotted the foundations of the family home. He wasn't going to send kids back to these nightmares against their will. And the boys and girls loved him and Huckleberry House for that.

There was something childlike about Beggs himself. He still looked boyish in his early thirties, and he spoke in teen-type bursts of wonder and feeling. If the runaway adolescents were struggling to find themselves in this new world, so was he.

Kids poured out their souls to Beggs in letters. They wrote to him from wrecked homes, juvenile halls, mental hospitals. Some of them had crashed at Huckleberry House, some of them longed to. Their hand-scrawled notes were a window into the bleeding heart of the American family in the 1960s.

In early September 1967, just before school started, a thirteen-year-old girl who called herself Deveron showed up at Huckleberry House. She was dressed all in black and was carrying a tiny black kitten and a battered five-string guitar. The counselor who took down her information noted that she was "obsessed with a desire to make it on her own": to enroll herself in school and get a job, a new ID, and an apartment. But at her age, there was no way she could be emancipated. She talked about a boy named Danny, but he never showed up. While walking the city, Deveron was picked up by the cops, who immediately took her to the old, city-run Youth Guidance Center on the slopes of Twin Peaks. She had no more tears left, but she cried for the kitten that the cops took away from her—she had named it after her sister.

Despite its name, the YGC didn't offer much in the way of guidance. It was a bleak, overcrowded warehouse for boys and girls who had fallen into the hands of the law, and there were more and more of them every day. Later, Deveron wrote the Huckleberry House staff to tell them what her life at YGC had been like.

"San Francisco juvenile hall cannot afford to be nice," she wrote. "It is two story's [sic] up. The rooms are steaming hot twenty-four hours a day. The windows are half an inch thick and through the tiny crack at the top you can maybe see a few lights at night outside of the barbed wire. There are no people there. Only animals. If it wasn't time to be let out they had to wet their floors. The only sounds are 'Be quiet!' 'Alright, girl—you're on tray!' and the sound of rattling trays and doors and keys."

One day, some girls stood on their cots, broke the windows of their cells, and squeezed out through the barbed wire. They were torn and bleeding, but for the moment they were free, running through the cool mists of Twin Peaks. Deveron looked out through the crack of her window at the bloodstained girls and began singing "The Star-Spangled Banner."

Now Deveron was back home. But she couldn't stop thinking about her days in San Francisco. "I worry about the children of Haight Street," she wrote Huckleberry House. "Haight Street is not dead, it never will be. But it will always be dying, so will its children. If someone doesn't help them to help themselves to live."

"You're helping them," she told Beggs and company. "You helped me . . . and mothers and fathers of lost children with windy feet. Just by being there and trying; if nothing more. Please never give up as long as children follow illusions and cities . . . And if Danny comes back, I love him."

Beggs was amazed by the heart and courage of these "lost children with windy feet." He knew what it took for them to leave everything behind and end up on his doorstep. Running away, he realized, was "an SOS—a flare in the dark"—for someone to step in and help resolve an agonizing family situation. The former minister was a godsend to the kids who found shelter at Huckleberry House. But to San Francisco's youth justice establishment, Beggs was a dangerous Pied Piper: a threat to the family structure that the city's heavily Catholic law enforcement hierarchy believed was the moral linchpin of society.

THE CHIEF ANTAGONIST OF Huckleberry House was Juvenile Court Judge Raymond J. O'Connor, who ran San Francisco's youth justice system with an iron hand and saw the upstart shelter as a challenge to his authority. Like Mayor Shelley and much of the city's hierarchy, O'Connor was a San Francisco native and a product of local parochial schools. After a long career in private practice, he was appointed to the bench by his old friend, California governor Edmund "Pat" Brown, the big-government Democrat whose political career was ended by Ronald Reagan in 1966. But despite his Democratic Party affiliation, Judge O'Connor was a crusty opponent of the decade's social activism. In 1964 the Superior Court Judge summoned newspaper reporters into his chambers to denounce the civil rights sit-ins sweeping the city as a criminal conspiracy. After he was named chief of the juvenile court the following year, O'Connor quickly made it clear that he was going to crack down on the youthful rebellion and lawlessness he saw spinning out of control in San Francisco. O'Connor began throwing teens and even preteens into the grim YGC citadel at a much higher rate and keeping them under lock and key much longer. He was particularly hard on black youths, and even jailed their parents when he felt they were lying to him. About two-thirds of the San Francisco kids behind bars at YGC were black.

In 1966 the judge ignited a furor when he tossed a twelve-year-old boy into jail for purse snatching, along with several other older boys—none of whom had ever been in trouble before. Family groups and civil liberties attorneys called for O'Connor's ouster. But police and business groups rallied to the youth czar's defense, and he held on to his post.

The following year, as San Francisco became a youth magnet, O'Connor scooped up thousands of young vagabonds and locked them up in his juvenile prison. The judge became a notorious villain in the Haight, denounced in one underground newspaper as a "sham . . . mentally and morally unqualified to sit in judgment on the young." O'Connor stuffed so many kids into his barbed-wire warehouse that they were forced to sleep in their own piss and shit on the floors of their cells and fight to defend their space. At an "emergency conference" on runaways held in the Straight Theater, a favorite Grateful Dead venue in the Haight, one boy explained bluntly what teens on the run could expect when they fell into O'Connor's net: "They get beaten up in the paddy wagon, then they get beaten up in jail . . . and then they get beaten up again when they get home."

O'Connor was determined to track down all of San Francisco's windy-feet children. In his eyes, storefront operations like Huckleberry House were a public nuisance, encouraging kids to defy parental authority and flee home. "Raymond O'Connor was a son of a bitch, and he wanted us closed," said Beggs. "This hippie minister was threatening his juvenile justice monopoly. That's how he saw it. 'Throttle the bastard!' In those years, you had complete control as a parent to force your kid to do many things. And judges like O'Connor were complicit in this. These brutal, alcoholic parents could be shit-faced drunk all week long, and then put on a suit and appear in O'Connor's court, and the judge would always take their side. He was sending these kids back home to be abused mentally and sometimes sexually."

The fifty-seven-year-old, gray-haired O'Connor was a father himself. He and his wife, Mary, had seven children. After one of O'Connor's own teenage sons ran away from the family's home in West Portal—a quiet mom-and-pop neighborhood that even today seems preserved from an earlier era—the boy ended up at Huckleberry House. The youth revolution had literally come home for Raymond O'Connor. It was only a matter of time before the judge slammed down his fist on the shelter.

The police raid took place on the night of October 19, 1967, several months after Huckleberry House opened its doors. An inexperienced night manager gave the cops their opening when she failed to make the obligatory phone call to the parents of a fifteen-year-old runaway, to get permission to shelter their son for the night. Suddenly there was a crying mother on the Huckleberry House doorsteps and a swarm of cops. The SFPD arrested everyone on the premises, including the runaways, for being without parental supervision; and the adult caretakers, for contributing to the delinquency of minors. Beggs, who was home at the time, turned himself in the next morning at county jail. Kissing his two young boys good-bye, he had to explain to them why "daddy is going to go to jail now."

Sitting in his cell, Beggs reflected gloomily on the fate of Huckleberry House, the nation's first alternative runaway shelter and, he thought, perhaps the last. But San Francisco in the sixties was not simply a bastion of Catholic law and order. There were other shifting forces at work, and it turned out that Beggs's sponsors at the activist Glide Church had some connections of their own. A young, politically ambitious, African-American attorney from the Fillmore named Willie Brown was retained to represent Huckleberry House. And within hours, Judge Joseph Kennedy—a black jurist who strongly supported Glide's social programs—released Beggs on his own recognizance. A couple of months later, the case was dismissed.

The raid on Huckleberry House was traumatic for its young staff. But it had a galvanizing effect on the community surrounding the shelter. "The overall effect of the bust," Beggs said, "was to dramatically communicate to the Haight that if we're being attacked by the police and the juvenile justice system and Judge O'Connor, that we were now legitimized as an authentic, counterculture operation." High school students went door to door to collect canned goods for Huckleberry. A printing company ran off several thousand promotional pamphlets for the shelter at no cost. An elderly woman in the Glide congregation gathered small soap bars from her residential hotel to donate to the shelter. Parents and former Huckleberry runaways mailed in small cash donations. As word spread about Huckleberry's resilience in the face of official harassment, more and more teenagers showed up on the shelter's doorsteps.

When Huckleberry House stood its ground and survived, it was a major victory for the new city growing within the old. The city's establishment didn't give a damn about the children on its streets. As an outraged editorial in the *Haight Ashbury Tribune* fumed, "If an individual treated a child with the [same] disregard for his health, safety, and welfare" that San Francisco displayed toward minors, "our law would punish that individual as a felon." But in the end, the community took care of its own.

They had flocked to San Francisco from all over the world, but they were now the city's children. And you take care of your children, particularly when they are lost and broken. That was the philosophy that took root in the new city during the Summer of Love.

6

STREET MEDICINE

As San Francisco braced itself for the Summer of Love tidal wave, a twenty-eight-year-old intern named David Smith was working as chief of the alcohol and drug abuse screening unit at San Francisco General Hospital. At night Smith drove across town to his apartment on Frederick Street in the Haight, near a donut store that sold LSD under the counter. The young doctor knew he lived and worked at ground zero. And he knew the city's public health system was woefully unprepared for the waves of drug-experimenting kids already washing up on its streets. In fact, Public Health Director Ellis Sox was openly hostile to the growing youth population, mirroring the attitude of Mayor Shelley's administration, which wanted to post "Hippies Not Welcome" signs on the bridge approaches to San Francisco.

If food and shelter were the most urgent needs in the Haight's rapidly expanding refugee encampment, health care was close behind. None of the medical facilities in the neighborhood wanted to treat hippies. St. Mary's, the big Catholic-run hospital on Stanyan Street, had a policy of turning away drug overdose victims. The Diggers once again tried to address the crisis but fell far short. They rounded up a few interns from Kaiser Hospital and an ex-mental patient named Doc, who served as a "witch doctor" to the Hell's Angels, to care for people at their free stores. But their makeshift emergency rooms were soon swamped with patients and quickly ran out of medical supplies. Grogan and his cohorts began ferrying young people who were hallucinating wildly on LSD and other chemical cocktails to Dr. Smith's small detox center. Smith would try to talk them through their nightmares, or if necessary, administer a sedative or a more potent antipsychotic like Thorazine.

But Smith's unit was open only during weekday work hours, and when high-flying kids were brought to General Hospital at other times, they were dumped across the street at Mission Emergency Hospital, where they were thrown in with alcoholics or gunshot victims, or locked in padded isolation cells. What began as a mildly bad trip could erupt into full-blown psychosis by the time a hallucinating patient made his way through the city's harrowing public health labyrinth.

Hippies who fell into the hands of public health doctors and nurses at Park Emergency Hospital, on the edge of Golden Gate Park, fared the worst. The hospital staff seemed to take pleasure in tormenting the young, disoriented patients, ignoring them or making them suffer through a long registration process. In the end, many of them were shoved into the back of ambulances and, sirens screaming, deposited on Smith's doorstep at SF General.

Like Rev. Beggs, David Smith felt estranged from his own profession. The truth was, Smith had never seemed at home in his surroundings. He had grown up "a jock and a square" in Bakersfield, the son of Okies whose families had fled the Dust Bowl for the oil fields and farms of California's Central Valley. Smith's father, Elvin, became a clerk for Southern Pacific Railroad, and his mother, Dorothy, grew up to become a nurse. But she always remembered the humiliations of working in the fields with her mother and sister during the Depression. When the farm boss would ask her mother what kind of work she would do, she answered, "Anything." Never say you will do anything, his mother told young David. She urged him to become a doctor.

In high school, David never tried to date "good girls" because he felt ashamed by his humble roots and his sickly mother, who was diagnosed with Hodgkin's disease when he was three. He was a good student and worked hard to make the varsity basketball team. But he always felt like an outsider. When his mother finally died of her illness during his senior year, David and his father, who both liked to drink, began to apply themselves to the bottle more seriously. Within a couple of years, his father had drunk himself to death, leaving David an orphan at nineteen.

Smith continued to drink heavily during the early 1960s as an undergraduate at Berkeley and as a medical student at the University of California campus in San Francisco. But he developed an interest in psychedelics while taking pharmacology courses in medical school, and after experimenting with LSD, he gave up alcohol for acid, mescaline, and marijuana. He would spend most of his professional life studying and treating the powerful effects of drugs. But he would never entirely condemn their dark magic. "It started as clinical, but it turned into a religious experience," Smith recalled. "I don't want to bad-mouth LSD, because I'd never have done what I did in my life had I not had that spiritual experience on LSD. I was the grandson of farm workers, and all I wanted was academic and financial success. The idea that I would leave the lab and risk everything to help these street kids was so foreign. But I broke on through to the other side. And it seemed to me like not only *should* I do it, but I *had* to do it."

Smith began feeling like he belonged for the first time in his life. He was a few years older than most of the ragged young people who roamed the streets of his neighborhood or found their way into his hospital office. But they were his tribe; his tribe of outsiders. The authorities had tried to block the Okies at the California border too.

As horror stories about the San Francisco public health system spread in the Haight, more and more young people refrained from going to city medical facilities, even though health-care problems in the community were reaching the crisis point. Smith knew he had to do something. Thanks to the Diggers, the idea of free medical service was blowing in the wind. A former girlfriend named Florence Martin, an African-American nurse, had also told Smith about her work at the Watts Clinic in Los Angeles, a community clinic established after the 1965 Watts riots. Before the clinic was built, neighborhood residents had to drive miles for medical care. Now they had a sense that their health-care system belonged to them. Smith was also intrigued by the stories that his Haight-Ashbury neighbor Terry Hallinan brought back from the South, where he had worked with the Student Nonviolent Coordinating Committee (SNCC) to set up free health clinics.

Brainstorming with a man named Robert Conrich—a physician turned private investigator who had dropped out of the professional world after becoming an LSD initiate—Smith developed the idea for a free clinic in the Haight. "I was pretty naïve about health politics then," he recalled. "But the concept of 'free' was all around me. I became the architect of the slogan 'Health care is a right, not a privilege.' That was the founding philosophy of the Haight-Ashbury Free Clinic. It was a very radical idea then. Now it's being debated in the mainstream. And it all came out of this area, the street university known as the Haight-Ashbury. I was learning more every day walking around in my neighborhood than I ever learned in the lab."

Smith and Conrich recruited doctors, nurses, and hippie volunteers to staff the clinic. They found an abandoned dental office on the second floor of a faded yellow Victorian at 558 Clayton Street, near the corner of Haight. Smith paid the lease out of his own pocket, with a $100 lecture fee and a $500 donation from Rev. Leon Smith, an activist Episcopal minister in the Haight. Smith and his crew then outfitted the office with scavenged furniture and medical equipment, including an X-ray machine so ancient that Smith thought it belonged in the Smithsonian.

Despite his growing emotional attachment to the hippie community, Smith was still an ambitious young medical professional who kept his curly hair closely cropped. He tried to keep one foot in the mainstream world while dipping his other into the crosscurrent. He thought he could be a bridge between the two realities. But it soon became clear to Smith that he was crossing a Rubicon. City authorities immediately resented the Haight-Ashbury Free Clinic because it was outside their domain. So bitter was city hall opposition that it seemed to Smith as if public health czar Sox "wanted to isolate the Haight-Ashbury and let its young residents die." Smith's former medical school mentors and colleagues urged him to abandon the free clinic project, warning him that he was ruining his promising career by treating drug takers and other undesirables. He was even told that someone would try to kill him.

But when the Haight-Ashbury Free Clinic opened its doors on June 7, 1967, it became instantly clear why the storefront emergency room was essential. A long line of patients in granny dresses, buckskins, and other light clothing stretched around the corner, shivering miserably in the wet fog. Eric Burdon and the Animals might have fantasized about warm San Franciscan nights, but only newcomers to the city expected to be greeted with summer sunshine. As the patients made their way up the hallway stairs to the clinic, Smith remembers, it soon turned into a "madhouse." Overdose victims clawed at phantoms in the air; runny-nosed babies wailed frantically, unappeased by their hippie mothers' bare breasts. A fever-flushed woman wrapped only in a pink blanket and racked with deep, bronchial coughs insisted that she could not be hospitalized because she had to hitchhike to Big Sur the next morning. The air was thick with marijuana, incense, and a rank mix of body odor and patchouli. Patients not utterly depleted by illness rattled tambourines and blew on wooden flutes. The cacophony went on and on.

The clinic treated more than 250 patients the first day, and more than 350 the next. By the third day, its stockpiles of bandages, antibiotics, and penicillin were depleted. When clinic doctors ran out of tranquilizers, all they could do was encourage patients freaking out on drugs to concentrate on flickering candles. The clinic's small detox room—wishfully called its "calm center"—was soon an overcrowded bedlam. An eighteen-year-old girl freaking out on acid was trying to hurl her body through the calm center wall. Another drug patient was prancing nude through the waiting room. Smith's volunteer staff—including some doctors who had served in the military—were already on the brink of burnout and comparing the beleaguered clinic to a field hospital in a combat zone.

The Haight was actually more like Calcutta, with its hordes of beggars in brightly colored rags and its stew of human misery. The Free Clinic staff treated a bizarre spectrum of infections and aggravations that Summer of Love, many of them more commonly associated with Third World slums than prosperous American tourist destinations. The young patients who came through the clinic doors were suffering from pneumonia, hepatitis, venereal disease, illegal abortion complications, skin infections, gum diseases, malnourishment, and intestinal disorders from eating rotten food.

Smith couldn't understand why the public authorities had turned their backs on the young people flooding his clinic. "Many of these kids came from traditional backgrounds," he recalled. "They were the establishment's own sons and daughters. They didn't come to Haight-Ashbury to go to the Free Clinic. They came for the music, for the freedom. And if you didn't take care of them, they'd get sick and clog up hospital emergency rooms. They certainly wouldn't go home."

When David Perlman, the science reporter for the *San Francisco Chronicle,* showed up to interview Smith for a story on the clinic, he was so stunned by the spectacle of suffering that he put down his notebook and began helping out, taking patient histories for several hours. His story, "A Medical Mission in the Haight Ashbury," ran on the front page, and it produced an outpouring of public support. Checks ranging from $5 to $100 came in through the mail. People arrived at the clinic hauling furniture, food, and medication. Celebrities volunteered to work in the clinic, including Bing Crosby's wife, Kathryn, who drove up from the family home in Hillsborough.

The *Chronicle* coverage put pressure on city authorities to support the clinic. But city hall responded only with smoke and mirrors. Public Health Director Sox vaguely promised to open a more "proper" health center in the Haight before the summer was over. And Mayor Shelley announced that in the meantime, the city was funding the Free Clinic. Both statements were untrue, and whether boneheaded or malicious, they had the effect of instantly drying up public contributions to the clinic and pushing it to the brink of financial ruin.

Meanwhile, other dark forces preyed on the struggling clinic. The police were a constant, harassing presence. Beat cops periodically roamed through the clinic's five rooms, hunting for runaways. And narcotics officers came around sniffing for illegal drugs. A sign posted in the clinic tried to avert police raids, pleading, "No dealing, no holding, no using dope—any of these can close the clinic." It concluded with a cheery, flower-decorated "We love you," because the clinic tried hard not to alienate its wary, young patients. But the sign was a reminder that everyone in the Haight was under surveillance, even in relatively safe zones like the Free Clinic.

Even more troubling to Smith and his staff were the street strongmen who tried to muscle their way into the clinic as it became established in the neighborhood. One such sketchy character called himself Papa Al. A successful speed dealer who lived in a Berkeley mansion, Papa Al roamed the streets of the Haight with a .38 revolver and a burly companion known as Teddybear. The two men began volunteering at the Free

Clinic soon after it opened up, passing themselves off as Good Samaritans. But it soon became clear that they intended to take over the clinic and use it as the base of their drug operation. When Smith confronted Papa Al and ordered him to leave, the drug dealer responded by putting out a contract on the lives of Smith and the clinic administrator, Donald Reddick. The word spread quickly on the street: any methamphetamine freak who knocked off Smith or Reddick would get $100 worth of speed.

"I freaked out," Smith said. "The neighborhood was so crazy then that if you put out the word like that, it could easily happen."

Smith went to the cops at Park Police Station, but they told him they couldn't do anything until Papa Al made a move. "So I learned the police were no protection. If Papa Al moved, I'd be dead. The cops' attitude was, Here's this insane asylum in the Haight, and whatever you crazed animals do in there to each other, we don't give a damn—just don't let it spill out into the rest of the city."

Reddick gave Smith a gun and holster, but his only experience with firearms was taking potshots at bottles on the banks of the Kern River as a kid. In desperation, Smith turned to the Hell's Angels: the hard guys in leather who brought a kind of rough justice to the neighborhood. Everyone was afraid of the Angels, including the police. But the bikers had their uses. The Haight had made a devil's bargain with the Angels. In return for protecting them from violent cops, bad drug dealers, and other rogue elements, the neighborhood turned a blind eye to the Angels' own bare-knuckled behavior. Heavy hippies like the Diggers admired the Angels for their outlaw integrity, the Dead and Janis liked their swagger and style. But people knew that bringing the bikers into the equation was like bringing a jungle cat on a leash into a party. It could all be cool—or not.

This time it all worked out. Smith phoned Hell's Angels leader Sonny Barger and told him his plight. The next day, two Angels visited Papa Al and told him how things stood. "You're David Smith's insurance policy," they said. "If anything happens to him—if he's hit by a car walking across the street—you're dead." The contract on Smith and Reddick was lifted. Papa Al disappeared from the Haight.

Smith knows everything that has been said about Barger and his gang. He knows that historians of the 1960s will have the final say. But for him, it's not complicated: "If you ask me, they saved my life."

IF SONNY BARGER SAVED Smith's life, it was another community icon—rock concert promoter Bill Graham—who saved his clinic. By July, the clinic was mired in debt. With the city still withholding financial support, the frontline medical facility was on the verge of closing its doors. But after reading about the clinic's crisis in the *Chronicle,* Graham phoned Smith, who invited him over to 558 Clayton. They were an unlikely pair: the Okie from Bakersfield and the Holocaust orphan who had raised himself on the streets of the Bronx. In the Haight's "free" circles, Graham was reviled as a moneygrubbing opportunist who was taking the neighborhood's free-floating music and selling it back to the people. But Smith saw the "heart of gold," as he put it, under Graham's snarly exterior. "He could be extremely tough, but if he decided you were one of his people, he loved you." Graham quickly sized up the young doctor as one of his people.

While talking with Smith in the clinic, Graham looked out the window and saw a phalanx of cops sweeping hippies off the street. "These kids have made my business possible," he told the doctor. "They don't deserve this treatment. Now I want to do something for them . . . We need the clinic. It's humanity—and the least I can do." Graham organized a benefit at the Fillmore Auditorium on July 13 headlined by Big Brother and the Holding Company that raised $5,000 for the clinic—a hefty sum in those days. "Without Bill Graham, the clinic would not have survived its fragile infancy that summer," said Smith. In October Graham followed up with a second benefit, this one featuring the Jefferson Airplane, that funneled another $5,000 to the clinic. Graham's largesse inspired a wave of other benefits for the clinic, including a free concert in a San Jose park again headlined by Big Brother.

"We literally built this clinic on rock 'n' roll," Smith said. It was a circular system. Many of the rock musicians who raised money for the Free Clinic were also its patients. Smith even saved some of their lives. He would get calls in the dead of night, sometimes from Graham, sometimes from friends, lovers, or bandmates. A beloved musician had collapsed and was turning a morgue-like pallor. Smith was needed right away. Years later, watching the movie *Pulp Fiction,* he instantly identified with the Harvey Keitel character—the man called in to clean up disasters.

No one required more emergency attention than Janis Joplin, whose dark romance with liquor and drugs long preceded her musical stardom. She was using up all her lives, one by one. Late one night, Smith got a frantic call from a girlfriend of Janis: the singer had overdosed on heroin and could not be revived. Smith rushed to Janis's house in the Haight and injected her with Narcan. This time Janis came back. When she opened her eyes and saw Doc Smith, she smiled and said, "Thank you."

Most of Janis Joplin's soul-wrenching music was ahead of her. Smith kept her going long enough so she could give the world those pieces of her heart. He was no miracle worker. But the young doctor built a haven that summer where America's lost children—from ragged panhandlers to rock stars—were made to feel that their lives were not disposable and that someone cared about them.

7

MURDER ON
SHAKEDOWN STREET

B EFORE BILL GRAHAM, there was Charles Sullivan. The king of
black music promoters on the West Coast, Sullivan signed up
the biggest African-American headliners for his concert circuit, which
stretched from Vancouver to San Diego. He presented them all: Louis
Armstrong, Duke Ellington, Count Basie, Billie Holliday, and, later, Ray
Charles, Ike and Tina Turner, Little Richard, James Brown, the Temptations. His long reign as a promoter began during World War II, when he
opened a joint in San Mateo, south of San Francisco, called Club Sullivan, and extended into the 1950s and 1960s, when he moved into San
Francisco and took over the lease on an old dance hall originally called
the Majestic Ballroom, renaming it the Fillmore Auditorium.

The Fillmore district was a hopping music scene in those years, with
jazz, blues, bebop, and rhythm and blues blasting out of dozens of clubs,
bars, and lounges all night long. Fillmore Street became "Swing Street."
And Sullivan was the ringmaster of it all: staging big shows at the Fillmore, running a hotel where black musicians felt welcome and a bar
where they jammed until dawn, and making another small fortune on
the side from liquor, jukeboxes, and gambling. He was the man to see;
they called him "the mayor of Fillmore Street."

In 1965 Sullivan launched Bill Graham in the concert business, loaning him his dance license—that essential city document—and subleasing the Fillmore to Graham on the auditorium's dark nights. Without Sullivan, Graham might never have cracked San Francisco's tightly controlled entertainment racket. Then Sullivan was suddenly, violently, torn out of the picture. And Graham made his move, taking over the Fillmore lease and turning the old dance hall into a hallowed name in musical history. "Behind every beautiful thing, there is some kind of pain": That's how Bob Dylan sings it. And, in the case of the Fillmore, it rings true.

Music was at the heart of San Francisco's magical transformation in the 1960s. And at the beginning of the decade, the Fillmore was the music's hot center. They called the Fillmore "the Harlem of the West." The streets were filled until the early morning hours with a parade of peacocks: men with diamond stickpins, satin ties, and long coats; women in slit dresses and furs. Adventurous white kids like Jerry Garcia would sneak into the Fillmore clubs and dance halls, this forbidden empire of cool, to hear the music they couldn't find on Top 40 radio.

And then it was all gone, destroyed block by block by the wrecking balls and bulldozers of the San Francisco Redevelopment Agency. As Jerry Garcia later sang, "Nothin' shakin' on Shakedown Street, used to be the heart of town." The agency launched the first phase of its massive urban renewal project in 1953, erasing stores, nightclubs, and churches and more than twenty-five thousand residents from hundreds of city blocks. Geary Street, a bustling commercial center, was turned into an eight-lane expressway, so that cars and buses carrying commuters downtown from the predominantly white west-side neighborhoods could hurtle directly through the Fillmore without stopping. Ten years later, the agency kicked off the second phase of its Fillmore blitzkrieg, uprooting an additional thirteen thousand people and shuttering thousands of more businesses over sixty square blocks.

The city called it urban renewal. But to residents of the Fillmore, it was "Negro removal." Redevelopment officials promised that dislocated residents would be moved back into the neighborhood. But those who were forced to sell their houses soon found that they were priced out of the Fillmore's rising real estate market.

The Fillmore was the heart of black San Francisco, and redevelopment tore it out. The Harlem of the West now looked like a war-ravaged city, pockmarked with empty, rubble-strewn lots, shuttered storefronts, and dreary street corners inhabited by lost and wasted men. After the middle-class home owners and business operators were forced out, all that was left was a crime-ridden ghetto.

As the wrecking balls turned the Fillmore into a wasteland, an ugly spirit began sweeping the streets. Cab drivers refused to take white tourists there anymore. White teenagers like John Goddard had crossed the Golden Gate Bridge from Marin County to see Little Richard (backed by a scrawny young guitarist named Jimi Hendrix) and other marvels at the Fillmore Auditorium. But now the neighborhood seemed forbidding. "It got to the point, around 1965, where I didn't feel safe coming to Fillmore Street anymore . . . people were angry—rightly so. But I didn't feel comfortable. Nothing ever happened, but it was a different vibe."

THEN, NEAR THE END of that year, Charles Sullivan loaned Bill Graham his Fillmore Auditorium dance permit. White kids began flocking to the desolated neighborhood to hear a whole new breed of musicians: the Airplane, the Dead, Quicksilver Messenger Service, Big Brother, Sopwith Camel, the Grassroots, Love, Velvet Underground, Frank Zappa and the Mothers of Invention, Van Morrison and his band Them. They all played the Fillmore in the first half of 1966. And suddenly the corner of Fillmore and Geary, the heart of the neighborhood, was jolted back to life with a surge of electric music.

The cops were not happy. They had written off the Fillmore as a no-man's-land. Now they suddenly had security headaches. More and more children of the white suburbs were venturing into the Fillmore after nightfall, which meant that the police had to patrol the neighborhood again.

Like all operators of liquor stores and late-night entertainment joints, Sullivan liked to keep everyone happy, particularly the authorities. Some of his enterprises required licenses from the city and the state. Others, like his after-hours speakeasies, depended on the look-the-other-way leniency of beat cops. Sullivan knew how to spread around the gravy. He always carried a roll of cash in his pants pocket, and he would take it out and peel off the bills whenever he needed to take care of somebody.

But this time, Sullivan couldn't smooth it over with the cops. They wanted him to pull his dance permit from Graham. They wanted the rock shows shut down. Or else they would shut *him* down: no more booze peddling, no more backroom gambling, no more vending machines. Sullivan caved. The next day he called Graham into his office and gave him the bad news. "They're leaning on me hard, and I got a business to run, and I got a wife and kids, and I have to pull my permit," Sullivan grimly informed the rock promoter.

Graham went home that night and told his wife, Bonnie: it was all over. The next morning, Graham returned to the Fillmore to pack up his office. When he arrived, Sullivan was sitting on the steps. The fifty-seven-year-old Sullivan always dressed like a gentleman, in suit and tie. And he would insist that his performers always look their best on stage too, picking up their suits after every show to make sure they were cleaned and pressed. But today Sullivan looked worse for wear. He was a big man—more than six feet tall, and close to two hundred fifty pounds—but now he seemed like a beat-down field worker. He was wearing the same suit, shirt, and tie from the day before, and it looked to Graham like he'd been up all night. "Bill," said the older man, "I want to talk to you."

They went upstairs to Graham's cubbyhole of an office. And Sullivan began pouring out his life story to him. How he had grown up on a farm in Monroe County, Alabama, raised by illiterate parents. How he had left home as a teenager and made his way out to the West Coast, washing cars in Los Angeles and then going to night school to become a machinist. How he had moved to San Francisco in search of work during the Depression, but was barred from the all-white machinists union and was forced to take a job as a chauffeur for a San Mateo socialite. It was only after years of tormented hustle that Sullivan finally began to get a leg up, saving a little money and opening a suburban hamburger stand, then adding a restaurant and a bar. Then, during World War II, as the Fillmore district began to boom, he saw his big chance to move into the city. All those black defense workers with cash in their pockets—and few places to spend it. He would become the king of swing.

All during his long trek to the top, Sullivan told Graham, the white man had messed with him. Finally, he thought, he had found his place in the sun: he was a wealthy pillar of his community with a booming entertainment business; a pretty, young wife; and a comfortable two-story house with Japanese décor near Alamo Square. But now the men downtown were messing with him all over again, making threats and telling him what to do. "Yesterday they really got to me," Sullivan said, and the big man began to shake.

"Bill, it's my life," he went on. "After I saw you last night, I started thinking about myself and what I been through and what they're making you do now." His eyes, red from lack of sleep, were fixed on Graham. "I can't do it. I can't. I just can't back off. I can't pull that permit from you."

Then Sullivan leaned forward. His voice was choked with pain and rage. "No, no, no. I just ain't going to let this happen now. You just go back downtown, man. And you beat those white motherfuckers."

Graham did just that. With typical sharp-elbows drive, the rock promoter finally finagled his own dance license out of city hall, lining up support from the *Chronicle,* neighborhood merchants, and even the rabbi of the temple next door to the Fillmore, who had complained about inebriated rock fans relieving themselves on his holy walls.

The smartest move Graham made was reaching out to San Francisco power attorney William Coblentz, who thought that the promoter was getting a raw deal and agreed to represent him for free. Coblentz hired a private eye, who snapped pictures of cops going in and out of a whorehouse across the street from the auditorium. The lawyer shared the revealing photos with the city board of permit appeals. He pointed out that the beat cops were in no position to charge that Graham was bad for the neighborhood. The board found this a convincing argument, and Graham was back in business.

But without Sullivan, nothing would have happened. "He was the guy, Charles," Graham said later. "He was *it*. I don't know if I could have *ever* found another place. Why would I have even tried? That *was* the place."

It should have been a triumphant time for Charles Sullivan too. He had stood up to the downtown bullies and won. He was at the top of his game, overseeing the West Coast tours for the top Motown Records acts and expanding into Los Angeles. But the Fillmore district, his base of operation since the 1940s, was becoming a dangerous ghost town. He was one of the few major business figures who stood in the way of the neighborhood's elimination. His turf was crowded by enemies and predators. Sullivan took to carrying a chrome-plated .38 in his briefcase.

It was a .38 that took Charles Sullivan's life. Sometime after midnight in the early morning darkness of August 2, 1966, someone stuck the gun's snub nose right against his heart and pulled the trigger. He was dead before he hit the ground. The homicide cops found him sprawled on his back at the scruffy corner of Fifth and Bluxome Streets, lying next to his rented car, a tan Chevy, with the gun inches away from his outstretched right hand.

From the very start, the cops seemed strangely confused about the murder. At first they put out the word that there was "a strong possibility of suicide"—until the coroner's inquest pointed out that it would be very "awkward" for a man to shoot himself in the heart this way. Testifying at the inquest, lead homicide inspector Ken Manley, a sixteen-year veteran of the force, could not be certain whether the gun found at the scene even belonged to Sullivan. And he was at a loss to explain why no fingerprints or gun smoke odor were found on the revolver.

The story that finally went down was that Sullivan was killed while being robbed. The promoter was reported to be carrying several thousand dollars in his briefcase after having staged a James Brown show in Los Angeles and a Temptations concert in Phoenix that weekend, and the empty briefcase was found in the trunk of his car.

But the SFPD never arrested a suspect, and—like the suicide theory—the robbery story never smelled right to the Sullivan family. After the murder, Charles's wife, Fanny, and his younger brother, Marion, found that the promoter had already stashed most of the weekend's receipts—some $25,000—in the safe at his Grove Street home.

Marion Sullivan, who had been raised by Charles during much of his adolescence and later went to work for him in his jukebox business, was convinced that his brother was killed by someone he knew. "Charles was involved with some shady people," he said.

Sullivan's family and the cops were quickly able to retrace his steps that night. He had taken a flight from LA after the James Brown show and landed after nine o'clock at San Francisco International Airport, where he rented the Chevy. Sullivan's wife was out of town, and, unsurprisingly, he was accompanied by an attractive young woman. "He loved women; there was no question about it. He'd always find a broad to take with him on his trips," said Marion.

Sullivan drove into the city, dropped off the cash at his home, and then checked in at the cocktail lounge he ran, inside the Booker T. Washington Hotel on Ellis Street. Later that night, he drove his female companion, a schoolteacher who lived in Oakland, across the Bay Bridge to her home on Twenty-third Street. They enjoyed each other's company for about forty-five minutes. She later testified that she had served Sullivan watermelon. And then, after midnight, he left. On the street outside her house, he shouted out, and she came rushing outside to see what was wrong. He told her that he had seen a "kid going down the street, and it had scared him for a minute." He was worried that the kid might have snatched his briefcase, which was on the front seat of his locked car. But nothing had been taken, and he drove off. That was the last she ever saw him, said the schoolteacher.

After that, Sullivan's trajectory became murky. For some reason, he apparently exited the freeway in San Francisco on Fifth Street, rather than taking the Fell Street exit closer to his home, and he turned left into the freight district. He was miles from the Fillmore, and he had no business in the neighborhood. But that's where they found him, splayed on the street between the Chevy and a wire fence, his body silhouetted in the macabre glow of his car's headlights.

The newspapers got excited for a day or two about the murder. The African-American paper, the *Sun-Reporter*, kept the story going a bit longer, with a two-page spread on Sullivan's lavish funeral. Belva Davis, a writer for the *Sun-Reporter* who later became a prominent local TV journalist, began digging into the mystery but was suddenly pulled off the story. There were powerful interests behind Sullivan's murder, she was told. Charles Sullivan, despite all his wealth and show business glamour, soon disappeared forever. He was dropped down whatever well there was in those days for colored people, prominent or otherwise, who got themselves shot.

Homicide inspector Jack Cleary, Ken Manley's junior partner on the case, always clung to the suicide theory. And he thought that Sullivan's schoolteacher girlfriend ("a broad who had legs eight feet long; could've been a model") knew a lot more than she revealed at the coroner's inquest. Cleary suspected that she was with Sullivan when he shot himself—maybe accidentally, during a lovers' quarrel—and then took off.

Cleary confronted the "witch"—that's how he saw her—after she stepped down from the witness stand. "Come here," he said. "You know what? I'm going down to the DA's, and I'm going to get a warrant on you for perjury. You were there when Charley killed himself, and you left him there to die and should've got him some help. And you just got up on the stand and lied. You raised your right hand under oath—"

"No, I didn't," the leggy schoolteacher broke in, cool as diamonds. "I raised my left hand."

Neither Cleary nor the coroner had caught that sly move. "We were pretty good, but she was better."

But the lover's suicide theory, which seemed right out of a B movie, did not find many believers—even in Cleary's own department. There was a lingering scent around Sullivan's murder, something hidden and rank.

Some prominent San Franciscans, including a rising young political leader named Dianne Feinstein, took an interest in the Sullivan case. Feinstein, a clean government crusader married to a Pacific Heights neurosurgeon, already had her eye on the mayor's office, and she liked to poke around the city's dark corners. Always intrigued by police affairs, Feinstein collared Cleary at the hall of justice one day. "Look, Jack, this is a murder," she told him. "Murder, my foot," he shot back at her, insisting on his suicide explanation.

Some time later, after the case was filed away, Marion Sullivan was running an after-hours speakeasy when it got raided by the police. One of the cops recognized him and brought up his dead brother. "He told me that he knew who killed Charles," said Marion. "But I wasn't crazy enough to ask him to tell me who."

There was always a seamy underside to San Francisco, even during the enchanted sixties. But Sullivan's murder did not stop the music. In his place came an even bigger showman: bruising, belligerent, big-hearted Bill Graham.

8

THE NAPOLEON OF ROCK

BILL GRAHAM ALWAYS seemed everywhere. Zooming around town on a motorbike and stapling concert posters to telephone poles. Mopping up spilled drinks on the dance floor. Struggling with a pack of roadies to heave an amplifier into place. Screaming at a band's hapless manager backstage. Now he was prowling the perimeter of the Fillmore Auditorium, his rock 'n' roll bastion in the heart of San Francisco's shrinking black ghetto. The line of ticket holders snaked down Geary Street and around the corner onto Fillmore: bearded young men with tie-dyed headbands and teenage girls in peacoats and bell-bottoms, carrying the bedrolls they had slept in to secure a good place in line.

Graham wasn't young, but he wasn't old. He wasn't big, and he walked with his shoulders slightly hunched. But he always seemed coiled and ready for anything that came his way. He had a brute handsomeness: with his thick, wavy ducktail spilling over his shirt collar and his sideburns, he looked like a guy who'd be cast as one of the Sharks in *West Side Story* if all the parts hadn't been claimed by gay dancers.

Now Graham was patrolling the Fillmore ticket line, counting heads—clipboard in hand; always a clipboard—when a kid with long, matted blond hair piped up, "Greedy fucking pig." Graham spun on his heels, like he was ready for it. "Who said that? Who *the fuck* said that?" With some weird street radar, the promoter instantly identified where the verbal assault had come from and was in the kid's face. "Do you know how much it costs to put on a show like this? Do you have any idea how many people have to be paid: the musicians, the roadies, the truck drivers, the sound people, the light shows? You don't have a *fucking* clue." The kid wilted under the harangue. Graham knew how to use his voice like a *New Yawk* jackhammer, and it was particularly effective against soft Californian ears.

Born Wolfgang Grajonca to Russian-Polish Jewish emigrants in Berlin, Graham was a refugee from European history. His mother and one of his five sisters were gassed to death by Nazis in Germany; another sister survived Auschwitz. Sent to an orphanage outside Paris, Graham escaped from the growing inferno at age nine by walking across Europe with his thirteen-year-old sister, Tolla. When she came down with pneumonia during the trek, he was forced to leave her in a hospital in Lyon, France, and he never saw her again. It haunted Graham for the rest of his life. He was put on an ocean liner in Lisbon, Portugal, and after a torturous voyage to Casablanca and Dakar, in Africa, he finally landed in New York. There he was plucked from an adoption agency by a couple, "as though they were going to a pet shop," he said. Of the sixty-four kids who'd set out on foot from the French orphanage three months earlier, only eleven made it to New York.

At age eighteen, Graham was drafted and sent to war in Korea. He hated the army and never figured out why we were fighting, but he did his duty, killed a man in combat, and won the Bronze Star and Purple Heart. By going to war, Graham finally gained his US citizenship, enabling him to bring two of his three surviving sisters to America from Israel. After his discharge, he worked as a New York cab driver and as a waiter in the Catskills. Graham first came to San Francisco to visit his oldest sister, Rita, who had settled there with her husband after arriving in America. Right away, San Francisco made him feel different. The hills, the Golden Gate Bridge, the soft sea light. There were horizons; there were opportunities. He breathed easier. "What I liked was that the game was not always on the goal line out there. It wasn't always life and death. There were time-out signs. It was a *nicer* game."

Graham had fantasized about a show business career ever since waiting tables on the likes of Marlon Brando, Eddie Fisher, and Jerry Lewis. But New York and Los Angeles were unassailable towns without the right connections. In 1964 he finally found his opening, in San Francisco's more freewheeling atmosphere, after he became the San Francisco Mime Troupe's business manager. When the actor-provocateurs were busted in the park by censorious cops, Graham organized a benefit at the troupe's South of Market loft to raise money for legal fees. The benefit was a runaway success: Graham crammed so many people into the loft that night, it was raided by fire officials. Seeing a new world open before him, Graham held two more Mime Troupe benefits, this time at the Fillmore Auditorium. He wanted to be the next Sol Hurok. But he would become the P. T. Barnum of the greatest show on earth, San Francisco's rock 'n' roll circus.

From the very beginning, Graham sparked wildly opposite reactions in San Francisco, where music was still regarded as a public resource. "He was a pure business guy out to make a buck," said Peter Berg, who worked with him in the Mime Troupe. "A total square. He didn't even like rock music; he was into Latin dance music."

But Berg's Mime Troupe–Diggers comrade Peter Coyote saw Graham very differently. It was Graham who repeatedly came to the troupe's rescue when the performers fell into legal trouble, Coyote pointed out. And it was Graham who let the Diggers take over the Fillmore for a "Stone Your Neighbor" night in 1967, an event that could have put everyone in jail. The crowd filing into the auditorium that night was funneled between two rows of Diggers who were blowing huge clouds of marijuana smoke from giant cardboard tubes into everyone's faces. "Bill walks into the hall," Coyote recalled, "looks at this big bong show, and goes, 'What the fuck!' But then he started to laugh. This was a guy who walked from the gas chambers as a kid. Nothing scared him. He was just authentic. I don't care if he wasn't San Francisco. He was just a great man—a huge-hearted, brass-balled man. I loved him dearly."

Graham had the blustery swagger of a man who didn't give a shit what anyone thought of him. But it wounded him when he was called a bloodsucker. The Grateful Dead's drummer Mickey Hart is among those who always thought it was a bad rap. Hart remembered the night after a show at the Fillmore East, the concert hall he opened in Manhattan in 1968, when Graham walked block after block in the rain-splattered city, handing out $100 bills to the homeless.

Graham wanted to be known as a consummate showman: the impresario who harnessed the uncontrollable musical furies of stoned-out San Francisco and created rock 'n' roll's most magical evenings, from the moment the doors opened and the crowds were greeted with baskets of red apples, to closing time, when they exited the hall to the auld strains of "Greensleeves." Instead he was widely seen as the music scene's "evil necessity," Graham once ruefully observed. "Many times, someone would tap me and say, 'Great show, Bill.' Then he'd give me a dig in the ribs: 'You really made a killing tonight, huh?' It was almost as if saying, 'I wish we didn't need you, but thank God there is a you to put this on.'"

Good Times, the San Francisco underground newspaper, once attacked Graham as "the Napoleon of the rock revolution," ruthlessly driving out competition and staging concerts that "were airtight, like a prison recreation yard." *Good Times* editors prepared for the inevitable Graham eruption and lifelong ban from the Fillmore premises. Instead he sat down for a long interview with the newspaper, talking about his "maniacal" drive to serve the music-loving public, how his marriage had become a casualty of that drive, his disenchantment with the growing corporatization of live music, and how he was the only San Francisco counterculture merchant willing to comply with a Diggers plan to donate 1 percent of his gross revenue to fund community projects. By the end of the cathartic interview, the underground reporters were thoroughly disarmed, telling their readers that Graham was not "the raging tyrant we had come to expect" but a worn-out and thoughtful man trying to do his best in a "monstrous industry."

THE ROCK JOURNALISTS WHO covered the San Francisco music scene over time had to endure the full Bill Graham treatment: the charm offensives, the tirades, the extravagant gestures of generosity, the threats to end their careers. The thin-skinned Graham had a long running feud with *Rolling Stone* magazine's Jann Wenner, once holding the publisher hostage in his South of Market warehouse office for nearly seven hours while he went line by agonizing line over an article he found objectionable. Throughout the siege, magazine staffers would periodically hear explosions of Graham fury reverberating through Wenner's brick walls.

Chronicle rock critic Joel Selvin, who also found himself on the

receiving end of Graham's tantrums, discovered a way to plug the vol-
cano one day: "I looked at him, and I said, 'Oh, Bill, don't be disin-
genuous.' He suddenly stopped ranting. There were these moments in
dealing with Bill when I suddenly remembered, 'Oh yeah, English is this
guy's second or third language.' And he's looking at me, trying to figure
out, 'Hey, was I just insulted or not?'"

Graham could be a vicious business operator, double-crossing partners and bullying music managers, lawyers, and vendors into submission. But he respected the ones who pushed back. One day Graham
blew up at Brian Rohan, who had built his early association with HALO
and the Grateful Dead into a thriving practice as an entertainment lawyer. "He was screaming at me," Rohan recalled, "and I grabbed him by
the throat. I said, 'Look, I don't work for you, and I'm not your child.
Don't ever talk to me that way!'" The two men grew to become frequent
business collaborators and close friends.

Rohan's law partner, Michael Stepanian, also was fond of Graham,
calling him the grown-up that the San Francisco music scene urgently
needed. "Bill was a fabulous character," said Stepanian. "He superim-
posed order on this chaotic world. Yes, he was tough. Yes, he wanted
to make money. But the fact of the matter is that his concerts were
magnificent. The shows started on time, the sound system was great,
the musicians got paid, the kids had a good time. Nobody was beat up
or stabbed, everyone felt safe. He was almost like a father figure of the
counterculture. Everyone was drawn to him."

Graham could be an especially intimidating figure to musicians. He
expected them to adhere to basic professional standards: to show up for
concerts on time, to be sober enough to play, to do encores when the
crowds demanded it. He was a self-proclaimed stickler for show business principles. But the musicians he promoted were often unpredictable children, and when booze or drugs were involved, which was often,
things could get even more erratic.

One night Graham fumed backstage, waiting and waiting for Jim
Morrison to lead the Doors onstage. The singer never showed. The next
afternoon, Morrison sauntered into Graham's cramped quarters upstairs
at the Fillmore and explained that while on his way to the concert,
he passed a movie theater playing *Casablanca*. He couldn't help it; he
went to see the movie instead. "I'm a big Humphrey Bogart fan myself,"

Graham told him, "but you should've called." Morrison thought this over. "Yeah, I *could* have called. But I saw it *three* times."

Musicians quickly learned that excuses didn't cut it with Graham. "Bill was great unless you were late," remembered guitarist Jerry Miller of Moby Grape, San Francisco's most talented but most star-crossed band. "If you fucked up business, he didn't go for that shit. I was waiting backstage at Fillmore East when the rest of the band got bogged down in a blizzard. And Bill was coming apart. He felt you should've told it not to blizzard."

Graham was the father figure that many rock musicians needed. "I thought he was a strong, good man," said Peter Lewis, Miller's bandmate. "He'd have football games on the hardwood floors at the Fillmore on weekend days. You'd have to play him and his beefy security guys. He wasn't a hippie."

"We were hippies, and we were pissed off at him for being a businessman," said David Freiberg of Quicksilver Messenger Service. "That is, until we got paid. He showed us you have to take care of business. Everything wasn't going to be free, not when you have to pay people who work for you."

Graham would become closest to the Grateful Dead, even though the band's barrel-of-monkeys ethos seemed diametrically opposed to his clipboard efficiency. He liked their dedication, the way Jerry Garcia would show up at eleven in the morning on the day of a gig to rehearse and check the sound. With their expansive and generous spirit, the Dead came closest to rock 'n' roll "utopia," in Graham's mind. Garcia, in particular, was, in Graham's words, "the big papa bear" of what the new music should be all about, but was often grubbily not.

Graham thought of the band as his children; particularly mischievous children. Garcia and Hart were always trying to dose him with acid, but the promoter was a control freak—someone had to stay sober to keep the party in bounds—and he was always on guard against the Dead's antics.

"He wouldn't take cookies from my grandma," said Hart. "But one day Jerry and me were standing backstage watching Janis rip up the crowd. We had a couple cans of Coke. Bill went rushing by with his clipboard and, without thinking, grabbed the Coke out of my hand and took a gulp. Jerry and I had anointed the lips of the cans. We had him. I yelled, 'Bill!' over the roar of Big Brother. He yelled back, 'What?' I said, 'The road you now travel will not be a familiar one.' Later that night, he started taking off his clothes, and he was wrapped around the gong onstage singing 'Death Don't Have No Mercy' with the rest of us."

Mickey Hart and Bill Graham went way back, to the days when they worked together as waiters in a nightclub in Atlantic City. Hart came to consider him one of his best friends. He and his bandmates trusted Graham, even when they didn't trust him. "We always laughed at Bill, even when he stole from us. He did it with such class."

One night the Dead finally caught Graham skimming the proceeds at a Winterland show. The band nailed him by positioning people with counters at the doors. "He tried to make up for what he did. He put the money in a paper bag and gave it to us for years."

Hart would find more forgiveness for Graham than he did for his own father, Lenny Hart, the Grateful Dead's business manager, who went to jail for embezzling from the band. Hart never talked to his father again. "What was there to talk about?" By that point, the band was Mickey Hart's family. "And he was the enemy."

But Graham somehow received the Dead's absolution. The band members knew how important he was to the temple of sound they were all creating. "Nothing would have happened without Bill," Hart said. "He made a home for the music. We were outlaws. Nobody trusted us. We were all crazies, and he was the responsible one. He was our big brother."

THE ADVOCATES OF "FREE" wanted the music to stay in the parks and streets. And it was there. Paul Kantner's favorite place for Jefferson Airplane to take wing would always be the sprawling greenery of Speedway Meadow in Golden Gate Park. Those "sunny day afternoons, acid, incense, and balloons" would forever be part of the San Francisco mystique. But the music also needed its sacred chamber, its magical proscenium of swirling lights and sounds, in order to resonate most deeply in the city's soul. And that was Bill Graham's Fillmore.

Graham was the radio tower that pulled in the sound from the crackling universe. There was a reason that the young crowd's eyes turned to him when he walked the ticket line, as if he were a Garcia or Clapton or Hendrix. He had the power to make it all happen. Without him, the exquisite notes would have drifted away in the fog. The crowds resented and adored him for it. But they never forgot the miraculous evenings he staged for them.

Graham shows had a special alchemy. The bills mixed English rock stars and American blues masters. He tried to revive Lenny Bruce's career, as it was nodding off into oblivion, by exposing a new generation to his hipster riffs. He once opened a Jefferson Airplane show with Ferlinghetti and Russian poet Andrei Voznesensky. He combined the sweet folk-rock harmonies of the Byrds with a production of *Dutchman,* playwright LeRoi Jones's screed on America's racial tempest. In the Summer of Love alone, Graham lit up San Francisco with a dazzling galaxy, including Jimi Hendrix, Otis Redding, the Who, Cream, Chuck Berry, Eric Burdon and the Animals, the Yardbirds, the Byrds, Buffalo Springfield, the Doors, Howlin' Wolf, Bo Diddley, Sam and Dave, the Paul Butterfield Blues Band, the Charles Lloyd Quartet, and the Count Basie Orchestra—in addition to all the best San Francisco bands.

Graham turned the Fillmore into holy ground. It was the core of what the city was becoming. For the young men and women who assembled under the old ballroom's chandeliers, it was sanctuary and salvation. This was why they'd trekked to San Francisco. It all came down to the music. They weathered the cold, the cops, the scruff of the streets just to stand inside the sacred walls of sound.

9

THE DAILY CIRCUS

S AN FRANCISCO'S CULTURAL revolution was not popular in city hall
or the hall of justice fortress at 850 Bryant Street. But it did find
some surprising allies downtown, inside the clock tower–topped bunker
at Fifth and Mission Streets that housed the *San Francisco Chronicle*.
The city's reigning daily was owned by a Republican clan that traced its
dynasty back to the gold rush founders of the paper. Yet readers opened
the *Chronicle* on many mornings to find the newspaper championing the
Haight-Ashbury Free Clinic or Huckleberry House, supporting the legal
rights of North Beach topless clubs, defending hippies' pursuit of happiness, and denouncing President Lyndon Johnson's deepening quag-
mire in Vietnam. All of this serious business came wrapped in a candy
box of gossip, carny barker promotion stunts, cheesecake photographs,
and eccentric musings that San Francisco readers found irresistible.
To browse the *Chronicle* each morning was to enter the portals of an
enchanted city that was more than slightly cracked. Fun was the paper's
first order of business, and any stuffed-shirt official who picked on the
city's clowns and misfits or otherwise rained on its cockeyed parade was
to be shunned and ridiculed.

The brilliant showman behind the *Chronicle*'s daily circus was executive editor Scott Newhall. His buttoned-down boss, publisher Charles de
Young Thieriot, might not have always seen eye to eye with his editorial

antics. But the Thieriot family could not argue with the financial results. After taking over the *Chronicle* in 1952, when it was a gray *New York Times* wannabe, languishing far behind the Hearst Corporation–owned *Examiner* in the circulation race, Newhall promptly began winning over San Francisco with his reinvigorated product and wild promotion campaigns. He made it his personal mission to defeat the Hearst newspaper empire, which he regarded as "something evil," preying on the ignorance and fear of the "Catholic, lunchbox San Francisco working man" with its "yellow peril" sensationalism, right-wing demagoguery, and shameless stories about "ghosts clanking their chains in English castles." Newhall would offer San Francisco something different: a progressive-minded and witty fish wrap that would appeal to the city's cosmopolitan aspirations and libertine tastes. His aim proved true: the *Chronicle*'s circulation soared, finally surging past the *Examiner* in 1960.

Scott Newhall's *Chronicle* was the perfect match between city and newspaper. The *Chronicle* did not just give voice to San Francisco; it invented the city. Newhall, who was born and raised in San Francisco, never got over his love affair with his hometown, and the paper was giddy with his passion. He thought of San Francisco as a "fairyland," and his newspaper spun what he frankly called "fairy tales" that added new layers of mythology to the city.

Newhall's *Chronicle* turned San Francisco into a city of fizz and fun. The cool clink of ice in a chrome shaker could always be heard in its pages. There was actor David Niven, spotted in his suite at the Stanford Court Hotel, raising his glass of Cristal to a full moon and murmuring to himself, "The moon's a balloon." There was Bobby Kennedy, at a rooftop party in the Haight with the Grateful Dead. It was the kind of city where anything could happen. Low-rent glamour girls were reborn as high-society hostesses. Square-jawed yachtsmen were inconveniently netted in raids on all-male nightspots.

When there was no fun to be found, Newhall simply made his own. He ran a story about an eccentric millionaire who was campaigning to clothe "naked" animals, which turned out to be a hoax. He ginned up an international incident when he launched a crusade to liberate Anguilla, a spit of sand in the Lesser Antilles, from the British Empire.

The mischievous editor's most famous stunt—an investigative series on the dismal quality of the coffee that was being served in San Francisco establishments—was actually his most legitimate. Newhall could remember when San Francisco was a coffee town, and the air was filled with the earthy aroma of roasting beans. "When I was a child, this was a huge shipping port. The ships came in from all over the world. As a small boy, going along the waterfront you could smell the coffee roasting: Hills Brothers, MJB, Alta Coffee, Folgers Coffee. And oh, it smelled so good, the coffee roasting. You could smell the spices in the old tramp freighters that were tied up along the waterfront—the copra, and jute, and teakwood logs and all that stuff." But things had gone downhill in San Francisco, and now its citizens were being served watery and rancid brews that were a disgrace to the city's richly fragrant heritage. So Newhall ordered a young reporter to investigate "what the hell San Franciscans were drinking today. [He] went up and down Market Street, he went to the hotels, and, my God, he found coffee urns with dead rats in them and everything else, or the coffee was three or four days old. And the stuff they were selling here was totally junk."

Newhall splashed the series across the front page under this opening cymbal crash of a headline: "A Great City's People Forced to Drink Swill." The coffee exposé became infamous in journalism circles, forever branding the *Chronicle* as a frivolous waste of newsprint. Berkeley media professors took to fulminating about Newhall's antics. Meanwhile, the sad-sack *Examiner*, now consigned to a distant second in the circulation race, scurried around trying to expose *Chronicle* "exclusives" as fakes—which, of course, they sometimes were.

Scott Newhall could be gravely serious when he had to. But he clearly preferred to live his life in an amusement park of his own making. And much of San Francisco wanted to join him there. "This guy was a complete wacko," remarked William German, who succeeded Newhall as editor of the *Chronicle*. "But a very talented wacko. And probably right for the time."

NEWHALL'S ESCAPADES SEEMED TO be his bulwark against life's inevitable vale of sorrows. By the time he made it to the top of San Francisco's newspaper racket, the miseries had piled up around him. Newhall was born into a pioneer ranching family that had multiplied its wealth in real estate and finance. He knocked around various California prep schools but didn't manage to graduate from any of them. He got himself into UC Berkeley, but, again, found it more amusing to drink and play than study. In search of adventure, he sailed out the Golden Gate with a friend on a forty-two-foot ketch called the *Mermaid*. They had 14 cents between them, but Newhall was a budding photographer, and he planned to underwrite the trip by selling freelance shots to the *Chronicle*, where he had been employed briefly. While tramping through Mexico, he was kicked by a horse (he kicked it first) and developed a bone infection in his leg. The rot went so deep that he nearly died, and he had to have the leg amputated when he returned to San Francisco. "Oh, well," Newhall thought to himself, he didn't want to be a photographer anyway.

The *Chronicle* took pity on him and gave him a job in the newspaper morgue, filing news clippings. It proved to be a resurrection of sorts. Hobbling around on crutches and filing stories about the city and the world he lived in gave Newhall the education he lacked. And deconstructing the newspaper each day with his pair of scissors taught him something about how to put one together.

From there, during the early 1940s, he began his relentless climb up the *Chronicle*'s editorial masthead. Newhall's ascent at the newspaper was interrupted only by a stint as a war correspondent with the Royal Navy. He found it harrowing on board the motorboat flotillas in the English Channel, running the gauntlet of Nazi submarines, and it made him question his own courage.

When he took over the *Chronicle* in 1952, Newhall surrounded himself with other young men from his generation. After the Depression and the war, newspapering seemed like a game. He was a ruggedly handsome, blue-eyed man, and, stalking the newsroom on his artificial leg, he had the swagger of a peg-legged pirate. Even after he got married and had four children—three boys (including a pair of twins) and a girl—Newhall still treated life like a party. His wife, Ruth, whom he had met at Berkeley, was a game sort with her own newspaper career. And the two of them would throw big parties at their *ranchito* in the Berkeley hills with a dazzling view of the Bay. Newhall loved jazz music and musicians, and his friend Earl "Fatha" Hines would often show up to play piano. Sometimes the parties lasted for days. Jon Newhall, one of the twins, woke up his parents one morning with this sober report: "The dean is asleep under the oleander."

One evening in 1955, during the Christmas season, Newhall's twelve-year-old daughter was caroling with some friends in the neighborhood. Suddenly a tow truck, its brakes having snapped, came roaring down a hill, crushing the girl against a house and instantly killing her. "It was the worst day of our lives," recalled Jon Newhall many years later. Ruth was devastated. Scott kept pushing forward. Sometime after that, he survived a heart attack. He and Ruth stopped going out much after that.

Readers of Scott Newhall's *Chronicle* were not protected from the world's daily onslaught of mayhem and grief. It was all there in easy-to-read packages, with bold-faced leads, surrounded by lots of white space. But embedded in the paper each morning was an absurdist sensibility that said, *You'd better find a way to laugh at life, because it will certainly make you cry.*

NEWHALL WAS A REGISTERED Republican, but it didn't mean much to him. He hated politics, and he thought religion was for pious hypocrites. He liked cutting against the grain. He called the *Chronicle* the country's only mainstream underground newspaper. It was the first major daily to come out against the Vietnam War. Grand newspapers like the *New York Times* and *Washington Post* liked to snicker at the *Chronicle*'s lack of gravitas, Newhall observed. But at least his paper got it right on the big issues. Year after year, the *Times* and *Post* kept toeing the government line on Vietnam, he pointed out, "braying about the communists or the domino theory and all this crap." The gullibility of the journalistic establishment never ceased to amaze him.

Like all lifelong San Franciscans, Newhall was deeply protective of his town. There was nothing about the hippie invasion of his beloved city that he found particularly endearing. He was strictly a jazz and martini kind of guy. But he knew that he didn't like to see the kids given shabby treatment. San Francisco was supposed to welcome "free souls" and "kooks," he thought. And so, as much to stick a finger in the eye of the civic establishment as anything else, Newhall made sure that the *Chronicle* rolled out the welcome mat for the young pioneers flocking into the city. The paper adopted an affectionate, even solicitous, tone toward the hippies. "Editorially, I have always felt that everyone should be free to express himself without any particular restraint as long as he doesn't bother the neighbors," the newspaper editor remarked. "Or, as they say, you can do it in the streets, as long as you don't frighten the horses."

The old expression was as succinct an expression of San Francisco's gold rush philosophy as you could find. *Just don't frighten the horses*. The *Chronicle* was the city's "water well" as Newhall put it, where everyone in town converged. By setting a tone of tolerance toward the hippies, the newspaper played a critical role in shaping the broader community's views. If long-haired boys and girls dancing beneath the diamond sky with one hand waving free was the kind of spectacle that ruined your day, the *Chronicle* told its readers, well, maybe you weren't a true San Franciscan. Curmudgeons, blowhards, and bullies were regularly treated to a good swift kick in the pants in Newhall's paper.

It was Ralph J. Gleason, the *Chronicle*'s legendary jazz and pop music critic, who brought the newspaper into the rock 'n' roll age. Newhall and Gleason were kindred souls. They roamed the streets of San Francisco together in the 1950s and 1960s, sampling the sweet sounds of the night. Gleason introduced his boss to jazz pals like Duke Ellington and Miles Davis. The music critic was a diabetic, and Newhall was trying to lay off the elixir, so they would drink tumblers of branch water on the rocks. One night Louis Armstrong—who was maintaining his own strict health regimen at the time, drinking a concoction that made him empty his bowels at regular intervals—received the two newspapermen in his backstage dressing room at Chez Paree, "a Mason Street G-string maisonette," in Newhall's words, while perched on his porcelain throne.

As the youth wave came rolling in during the sixties, Gleason immediately recognized that something shimmering was happening in the city. The music columnist was pushing fifty when the revolution hit, but he had the spirit of a man who "kept bathing his soul in the fountain of youth," said a friend. Gleason was there in 1965 when the Jefferson Airplane made its debut at a small club in the Marina district called the Matrix, and later that year when the Family Dog collective held its historic dance concert at Longshoremen's Hall, where he met a young fan of his column named Jann Wenner. Gleason used his daily column as a platform to champion the kids' right to dance in Golden Gate Park, and he talked Newhall and the *Chronicle* editorial board into siding with Bill Graham against the cops. He never indulged in drugs, but he cultivated his own unique personality, with his Sherlock Holmes hat, tweed coat, pipe and handlebar mustache. He was the patron saint of San Francisco's emerging rock scene. "There would have been no Jefferson Airplane without Ralph Gleason," said singer Marty Balin. There would have been no "San Francisco Sound" at all, added the Airplane's manager, a former *Chronicle* copy boy named Bill Thompson. "He was the grown-up who got it," said Wenner, whom Gleason affectionately called Yanno. The ambitious Wenner and his mentor would later co-found *Rolling Stone* magazine.

The *Chronicle* of the 1960s—witty, offbeat, bemused—was a Scott Newhall production. But Newhall preferred to stay behind the curtain, relying on his colorful menagerie of columnists to vocalize the *Chronicle* point of view. If he was the impresario, the columnists were his players, and he cast them as carefully as a Broadway producer. Trawling for a sports columnist, he found rewrite man Charles McCabe, who didn't like sports. Exactly what Newhall was looking for. Billed as "the Fearless Spectator," McCabe would become a *Chronicle* institution. He was pictured above the column in a bowler hat, like a member of the London Stock Exchange. But he churned out his copy each afternoon from his perch at jovial Gino and Carlo's saloon in North Beach. McCabe's column offered up an eccentric goulash of opinion—sometimes royalist, sometimes radical—on public affairs, the human heart, or any other damned thing that crossed his mind between scotch and sodas at the bar.

For the women's page, Newhall hired a former hairdresser named Marc Spinelli, rechristening him Count Marco, a bitch queen columnist who scolded women for being too fat and whiny, and instructed them how to emerge from a bathtub without looking like a cow. "It was weird," even Newhall had to admit. Female readers were outraged, but they couldn't seem to get enough of the count's acid-tongued Bette Davis routine.

Newhall's biggest star by far was three-dot columnist Herb Caen, San Francisco's beloved deadline bard. Every day but Saturday for more than a half century, Caen spun a yarn about San Francisco and its peculiar denizens that was so enchanting, the city still remains in its thrall years after his death. He called the town "Baghdad by the Bay" in his column, conjuring the exotic wonders of ancient Babylon. But his San Francisco was more like Oz, Wonderland, and Gotham City all rolled together. If much of it was Caen's own creation, it's the city that San Franciscans wanted to live in.

The columnist concocted a fizzy drink of a city, full of witty and beautiful people and equally amusing scoundrels. It was a shining metropolis with enlightened values and wide-open sensibilities, where Chinese waiters and black cable car bell ringers were as fascinating as Nob Hill playboys. Most of his columns were bird-cage ephemera: Pacific Heights marriages on the rocks, celebrity sightings, and punch lines too good to be true, like the 1962 item about San Francisco's most famous madam. ("Sally Stanford is off tomorrow for a month in Europe. 'Have you ever been abroad?' she was asked. 'Always,' she replied tartly.") But in between the bold names and the patter, there was an epic poem about San Francisco.

John Steinbeck got it. "Herb's city is the one that will be remembered," he said.

10

SAN FRANCISCO'S MORNING KISS

ERB CAEN WAS born in Sacramento, California, a town that combined all the glamour of a farm fair with the dazzle of a state franchise board hearing. But he carried a different story in his genes. His father was a Jew from the Alsace-Lorraine region of France whose American dream turned into a liquor wholesale business. His mother had been an opera singer in Germany. They moved to Sacramento to give their children an all-American upbringing. But even as a boy, Caen knew he didn't belong there. He subscribed to the *San Francisco Call-Bulletin* just to read Walter Winchell's column, that staccato drumbeat of metropolitan energy.

San Francisco was a revelation whenever his family visited. Known to everyone in the surrounding hinterlands simply as the City, it rose up on the hills, some of it white and gleaming, the rest wrapped in fog and mystery. Every time Caen came back to San Francisco, it was like he was arriving for the first time. Throughout his life, he carried the arriviste's desperate love for the city. It always seemed to loom slightly above him, beyond his grasp. Summoned as a young man by the *Chronicle* for a job interview in 1938, he bought a new suit and hat for the occasion. But as his big, white ferryboat steamed toward the city, while Caen once again marveled at the skyline, his hat was blown into the choppy bay. Caen would always worry whether he was sophisticated enough to fit in.

The "Sackamenna Kid," as he humbly anointed himself, found it rough going in the early years. One day the young columnist, playing the suave host, tried to introduce an heiress from the de Young family, owners of the *Chronicle*, to an heiress from the Spreckels family, the wealthy sugar barons. "Oh, we know each other," sniffed the de Young heiress. "It's just that we haven't spoken since her daddy shot my daddy." Caen was beaten up twice, both times in the lobby of the Mark Hopkins Hotel, by wealthy playboys who objected to his snappy items on their romantic peccadillos. On another occasion, he was nearly killed by a Mickey Finn heavily laced with horse laxative. The knockout punch was slipped to him by the owner of a secret Turk Street gambling joint—one of the few night spot operators whose business was hurt by a mention in Caen's column. The columnist managed to crawl out of the dive and get home before collapsing on his floor.

But Caen ultimately found his groove, working the city more tirelessly each night than Sally Stanford's girls—who, coincidentally, often appeared in the column, in the prim Junior League dresses and corsages that the madam insisted they wear as they greeted clients in her Russian Hill mansion. The columnist's nightly circuit changed over the years. In the beginning, he trawled for items at the city's swanky Nob Hill hotels and the more colorful watering holes down below, like Shanty Malone's—whose massive floor was marked out with white lines like a football field—and the Black Cat, where drag diva José Sarria would lead patrons each night in a rousing version of "God Save Us Nelly Queens" sung to the stately tune of the British anthem. In later years, Caen preferred North Beach jazz clubs like El Matador, the hungry i, and Enrico's, where sometimes he sat in on drums.

Caen lived and breathed the city. He was so devoted to it, that his first wife, Bea, a bright-eyed showgirl with a blond bubble, threatened to name San Francisco as a co-respondent when she sued him for divorce. In his columns, he was always trying to find the city's heart. His three-dot patter had the swinging rhythm of his friend big-band drummer Gene Krupa. He was cool enough to be thrown out of Tosca in North Beach with a barefoot Allen Ginsberg. "You can't throw out Allen Ginsberg!" Caen objected. "He's a famous poet." To the Italian proprietors, however, he was just another filthy beatnik. Caen might run with a 'round-midnight crowd, but he always imagined he was writing the column for a simple housewife out on the city's westerly, windswept avenues. "Effie Zilch," he called her, and she would read his column after getting her husband off to work and making herself a pot of coffee, as she rested her slippered feet on the breakfast table.

Caen gave the tourists' San Francisco its due, with nods to sourdough aromas, the crab pots of Fisherman's Wharf, and the "ceaseless click-clacking of the cables in their slots." But he never stopped looking for some deeper truth about the city. Maybe he came close late one night in the spring of 1961.

"The other midnight, in a Chinatown bar," he wrote, "I met a real San Franciscan. He was a middle-aged longshoreman from the Mission, and he wore a zipper jacket and open shirt. While he quietly sipped a Scotch, he talked of Harry Bridges, Bill Saroyan, and Shanty Malone. He was curious about Leontyne Price and Herbert Gold. He wondered if the Duke of Bedford's paintings were any good, he missed Brubeck, and he discussed Willie Mays down to his last spike. He seemed to know everybody in town, by first names—and it was only after he'd left that we discovered he'd bought a round of drinks for the house. For want of a better phrase, he had that touch of class—the touch of a San Franciscan."

Caen found his full stride in the sixties, the decade that began with the jazzy energy of Lenny Bruce and Miles Davis and swung seamlessly into the glorious, furious wails of Janis and Grace. San Francisco's bard made the transition to the new, psychedelic city in smooth style. His column pulsed with everything San Francisco was becoming. He welcomed in New Year 1967 at the Fillmore, showing up in a tuxedo with some high-society friends to dance to the Jefferson Airplane. Despite his stiff, black-tie attire, he was warmly welcomed by the young crowd. "They think you're in costume," said his friend, novelist Herb Gold.

Caen genuinely loved the kaleidoscope scenes at the Fillmore and Winterland. And he was a big fan of the Airplane, even after an unfortunate incident at the band's Fulton Street mansion, across from Golden Gate Park. Caen and his young third wife, Maria Theresa, were among the guests one night in the fall of 1968 for a decadent banquet at the Airplane's black-painted Greek Revival mansion. The feast included a roast suckling pig (complete with apple in mouth) and a punchbowl liberally spiked with LSD. During the evening, as psychedelic wizard Owsley Stanley repeatedly blared the Beatles' new release, "Hey Jude," throughout the wired mansion's multitude of speakers, a blissfully unaware Maria Theresa dipped her cup into the punch bowl several times and was soon weeping uncontrollably about the radiant beauty she felt all around her.

Maria Theresa remained fond of rock musicians, despite her nonconsensual LSD initiation. A number of them visited the Caen residence, which by then was a Pacific Heights house big enough for the columnist's voluminous book and record collection as well as his wife and son, Christopher. "When I was growing up, Jim Morrison would drop by," recalled the younger Caen. "He'd drink all of our cognac."

Sixties San Francisco, as portrayed in Caen's column, was a room full of balloons. There was golden Julie Christie, in town to film *Petulia*, adrift in her rainwater pool in Sausalito and dancing to the Grateful Dead on a ferryboat in the bay . . . there was Paul McCartney wandering Haight-Ashbury with girlfriend Jane Asher, carefree and unbothered, and sitting in with the Jefferson Airplane . . . there were Marshall McLuhan, Tom Wolfe, and Caen doing some sociological research at a topless bar in North Beach, where the esteemed professor observed that the blushing newspaperman couldn't bring himself to look at the waitresses' bare breasts . . . and there was ballet dancer Rudolf Nureyev, swanning around the SFPD's Park Station, after being rounded up in a pot party raid, serenading the cops with "San Francisco" in the flamboyant old MGM style of Jeanette MacDonald.

But it wasn't all incense and peppermints. The decade also brought out a political edge in Caen that gave his column a new sharpness. He fulminated against the Vietnam War and picketed with Marlon Brando outside San Quentin to protest the gas chamber execution of a thirty-nine-year-old rapist and thief named Caryl Chessman. "Why isn't Caryl Chessman gassed in the middle of Union Square at high noon?" wrote an unusually bitter Caen, who as a young reporter had witnessed a hanging at Folsom State Prison. "But no, that would be an indecent spectacle, abhorrent to those who prefer to live by euphemisms. He must be done away with in a gloomy little room surrounded by a protective nest of walls—as though the act itself, the final demonstration of the majesty of law, were some dark and dreadful thing. And a dark and dreadful thing it is."

He scolded the San Francisco snoots who turned up their noses at hippies—"Goldie Locks and the Three Bores," he called them—and the cops who cracked open kids' heads on Haight Street. And, to the dismay of many of his high-society friends, he raised a ruckus over the massive high-rise developments that were beginning to overshadow the gleaming white skyline he fell in love with as a boy.

Caen had a complicated relationship with blue-blood San Francisco. He was a union man at heart, and he had a weak spot for the underdog, walking the picket line during the 1966 newspaper strike and giving Harry Bridges some of the only good press he got in town. But the Sackamenna Kid also longed to be embraced by the swell set. He certainly dressed and acted the part, gliding (not walking) about town in his Wilkes Bashford suits, and smoothly tipping two light fingers to the brim of his hat to passing ladies. But the WASP types never could fully accept a wise-cracking Jew from the Central Valley. And Jewish society was perplexed by an atheist who never went to temple, married only shiksas, and christened his son "Christopher."

When Caen joined the first anti–high rise campaign in 1968, aimed at blocking a U.S. Steel office tower on the waterfront, he helped terminate the project but also gained some powerful enemies. Sometimes it's necessary to shame the city's business class, the columnist later remarked, to remind them that a city like San Francisco is more than just a real estate opportunity—it's "a precious, special, fragile place." Walter Shorenstein, the wealthy San Francisco developer, was one of those who took strenuous exception to being labeled a money-grubber by Caen. The real estate magnate's equilibrium was not improved by the fact that he lost $5 million when the city board of supervisors voted down the U.S. Steel project. It was not the first time, and would not be the last, that Caen seemed to wield more power than the city's mayor.

A couple of nights after the board decision, Shorenstein—a distinguished-looking gentleman with thinning, silver hair—spotted Caen at a gala event and came charging across the room to throttle him. "I'm gonna run you out of town, you sonofabitch!" screamed Shorenstein, while his political sidekick, newly elected mayor Joe Alioto, tried desperately to peel him off Caen. Throughout the tempest, Caen couldn't stop laughing, which only made Shorenstein more berserk.

Caen was no muckraker, and when he vented too much steam about Vietnam or the changing San Francisco skyline, he worried about being a bore—one of the worst sins the three-dot columnist could imagine. He knew his job was to gently tickle the morning reader as his caffeine juiced him awake. But every now and then, the column performed a different duty. Amidst the daily assembly line of amusements came an important reminder of what San Francisco was all about. Caen was the city's convivial conscience, and the chatty, shameless *San Francisco Chronicle* was the perfect platform for his disposable, indispensable wisdom.

11

RADIO FREE AMERICA

THE 1960S WAS essentially a cultural dialogue between San Francisco and London. The music, art, fashions, comics, drug experimentation, sexual innovation—it was all driven by the creative interplay between the two cities (with some heavy assistance from Detroit, in the music department). In America, if you were young and longing for more, if you felt like a vagrant in your own hometown, if your life seemed elsewhere, then you headed for "Gold Mountain," as Chinese fortune seekers once called the city by the bay. Otis Redding condensed all this longing in "(Sittin' On) The Dock of the Bay," which he began writing on a Sausalito houseboat in the Summer of Love, with the city gleaming in the distance. San Francisco beckoned to dreamers and losers everywhere. Many of them found the paradise they were seeking, free of the small voices that had hobbled them. Stewart Brand, Chet Helms, Janis Joplin, Jann Wenner, Hunter S. Thompson, Robert Crumb. More and more rebels arrived every day. They found one another, they formed bands, they started underground enterprises, they made history. San Francisco was Radio Free America, beaming its message of liberation around the world and summoning an endless army of outcasts.

Crumb's exodus from the Midwest was fairly typical. His father, a twenty-year veteran of the marine corps, never got over the fact that he had produced three awkward, arty sons. To escape his old man's anger and bafflement, young Crumb moved in with a friend in Cleveland and went to work doing color separations for a greeting card company. Month after month, he woke up every morning in blank, wintry Cleveland and punched the time clock. In June 1965 deliverance finally arrived in the form of a little blue vial of Sandoz pills that his wife, Dana, brought home one day, courtesy of her psychiatrist.

"LSD knocked me on my ass," said Crumb. "It was my road to Damascus. The next day I had to go to work, but it all seemed like a cardboard world to me; people seemed like they were just going through the motions. After a couple years, I fled to San Francisco. I remember showing up in Golden Gate Park—some guy dressed like Peter Pan was flitting around dropping strange pills in people's mouths."

Crumb abandoned his old life—"deserted my job, deserted my wife. I was not a good man. I ran away from it all." And he never looked back. In the fall of 1967, a broke Crumb, sitting in his Haight-Ashbury apartment, drew *Zap No. 0* and *Zap No. 1* and sold the underground comic books out of a baby carriage on the street. It was the beginning of Mr. Natural, Angelfood McSpade, Fritz the Cat, and other warped creations of Crumb's brilliant, drug-assisted imagination. The legend had begun.

Wes "Scoop" Nisker showed up in San Francisco after coming west in June 1967 to cover the Monterey Pop Festival for a student magazine at the University of Minnesota, where he was enrolled in graduate school. The festival was a celebration of the West Coast and UK musical renaissance, with historic performances by Jimi Hendrix (who was introduced onstage by the Rolling Stones' Brian Jones), Janis and Big Brother, Otis Redding, and the Who. An eight-foot statue of the Buddha greeted festivalgoers as they entered the luminous grounds. Nisker was utterly transformed by the "colorful, joyous, quasi-spiritual explosion." Afterward, he and some Minnesota friends drove up to the city, along the winding, rocky coast studded with cypress and pines, with the Pacific crashing below. In San Francisco, he ambled through the labyrinthine greenery of Golden Gate Park and, as a young devotee of beat culture, made a trek to one of his meccas, City Lights Bookstore. Nisker quickly realized that San Francisco was where he belonged. "I knew I'd found my family. I wanted to be part of this tribe."

Nisker moved into a coffee baron's old mansion at the corner of California and Franklin Streets that had been subdivided into a hippie warren. He felt he was living in a storybook castle, with a sweeping, polished redwood staircase and majestic bay windows. The Victorian house crackled with youthful creativity. "We were remaking culture," he recalled. "The revolution was weeks away." Nisker could hear it when he tuned in to San Francisco's FM radio.

San Francisco was the center of the underground radio revolution. Until the late sixties, American radio was dominated by Top 40 AM radio—a tightly formatted Wall of Sound that allowed only the occasional Beatles or Stones song to break through with hints of the musical revolution outside. But then Tom Donahue—the gargantuan, bearded DJ and music promoter—lumbered into the San Francisco radio world.

The big man came west from Philadelphia's pioneering WIBG in 1961, on the run from the radio payola investigations that had destroyed the careers of Alan Freed and other celebrated DJs. In San Francisco, his ears quickly picked up the new hum and thrum in the universe. Listening to the Doors' first album at home late one night, Donahue wondered why the hell radio was not playing this kind of music. In 1967 he issued his revolutionary manifesto in the pages of a new San Francisco magazine called *Rolling Stone*: "AM Radio Is Dead and Its Rotting Corpse Is Stinking Up the Airwaves." Donahue convinced the owner of KMPX, a backwater FM station, to allow him to take over its programming. At that time, FM radio was lunar terrain, a rarely tuned-in world of AM station simulcasts and educational broadcasts. But when Donahue took control of the KMPX airwaves, free-form, alternative radio was born, with the DJ promising "no jingles, no talkovers, no time and temp, no pop singles."

Tuning in to KMPX in his room in the coffee mansion, Nisker knew immediately that he wanted to enlist in Donahue's revolution. For Nisker and his friends, underground FM radio was like the dawn of the web for a future generation: a hardwire connection to the essential sounds and secret ideas swirling around the globe.

One day in late 1967, Nisker got up the nerve to march down to the KMPX office at Sutter and Montgomery Streets. He talked Donahue into letting him launch an experimental news program on the station. Nisker began creating news collages, cutting up politicians' fatuous pronouncements and laying appropriately ironic music underneath them. He brought counterculture guests into the studio—like Allen Ginsberg,

Abbie Hoffman, and Alan Watts—and gave them the kind of media platform they never had before. He drew on his own unique blend of Marxist (Karl *and* Groucho) and Buddhist philosophy to create a wacky, spiritually enlightened, politically engaged news program that was a perfect fit for San Francisco's rock audience. He told his listeners, "If you don't like the news, go out and make some of your own."

For a brief and glorious moment, the inmates were in charge of the asylum at KMPX, voting on which ads to run and rejecting military recruiting spots. When the station owner suddenly tried to tighten the reins in early 1968, even instituting a staff dress code, Donahue promptly resigned. His DJs began picketing the station, with local bands like the Grateful Dead and Blue Cheer rallying around them. Soon afterward, Donahue, Nisker, and their merry band took their act to rival station KSAN-FM, which recognized the commercial potential in San Francisco's underground sound.

NURTURED BY FM RADIO and concert promoters Bill Graham and Chet Helms, San Francisco bands proliferated like fungi in the deep, wet woods. *Rolling Stone* later estimated that there were about five hundred rock groups playing in the San Francisco area during the sixties golden days. "We felt the city was the center of the universe," said Jann Wenner. "It was one great big ball."

Most of these San Francisco bands have long since faded into the mists of time—even some of the great ones, like Moby Grape, a group that many rock fans thought would soar the highest of all. But it's important to conjure the sense of *excitement* and *importance* that once swirled around these young musicians.

Moby Grape married the sweet folk-rock harmonies of the Byrds with the ballsy rage of the Rolling Stones. They were musicians' musicians: five men who, after honing their craft in various musical incarnations, created a perfect chemistry when they came together. The quintet began rehearsing together in the fall of 1966 at the Ark, a Sausalito club that had been converted from an old paddleboat. Working all night long, they perfected a slashing, symphonic sound composed of intricate, five-part harmonies and three distinctive guitar styles. The band members knew from the very start how good they were. "There was something about this particular combination of people, coupled with this magical San Francisco environment," recalled singer and guitarist Jerry Miller, who had knocked around Seattle with a young Jimi Hendrix and had played the Southwest circuit with the Bobby Fuller Four ("I Fought the Law") before joining Moby Grape. "We knew right away. Everybody in the band knew they'd better start playing better, writing better. We had to pick up our game. Each guy was better than the other guy."

The word immediately began to spread in the Bay Area's febrile music environment. Something phenomenal was happening at the Ark. Other musicians began dropping in to hear what Moby Grape was assembling: David Crosby from the Byrds, Steve Stills and Neil Young from Buffalo Springfield, Janis Joplin and Sam Andrew from Big Brother. They had never heard anything like it. Tightly constructed two-and-a-half-minute songs that came roaring through the billowing psychedelic haze of the day. "Listen my friends!" Moby Grape demanded in its swooping, breathtaking anthem "Omaha"—a song written by the group's mad genius, Skip Spence, former drummer for the Jefferson Airplane. And the entire San Francisco music scene *did* listen. "You guys are better than the Beatles," gushed a bedazzled Andrew after taking in one of the band's rehearsals.

Right here, right now—there was no other place to be for a young musician in the late sixties. That's how Peter Lewis, the son of screen legend Loretta Young, felt. The feeling came rushing into his heart as the Moby Grape singer-guitarist sat with his bandmates and other musicians on a deck in Sausalito late one afternoon, watching the fog cascade over Mount Tamalpais. He loved the fog; it was certainly more bracing than LA's suffocating smog. He loved that he was no longer "Loretta Young Jr." He loved listening to Stills and Young as they sat there playing "Mr. Soul" and "Bluebird" and other new songs from their unreleased second album.

Like Big Brother, Moby Grape was scooped up by Columbia Records. The band was going to be the Next Big Thing. The young musicians were feted at Columbia parties like dauphin princes. Columbia president Goddard Lieberson entertained the San Francisco rockers at his home, but the host and his guests didn't know what to make of one another. Lieberson, who sported a Caesar haircut and a gold chain with the letters G-O-D around his neck, was known for his cast recordings

of Broadway musicals. Joplin felt discombobulated by the glittery surroundings. She went into Lieberson's bathroom, piled all his expensive
toiletries on the floor, and pissed on them. "Go in there and check it
out," she told Peter Lewis and the other musicians when she came out.
"I really got this guy good."

"It was disgusting," said Lewis. But he understood. "Janis had been
kicked around all her life." And now the court minstrels were suddenly,
inexplicably, in command. "She knew she could put her cigarette out on
the king's rug and get away with it."

THE MUSIC HAD THE power. The music was the signal. It called out to
young people everywhere. It lured them to San Francisco—if not to the
city itself, then to its empire of dreams. San Francisco was a youth fantasy, not just a seven-mile-by-seven-mile metropolis on the tip of a peninsula. The city of dreams even called out to Ronald Reagan's children.

Reagan was the leader of the 1960s' political backlash—a backlash
that came whipping into existence almost simultaneously with the cultural revolution itself. The conservative movement's new hero was the
product of a dreary Midwestern upbringing, the son of an alcoholic
father and a pious mother. He had learned early on to create a fantasy
life, a skill that was put to good use in his Hollywood career, but even
more so in his political one. In Reagan's storybook America, San Francisco was a freakish outpost. He mocked the young people who idealized
the San Francisco way of life. Hippies, he sneered, "dress like Tarzan,
have hair like Jane, and smell like Cheetah." And yet Ronald and Nancy
Reagan's own children, Patti and Ron, were among those disaffected
teens. Raised in the lush suburb of Pacific Palisades, Los Angeles—in
a model home outfitted with the latest gadgets from General Electric,
one of their father's perks for working as the company pitchman—the
Reagan children fantasized about escaping to the Haight.

"My father became governor of California in 1966, when I was
fourteen—just as I was longing to be older and run off to the Haight
and plait flowers in my hair," recalled Patti Reagan Davis. "When he
got elected, I felt humiliated, devastated; I felt more trapped than ever.
I never did get the chance to run off to the Haight during its glory
years. Everything I believed in and wanted in those days was just out

of reach because of my age. And then my father was elected governor, and in such splintered times."

Reagan was swept into office in Sacramento on a tide of resentment against Berkeley student protests and other youthful rebellion. He threatened student radicals with a violent crackdown: "If it takes a bloodbath, let's get it over with." In later years, as president, he was known for putting a genial face on his callous policies. But the 1960s brought out Reagan's mean streak. "He was a lot more mellow as president than he was as governor," Patti said. "He was such an angry Republican in those years—he had that hard set to his mouth that you saw on the antiwar posters at the time."

It was Patti who brought the sixties home to the Reagan household. She felt suffocated in the family home's quiet, immaculate "glass atmosphere" and was constantly trying to crash through to something real. In her memoir, Patti recalled that she and her mother, Nancy, fought constantly—volcanic clashes that frequently ended with Patti being smacked across the face. Patti sought emotional solace from her father, but there was nothing there. His "presence felt like an absence."

Nancy, the future "Just Say No" antidrug crusader, used a string of mother's little helpers to get her through each day. Through the years, her medicine chest was stocked with vials of Miltown, Librium, Valium, Seconal, and Quaalude. Reagan blamed his wife's frayed nerves on his daughter. "Do you think a child can be born evil?" he once asked Ron. He was talking about Patti.

Patti was the outcast. She felt that her own parents treated her like a "trespasser." She was the daughter who probed the family lies and secrets, who questioned her father's political opinions, who stood up to her mother's bullying. And the Reagans—like so many American families at the time—were utterly incapable of dealing with her. Before Patti could run off to San Francisco, like thousands of other kids, the family packed her off to a boarding school.

Ron, the younger child, worked out a different stratagem for handling his parents. He avoided the "operatic" confrontations, and tried to finesse the conflicts instead. One day he put the *Woodstock* album on the family's state-of-the-art GE sound system, with speakers throughout the house. But he made a mad dash to the living room turntable from his bedroom before Country Joe and the Fish could give its "F-U-C-K" cheer, to spare his parents the aggravation. Ron saw his father in a more forgiving light, observing, "My dad did not have a mean bone in his body. He was just completely baffled by the sixties."

Both Reagan children found sanctuary in the San Francisco of their dreams. Exiled to a prep school on an Arizona ranch, Patti daydreamed about running off to the Haight, where she would fall in love with a musician or poet and wander the streets, handing out flowers to tourists. Meanwhile, at home in Pacific Palisades, Ron grew his hair longer, to his parents' dismay, and borrowed his sister's Jefferson Airplane albums. The music set you free.

When the truth is found to be lies, and all the joy within you dies, don't you want somebody to love.

12

THE PALACE OF GOLDEN COCKS

ONE SPRING MORNING in 1969, a doll-faced teenager named Pam Tent found herself lolling in the grass next to a pond in a remote green cove of Golden Gate Park surrounded by palm fronds and ferns. She had just hitchhiked to the city from Boulder, Colorado, and was dreamily mulling over her next move. The Haight seemed more raunchy than it was during her first trip to San Francisco the year before, and this overgrown corner of the park was an oasis of peace and quiet.

Suddenly her reverie was interrupted.

"We're having a heat wave . . ." Pam recognized the song right away. It was the Marilyn Monroe tropical dance number from *There's No Business Like Show Business*. Pam knew her show tunes. As a kid, after abandoning her original ambition of becoming a nun, she decided to become a showgirl. Now she cracked open an eye and gazed across the pond. Three young men were folded into the crook of a gnarled cypress tree, making like they were Marilyn's Caribbean chorus boys. One of the men wore lipstick.

"Yoo-hoo!" he called out to her. And Pam Tent's life changed forever.

"HE WAS A STUNNING apparition: half child, half temptress," Pam recalled. "He giggled through glamour-girl lips. His blond hair was a tousled mane, crowned with a garland of wild flowers. Coquettish in dark eyeliner, bare feet, and a white muslin caftan, he looked like a cross between Marlene Dietrich and Puck from *A Midsummer Night's Dream.*"

As Pam approached the tree, the man danced along one of the branches in his bare feet like a wood faerie, sprinkling gold glitter in his wake. She was dazzled by his radiance. He called himself Hibiscus, and he invited her home—which turned out to be a commune in a three-story Sutter Street Victorian mansion on the edge of Japantown that was slated for destruction by the city's redevelopment bulldozers.

Pam quickly accepted his offer to move in. And she dropped like Alice down the hole in the earth, disappearing into a world that would grow curiouser and curiouser by the day.

Hibiscus was the "divine dictator" of this world. Born George Edgerly Harris III to a theater family in Bronxville, New York, he began displaying a dramatic flair at an early age, staging backyard musicals and Hollywood epics. "We knew he was gay even as a kid, when he started to give our Barbie dolls transsexual makeovers," said his sister Mary Lou. After a brief romp in the New York experimental theater world, Harris headed west in 1967. He took a detour through Washington, DC, for the big antiwar demonstration outside the Pentagon, where he was captured in an iconic sixties photo, placing a carnation in the barrel of a soldier's gun. Shortly after arriving in San Francisco, he reinvented himself as Hibiscus, a vision in sequins, glitter, flowers, and diaphanous robes. "He came out of the closet wearing the entire closet," said his friend Nicky Nichols.

Hibiscus's Sutter Street commune was led by a short, severe rabbinical figure named Irving Rosenthal, who had dedicated himself to following the Diggers' free philosophy. Nicknamed the Kaliflower commune, after the weekly newsletter published every Thursday in its Free Print shop and distributed to other San Francisco communes, Rosenthal's group led a disciplined, ascetic existence. Once Pam brought home a sweet indulgence—a can of lemon pie filling—only to later discover that the Kaliflower chef had redistributed the luxury item among the commune's entire, ravenous membership while she was gone.

"If you could live communally and cheaper," thought Rosenthal, "you didn't have to bore yourself to death working in an office job."

The author of a homoerotic novel, *Sheeper*, and the sometime publisher of Ginsberg and onetime lover of William S. Burroughs, Rosenthal enjoyed a cultish cachet and was able to bend his hippie communards to his stern will. Everyone, that is, except Hibiscus. Rosenthal agreed to take in Hibiscus as a favor to a good friend—a lover of the hothouse creature who begged Rosenthal to take him off his hands. Rosenthal the disciplinarian soon fell before Hibiscus's anarchic charms. He began to indulge Hibiscus as the commune's "delicato" and allowed him to opt out of Kaliflower's strict regimen of household chores and meetings. "I don't scrub floors," Hibiscus announced merrily as he skipped in and out of the house, collecting colorful rags and trinkets from thrift stores and flea markets and assembling a wardrobe big enough for the cast of *Scheherazade.*

Hibiscus created a circle of magic wherever he went in San Francisco. He dressed like Isadora Duncan and danced in Golden Gate Park. One day a concerned young man came up to him and warned him that he should move deeper into the park because the police were beating up freaks like him. Hibiscus batted his long, false eyelashes at him. "They would do that to *me?*" he trilled in a voice as sweet and delicate as a nymph.

Hibiscus staged free kiddie shows in the park with Pam, whom he rechristened Sweet Pam. Together they sang "Tender Shepherd" from the musical *Peter Pan* and tunes from *The Wizard of Oz* and made flower headdresses for the children.

He was an angel of light. Wherever he went, he dusted the world with glitter and sequins. His lovers, including Ginsberg, had to accustom themselves to being glitter encrusted after spending a night with him. "It was difficult to sleep on [his] sheets because there was this sort of like difficult glitter stuff there," recalled the poet. "And it was always in our lips and in our buttholes . . . You couldn't quite get it out."

Hibiscus kept an enchanted scrapbook, filled with glittery scenarios for future musicals that were taking shape in his florid imagination. He pasted old publicity shots of Hollywood idols in its pages, alongside images of Eastern and Western deities. Many of the pictures were torn out of books from the San Francisco Public Library.

Over dinner at Kaliflower on New Year's Eve 1970, Hibiscus shared his vision with Fayette Hauser, a curvy and creamy young artist from New Jersey, and his other guests. It was time to put on a show. "A new theater for a new decade!" he gushed to "Fayett-ah," as he operatically pronounced her name. In fact, he wanted to do a dry run that very evening at a late-night movie house in North Beach called the Palace. They would play dress-up, jump onstage, and see what happened.

Rosenthal kept a large, locked room in the Kaliflower attic that was stuffed with feather boas, petticoats, wigs, and other drag paraphernalia— costumes for an underground film he was producing. Since Rosenthal was conveniently out of town at the time, Hibiscus quickly convinced the commune's keeper of the keys to unlock the door. The drag queens fell on the lacy frills like jackals on a fallen zebra. What would they call their troupe? The keeper of the keys pulled Hibiscus aside and whispered, "How about the Cockettes?"

Dolled up like Dorothy Lamour on acid, Hibiscus and his colorful crew piled into their motley fleet of vehicles and headed for the Palace. There was no better venue for the Cockettes' debut. The post-earthquake relic was a collision of visual fantasies. The old Italian opera house still featured its original gold leaf designs, art deco chandeliers, and curved staircases. But overlaid on all this Italian brocade were Oriental design themes that fit the theater's current role as a Chinese-language movie house. In the auditorium, a gilded lotus fresco was splashed across the ceiling, and golden dragons roared fire on the lobby walls. Around midnight, after the Chinese patrons filed out of the final show, the Palace was taken over by a very different crowd for the screening of campy Hollywood classics and experimental films. This late-night audience was part of San Francisco's emerging underground culture—hippies with a taste for more glamour than a Dead concert could provide, sexually flamboyant men and women searching for others like themselves, renegade artists looking for brave new ways of communicating. They were all hungry for something like the Cockettes.

Hibiscus and his dazzling coconspirators took the stage in a mad rush, aided by the ample hallucinogens coursing through their bodies. Someone put on a record—the exact tune is a matter of hazy dispute, either the Stones' "Honky Tonk Women" or "Jumping Jack Flash," or an old 78 rpm of a French burlesque song. And the Cockettes formed a rowdy cancan line, kicking up their heels and swishing their skirts. As the troupe finished its performance, the crowd shot to its feet, erupting in cheers and wolf whistles. "Now what?" the Cockettes wondered. Hibiscus and Fayette stared at each other. But Hibiscus knew instantly. He put on the record again, and the Cockettes began shedding their glittery costumes. A whole new galaxy of San Francisco stars was born that night.

DRAG QUEEN SHOWS HAD a long, luxurious history in San Francisco, dating back to the 1860s and 1870s, when vaudevillians like Paul Vernon, wearing lacy gowns and Goldilocks wigs, wowed local audiences—made up largely of lonely frontiersmen. At the turn of the century, the city's first openly gay bar, the Dash, featured female impersonators. The club, in the Barbary Coast, managed to stay open until 1908, when city officials shut it down as the "most notorious and disreputable establishment" in San Francisco. In the 1930s drag broke into the city's thriving sex tourism market when an Italian immigrant and former speakeasy owner named Joe Finocchio opened a dazzling female impersonator show on Stockton Street, which he later moved to a bigger venue on Broadway. Finocchio's became a major tourist attraction, drawing suburban thrill seekers as well as Hollywood celebrities such as Frank Sinatra, Bob Hope, Bette Davis, and Tallulah Bankhead. In the 1940s nightspots like Mona's Club 440 in North Beach, the city's first lesbian club, flipped the Finocchio's formula, billing itself as the place "Where Girls Will Be Boys." Mona's biggest star, in more ways than one, was a 250-pound African-American singer-pianist named Gladys Bentley. Advertised as the "Brown Bomber of Sophisticated Songs," Bentley packed her voluminous figure into white tails and top hat, flirted with women in the audience, and dedicated songs to her female paramour.

José Sarria, a hometown boy who plucked his eyebrows, slipped into a basic black dress and a pair of Capezio stilettos, and began singing torch songs at the bohemian Black Cat in the 1950s, was the first to politicize the drag world. In between songs, he started preaching that "gay is good," and at the end of each performance, he had the audience stand and belt out a parody of "God Save the Queen"—"as a kind of anthem," he later recalled, "to get them realizing that we had to work together, that . . . we could change the laws if we weren't always hiding." In 1961 Sarria took his campaign public, running for the city's board of supervisors with an early gay pride message. The campaign fell short of victory, but the gay genie was released from San Francisco's bottle.

During the 1950s and early 1960s, San Francisco had a blossoming but largely secret gay life. Indeed, the song that would become the city's anthem, "I Left My Heart in San Francisco," was written in 1954 by two gay lovers who were pining for "the city by the bay" after moving to Brooklyn Heights. Tony Bennett made the song famous, singing it for the first time at the Fairmont Hotel's Venetian Room in December 1961, with future mayor Joe Alioto in the audience. By then, the songwriters—Douglass Cross and George Cory—had moved back to the Bay Area, where Cross died of a heart attack and a grief-stricken Cory later took his own life.

By the midsixties, gay liberation was busting out in San Francisco, with picketers circling the downtown Macy's in 1964 to protest the police entrapment of men in the store's restrooms and demonstrators rallying outside the Federal Building in 1966 against the exclusion of homosexuals from the armed services. That same year, drag queens ignited a violent blowup at a Tenderloin eatery called Compton's Cafeteria— three years before the Stonewall riots in New York that are credited with launching the gay rights movement. The Compton's tempest began when a cop tried to arrest one of the queens who frequented the cafeteria, and, sick of the constant harassment, he resisted by throwing a cup of coffee in the policeman's face. In the ensuing melee, angry queens flung dishes and trays at the police, smashed the cafeteria's plate glass windows, and burned down a nearby newsstand.

Despite this colorful history, San Francisco had never seen anything quite like the Cockettes. Hibiscus and company broke down all the drag queen traditions. They were not clean-shaven men costumed as women, but all sorts of imaginative—and often furry—creatures. Hibiscus liked to resurrect Jayne Mansfield, with enormous golden balloon breasts, and a glitter-sparkled beard. Fayette once turned herself into a singing vagina. They were pirates and nuns, Betty Boops and motorcycle greasers, dominatrixes and harlequins. The audience at Cockettes shows "couldn't tell if it was a man or a woman" onstage, marveled filmmaker John Waters, who rode the drag troupe's long, sequined train to notoriety in San Francisco. "It was complete sexual anarchy—which is always a wonderful thing."

"We're not queer," explained one Cockette to the press. "We're just chicks with cocks." Which made all the sense in the world once you went through the looking glass.

AFTER THE COCKETTES' IMPROMPTU debut at the dawn of the 1970s, the troupe plunged into a frenzy of creativity, mounting sixteen different shows in two and a half years. "Hibiscus's charisma is what brought us together," recalled Rumi Missabu, a Cockette who had grown up on the edges of Hollywood show business. "Every month, he'd come up with a new theme from his jeweled scrapbook of fairy tales and fever dreams. 'We're going to do this next month—on LSD!' he would announce. The Cockettes were like the Little Rascals in drag doing Busby Berkeley on acid."

Some shows, like *Pearls Over Shanghai*—the tale of three perky, all-American sisters who fall into debauched white slavery in the Orient—featured well-crafted original scores and the makings of an actual plot. But Hibiscus, who was wedded to his wildly funky theatrical vision, made sure that the shows never could be accused of slick showmanship. He resisted rehearsals, which, in any case, often had a way of deteriorating into hissy fits and huffy walkouts. And when show business stars started to emerge from the Cockette free-for-all—like the future disco queen Sylvester—he had a way of popping their balloons. Once, as Sylvester sang a torrid solo version of "Someone to Watch Over Me," Hibiscus wandered onstage in a zebra costume. The furious diva slapped Hibiscus across the face as he stalked offstage.

There were no taboos, no politically correct inhibitions. The Cockettes did their version of *Gone With the Wind* in blackface, and *Madame Butterfly* in pidgin Cantonese. One afternoon the troupe performed *Pearls Over Shanghai* before a stunned audience on the Berkeley campus. The politically earnest young crowd grew increasingly restive as it took in the wild pageant of scheming dragon ladies, horny coolies, and virginal white victims, until one outraged woman suddenly jumped up and yelled, "This is the most sexist, racist piece of shit I've ever seen!"

The Cockettes' "nocturnal dream shows" at the Palace soon became the talk of San Francisco. Crowds whose peacockery rivaled the drag stars' themselves crammed into the 1,200-seat theater. Janis and other local rock stars began showing up. Herb Caen, a longtime fan of the North Beach drag scene, began touting the Cockettes' gender-bending chaos in his column. Denise Hale and other Pacific Heights socialites dropped by with out-of-town friends like author Truman Capote and film critic Rex Reed. "Hibiscus, we love you!" screamed the crowds as the leader of the drag queen pack made his grand entrance each night, buoyed by his shiny balloon boobs.

But as the Cockettes' star soared higher, Hibiscus resisted the siren call of commercial success. He may have dressed like Monroe and Mansfield, but he didn't want their gilded cage lives. Hibiscus had taken a vow of poverty during his days at the Kaliflower commune, and though he finally moved out of its monastic environment, he was still honoring Irving Rosenthal's "everything free" belief system.

No one was getting rich off the Cockettes' success. Sebastian, the late-night impresario at the Palace, charged only $2 a ticket. Each member of the troupe was lucky to earn a few bucks off the shows—"enough to keep us in false eyelashes," as one Cockette put it. But Hibiscus thought even this was too big a concession to Mammon. He wanted the shows to be entirely free. When Sebastian resisted, Hibiscus and his cohorts ran around the theater flinging open the exit doors to the swarming crowds.

John Waters, who would find a way to make a good living off his cultural subversion, never understood Hibiscus's "hippie Communism." As time went by, more of the Cockettes began to share Waters's view, finding their leader's free philosophy and unpredictable antics increasingly tiresome. Their frustration finally erupted in the summer of 1971, as the troupe pondered traveling east for its big New York stage debut. At an emotional meeting in the second-floor flat of the Cockettes' upper Market Street commune, several performers turned on the troupe's founder. Hibiscus was slapped and kicked and pushed down the flight of stairs.

Fayette found him there, at the bottom of the stairwell, in a puddle of tears. He had been violently ejected from his own dream. Fayette thought it was a devastating blow—not only for Hibiscus but also for the entire troupe. "Yes, he had a way-over-the-top personality," she reflected, "but they didn't get it. They didn't want anyone to mess up their makeup. My feeling was, 'Please, mess it up!' They were ego driven and uninteresting. Hibiscus wanted to do something more fantastical and revolutionary."

To make matters worse, Fayette thought, Hibiscus was the only Cockette with any real stage experience. She smelled disaster. Which is exactly what New York turned out to be.

When they landed in Manhattan, the Cockettes were greeted by the city's glamour crowd as visiting royalty. They were treated to parties with the Warhol circle, fashion magazine editor Diana Vreeland, clothing designer Oscar de la Renta, and artist Robert Rauschenberg. But when the curtains opened on the Cockettes' *Tinsel Tarts in a Hot Coma* at the Anderson Theater, a sad and tatty old barn on the Lower East Side that once featured Yiddish dramas, the celebrity-packed audience didn't know what to make of the San Francisco queens' big mess of a show. The Cockettes were accustomed to audiences that were as raucous and psychedelicized as they were—with some ardent fans even jumping up on stage and becoming part of the show. But the New York audience members expected to sit back and be entertained, and when they weren't, a snarky chill settled over the old theater. As *Tinsel Tarts* grinded on, hoots and howls echoed off the walls. By the end of their opening-night performance, the Cockettes were dead in New York. "Having no talent is not enough," sniffed Gore Vidal as he left the theater. The reviews the next day were equally merciless.

New York just wasn't the Cockettes' scene. One gay bar in Brooklyn Heights even barred Sweet Pam at the door when she tried to enter with her pack of boys—because she was a *girl*—something that never would have happened in loosey-goosey San Francisco. The troupe hung on in Gotham for another month—long enough for several members to get addicted to the cheap heroin that was all over town. Every bellhop seemed to be pushing the stuff.

By the time they got back to San Francisco, the Cockettes felt like Dorothy: that there was no place like home. "New York was nihilistic and cynical—there's a sweeter spirit here," sighed Rumi. "New York was all concrete; San Francisco is lush, plush, velvet, warm, cozy," gushed troupe member Scrumbly, who by then was expecting his first child with his new bride, Sweet Pam—a development that seemed to catch them both by surprise.

San Francisco clasped the Cockettes to its plush bosom after they returned, and they continued to perform at the Palace for several more months. But they never recovered from New York's ice-cold reality check. The pre–New York days were a topsy-turvy dream that could never be repeated.

Hibiscus went on to start a rival drag company, the Angels of Light. But it never achieved the same giddy level of phantasmagoria. He eventually drifted back to New York, where he became a high-priced rent boy in sleek Armani suits. Nothing was free anymore.

Among all the "end of the sixties" moments that would rain down on people's souls, the collapse of the Cockettes was as dreary as any. Hibiscus was the Peter Pan of Golden Gate Park. He should never have grown old or turned a trick. But there would be many more such turns of the screw.

At the end of the 1960s, Jerry Garcia was asked by a reporter to look back at everything he and his crΔowd had been through and to make some kind of sense of it. Garcia said it was too soon. For the rest of his life and longer, he predicted, America would struggle to absorb the convulsive changes of the previous five years.

No city would go through more convulsions than San Francisco as it processed the 1960s. Like the mystics who eat from strange and sacred plants to let their minds touch God, the people of San Francisco first had to know hell.

As the decade expired, the drugs became harder, the sexual freedom more rapacious, the demands on the human psyche more severe. Meanwhile, the outcasts from America—and its domestic and overseas wars—grew more damaged. They carried within them a hot and reckless lust for salvation as they showed up on the streets of San Francisco. The city was still known for its enchantments, but it would soon become notorious for its terrors.

PART TWO

TERROR

Darkness, darkness, be my pillow.

13

A DEATH IN THE FAMILY

WHAT BEGAN IN San Francisco as a celebration of life would become the opposite. Like the moon pulls on the tides, more and more young people were drawn inexorably to the darker shores of oblivion. Looking back, the death of Nancy Gurley seems an omen of all that was to come.

Born Nancy Felice Reisman in 1938, she was the second of three children in a secular Jewish family in Detroit. Her father was an ear, nose, and throat doctor, and her mother was a schoolteacher. She was at odds with the world from the very start. Dinners in the Reisman home often ended with Nancy exploding and running upstairs to her room. She began playing sexually with boys at thirteen or fourteen. One summer she was fired as a camp counselor and sent home after she was caught giving a blow job to another counselor. Dr. and Mrs. Reisman were mortified by their daughter's behavior. "My parents were so upset with Nancy that they were almost sitting shiva for her," recalled her younger brother, Alex. "They didn't trust therapy, and they didn't have the tools to deal with someone like Nancy. My mom started getting migraines because of her."

But to Alex, Nancy was an exciting, beautiful, older sister. She was an elfin five foot one and one hundred pounds, with wavy, auburn hair and deep, brown eyes that were "totally alive." And she was always turning life into an escapade. "When you were around Nancy, you always *felt*," said one of her friends. After graduating from high school, she took off for Hawaii, where she ended up marrying a Zen Buddhist poet—"a Leonard Cohen type," as Alex described him. But the marriage was quickly annulled, and she returned home, her spirit undiminished. She brought back a hula skirt and taught everyone how to shimmy like a palm tree in a tropical gale.

In Detroit, Nancy enrolled at Wayne State University, where she became a straight-A student and eventually pursued a master's degree in English literature, writing her thesis on Yiddish phrases. She had the kind of temperament that bounced between emotional extremes, and she found a philosophical home somewhere between nihilism and existentialism. "She worked hard at being positive, but she could get very down," remembered Alex.

While going to Wayne State, Nancy worked nights at a beat coffeehouse drolly named the Cup of Socrates. That's where she met James Gurley, the young man who would entrance her for the rest of her life. He was as beautiful as Nancy, a tall, lean man with a strong nose and chin, and soft, feminine eyes. His face, which had traces of his Cherokee grandmother, had the romance of a Wild West hero. James came from poor people. His father was a demolition derby driver. He worked young James into his act, tying him to the hood of his jalopy and crashing through a flaming plywood barrier at local speedways. James wore a helmet, but he would be routinely knocked out by the stunt. Once he lost his front teeth, and another time his hair was scorched to the scalp.

At age fourteen, James found sanctuary in a Detroit monastery run by the Catholic Brothers of the Holy Cross. He would live there until he was eighteen, getting up every morning at five-thirty for church and going to Mass every night before bedtime. "I was brought up in the Middle Ages," he would later say. "It may have kept me from a life of crime. I don't know what I would have gotten into."

James also found solace in music. His uncle had a guitar, and he let James play it. He taught himself chords by listening to Lightnin' Hopkins and other blues masters. One night James heard John Coltrane in a Detroit nightclub, and he tried to make his guitar wail as ecstatically as Coltrane's sax.

A man of few words, James let his music speak for him. But he was immediately drawn to Nancy, who was a cauldron of words and feelings. They moved in together in a kind of bohemian rooming house in downtown Detroit inhabited by artists, philosophy students, and drug dealers.

Nancy would return to her family's home for Friday night dinners and always leave loaded down with two bags of groceries. She was still in and out of favor with her parents, who didn't approve of James or his family. "They thought he wasn't good enough for her," Alex said. "They thought she'd come to her senses and marry a nice doctor."

But Nancy and James were paragons of cool. They tripped down the streets together, wrapped in each other's arms, the center of each other's story. She carried around a big, green, stuffed frog with her, wrapped up like it was their baby, just to see people's bug-eyed reactions. They were not made to settle down in Detroit. In 1962 they took off for San Francisco, where James eked out a living playing folk and blues in North Beach cafes.

ONE AFTERNOON IN LATE 1965, Sam Andrew and Peter Albin—the beginnings of the band that would become Big Brother and the Holding Company—were noodling on their guitars in the redwood-paneled, ballroom-sized basement of 1090 Page Street, the Victorian rooming house where Albin lived. Chet Helms—the bespectacled, soft-spoken, Texas-born rock promoter who would become the yin to Bill Graham's yang—suddenly appeared with a striking entourage in tow. The handsome young man with Helms was clad entirely in black, and he wore Indian feathers in his heroically long hair. The petite woman who accompanied him was dressed like an Elizabethan lady in waiting, in velvet and lace. She was "wild and noisy," as Sam Andrew recalled. They had a big German shepherd who seemed as untamed as a wolverine, and a baby who appeared almost as feral. The couple were James and Nancy Gurley—they were married by then—and they were about to join shining forces with San Francisco's cultural revolution.

James brought his singularly savage guitar style to Big Brother, playing at furious speed with fingerpicks, instead of the one flat pick favored by most guitar players. He soon became known as "the fastest guitar slinger in the West." The sonic explosions that James set off with his rapid-fire fingerpicking and his primitive effects, which usually involved a swift kick to his amplifier, came to define psychedelic rock. "It sounded like thunder in a Wagner opera when James shook his amplifier," said Andrew.

James was the star of the early Big Brother lineup. A photo of him taken by Bob Seidemann—staring soulfully ahead, wearing a double-breasted Civil War shirt and an Indian feather in his hair—instantly became a popular Haight Street poster, the definition of hippie masculinity. But Big Brother was incomplete until the day in June 1966 when Helms—the man who pieced together the band, player by player—brought a fellow Texan named Janis Joplin to the band's rehearsal hall in an old firehouse on Henry Street. At first look, James was not impressed with the band's new singer. "She looked like a punk or something," he recalled. "She had Levi's that had the knees turned out. She had Mexican huaraches sandals on, and her hair was pinned up in a bun. She had no makeup, and her face was really broken out. She had a bad complexion, and she had this blue sweatshirt on that was all torn and covered with paint because she had been a painter. Nobody would have looked at her and thought, 'In a few years, she's gonna be the biggest thing on the planet.'"

BUT THEN JANIS BEGAN singing, and it was unlike anything the band members had ever heard. Her voice was a wail from somewhere too deep, the saddest, most desperate orgasm ever wrenched out of a woman's body. It was as disturbing as it was exciting, equal parts sex and death. One day, while the band was rehearsing, it was interrupted by loud thumping on the firehouse door. When a man in the band's extended family opened the door, five policemen were braced to enter, straining their necks to look inside. "We have a complaint that there is a woman screaming here," said one of the cops. "That's not a woman," replied the man, "that's Janis Joplin." Men never knew what to make of Janis.

In early summer 1966, Alex Reisman moved to California. He was going to attend Stanford Law School. But he also wanted to be around his ever-dazzling sister. By then Nancy and James were living at 459 Oak Street, on the edge of the Panhandle, with their toddler, who was named Hongo Ishi Gurley, after the last of the free Indians. Nancy was an advocate of the Summerhill philosophy of child rearing and didn't want to place any constraints on Hongo. The boy roamed the house without a diaper accompanied by the family German shepherd, who also crapped on the floor whenever the need gripped him. Big Brother wasn't making any money yet, and the family seemed to get by on food stamps and various hustles.

The Big Brother orbit was becoming an exciting place to be. Nancy kept telling her brother about the volcanic new singer who had joined the band. In June 1966, Janis made her debut with the band at Chet Helms's Avalon Ballroom. It was the first time that Alex had seen Big Brother, the first time he had seen James play rock music, the first time he had seen a light show. Old Betty Boop cartoons and Harold Lloyd silent films flickered on the walls. Nancy was his magic ticket.

Before the show, Alex went backstage with his new wife, Dorothy, and smoked dope with the band in their cramped dressing room. Janis was terrified—she had never performed with a rock band before, only in coffeehouses with an acoustic guitar. Alex couldn't see what the buzz was all about. "I remember thinking Janis was not that great looking, especially compared to someone like Grace Slick. Then she went onstage and opened her mouth, and I thought, 'I get it.'"

Janis was blasted into air by the band's rocket of sound. "What a rush!" she felt. "A real drug rush. The music went boom, boom, boom, and everyone was dancing, and I stood there and clutched the mike, and I got it." There in the spotlight, that's where she belonged. It would become the only place she did belong.

JANIS NEVER STOPPED THINKING of herself as just an "ugly chick from Port Arthur with not too much talent." The girl nominated most "ugly man on campus" by her stupidly cruel fellow students at the University of Texas. She had what Big Brother drummer Dave Getz called a bottomless "hole in her gut" that she was forever trying to fill with men, women, whisky, and drugs. Her hunger swallowed the room, she wanted to suck down everything around her. "She was scary," recalled Fayette Hauser, the young artist and future Cockette who had followed Nancy to San Francisco. "She was so intense and butch. She'd come right into your face. I was shy. She was way too heavy for me."

Within weeks of joining Big Brother, not only had Janis replaced James as the star of the band but she had also claimed him as her lover. Lanky, soulful James was a magnet for women. "After shows, women would often ask me whether James would be in my room later," recalled bandmate Peter Albin. The quiet former Catholic boy was overwhelmed by the sexual attention. James's monastic adolescence had left him feeling, in his words, "shy, repressed, and screwed up." He proved an easy mark for voracious Janis. In the summer of 1966, James moved in with the band's new star, leaving Nancy and Hongo back in their Oak Street flat.

But Nancy Gurley had her own magnetic power. A couple of weeks later, she came marching into Janis's bedroom with Hongo and the German shepherd, and she took James back.

Nancy and Janis began as sexual rivals, but they quickly became a dynamic duo. They were both strong-willed, whip-smart women who loved to read. Janis always carried around her San Francisco Public Library card with her. And they both grew up feeling like angry and tormented outcasts. Janis was "very, very smart," said Getz. "And Nancy was one of the few people who was up to her caliber."

Nancy was the Big Brother tribe's mesmerizing gypsy queen. In her "long gowns of lace and velvet" and with her "many, many necklaces draped colorfully from the porcelain gracefulness of her neck," as the band's publicist, Myra Friedman, described her, Nancy set the standard for femininity in the band's circle. She took the scruffy girl from Port Arthur and made her over in her lushly romantic image.

Not long after Janis joined Big Brother, the band and its retinue of wives, girlfriends, and children all moved into an old redwood hunting lodge at the end of a road in woodsy Lagunitas. Nancy and Janis would spend hours together, talking late into the night and stringing bits of antique glass and crystal beads, which they decorated themselves with like Christmas tree lights. By this point, Nancy's natural exuberance was further amped by regular injections of speed. Janis was trying to stay away from her hard drug demons. When Chet Helms lured her back to San Francisco from Texas earlier that year, he assured her that the scene had been taken over by psychedelics, which never particularly interested her. But Nancy's speed-driven dazzle was too enticing, and during the band's Lagunitas sojourn, Janis fell back into her old meth habit.

Nancy had developed a strong affinity for speed as a girl, after her mother began freely dispensing Dexedrine capsules to all three of her children to manage their weight. The family had a cabinet that was well stocked with prescription drug samples brought home by Dr. Reisman. "We called it the drug store," Alex said. "The result was that all three of us kids developed a strong liking for uppers." For the rest of her life, Nancy would always prefer drugs that took her fast-forward rather than down.

In the beginning, San Franciscans felt they owned Janis and Big Brother. They were like the Dead, neighborhood minstrels, the Avalon house band. She was the type everyone knew from high school: the brassy bad girl rejected by the cheerleaders but beloved by losers everywhere. After shows, she would jump down from the stage and mingle with the audience. You could see her down on the Panhandle, amid all the harlequins and gypsies, smoking a cigar and swigging from a bottle of Jack. If you hadn't slept with her, you knew someone who had.

But after the Monterey Pop Festival in June 1967, when Janis stole the show along with Hendrix, Otis Redding, and the Who, everything changed. The star-making pressures grew unbearable, and the corporate sirens began wooing Janis away from the band. She couldn't walk her old neighborhood anymore. "These days Haight Street is so weird," she told San Francisco journalist David Dalton after the festival. "Remember that *Suddenly Last Summer* movie, where that guy gets eaten by cannibals? Well, that almost happened to me the last time I was there. I got out of my car. 'It's Janis Joplin, it's Janis Joplin! Hey, give me this, give me that.' Pushing, pulling on me, trying to aggravate me."

Heroin began creeping into the band's circle. Soon Janis, James, and Sam Andrew were all using. Nancy was more leery of heroin's catacomb lure, but she too started alternating speed and smack. How could people so smart put themselves at such risk? A lifetime later, Fayette Hauser could still see method in her friend Nancy's madness. Nancy and her San Francisco troupe were remaking the world by tapping into the deepest recesses of their souls. Drugs were an essential tool in the process, and each one had its own unique use. It was all about finding the right alchemy. "These were people who considered acid trips and speed as their work," she explained. "It was a serious matter with them. People had made discoveries through acid that had reshaped them. They were very consciously exploring life. The heroin was the perfect counterpart. It would put you right back to where you were on your last acid trip."

But the balancing act proved elusive. The band lost its core discipline, began to get sloppy. Janis grew crazier, becoming dangerous to herself and others. She was so desperate for a fix one time that she drew water from a toilet into her syringe. She could be equally reckless with others. One night Terry Hallinan dropped by her Noe Street apartment with Peggy Caserta, a bosomy clothing store owner with whom they were both sleeping. Janis—already high, and burning with jealousy—convinced the young lawyer to sample smack for the first time and then injected him with an extra-stiff shot. Hallinan's eyes immediately rolled upward, and he collapsed to the floor. Caserta was frantic. "Oh Jesus, Janis, he's gonna die on us!" But the singer simply began undressing Caserta and took her to bed, while Hallinan was sprawled unconscious at their feet. "Aren't we naughty girls?" Janis giggled. Only after they had finished with each other did Janis revive Hallinan with a cold towel.

Hallinan never forgave Janis. "I didn't think she was a great person," he smiled wryly many years later. "Of course, we didn't exactly get off on a good foot. She was an arrogant person. She was the Queen Bee by then." Only in San Francisco could a young man who took a near-lethal dose from Janis Joplin's needle wind up overseeing the city's criminal justice system—but that's precisely what Terry "Kayo" Hallinan did three decades later when he was elected San Francisco's district attorney.

Nancy felt that James too was disappearing into the heroin netherworld. What began as a conscious exploration of life's mysteries was becoming an endless half slumber. She was losing the love of her life to drugs and other women—there was always too many of both. It only got worse after Janis left Big Brother to form her own band in fall 1968—just as Big Brother's album, *Cheap Thrills,* was rocketing the band into the music industry heavens. Janis's abrupt departure was a betrayal that neither she nor the rest of the band ever recovered from. Now heroin was the only organizing principle in James's life.

Nancy tried leaving James. She ended up in Colorado for a while, taking up with a hippie surfer on shore leave. It was there that Fayette Hauser met her one day, while hitchhiking to Aspen. Nancy and her surfer boy picked up the young art student in their panel truck. There was a whole, exotic world in that truck. Dark velvets hung over a double mattress bed. The dashboard was covered with dried flowers and tiny bird skulls. When Fayette opened the truck door, she was greeted by Nancy with a hash pipe. "I climbed in, took the pipe, and thought, 'I'm never getting out.'"

Fayette immediately became another of Nancy's acolytes. She loved to go walking with her and listen to her discourse on literature and philosophy. "Listening to Nancy tell stories was like a walking novel. It was like taking a stroll with Jane Austen."

By the time Nancy returned to San Francisco, she had so enthralled the younger woman with stories about the Emerald City, Fayette knew she had to follow her. Nancy installed her in a Victorian flat in the Duboce Triangle neighborhood, where she became roommates with a drug dealer named Paula and a teenage groupie named Patty Cakes, who alternated between Janis and Jimi Hendrix. Nancy taught Fayette how to dress. And she showed her how to fix, warning her never to shoot up alone and always to inject herself. They were both high when they went to see Janis's final performance with Big Brother.

NANCY WAS STILL TRYING to stay away from James. "James had so many groupies that it drove Nancy crazy," Fayette said. "They were so crazy in love." At last, they fell back into each other's arms. Nancy and Hongo moved back in with James. She was euphoric; it was their destiny to be together. Their story had the inevitability of one her Austen novels. She got pregnant. She cut back on heroin. James was determined to get clean too, to start over.

On the Fourth of July weekend in 1969, James and Nancy took Hongo and drove up to the Russian River for a family outing. James loved the country; it made him feel healthy. He took along a $100 bag of heroin, but he made a junkie's bargain with himself. This would be his final trip to the underworld.

They spent the day floating lazily down the river, drinking wine. By the time they camped outside Cloverdale, James was drowsy with the day's sunny pleasures. Around ten o'clock, he drifted over to his Toyota jeep, where he had left his works, to cap off the night with a syringe full of milky sweetness. In his hazy state, he missed his vein on the first try, and, trying again, once more plunged the needle into muscle.

Nancy walked over to the jeep. She wanted to share this final journey with James. She forgot her own lesson and asked him to take care of her too. James didn't realize it—because he'd missed his own vein and hadn't felt the injection's full effect—but his heroin was more potent than Nancy was used to.

This time his needle found its mark. Nancy walked back to the campfire to read Hongo a bedtime story. Suddenly she pitched forward, in front of her little boy. When James came drifting over moments later, he found his wife sprawled in the dirt.

The rest of the night was so harrowing that, even in the clinical language of court documents, it reduces the reader to tears. James, jolted out of his haze by the sight of his wife on the ground, carried her and Hongo to the jeep and went roaring into Cloverdale. He stopped at a gas station, frantically asking where he could find a doctor in town, and was directed to the office of Dr. Lombard Sayre. The doctor, having been tipped off by the gas station attendant, arrived at his office shortly after James, who swept Nancy into his arms and took her inside. Dr. Sayre quickly realized that Nancy was beyond his help, and he quietly told James that she was dead. But James refused to believe him. He bent over his wife, put his lips to hers, and kept trying to breathe life into her. He didn't stop until two Cloverdale policemen, notified by the doctor, showed up and pulled him away from Nancy's body.

After being led into an adjacent waiting room by the policemen, James slumped into a chair, with a naked Hongo in his lap, and rocked back and forth, sobbing, "Nancy, Nancy, Nancy, no, no, no." Dr. Sayre was so concerned about James's state of mind that he urged the policemen to have him committed that night to a psychiatric ward in a nearby hospital. All during the half-hour ambulance ride to the hospital, James wept over and over to his three-year-old son, "What are we going to do? Nancy isn't here, Hongo, what are we going to do? Nancy isn't here."

The next morning, James was arrested on murder charges. Janis hired the best lawyer she could think of—the rugby-tough Vincent Hallinan–schooled drug attorney Michael Stepanian—to represent her former bandmate and fellow heroin casualty. Alex Reisman testified at the coroner's inquest where Nancy's death would be ruled either a homicide or an accident. The hearing was trying to determine whether Nancy could have given herself the fatal injection, and a key question before the court was whether she was left- or right-handed. After conferring with his family, Alex testified that his sister was ambidextrous. "We didn't want James to get pinned for giving her the shot," he said later. "We thought the worst thing for Hongo would be to have his father locked up for years."

The charges against James were later reduced to heroin possession, and he was given probation. Some regarded James Gurley as a very fortunate man. But the court didn't see it that way. "Some [life] consequences furnish greater penalties than the law can impose," read a court document in the case, a beautifully concise appraisal of the hell that James would go through after that night on the Russian River.

James never got over Nancy's death. It was a mournful note that echoed through the rest of his life. It was not the first overdose in San Francisco's hippie community, and it would not be the last. But it quickly took on a darkly mythic quality. People who knew her tried to make sense of it. Some saw it as an early feminist parable, the story of a sparkling hippie earth mother who overdosed on love for her old man.

But others simply saw a young woman who had demanded much from life and then taken her leave. There was always a brutal toughness in the beat and hippie cultures, a shrugging awareness that casualties were inevitable when you challenged life's limits. One San Francisco poet wrote a "dry-eyed" requiem for Nancy, which even suggested there was something "graceful" about her exit.

James believed that Nancy's family would never forgive him. But it was never that simple for Alex. "I never felt he was responsible. Nancy did these things on her own."

James had been a big brother to Alex. Nancy and he had been magical presences in his life, warmly welcoming him into their highly charged force field. For two or three years after Nancy's death, Alex had no contact with James. Then one day, Alex—by then a young activist lawyer—found himself at a friend's house in Marin, down the hill from where James was living with his new wife and Hongo. Alex dropped acid and found himself being drawn up the hill, where he knocked on James's door. When James opened it up, Alex told him he was tripping, and James invited him in. Alex wanted to talk about Nancy. "It was still raw," he recalled, "and his new wife was uncomfortable. But it was important for me to talk to him."

In the final years of his life, James Gurley conjured his long-lost wife in a song called "For Nancy (Elegy)." It was a sad and wispy blues-rock tune, lamenting what could have been. "In my life, you were the only one. In my life, my life had just begun." He wrote a couple of "bucket list" letters to Alex near the end, telling him how much he loved his sister. James died of a heart attack in 2009, two days before his seventieth birthday.

Nancy Gurley—this "burning star in a wild firmament," as Alex saw her—was not destined to live into a wistful old age. Nor was Janis Joplin, who, after getting word in New York about her close friend's death, said, "Well, I guess I'll go score some smack." Fuck you, death.

There's an exhilaration in that kind of recklessness. It takes a reckless kind of soul to tear down monuments and torch bridges, to shake the dead grip of the past. But by the end of the sixties, the revolution was entering its Jacobin phase, and the wreckage was growing wanton. If the revolution liberated the human imagination, it also unleashed humanity's demons. San Francisco—capital of the new world—was descending into its Season of the Witch.

14

LUCIFER RISING

ONE NIGHT IN 1969, Peter Lewis of Moby Grape peered from onstage into the cavernous darkness of the Fillmore ballroom. A sea of young faces was staring back at him. The faces were not joyous. They looked "lost and worried" to Lewis. "They looked like they were going to freak out." It unnerved Lewis; it disrupted his musical flow. "When you're trying to concentrate on a song and the crowd looks at you like they don't know what's going on, you get lost too. There was so much pain in that room." Lewis stumbled through the rest of the show, holding on until the band reached the end.

There was always a dark shadow around the San Francisco rainbow. From the very beginning, violence, desperation, and fear stalked the streets of the Haight, side by side with the euphoria. "When I hear about the Summer of Love, I say, 'Where was that?'" remarked Lewis. "It was there, but always lurking below was this seething hatred and fear from Vietnam and the Cold War. There was always this feeling that we were going to die."

As the 1960s drew to an end, and America's pain intensified, more and more of the suffering washed up in the Haight. Runaways who could never go home, strung-out Vietnam vets, draft dodgers terrified of what awaited them when they were caught, teenagers sickened by what loomed ahead of them in adult America. The war was dragging on and on, the country's most promising leaders had been mysteriously assassinated, racial divisions were growing more bitter, inner cities were smoldering.

San Francisco's cultural revolution was launched with the grandest intentions. As the Human Be-In visionaries proclaimed, they were giving birth to "a new nation . . . inside the robot flesh of the old." The great notions spawned by San Francisco's revolution—peaceful coexistence, racial harmony, sexual liberation, ecological consciousness, organic food, communal living, alternative commerce, free culture—did indeed spread throughout the country, where their green tendrils could be seen sprouting here and there in the stony ground.

But as San Francisco's revolution spread—carried by the music, the drugs, the underground railroad of wandering youth—the poison in America's soul was also billowing. You could feel it more and more on the streets of the Haight. San Francisco was no longer only a haven for the country's restless dreamers but also for its wrecked and ruined.

The 1960s turned sour in large part because of the endless bloodletting in Vietnam. The soul sickness leached everywhere as the war came home, but nowhere more than the Haight, where many ravaged veterans sought solace. The music that GIs listened to in Vietnam, and the magazine spreads of hippie revelry, promised a halcyon world far from the blood and mud. But many of them found it was not easy to leave the war behind; they brought it home with them.

Life in the Haight grew more violent and disturbing. The drugs got harder. By 1971, 15 percent of the servicemen returning from Vietnam were addicted to heroin. Smack and speed began to shove aside psychedelics. The harried staff at the Haight-Ashbury Free Clinic was seeing more and more hard-core drug abusers. The speed freaks were the most harrowing cases: amphetamines worked their dark magic on the brain with power-drill intensity.

Speed freaks were loathe to approach the health system when their bodies started breaking down. But one day a meth head named Randy ventured into the Free Clinic in search of help for an AWOL soldier who was too wasted to come in. Dr. Ernest Dernburg, a clinic psychiatrist who had won the trust of the meth addict subculture, agreed to follow Randy back to his residential hotel—a crystal palace on Haight Street. It was a mission of mercy into San Francisco's darkening drug underworld that only a doctor like the Free Clinic's Dernburg would have been willing to risk.

In the hotel lobby, Randy had to convince the heavily armed and suspicious manager at the front desk to let the doctor enter the premises. Dernburg continued to run a hostile gauntlet as he mounted the staircase to the AWOL soldier's third-floor room. "Gaunt and menacing faces peered out" from half-open doors, he later told his colleague, Dr. David Smith, and he could see "corpselike figures stretched out on the floors and the furniture in several shuttered rooms."

When Randy and Dernburg reached the third-floor landing, they were again stopped, this time by a handful of half-naked phantoms, who grilled Randy about the doctor's identity for a full ten minutes and then demanded to see his medical credentials before they were finally allowed to proceed. As Dernburg approached the GI's door, he could hear high-pitched wails. After Randy and his wraith-like companions shouted through the locked door, it was finally opened by another specter with "a thin, deathly white, female face," the doctor recalled. Dernburg entered and picked his way through a room littered with needles, piles of white powder, filthy bedsheets, sleeping bags, soft-drink cartons, and cat shit. The doctor was guided to a bed where the soldier lay. He was once a robust, six-foot-tall young man, but he had been shriveled to a twisted knot of human misery.

"He was lying in a foul pool of sweat," Dernburg recounted. "Beside him was much-used needle with a broken, rusty tip. His jaundiced face glistened with perspiration and was sunken around the eye sockets. His heart raced. His arms, visible under the shreds of a long-sleeved uniform, were covered with fresh tracks or needle punctures and swollen with abscesses the size of baseballs. Running up to one shoulder was a darkened blood vessel, the sign of septicemia, or blood poisoning. He mumbled incoherently and writhed under [my] touch. He screamed, 'Let me die! Don't bust me; I've had enough!'"

This is as good a portrait as any of what the Vietnam War did to the young men who fought in it.

Dernburg knew that somehow he had to extricate the young soldier from the meth den and get him immediately to a hospital. He sent Randy back to Clayton Street to fetch the clinic's "ambulance": an old Peugeot station wagon. He then picked up the emaciated GI, who was

too weak to walk, and carried him to the third-floor landing. Here Dernburg's path was blocked by a raving young man in a greasy trench coat,
who, thinking he was a narcotics agent, assaulted the doctor. Dernburg
finally pacified the violent man by again fishing his medical credentials
out of his pocket. He continued to run the meth hotel's grim gauntlet,
with the soldier in his arms, until they finally emerged onto the street.
By this time, Randy and a Free Clinic colleague had arrived with the
ambulance. But before they could load the wasted man into the back
of the vehicle, they were again confronted: this time by a half dozen
Hell's Angels, who demanded to know what was going on. One of the
Angels recognized Dernburg's colleague, who explained the emergency,
and the bikers offered to escort the ambulance on their Harleys, plowing
through traffic on the way to San Francisco General.

And this is as good a picture as any of how counterculture communities like the Haight took care of the war's mangled souls: a doctor from a
hippie clinic carrying a dying, emaciated soldier in his arms. For decades
after the war, up to this very day, right-wing politicians and pundits have
spread the libel about how peace activists and hippies greeted returning
Vietnam vets with gobs of spit and contempt. The truth is that many
survivors of the war headed directly to havens like the Haight, where
they found more comfort than they ever could in veterans' hospitals or
bastions of flag-waving patriotism.

VETS AND OTHER REFUGEES from the American wasteland continued
pouring into the Haight, even as its streets grew meaner. Much of the
neighborhood's growing craziness was fueled by new waves of drugs.
Even the psychedelics were getting more potent and exotic. Superhal-
lucinogens like STP and PCP, which were developed and tested in military laboratories, were suddenly and inexplicably flooding the Haight.
STP made a particularly insidious debut in the Haight, sending users on
a three-day trip that was "like being shot out of a gun," according to one
unsuspecting victim. The nightmare was intensified for those who were
treated with Thorazine, the standard remedy for LSD freak-outs, which
only compounded STP's effects. Some of the superpsychedelics coursing through the neighborhood were cut with poisonous additives such as
strychnine and insecticide.

The Central Intelligence Agency and the military had long been fascinated with LSD and other psychedelics as potential mind control weapons. Beginning in the early 1950s, the CIA became the leading sponsor of LSD experimentation, using agency personnel and civilians as unsuspecting lab rats. The army followed in the CIA's footsteps, testing drugs at its Edgewood Arsenal and Dugway Proving Ground facilities.

The CIA and the military became unwitting birth mothers for the psychedelic revolution when they began expanding their drug test groups to include bohemians, artists, and students. One of the research scientists who administered Allen Ginsberg's first acid trip in 1959 had conducted hallucinogenic drug experiments for the US Navy. Moloch, the vast stone of war, was everywhere.

LSD's leading apostle in the 1950s and early 1960s was, in fact, a former OSS (Office of Strategic Services, predecessor to the CIA) officer with strong ties to the espionage establishment: Captain Alfred M. Hubbard. He traveled the world, introducing acid to an elite spectrum of statesmen, corporate chieftains, church leaders, and writers, including Aldous Huxley, who became another influential advocate for the drug. "They all thought it was the most marvelous thing," said Hubbard about his acid evangelism among the elite. "And I never saw a psychosis in any one of these cases."

As psychedelic drugs jumped from agency labs into the general population, the CIA had an ambivalent reaction. On the one hand, it feared that the counterculture might try to use the drugs against the political establishment, including the agency itself. Ginsberg was not the only underground figure who fantasized out loud about turning on the world's warmongering leaders and saving the human race from nuclear extinction. These pipe dreams even made their way into intelligence circles, where Mary Meyer—the ex-wife of high-ranking CIA counterespionage official Cord Meyer—sought Timothy Leary's help to conduct acid experiments in her Washington circle. Among Meyer's circle was none other than her secret lover, President John F. Kennedy.

On the other hand, as LSD consumption began spreading widely in the youth culture, the CIA welcomed it as an opportunity to test its mind control techniques. One CIA agent referred to the Haight-Ashbury as a "human guinea pig farm." As early as June 1967, the dawn of the Summer of Love, a CIA-sponsored psychiatric researcher named Dr. Louis Jolyon "Jolly" West set himself up in a safe house in the Haight to monitor the neighborhood's young drifters and their drug intake. Bearded, ruddy-cheeked Jolly West had a peculiar resumé. In the fifties and early sixties, as the head of the University of Oklahoma's department of psychiatry, he had turned the campus into a center of CIA experimentation on LSD and brainwashing. One of his more notorious stunts was injecting a circus elephant with lethal doses of LSD. In 1964, when Jack Ruby, the murderer of Lee Harvey Oswald, began intimating that President Kennedy was the victim of an ultraright conspiracy, the CIA dispatched West to examine Ruby in his jail cell. West diagnosed Ruby as "paranoid" and delusional.

In the Haight, Jolly West later wrote, he rented a "typical, large apartment, or pad" which he "cleaned, disinfected, and humbly but suitably furnished and decorated with posters, flowers, and paint. For the next six months, an ongoing program of intensive interdisciplinary study into the life and times of hippies was undertaken . . . The Haight-Ashbury district proved to be an interesting laboratory for observations concerning a wide variety of phenomena."

It is still not fully known what West's research entailed, but one visitor to his CIA "pad" recalled a bizarre, "messy" scene, with tangles of young people lying about, "blasting off" on various chemical fuels.

After his Haight experiment in the summer of 1967, West predicted the demise of the counterculture: "The very chemicals they use will inevitably enervate them as individuals and bleed the energies of the hippie movement to its death." Some counterculture figures thought the death of the movement was, in fact, a primary goal of the CIA's drug experimentation. The ever-stronger drugs, the hollowed-out zombies walking the streets, the violent psychotics. The point, they alleged, was to kill the surge of youth rebellion before it became any more of a threat to the established order. New Left activist Tom Hayden, beat writer William Burroughs, and radical White Panthers leader John Sinclair were among those who denounced the drugs cooked up in CIA labs as instruments of social control. "The new drugs were reminiscent of the distribution of alcohol for American Indians, gin for the 'gin mills' of Irish and British workers, and Britain's introduction of opium into China," Hayden later wrote.

As hard drugs took their toll on Haight-Ashbury, the neighborhood descended into crime and squalor. By 1969, most of the stores on Haight Street were boarded up and vacant. Cats were said to be hard to find on the streets, because starving junkies were hunting them for food. The neighborhood was hit by a wave of grisly drug murders. A twenty-three-year-old biker who claimed he had been high on acid for eighteen straight months was pulled over by police one day. He was driving a stolen black Volkswagen owned by an unemployed flute player turned drug dealer. The severed arm wrapped in blue suede that police found in the back of the car also turned out to belong to the flute player. "I'm very, very hazy about that arm," the biker told his lawyer after he was arrested on murder charges.

Guns were suddenly everywhere in the neighborhood that had been, until very recently, the capital of peace and love. The SFPD reported confiscating more weapons in the Haight than any other San Francisco district. One day a gunfight broke out between hippie dealers and black teenagers from the Fillmore who were trying to rob them. A long-haired dope peddler blasted away at the teenagers with a .22 pistol as they crouched behind garbage cans.

The homicide cops who worked the Haight called it "Hippieville." Most of these inspectors were born and raised in San Francisco, like Jack Cleary, a graduate of Archbishop Riordan High School. Cleary wasn't a hard-on. In the old days, when he and other cops saw burnouts and rummies on the streets, they'd put them in the back of their patrol cars and drive them home. Young Cleary's sergeant would remind him that a lot of these sad cases were World War II vets. "You gotta always remember: they fought for their country."

But the Haight was a different world. Cleary saw unspeakable things there; the sort of things a man can't tell his wife. "I had a guy who put his cowboy boots in this girl's vagina. He killed her that way. It was out there in Hippieville."

There was a carelessness about life among these young people that Cleary found stunning. One day he and his partner got a report about a body sprawled outside a big boardinghouse near Haight Street and Masonic Avenue. It turned out that a young man had plummeted to his death from a third-story window. When Cleary entered the building to investigate, he found a party in full swing. "I go into the bathroom to check it out, and here's a hippie making some kind of Kool-Aid in the bathtub—with a fucking oar! This other guy has just died, but there's a party still going on!"

MORE AND MORE LOST children kept arriving in the Haight, even as the streets grew rougher. Many were looking for the families they never had. One of those who found her way there was Susan Atkins, a sad-eyed, oval-faced teenager from the drab suburbs south of San Francisco. She had a high, sweet, wispy voice, and she sang in her church choir. But when she was fourteen, her mother died of cancer, and afterward her hard-drinking father sank deeper into alcoholism. Susan herself struggled with depression, liquor, and pills. Her family began coming apart. Her older brother went off to join the navy, and she dropped out of high school. By the time she arrived in San Francisco, Susan had survived a codeine overdose, an endless string of men—some bad, some just faceless—and a hard stretch in county jail for robbery. She was hired as the youngest topless dancer on North Beach's neon strip after her boyfriend of the moment talked her into getting onstage for an amateur show. She was girlish and full breasted, and she knew how to turn off her mind and sink her hips and ass into the music. She did whatever her nightclub boss asked her to do.

One afternoon Susan's boss brought an eerie-looking man into the bar. He was dressed all in black and had glistening, black eyes and a devil's goatee, and his shaved head gleamed a ghostly white in the shadowy bar. Her boss introduced the man as Anton LaVey and asked her to dance for him. The name meant nothing to Susan, but LaVey had achieved local notoriety as the Church of Satan's "Black Pope." A one-time crime-scene photographer and carny musician, LaVey played the calliope and Wurlitzer organ on dozens of midways and in numerous strip palaces. But he found his true showbiz calling as San Francisco's celebrity Satanist.

LaVey tooled around town in a black 1949 Citroën and bought a two-story Victorian mansion out on the windswept avenues, which he covered with a thick coat of black surplus submarine paint. A stream of devil worshippers and curiosity seekers frequented the satanic services and séances at his house, where they were greeted by dangling skeletons, a stuffed werewolf, and a mangy, roaring lion named Togare, who roamed the backyard. Among LaVey's followers were eccentric socialites, city officials, artists, and Hollywood celebrities, including the monumental blonde Jayne Mansfield. LaVey, like all violators of social convention, also found it useful to cultivate cops. One of the retired police inspectors in LaVey's thrall never forgot the night he dropped by the black mansion and saw a naked Mansfield draped on top of the grand piano. "She liked to be humiliated," LaVey said of the B-movie queen. "She longed for a stern master."

LaVey recruited Susan Atkins to perform in another of his spectacles, a topless Witches' Sabbath that he staged in the North Beach nightclub where she was working. She played a voluptuous vampire, rising out of a coffin with jet-black hair, bloodred lipstick, and bare breasts. Susan couldn't bring herself to climb into the coffin until she dropped a tab of acid. During the show, she remained motionless in the coffin, taking in every sound, the audience's footsteps, sighs, and breathing. She found that she liked playing dead. When it finally came time for her to rise up, she freaked out the men and women who were packed into the club. They gasped loudly as she stood up and pointed a long, red fingernail at them to mark them as her next victims.

To LaVey, Susan was just another hippie burnout—"perhaps a bit more drug befuddled than some," as he later recalled. LaVey had contempt for San Francisco's hippie culture, which he found "a mire of ignorance, stupidity, and egalitarianism." His Witches' Sabbath was just another carny show. But Susan felt something deeper. She liked the way the gaudy ritual made her feel each night; she liked her role's wicked power to shock and excite. Her new boyfriend thought it was all too creepy. He told her she was losing herself to LaVey, and he moved out.

After the Witches' Sabbath show closed, Susan once again found herself without a home, with no direction home. Inevitably, she ended up on the streets of the Haight, among crowds of other young drifters who shared her feelings that the world was "crooked and perverted." By now, the Diggers had scattered. There were no more street guardians to look out for the lost children. With no one to guide them, the kids fell into the hands of long-haired Fagins and worse. One day, standing in front of the Drugstore Café, a neighborhood institution, Susan was scooped up by an old girlfriend from the suburbs and taken to her communal house at the corner of Oak and Lyon Streets. She quickly fell into the house's hazy routine, binging on an endless supply of marijuana, hashish, and acid, and sitting stoned on the front balcony, listening to her next-door neighbor Janis Joplin sing blues arias.

It was in the living room of the old two-story brown house where Susan first met the scrawny, bearded little man who would change her life. He introduced himself as Charles Manson, and as they talked, Susan felt he was seeing right inside her. He took off her clothes and stood her in front of a full-length mirror. She wanted to look away, but he made her look. "Look," he whispered to her. "Look at yourself. You're beautiful."

He asked her if she ever imagined making love to her father when she was a little girl. She giggled. "Don't be silly."

He kept staring at her, unblinking. "I know you have. You must be honest. Every girl at some time wants to make love to her father."

He told her she had to break free of the inhibitions that were choking her. "Make love with me," he said, his voice getting lower. "Make love with me and imagine that you're making love to your father. You must break free from the past." Charlie would be her new father.

Even though he was a hardened, thirty-two-year-old ex-con, Manson was just as lost as the other young drifters when he arrived in the Haight after being released from McNeil Island penitentiary in March 1967. Manson, the son of a teenage prostitute, was the survivor of a childhood even more obliterated than Susan's. He had spent most of his life behind bars. "I still didn't know anything about marijuana or LSD or any kinds of drugs," he said later. "In fact, I didn't really want to come out of jail—I was frightened and didn't know where to go."

The Haight-Ashbury folded Manson into its arms. The ex-con became a well-known figure on the streets, collecting young women like Susan and becoming the father that they—and he—had never had. They created a "nest" for themselves in a two-story building at 636 Cole Street, near the Free Clinic, which he would frequent with his female tribe. Manson never seemed to require medical attention—"sickness is the product of an impure mind," he told the clinic staff. The Manson women were treated for vaginal infections, and they often asked for advice about natural childbirth.

As his reputation and strangely obedient family grew, residents of the Haight began to recoil from Manson. "I met Charlie Mason," recalled rock attorney Brian Rohan. "He was a little troll. He kept his girls on drugs all the time; they didn't know what they were doing." Susan later estimated she dropped acid at least three hundred times during her days with Manson.

Peter Lewis recalled meeting Manson at the home of Los Angeles record producer Terry Melcher "He didn't have an immediately weird vibe because there were a lot of guys like that. There were a lot of people coming back from Vietnam like him, and they headed right for the Haight. They were like the war casualties in Robert Stone's *Dog Soldiers*. So in the context of the sixties, Manson didn't really stick out. Who the hell was Manson? Maybe the CIA worked on him, you know, with one of its drug programs. I don't know who Manson was. Manson might not have known who Manson was."

Susan, though, knew who Manson was: the man she was supposed to follow. "I was eighteen but older inside. I was free. My father, brothers, and I were irreparably torn apart, it seemed. I had come close, but so far had found no substitute. Charlie had instantly seemed more of a father to me than my own father. He not only preached love, he had power. What he wanted, he could get. He often sounded like God."

As time went by, Manson was feeling less comfortable in the Haight. He thought the streets were getting "ugly and mean." He didn't feel safe in San Francisco anymore. One day in 1968, he sat down with Susan, whom he called "my right-hand man." He said, "Come on, we're going to LA." She didn't hesitate. She followed her destiny.

15

A KNIFE DOWN YOUR THROAT

A YEAR LATER, THE whole world knew Charles Manson—and Susan Atkins, too, as the giggling, witchy-eyed Sexy Sadie.

"Woman, I have no mercy for you," she told Sharon Tate as the actress begged for her life and the life of her unborn baby. Susan held down Tate as her accomplice, Tex Watson, plunged a knife into her belly sixteen times. They both had been snorting crystal meth for the past three or four days. When Susan and her Manson family accomplices showed up that night at the house off Benedict Canyon, one of Tate's houseguests asked them, "Who are you?" Watson replied, "I'm the devil, and I'm here to do the devil's business." Despite all the speed racing through her bloodstream, Susan felt strangely immobile, like "even if I had wanted to run, I couldn't." She felt "caught in something that I had no control over . . . it was like I was a tool in the hands of the devil."

The media coverage of the Manson mayhem wallowed in satanic hippie mythology. But the most horrific explanation was the one offered by Manson himself: "These children that come at you with knives, they are your children. You taught them. I didn't teach them . . . You made your children what they are."

The Manson family's gory helter-skelter in August 1969 was followed by the bloody debacle of Altamont in December. That's how the 1960s ended, with Manson and Altamont. "No more peace and love," reflected Peter Lewis. "It was stabbing people thirteen times just to see if the fourteenth time would make you feel funny."

By 1969, Lewis's own band was going to hell. Moby Grape was once the tightest, most promising rock group in San Fransisco. "For one second, they were great," said Mickey Hart. "They had chemistry. I saw them play. They were a *powerful* band, but they burned out in a second. They were just like a flash." Moby Grape began coming apart as soon as it burst on the scene—a victim of Columbia Records' overhype in a distinctly antihype environment, bad management, and perhaps most of all, the band members' own manias and drug excesses. Like the Cockettes' meltdown, the band's dissolution took place in New York, where they went to finish recording their second album. The city seemed to infect the band with poisonous spirits. While they were holed up there, the group began hanging out with the Rolling Stones and their ghoulish retinue, including a group of "sex witches," as Lewis described them, "who dabbled in black magic and various shit. The Stones didn't believe any of that. But the chicks really believed the Stones were satanic."

Skip Spence, Moby Grape's manic spark plug, fell into the sex witch darkness, and never really came back. "He went from a jolly, cool guy to a guy with a leather jacket, no shirt, and a big old dangly hanging from him," said bandmate Jerry Miller. "He looked like he'd shaved with a battleaxe. He was sweating all over the place."

After lunging at a Columbia executive with a pair of scissors and chopping through drummer Don Stevenson's hotel door with an axe in pursuit of the drummer, Spence ended up in the criminal ward of Bellevue Psychiatric Hospital and was later diagnosed with schizophrenia. Following Spence's breakdown, other members of the band also wrestled with their sanity. Moby Grape released their second album, appropriately titled *Wow,* and went on to record several other LPs over the years, mostly without Spence. But they never fulfilled the enormous expectations that swirled around them during those long, foggy nights at the Ark.

When the music scene withered, so did San Francisco's soul. Sages of dubious distinction began declaring the end of the sixties before the decade was even done. Except that it really wasn't. The 1960s would have many endings and beginnings, up to this very day. But, like the Manson bloodbath, the Altamont "festival"—if that's the right word for the macabre event—was undeniably a funeral of sorts.

The Rolling Stones, inspired by Woodstock, and sensitive to the charge that they were ripoff artists, decided to stage their very own free festival at the end of their 1969 US tour. San Francisco was the obvious location. The Stones' organization consulted with the right people: the Grateful Dead and what was left of the Diggers. At the Dead's suggestion, Stones tour manager Sam Cutler lined up the Hell's Angels to provide security. That's the way it was done in San Francisco: no cops, no professionals, just the badass bikers whom the longhairs always kept wanting to be their heroes. The free concert was supposed to take place in Golden Gate Park, as usual. But city officials knew that a Stones crowd would strain park facilities, so the venue shifted at the eleventh hour to Altamont, a speedway in the remote, tumbleweed hills of the East Bay.

Every headlining rock band in those days had its own karmic aura. San Francisco bands like the Grateful Dead and Jefferson Airplane gave off a life-celebrating shimmer that made even the Hell's Angels want to dance. The Rolling Stones cultivated a different identity. They played with the dark side. Mick Jagger became the midnight rambler, jumping your garden wall. He was in character when he screamed, "I'll put a knife right down your throat, baby, and it hurts!" He was a sinuous East End actor with a stage dagger and a crimson cape. But in America, the savage song sounded like the evening news. He had no idea what he was conjuring.

Earlier that year, the Rolling Stones had used a group of self-styled British Hell's Angels for security at a free concert in London's Hyde Park. But that crew, which simply liked strutting around in the outlaw bikers gear, was far from the real deal. The Stones were soon to find out what the real Hell's Angels were all about.

By the time the World's Greatest Rock 'n' Roll Band rolled into San Francisco on its long-awaited 1969 tour, its first in three years, Peter Coyote and Emmett Grogan were strung out on heroin, and the Diggers were fading fast. But Grogan, hanging on to his old role as ringmaster of all things free, began lining up the usual suspects for the concert, including the Angels. As the plans for Golden Gate Park began falling apart and the event began spiraling out of control, the Diggers got nervous.

"We tried to warn the Stones before Altamont," said Coyote, "but they were too rich, too powerful, and there was too much flow of multinational capital to listen to us. We warned the Dead too. They should've known better. We were the experts at bringing thousands of people together with no violence. But mainly I blame the Stones, who were planning to make a fortune off the movie rights, for trying to put on a phony free concert, with the Angels and all these kids as their extras. And I blame Mick Jagger for fucking with black magic. They reaped what they sowed. So you want to go strolling on the dark side, boys? This is what it fucking looks like."

As the helicopter carrying Jagger and drummer Charlie Watts across the bay from San Francisco hovered over the Altamont Speedway, it looked like the end of the world. More than three hundred thousand people were packed into a dust bowl ringed by scrub-covered hills. A poisonous-looking vapor blanket, combining the first wisps of tule fog from the Central Valley and the choking fumes from thousands of camp-fires and burning tires, hung over the bleak landscape. The copter made a bumpy landing, and Jagger—dressed like a medieval prince reviewing his battlefield, in yellow crushed-velvet pants, red silk shirt, and a leather cape—emerged into the crowd. A young, wild-eyed man immediately rushed up to him and hit him square in the face. "I hate you! I hate you!" he screamed at the rock star.

Jagger and his entourage pushed their way through the crowd to a trailer behind the low, makeshift stage. The scene already crackled with madness. Hell's Angels hovered around the trailer, binging on speed, acid, and red jug wine, and brandishing lead-weighted pool cues. Blood pulsed from the nose of a fat, naked boy. Inside the crowded trailer, guitarist Keith Richards—who had spent the previous night on the festival grounds, dropping acid and smoking opium—was sprawled on a bed, exchanging banter with a two-year-old girl.

"I'm gonna beat you up," she kept telling him.

"Don't beat me up," he pleaded.

Reports of the growing mayhem kept filtering back to the Stones' trailer—of Hell's Angels running amok in the crowd, cracking skulls and bloodying faces with fists, those pool cues, even full cans of beer. They heard that Marty Balin, the Jefferson Airplane's founder and singer, had been knocked out cold by the Angels when he jumped off the stage and tried to stop one of their gang assaults. It was the one heroic act by a performer during the entire sickening spectacle. As the Airplane broke into "Somebody to Love," Balin looked into the throng and saw the Angels—not known for their racial enlightenment—flailing away at a bare-chested black man with their pool cues.

"I saw the whole crowd, this mass, just back up and allow it to happen," Balin recalled. "I said, 'To hell with the song, this guy needs help.' So I went down there and started fighting, helping the guy out. When I woke up, I had all these boot marks tattooed all over me." Afterward, "Animal," the Angel who slugged Balin, tried to explain himself backstage to the singer. "Fuck you," spat Balin, who was promptly knocked out again.

Balin's act of courage didn't save the day, but it saved a small piece of San Francisco's soul. "That was a stand-up thing to do," Coyote said. "Brave man."

Years later, Balin's bandmate Paul Kantner resisted the idea that Altamont was a tragic watershed. "It didn't end the sixties," he insisted. "It was just a bad day with a bunch of drunken Hell's Angels who couldn't hold their liquor. I thought Marty did the right thing by jumping off."

Why didn't Kantner plunge into the melee too?

"Because Marty did."

As night fell, and the Rolling Stones finally prepared to take the stage, Sonny Barger and the Hell's Angels' high command began plowing through the crowd on their roaring Harleys to get to the front of the stage. Rock photographer Michael Zagaris never forgot their terrible entrance. "Barger was wearing a bear's head on his head. The crowd parted, people were trying to appease the Angels, offering them bottles of wine as they passed through. You could tell everyone hated them. As stoned as I was, I was thinking, 'This is like Poland when the Nazis marched in.' Everyone hated them but felt they couldn't do anything."

Once upon a time, the Angels had offered some kind of protection and rough justice on the Haight's wild streets. San Francisco bikers lived among the hippies, like wolves among lambs. But now the red-fanged realities of nature were making themselves clear. "I used to hear all the time in the Haight, 'Hey, the Angels are our brothers,'" said Zagaris. "But I thought most of these guys are killers—they could've hung with Attila the Hun, Genghis Khan. How the fuck are these guys our brothers?"

By the time the Stones took the stage, hours late, it was cold and dark, the crowd was surging toward the music's hot center, and the Angels were angry, fucked-up, and ready to pounce. As Jagger began singing and dancing in his "prissy clothes," Barger glowered at him from his corner of the stage. The top Angel was furious at the Stones' diva-like delay, while the crowd grew increasingly frantic and unpredictable. "I could no longer picture the Hell's Angels playing the part of bodyguards for a bunch of sissy, marble-mouthed prima donnas," Barger later remarked. He and his gang quickly made clear who controlled the stage.

When some Angels began manhandling a fat, drug-crazed, bare-breasted girl who kept trying to crawl onstage, Keith Richards leaned into Barger's face and said, "Man, I'm sure it doesn't take three or four great big Hell's Angels to get that bird off the stage." Barger responded by walking over to the edge of the stage and kicking her in the head. "How's that?" he asked Richards.

Then came the final descent into the jungle. Meredith Hunter, a black teenager with a flashy lime-green suit and a white girlfriend, was a target for the Angels' resentment all day long. Finally, while he was being roughed up, Hunter pulled the gun he was carrying with him—"but only to make them stop and think when they were beating him," said his girl-friend, Patty. "I know he would never have used it." An Angels desperado named Allen Pizzaro responded the way you do on the street. He spun the teenager around and knifed him in the back with his long blade in one smooth, acrobatic move. And then the other Angels of Death were flocking all over Hunter. They kicked the fallen boy in the face, they smashed him over the head with a metal garbage can, then they kicked his head some more with their heavy boots. His last words came in bloody bubbles from his mouth: "I wasn't going to shoot you."

Onstage, Jagger was the midnight rambler, he was the devil asking for sympathy. As the savage frenzy rose and fell in front of the stage, he broke character to plead for civility. "Everyone just sit down! Keep cool! Let's just relax, let's get into a groove. Come on, we can get it together, come on!" His voice was pleading, desperate. But it was his singing that weaved a deeper spell that night. "I'm called the hit-and-run raper in anger, the knife-sharpened tippy-toe." He was Charlie Manson invading a family's quiet sanctum.

The Rolling Stones were at the height of their artistic power at the time. America wasn't their native country, but they had mastered its roots music and made it uniquely their own. Their songs surged with the country's violent energy. But Altamont shook their souls. It exposed the utter artifice of their bad-boy act.

At one point during the Hell's Angels' bloody carnival, a disgusted Keith Richards walked across the stage to Barger and announced, "Either these cats cool it, man, or we don't play." But star power had no pull in that mad abyss. Barger stuck a gun in the guitarist's ribs and told him to start playing or he was a dead man. "He played like a motherfucker," the head Angel recalled.

After it was all over, and the Stones had fled back to the safety of their San Francisco hotel rooms, they tried to make sense of it all. But they simply sounded stupefied, like English schoolboys who'd found themselves in some unspeakably barbaric outpost of the empire. Talking to a San Francisco radio station, Jagger sounded on the verge of tears: "I thought the scene here was supposed to be so groovy. I don't know what happened, it was terrible. If Jesus had been there, he would have been crucified."

SOME HEAVY HIPPIES SHRUGGED off the bloodshed at Altamont as collateral damage. Stewart Brand was an old Merry Prankster. He had been around the cosmic block and prided himself on being unshockable. He knew the Angels, they had partied together at Pranksters ringmaster Ken Kesey's compound in the hills above Palo Alto, they were fixtures at the early Acid Test happenings. The counterculture was always a mix of ecstasy and depravity, Brand noted. "If you're going to have a Ken Kesey, you're going to have a Charles Manson—the one basically gave permission to the other. I went to Altamont and thought it was terrific. The hubris of hiring the Angels to work as security was both ballsy and bad judgment, but that's what the period was all about—exploring the limits of bad judgment. I remember a woman shrieking and humping the stars, losing herself orgiastically into Jagger's lips as the Stones bashed away onstage. It seemed entirely appropriate that there'd be people beating each other to death in the midst of all that. Dionysus leads people to being shredded and eaten. Those were the death-defying leaps we were about in those days, and some people die in the process."

But few in San Francisco's underground culture were philosophical enough—or perhaps hard souled enough—to take Altamont in stride. People were dispirited, angry, dazed. Everyone was talking about it, trying to sort through it, and figure out what it meant for the future of the counterculture movement. One of the more perceptive commentaries on Altamont popped up in the letters section of *Good Times,* the underground San Francisco newspaper that began in hippie bliss but became increasingly hard-bitten and radical as the years went by. The letter was written by a twenty-seven-year-old reader named John Peters, who had attended the festival. It's worth quoting at length, because of the way it captures the darkening mood of Hippieville.

> What's made Mick and his boys rich and famous and great is their whole fantastic trip of power and violence, and it's a very American trip by the way . . . For [the Rolling Stones], the power and violence is fantasy, something close to pornographic literature. But Americans just ain't like that. The real Americans want to get their hands and faces in the mud and the blood and the beer.
>
> The Love Generation never made it, except in a few communes way off by themselves, because it had no roots. The Pranksters and the Angels and the tough blacks, whatever their differences, they all have roots. Put any of them in a frontier town and they'd be running around with the worst motherfuckers around within a week. Their power and violence isn't a fantasy.

There was a burning desperation in the Altamont crowd, wrote Peters, like the hollow-eyed mob in *The Day of the Locust,* crowding desperately around its Hollywood idols, threatening to devour them. The young people jostling with the Hell's Angels for the prime turf around Mick Jagger's stage were the craziest of all. "At Altamont," Peters wrote, "you had to fight your way tooth and nail to the front if you wanted to be where the action was. If I were 18 instead of 27, with a sharp edge of despair in my stomach, I might have done the same." The people up front, in the killing pit, "were there because they wanted to be. In spite of what Mick says, sometimes you do get what you want. But when you do, it can hit you in the face."

Sensing the strong need of people in the Haight to discuss Altamont, Stephen Gaskin, a popular counterculture medicine man, resumed his Sunday morning gatherings at the tip of Golden Gate Park, across the highway from the ocean. Gaskin, a former semantics teaching assistant at San Francisco State College, attracted a large following that spilled out of the classroom and into the park when he began exploring the mysteries of sex, drugs, and consciousness. With his hollow cheeks, long, stringy brown hair, scraggly beard, and wiry body, Gaskin looked like a blazing-eyed Confederate cavalryman, still haunting the Tennessee woods long after the war was over. His followers hung on his every word.

San Francisco's "vibes" were seriously damaged by Altamont, Gaskin told his flock. He said the Stones' music was "sadistic," and he had stopped listening to it after it sent him spiraling downward during a frightening acid trip. Those who attended the concert were on a death trip, which inevitably ended in the human sacrifice of young Meredith Hunter.

The Stones, however, were not to blame for America's wretched state. "Let's face it, this country is weird right now." It was an empire reveling in its savage glory. During the height of the British Empire, Gaskin observed, "flagellation was a popular sport."

Gaskin announced that he would try to counter Altamont's morbid vibes on Easter Sunday in March 1970 with an enormous celebration of life in the Polo Field, where—an eternity-seeming three years earlier—the Human Be-In had ushered in a new era of higher consciousness.

But, in the end, Stephen Gaskin gave up on San Francisco, rolling out of the Haight with his congregation in October 1970 in a caravan of thirty-two rebuilt school buses and dozens of other motley vehicles. Gaskin's great exodus ended in Tennessee, where he established one of the most successful and longest-running communes in American history, the Farm.

Peace and love no longer held dominion in San Francisco, Gaskin decided. "The information we got in San Francisco was that folks were buying into violence in a wholesale lot," he said in explaining his flock's mass departure. His apocalyptic vision extended to American cities in general. They were falling into brutishness and depravity. And the only solution, according to Gaskin, was to withdraw from their destructive vortex and lead a simple, communal life in the country.

Gaskin's declaration of rural retreat marked another key turning point in the San Francisco counterculture's long, strange trip. Most of the Haight's original wave of visionary settlers were now gone. The bands were broken up or had dispersed to sunny hillside mansions in Marin. The Diggers were no more, and Grogan wound up back in New York, deeply enslaved by his heroin habit. He died on April Fool's Day 1978, nodding into the afterworld on a subway car, at the end of the Coney Island line.

Without its street-smart leaders, the Haight—capital of the counter-culture—was at the mercy of the growling packs of hustlers and thugs who began overrunning the neighborhood. Even more ominous, the same powerful redevelopment forces that had erased the Fillmore were now maneuvering to exploit the Haight's decay and do the same to that once robust district.

The Haight now found itself confronted by its most sophisticated antagonist: the new mayor of San Francisco, the brilliant dynamo Joseph L. Alioto. A bridge from San Francisco's old order to the new, Alioto was a strong defender of civil liberties and artistic freedom. But he regarded the youthful rebellion sweeping San Francisco as borderline anarchy. And he was prepared to destroy the Haight in order to save it. The strug-gle between Mayor Alioto and the street rebels of the Haight-Ashbury became an epic battle for the city's soul.

16

BENEVOLENT DICTATOR

J OE ALIOTO GREW up in North Beach in the 1920s and 1930s, when San Francisco was wracked by labor violence and civil turmoil. So the upheavals of the 1960s and 1970s—many of which shook the city during his eight-year mayoral reign, from 1968 to 1976—did not seem to undo him the way they did many political leaders during those years.

In 1926, when Alioto was ten years old, anarchists bombed the majestic Saints Peter and Paul Church on North Beach's Washington Square on four separate occasions, rattling the windows of his family's apartment a block away at 572 Filbert Street. To Italian Catholics in the neighborhood, the church—built in Romanesque Revival style, with twin cathedral-like spires and a massive Carrara marble altar—was a towering symbol of their faith and national heritage. But to labor militants, including the anarchists who targeted the church, the looming edifice stood for reaction and superstition. The Catholic Church was a mighty cross of gold that bent the shoulders and buckled the knees of San Francisco's immigrant working families.

During the Depression, San Francisco became even more violent a battleground. The Catholic Church and the Communist Party competed bitterly for the hearts and minds of San Francisco's Irish and Italian working class. After Harry Bridges's longshoremen's union closed down the waterfront and set off a general strike in 1934, Catholic officials condemned extremism on both sides of the bloody conflict and moved aggressively to mediate an end to it. When the eighty-three-day strike was finally settled, the church stepped up its efforts to counter labor militancy in San Francisco, organizing rival Catholic unions, staging mass rallies at Kezar Stadium, and sharing intelligence information about left-wing activists with the shipping companies, the right-wing American Legion, and the SFPD. Many of these church actions were carried out under the banner of Catholic Action, a global crusade to counter the rise of social democracy and Communism and inject traditional church values into civic life. The crusade was embraced by San Francisco archbishops Edward Hanna and John Mitty. And it was led by Sylvester Andriano, an Italian-born San Francisco attorney and a tireless soldier for the church.

Andriano, a Fascist sympathizer with close ties to both the Vatican and the Mussolini regime, was drafted to evangelize among San Francisco's Catholic youth. The Catholic activist told Archbishop Mitty that his goal was to steer young church members from "the evil influence of liberalism and laicism" and build in them "discipline, obedience, and respect for authority."

Among the young men caught up in Andriano's Catholic Action crusade was Joe Alioto, who—after graduating from Sacred Heart High School in the city—had enrolled at Saint. Mary's College in the East Bay, Andriano's alma mater. Alioto, a gifted debater, was assigned a prominent role in the church's social campaign, giving speeches against Communism, which he denounced as a "soulless philosophy [bent on] destroying Christianity, civilization, and all the sweet fruits which art and culture have bequeathed."

This would always be one side of Joe Alioto: Manichean, implacable, brutal in his opposition. You could see it on display when he became a lawyer—first as a young antitrust litigant in FDR's Justice Department, and later as a wealthy, corporate attorney for clients like the wine industry, rice growers' association, and Hollywood studios. And it was there in full fury—with his shiny, balding head radiating heat—as mayor of San Francisco, confronting the young militants in the Haight who screamed "Mussolini!" and "Pig!" at him, as well as the student radicals who shut down San Francisco State College during the longest campus strike in American history, which dragged on for five months in 1968 and 1969. Alioto's religious upbringing had instilled in him a deep sense of sin in the world, and also the will to combat it to the end.

But there was always another, big-hearted side to Alioto. He was a son of North Beach's "rich Italian peasant life," as he called it—a life centered on family, food, and the arts. Alioto came from Sicilian stock. His father, Giuseppe, sailed to America from Palermo, alone, at the age of ten. When he was eighteen, Giuseppe met his future wife, eleven-year-old Domenica Lazio, in the midst of the 1906 San Francisco earthquake. Fleeing the fiery chaos, young Giuseppe ran down to the wharf, where he saw Domenica's father shoving off the family boat into the bay. "*Salta, giovanotto, salta!*" yelled old man Lazio at Giuseppe, and the teenage boy did just that, leaping aboard the fishing boat, where he and the family floated for two days until the fires subsided. There were three Lazio daughters on board. By the time they docked, Giuseppe knew he would marry Domenica. His two brothers married the other two Lazio girls. The three young Alioto-Lazio couples moved into the same Filbert Street building, a different family in each of the three flats, and their children began arriving at regular intervals, including baby Joe in 1916.

The Aliotos and Lazios built the San Francisco fishing industry, opening wholesale fish companies and restaurants on the wharf. The families were not rich, but they were comfortable, even during the Depression. At home, the Aliotos dined on the sea's bounty—Dungeness crabs, clams, oysters, shrimp—and the red wine they made in their backyard, with the kids stomping the grapes, laughing and splattering themselves with plummy juice.

Prohibition turned many law-abiding San Franciscans into outlaw bootleggers. The Mafia was intertwined with Italian immigrant life in North Beach. "My father never forgot where he came from," said his daughter Angela, who later followed him into city politics. But this is one aspect of his North Beach background that Alioto never dwelled upon in public.

Joe Alioto grew up to become a symbol of Italian-American success in San Francisco, the political leader who represented the second-generation bridge to the American Dream. He might have risen even higher, to the nation's summit, but he could not untangle himself from his tribal past.

ALIOTO WAS A WEALTHY, fifty-one-year-old antitrust lawyer in 1967 when he was selected by a backroom group of city power brokers to replace Jack Shelley as mayor. He was the candidate of the downtown elite, but he was no shoo-in. Relatively unknown to the general public, he knew he had to win over the city's powerful unions—particularly Bridges's International Longshoremen's Workers Union (ILWU) and the Laborers' International Union of North America (LIUNA)—to rally voters. The political novice was smart enough to hire campaign staffers with strong labor ties, including press secretary Hadley Roff, a stocky, glad-handing former newspaperman who was chummy with longshoremen union officials Jimmy Herman and Dave Jenkins.

But Roff thought he had picked the wrong horse when he showed up at Alioto's elegant Presidio Terrace house one evening to accompany him to a make-or-break ILWU meeting, where the mayoral candidates were to vie for the union's endorsement. Alioto told Roff to pile into his car—to the press flack's horror, it was a shiny, brand-new Rolls-Royce.

As the two men cruised through a pea soup fog straight out of Dashiell Hammett, on their way to the Longshoremen's Hall building near Fisherman's Wharf, Roff stared glumly through the Rolls's window, which Alioto—unable to decipher his gleaming 747-like dashboard—could not defrost. Finally, Roff voiced his concerns to his new boss.

"Jesus, Joe, we're going to the ILWU!"—which, he did not need to remind Alioto, was San Francisco's toughest, most battle-scarred union. "And they'll see you in your pinstripes stepping out of a Rolls-Royce, for God's sake."

"Well, what do you wanna do—walk?" said Alioto, fumbling with the knobs on his dashboard.

Sure enough, when they pulled up in front of the building and Alioto emerged from his luxury car, he was greeted with a lusty chorus of boos from the rank-and-file stevedores filing into the building. The meeting hall inside was packed, and the air was filled with stale smoke and angry mutterings as the candidate made his way to the stage. Opposing him was Jack Morrison—a balding, bespectacled Adlai Stevenson–type—who spoke first. As the leading liberal tribune on the board of supervisors, Morrison was articulate, knew the city issues, and knew what mattered to the union. The crowd gave him a big round of applause.

Then Alioto got to his feet. He had served on the San Francisco Board of Education, but this was his first real campaign. He had never been in a position of courting hostile voters before. But he did know how to win over a jury. He quickly turned the cavernous room into his own chamber, and he took complete control of it.

"Can you guys hear me?" he yelled.

"Yeah!" came the booming response.

"Well, then, we don't need this microphone," he said. With that, Alioto jumped off the stage—looking more like a working stiff than an executive—and began prowling the hall.

"I had no idea what he was going to do," recalled Roff. "No talking points had been provided, no notes had been made. He talked for about fifteen minutes, walking down the center aisle. There must have been over a thousand people there that night, but he seemed to be talking to everybody like he was talking to them personally. He was talking to the proverbial jury. The next day, we had the endorsement of the most integrated, leftist union in town. And through the ILWU, he had access to the black community too. The number of blacks who got involved in the campaign was unheard of in San Francisco."

Putting together a formidable coalition of downtown business interests, organized labor, and black voters—along with his base in Italian North Beach—the centrist Alioto swept to victory on November 7, 1967, beating businessman Harold Dobbs on the right and Morrison on the left. Despite his political inexperience, Alioto proved to be a natural politician. He brimmed over with an infectious passion for the city of his birth, and he moved easily through crowds, touching and loving to be touched.

"Joe had an extraordinary physical electricity," Roff said, "and I say that not as an ex–press secretary who's strumming the usual violin, but as a fair observer. He was one of those guys who had an open heart to people. He had instant empathy. Once we were walking into the press club, and a couple of ambulance drivers were just coming out with somebody on a gurney, with the sheet pulled over him. The man's wife—or widow—was following behind. And Joe immediately rushed over to her and put his arms around her, so she wouldn't have to see her husband's lifeless form being clunked into the ambulance. Joe was crisp."

Shiny headed, bull shouldered, and encased in sleek suits, Alioto seemed as dynamic as a missile. His intensity was a tonic to the city after the fatigue of the Shelley administration. Charles McCabe, writing in the *Chronicle,* greeted Alioto's election as a welcome power shift to robust, Italian North Beach—away from the tired "Irish politicos who have been running this town for practically all of its history . . . It is an honored tradition to permit the Italian-Americans to take over when the harps have become bored, or otherwise rendered themselves useless."

Alioto started fast, promising to lift all boats with redevelopment dollars and federal aid. He also vowed to shower money on the arts and make San Francisco a world-class city. It was still a time when mayors could think big, and he wanted the whole city to share his gusto.

Alioto, the immigrant's son, brought a wider spectrum of people into the city's political establishment than ever before, appointing the first African American as deputy mayor and the first Latino and Chinese-American to the board of supervisors. He also paid off his big campaign debt to the unions that helped carry him into office, especially the Longshoremen's Union, giving their leaders key roles and advisory positions in his administration. Alioto named Harry Bridges to the port commission—a long overdue honor for San Francisco's legendary labor warrior, but a move that certainly sent the mayor's old Catholic Action mentor, Sylvester Andriano, twirling in his grave.

ALIOTO'S BOUNDLESS OPTIMISM ABOUT the city was immediately challenged by a series of stormy events. During his first year in office, rioters clashed repeatedly with police in the Haight and on the San Francisco State campus. A lecturer at State named George Murray, who belonged to the Black Panther Party, called publicly for the assassination of "slave-masters" Alioto and Police Chief Cahill. Three San Francisco policemen were shot after they pulled over a van filled with armed Panthers three blocks from the hall of justice. A police station in the Richmond district was bombed.

Throughout the tumultuous year, Alioto kept his cool. He affirmed protesters' right to express themselves. "Persons have the right to use the streets to say anything, no matter how unpopular," he announced in the midst of the Haight-Ashbury riots. But he just as firmly drew the line at violence. "There is no constitutional protection for throwing rocks and bottles," he pointed out.

Alioto strenuously avoided the provocative rhetoric of Governor Ronald Reagan, with his threats of a "bloodbath" and other extreme responses to youth protests. But while he tried not to demonize dissenters, the new mayor was not afraid to send the infamous tactical squad—a riot control unit whose black-helmeted, heavily padded members looked like storm troopers from an Orwellian nightmare—into the Haight or onto the San Francisco State campus when protests verged on chaos.

The mayor had a confidence about himself that allowed him to engage with protesters, even when they were enraged and foul mouthed. Some saw it as a cocky Il Duce swagger. But its true sources were his street-tough upbringing in North Beach, his finely honed skills as a Catholic school debater, and his deep love of San Francisco—which he assumed anyone of sound mind must share.

When Alioto heard about the assassination of Martin Luther King Jr. on April 4, 1968, he immediately called for a memorial service to be held on the steps of city hall the following day so that people from all over the city could grieve together in public. Police Chief Cahill was panic-stricken. A crowd could lead to a riot. But the mayor was unswerving.

The next afternoon, as thousands of people of all races crowded into the plaza in front of the city hall steps, a police official came rushing into Alioto's office. "There's a bunch of young kids from one of the high schools in Daly City, and they're all armed," he told the mayor.

"Well, invite the leaders up here right now. Right in my office," Alioto said.

When the four African-American students were ushered into the mayor's office, he told them, "I want you to march downstairs with me and sit on the platform." And that's what they did. Alioto and the students sat together on the makeshift stage on the city hall steps, next to a row of priests, ministers, rabbis, and a robed monk, as speaker after speaker offered prayers for King and pleas for the peace and racial harmony for which he had given his life.

The crowd, eerily silent, could see police snipers silhouetted on the roof of San Francisco Civic Auditorium across the plaza. The police had informed Alioto that there were many armed people in the crowd, just a few feet from the stage. Everyone seemed ready to explode. A firecracker could have set off a bloodbath. But at the end of the ceremony, people in the crowd joined hands and swayed in unison like a giant wave as they sang "We Shall Overcome." San Francisco did not blow up that day. It was one of the few major American cities that did not.

Alioto was a loyal mainstream Democrat, and he supported Lyndon Johnson's war in Vietnam. But he respected antiwar students' opinions, and he engaged in give-and-take sessions with them about the war and the limits of dissent. He arranged for KQED, the local public TV station, to host a seven-hour public forum for all sides in the San Francisco State strike to air their views. He also challenged Black Panthers leader Eldridge Cleaver to a debate on KQED. The ex-convict had become a literary sensation with his bestselling book *Soul on Ice*. And Cleaver used his badass, black-shades image, and his assaultive eloquence, to intimidate his critics into submission. But Alioto stood toe to toe with him on the studio stage.

"When everybody else was afraid to talk to this guy, I told him that I had seen tougher kids at Fisherman's Wharf," Alioto recalled years later. "He didn't bother me, and what the Black Panthers were doing was wrong. They were espousing violence, and violence was going to be met, no matter who was creating the violence."

As the 1968 Democratic Convention approached, Alioto's star was on the rise. Just a few months into his job as San Francisco's mayor, he was already being talked up as a potential running mate for presidential nominee Hubert Humphrey. He was an ethnic Catholic with impeccable labor and civil rights credentials, and he also brought a strong law-and-order reputation that could deflect Republican charges that the Democrats were soft on crime. But the vice presidential nomination went elsewhere, and the party, presiding over a disastrous war and torn by the violence-wracked Chicago convention, suffered a close defeat at the hands of Richard Nixon.

NIXON'S VICTORY IN NOVEMBER did not dampen Alioto's political ambitions. The following year, he began to position himself to challenge Ronald Reagan in the 1970 California gubernatorial race. San Francisco's tough-love mayor would have been Reagan's most formidable opponent. But in September 1969, *Look* magazine dropped a bombshell on Alioto that knocked him out of the governor's race and shadowed the rest of his political career. An investigative feature charged that Alioto was caught in a "web of relationships" with the Mafia that dated back to the days of the mayor's father, Giuseppe, who was partners with a San Francisco gangster in a Fisherman's Wharf restaurant. According to the magazine, Alioto himself had provided a variety of legal and financial services to mob figures. The most damaging charge against Alioto was that in 1965, as the board chairman of the newly opened First San Francisco Bank, he arranged a series of loans totaling $105,000 for a notorious Mafia executioner and ex-convict named Jimmy "the Weasel" Fratianno, who was trying to muscle his way into the California trucking business.

Alioto, fighting for his family's reputation and his political life, filed a $12.5 million libel suit against the magazine. The legal battle consumed nearly a decade of his life. He finally won, but it was a pyrrhic victory. His political career was finished, and his reputation carried the faint marks of a stain until his dying days. Alioto later claimed that he was a political victim of the conniving Nixon administration, which saw the mayor as a rising threat following his star turn at the Democratic Convention. Alioto said he obtained federal documents under the Freedom of Information Act showing that the Mafia allegations were leaked to *Look* by Nixon officials.

But the story grew complicated in 1981 when Mafia chronicler Ovid Demaris published Fratianno's life story, *The Last Mafioso*. In the book, the mobster declared that the *Look* exposé was "basically accurate." Alioto was not "a made guy," Fratianno told Demaris, but in the gangster's view, he "had impeccable credentials." The mobster described how he would drop into Alioto's offices at 111 Sutter Street—unannounced, to avoid FBI surveillance—where the two men would discuss various business schemes to enrich themselves.

The Weasel's confessions, which were published while he was in the federal witness protection program, became a bestseller. Alioto later dismissed him as a "notorious stool pigeon . . . who was paid more for being a stool pigeon than for any criminal activities he engaged in." But this time Alioto chose not to sue.

After the *Look* article exploded, Joe Alioto never seemed to bring the same sharp focus to his job as mayor. Throughout his life, he had wrestled with theological questions about good and evil. Now that he was accused of sin, he became obsessed with absolving himself. The strenuous attention that he devoted to his libel case went beyond the legal requirements, he was a man on a spiritual crusade to define himself.

WHILE THE MAYOR WAS distracted by his legal mission and his lingering political ambitions, his city grew more feral. The Haight, in particular— with its hard drugs, crime, and decay—was becoming a no-man's-land. Alioto's responses to the city's growing problems became less imaginative. With protesters, he began using the iron fist more than the velvet glove.

One day Alioto summoned an energetic Fillmore community activist to his office. The day before, the activist had organized a sit-in occupation of the mayor's office. Now, as he walked into the mayor's suite, he was greeted warmly by Alioto, who was flanked by two policemen.

"I like your style," said Alioto. "Do you want to come work for me?"

"No," the activist replied—his job was on the streets.

"Oh, come on, you can do a lot for those kids in the Fillmore by working for me," Alioto pressed. "You're a very bright person."

The community organizer held his ground.

"You sure?" asked Alioto, giving it one last shot. He was sure.

Alioto immediately had the organizer thrown in jail, where he spent the next ninety days for his illegal takeover of the mayor's office.

Early in his administration, Alioto attempted a balancing act with protesters, mixing force with reason. But as the civil disturbances spread, he grew more exasperated, and he gave the SFPD's fearsome tactical squad full rein to run riot, chasing down student protesters at

San Francisco State and Haight hippies and beating them at will. When riot cops roughed up Terry Hallinan, the lawyer for the SF State demonstrators, putting a gash in his head that required sixteen stitches, Alioto declared that the young attorney got what he deserved. After the Hallinans threatened to drag the mayor into court, he wisely made a conciliatory gesture toward the famously combative family, saying that he had "respect and admiration" for paterfamilias Vincent and "for the spirit of the entire family."

But Alioto continued to make war on the young settlers in the Haight, vowing that "a few thugs and malcontents are not going to turn the Haight-Ashbury into a war zone." Actually, the mayor's police department was doing exactly that. One evening, the tac squad even laid siege to the Free Clinic when a group of badly battered young longhairs sought sanctuary there. The police unit—high on its own testosterone and unhinged authority—surrounded the Clayton Street building, smashing the front door and manhandling clinic staff.

As far as Alioto was concerned, the Haight-Ashbury was enemy territory. And he was intent on occupying it. Neighborhood activists were convinced that he wanted to go further. They believed that city hall was allowing the district to sink deeper into decay, so that redevelopment officials could send in the bulldozers and erase it from the map, as they had done with the Fillmore.

The mayor took the first step toward remaking Hippieville in fall 1970, when he appointed a Mayor's Committee to Restore the Haight-Ashbury, composed of the same business, labor, clergy, and academic types who had given their blessing to the leveling of the Fillmore neighborhood. The mayor boldly decided to venture into the Haight to unveil the committee, sweeping into the Polytechnic High School auditorium across from Kezar Stadium one evening in October flanked by twenty-seven police bodyguards.

Alioto assured the hostile audience that city hall would not "shove anything down your throats." The redevelopment project would be a "grassroots" enterprise, he declared. But Haight activists—some of whom were refugees from the blasted Fillmore—had heard that before. "You wouldn't know a grassroot if you saw it, pig!" screamed one heckler.

The mayor stood on stage, peering into the crowd of some five hundred people, as the jeers and catcalls washed over him. "Motherfucker!"

"Thief!" "Mafioso!" That latter dagger found his soft spot. But he kept standing there in the sharp glare of the TV lights, with his jaw clenched and his eyes flashing. He was the one in control. His opponents seemed crazed, disorganized. At one point, a group of his loudest hecklers stormed out of the public meeting, a staged walkout that only left Alioto in more command of the battlefield.

A reporter from *Good Times* took note of Alioto's frozen smile, his self-confidence, his empty promises. "Patronizing prick," thought the underground journalist. Everyone knew where this was going to end: with the neighborhood razed, and high-rise condominiums and office buildings replacing the old Victorians. With the colorful, ragtag circus on the street replaced by white-collar commuters.

Only it didn't. Not this time.

17

LOVE'S LAST STAND

THE HAIGHT WAS a war zone by the time that Robert McCarthy found his way there on Christmas Eve 1969. But he had seen worse. McCarthy had served in Vietnam as a gunner's mate on a patrol boat on the upper Mekong River, near Cambodia. "It was the whole *Apocalpyse Now* experience," he said many years later. "I was terrified the whole time."

McCarthy lost a number of mates there. "And I killed a lot of people. I never said that until recently."

When McCarthy returned to the United States, he was stationed on Treasure Island in the San Francisco Bay. He tried faking mental illness to get a medical discharge, but it wasn't that far from the truth. One time, while way too high on white lightning acid, he considered suicide. "The reality was setting in, and it felt good to have a gun," he recalled. The truly crazy ones at Treasure Island were the guys who clutched pouches they had made from the scrotums of dead Vietnamese. The navy patched up their heads and sent them back into action.

The Haight beckoned to McCarthy from across the choppy, cold waters of the bay. On Christmas Eve, he went strolling in the hippie haven that he had read about years before in *Life* magazine. He wasn't looking for sex but for "mystical camaraderie." It was a harder connection to find in those days. As he walked down Haight Street, some ratty-looking speed freaks were hanging out in front of him, hassling anyone who went by. When a hooker passed them, the jitterbugs grabbed at her, trying to pull her into their doorway. She broke away, and the freaks started to go after her. But the navy man, high on LSD, fixed them with a look of death, and they backed off the woman. After Vietnam, it was a look that came naturally to McCarthy, and it was only enhanced by the acid.

Twenty yards past the meth head toll bridge, McCarthy heard a loud scuffle behind him and then the sharp crack of a gunshot. As he spun around, a young man stumbled past him, blurting out, "My God, they shot me!" The kid, who had ventured into the Haight from an outlying suburb to score some drugs, had been shot through the thigh. Snapping into action, McCarthy threw him over his shoulder and carried him to the corner, where his frantic girlfriend was waiting in her father's T-Bird.

McCarthy's introduction to the Haight started out as pure misery, but then he got lucky. He stumbled upon a store called the Ever Lovin' Trading Post, where a swarm of young men and women were caught up in the Christmas Eve mood of celebration, singing and dancing and exuding good cheer. He began talking with them. They had long, flowing hair, and all of them—men and women alike—looked beautiful to McCarthy. Even though he was trying to hide where he was from, they took one look at him and knew he was military. But they received him warmly. "They understood," recalled McCarthy. "They knew that I was looking . . . for . . . it."

McCarthy spent that night in a dilapidated house in the Haight—"no vibes, no love, just junkies crashing around." On Christmas morning, he woke up and went back out on the streets, still searching. He ran into Steve Kever, one of the young men he had talked to the day before at the Ever Lovin' Trading Post. Kever had a strong, compact body, and with his long blond hair and beard, he looked like Thor. "I just wanted to touch that: not his hair, his vibe. Steve had an enormous, open heart." Kever asked the sailor if he had found what he was looking for. He said no. So Kever invited McCarthy for Christmas dinner at his communal house that evening.

When he showed up at 1915 Oak Street, headquarters of the Good Earth commune, McCarthy instantly felt he was stepping into his dream of what the Haight was supposed to be. The ornate, three-story Victorian was beautifully kept, with shiny, oiled wooden floors and staircase, and heavy velvet curtains. The high-ceiling dining room was dominated by a huge table that looked like it was constructed of railroad ties that had been bolted together. The table was filled with steaming platters of food—roasts, winter vegetables, mashed potatoes—and the room was spilling over with people. Men, women, babies of all races—white, black, brown, yellow, red. McCarthy just stood there quietly in the midst of the festive chaos and took it all in. He knew that he had found home.

McCarthy began spending all his free weekends at the Good Earth commune. And when he was finally discharged from the navy on October 12, 1970, there was a blue hippie bus filled with his Good Earth mates waiting for him outside the Treasure Island Naval Base. As he left the base for the last time, McCarthy flung off his white cap and the rest of his uniform piece by piece. By the time the sailor reached the bus, he would recall, he was "butt-fucking naked." Climbing aboard, he was handed a fat joint by a commune member called Kentucky Jim. "It was the beginning and the end," said the Vietnam veteran. Robert McCarthy was gone: "killed in Vietnam." From that point on, he would be Mouseman, a nickname from his childhood days in Chicago.

The Good Earth commune was a central part of the second wave of Haight-Ashbury's hippie settlement. The commune was founded in 1968 by Kever and a fellow ex-convict named Cyril Isaacs, whom he had met in Susanville State Prison, where Kever served four and a half years for armed robbery. The idea came to Kever while he was on parole and working on the rapid-transit tunnel that was being constructed under the bay. He and his ex-con friends would pool their resources and live communally in the Haight. At first it was just a small group of Kever's and Isaacs's friends and the women who loved them. But Good Earth rapidly grew until it was a sprawling network of more than a half dozen houses in the Haight and a loose, ever-changing membership that was estimated at its height to number over seven hundred people.

The Good Earth communards took up where the Diggers left off, but in many ways they were tougher and more resilient. The core group within the commune were life-hardened young men and women—ex-cons, Vietnam veterans, streetwise runaways—who knew how to survive. They called themselves a church and claimed pot as their sacrament, and they preached the usual peace and love philosophy. Still, they were no pushovers. They loved their neighborhood, but they knew it was turning into a jungle, with violent predators and vicious cops around every corner. Good Earth made it widely known that it was prepared to defend its turf.

At first this self-defense took the form of simply escorting female commune members at night from house to house through the Haight's mean streets. But then it became a campaign to clean up the streets themselves. By 1970, the neighborhood was swimming with heroin and speed. A scruffy crew of junkies had moved into a boarded-up house directly across from the Good Earth house at 409 Cole Street. The commune decided that they had to go. Calling the police was not considered an option, since they would probably take the opportunity to raid the Good Earth house too. Besides, the police had closed down nearby Park Station and had apparently abandoned the Haight-Ashbury bestiary to the reddest in tooth and claw. So one day, a group of the commune's tougher members, including Mouseman/McCarthy, simply paid the junkies a visit and convinced them to leave. Good Earth took over the house, fixed it up, and moved in its own members.

Heroin dealers still roamed the neighborhood as if they owned it. But Good Earth began to run them out too. One afternoon, a smack pusher named Rico came roaring down the street in his flashy car, nearly running over several commune members, including Kever. The Good Earth crew loudly let the dealer know what they thought of him. Ten minutes later, Rico returned and stepped out of his car with a gun. "What are you going to do now?" he said. Kever and several other commune members began walking straight at him.

"They had no fear. Rico freaked out and raced away," said Will "Wild Bill" Huston, a commune member who was there that day. Kever and his posse knew they had backup. Huston—who had grown up in a Missouri Bible-thumping family and had served briefly in the air force—was stationed on the roof of the Good Earth house with a rifle. "I was ready to shoot if necessary," he recalled. "I knew how to use a rifle from my military and hillbilly background." Not long afterward, Rico moved out of the Haight, never to be seen again.

On another occasion, "Sag" Darel Ferguson and "Leo" Ron—known, like many Good Earth members, by their astrological nicknames—witnessed a gangster roughing up his girlfriend on the street. "We stepped in," said Ferguson. "We didn't tolerate that kind of behavior. You beat a girl, and you're going to pay for it."

The thug aimed a shotgun at the Good Earth men. "Big mistake," said Ferguson, who had learned how to handle himself on the streets after being kicked out of his family's house when he was sixteen. "We chased him like lightning down Haight Street, and he kept pointing it at me like he was going to shoot me. When we caught him, we smashed him over the head with the gun and beat the hell out of him, then dumped him in a trash can and left him for dead."

Good Earth became a solid community bulwark in a neighborhood battered by crime and decay and deserted by city authorities. Some longtime residents, like the Free Clinic's Dr. David Smith, credited the commune with saving the Haight. Smith said he knew of no other urban neighborhood that had been rescued this way once the scourge of heroin had taken hold on its streets. "Good Earth won, they beat the heroin dealers, because they were a warrior tribe," marveled Haight-Ashbury activist Calvin Welch. "They knew how to fight."

GOOD EARTH'S BIGGEST FIGHT turned out to be with Mayor Joe Alioto, whom commune leaders accused of letting the Haight decay so that he could bulldoze it and turn it over to his real estate cronies. "It was the same old story," said Larry "The Hat" Lautzker, a savvy Brooklyn-born commune member. "The government basically targets a neighborhood, they pull out the police and let the bad drugs flood the streets, they let crime go rampant, they let abandoned houses fall apart, they let the neighborhood go to hell—and then the redevelopers come in."

The commune took the lead in resisting city hall's redevelopment plans for the Haight. It was Good Earth members who had led the heckling and walkout when Alioto showed up at Polytechnic High in 1970 to announce his new citizens' committee to "restore the Haight-Ashbury." Later they infiltrated the committee and convinced it to disband. In the Fillmore, this kind of grassroots resistance had sprung up too late to save the neighborhood. But because of troublemakers like the Good Earth's "heavy hippies," this time the redevelopment juggernaut hit a wall.

Alioto was not happy with the commune's pesky interference. "He gave us thirty days to get our hairy asses out of town," recalled Mouseman. When Good Earth didn't budge, the mayor unleashed the police department on the commune, subjecting the tenacious hippies to a withering harassment campaign that would go on throughout the early 1970s. Commune members were stopped on the streets, shoved against the wall, and taken into custody on the slimmest charges. The Ever Lovin' Trading Post, the Good Earth store on Haight Street, was padlocked by the city. The commune's old vehicles were pulled over and ticketed.

The city crackdown on Good Earth culminated one evening in January 1971, when plainclothes SFPD narcotics officers raided the Oak Street house, arresting twenty-three people on charges of possessing marijuana, hashish, and LSD. Women were dragged onto the streets, and babies were torn from their arms. Men were roughed up, and some were smacked with billy clubs. The cops confiscated Good Earth property and over $1,200 in rent money from the commune treasury during the raid. They later returned the money, but by then, Good Earth members had been evicted from one of their houses for nonpayment of rent.

Good Earth leaders, increasingly frustrated by the police harassment, turned their arraignment a week and a half later into a near riot. As helmeted police tightly gripped their batons in the courtroom, Steve Kever and other commune leaders traded barbed comments with the presiding municipal court judge. Kever's heated exchange with the judge, which resulted in multiple contempt citations and jail sentences, began with this frank remark: "Fuck the court. You're a bastard and pig and fucker."

It spiraled downward from there.

Good Earth members briefly considered turning to armed resistance against the police brutality. But, they decided, that's not who they were. Instead of going down the violent path of the Weather Underground, the Black Panthers, and other armed groups on the radical left, Good Earth found a good lawyer. His name was Tony Serra, and with his long Native American–looking hair, pirate's gold tooth, and stoner aura, he seemed every bit the spacey hippie that the Good Earth hard hippies disdained. But when it came to the legal battlefield, Tony Serra was a brilliant warrior.

Serra, a San Francisco native, grew up in the outer Sunset district in an artistic, blue-collar family that also produced a younger brother, Richard, who would become a world-renowned sculptor. Their father, an immigrant from Mallorca, Spain, made jelly beans. Their mother, a Russian-Jewish bohemian aesthete, later killed herself, walking straight into the ocean at the end of Taraval Street, where she had taken her boys to the beach when they were growing up. Serra majored in philosophy at Stanford and threw himself into combative sports, joining the boxing and football teams. After graduating from law school in 1962, he tried to avoid his professional destiny, bumming around Morocco and South America and writing bad poetry.

It was Vincent Hallinan who convinced him that he had chosen the right profession. Two weeks after beginning his career as a criminal law-yer, Serra was walking past a courtroom in city hall, when the doors flew open and two men came spilling out like brawlers in a gold rush saloon. One man had the other man—a distinguished, corporate attorney type—by the throat. He slammed the unfortunate gentleman against the wall in the hallway and popped him in the mouth with a right jab.

"Who's that?" young Serra asked, staring at the pugilist wide-eyed.

"Oh, that's one of the best lawyers in town," a face in the crowd told him. "That's Vincent Hallinan."

"I'm going to like this profession," Serra thought to himself.

He brought Hallinan's combative style and poetic oratory to the courtroom on behalf of his Good Earth clients. The Haight-Ashbury communards grew fond of their legal champion, as he repeatedly suc-ceeded in getting charges against commune members thrown out of court. After the Oak Street raid, they hatched a plan with Serra to fight back against Alioto on his own turf. Good Earth would challenge the incumbent mayor in his November 1971 reelection bid, running none other than the commune's attorney on its "Platypus Party" ticket.

Alioto faced a typically colorful field of San Francisco opponents in his race for a second term, including one serious challenger: Dianne Feinstein, the ambitious president of the board of supervisors, who ran against the incumbent from the left, attacking him for his opposi-tion to school busing and courting the gay vote. But Alioto succeeded in slapping the limousine liberal label on Feinstein, who resembled a prim Snow White and was squired around town to political events in a Rolls-Royce. Once Feinstein was marginalized, the race became more entertainment than politics. Scott Newhall, the *Chronicle*'s mischievous former editor, injected a weirdly honest and even literary note into the campaign when he entered the race. But the real fun in the campaign came from Tony Serra.

Good Earth campaign workers scurried around the city, tacking up Serra posters and distributing the Platypus Party's unique platform, which called for abolishing victimless crimes such as drug possession, prostitution, and all consensual sex acts, and turning San Francisco into a city-state sanctuary against the war and the draft. The party also envisioned transforming San Francisco into an eco-friendly urban model, banning cars from the downtown area and replacing paved streets with green spaces.

Good Earth held a rock 'n' roll rally outside city hall to promote its candidate, who was photographed dancing exuberantly to the music, with one hand waving free. Commune members provided security at the campaign events, decked out in long, tie-dyed underwear. The rock fund-raisers staged by the Serra campaign failed to fill the candidate's coffers, but he shrugged it off. "I've always been nonmaterialistic, and I don't give a damn," Serra told the alternative press. "Also, I represent a lot of dope dealers, and they lay many thousands of dollars on me."

Serra had no illusions of knocking off Joe Alioto in the race. "I don't expect to win. But before I entered the race, I consulted the I Ching. The Ching referred to the planting of a seed—all I want to do is to make my ideas known." And Platypus Party ideas about greening the city and decriminalizing consensual sexual behavior would indeed seep into San Francisco's political mainstream a few years later.

After Alioto was reelected, he escalated his war on Good Earth. In May 1972, the SFPD launched its biggest raid on the commune, bursting into several Good Earth houses in the Haight in a predawn raid and sweeping off eighty-seven people to jail. Dan "Spud" Moore, a Vietnam vet from Boston, opened the Cole Street door when he heard the police pounding. "I just stood there; I thought we had nothing to fear. Little did I know." A long-haired narcotics cop came rushing into the house with a small army behind him, yelling, "Let's get these hippies!" He began to beat up Moore, breaking one of his front teeth.

Serra again quickly got the charges dismissed against the incarcerated commune members. But when they returned home, they discovered that the cops had trashed their living quarters, smashing guitars and other possessions and overturning furniture. Steve Kever and Tony

Serra held a press conference to denounce the police mayhem and filed suit against the city for $240,000 in damages. Good Earth leaders also rounded up support from community organizations such as the local Catholic Social Services, which complained in a letter to Police Chief Al Nelder about the raiders' "brutality" and "wanton" destruction of property.

Good Earth's pressure campaign put Alioto and the police department on the defensive. One day Supervisor Feinstein and Richard Hongisto, the city's maverick sheriff, even showed up at the Cole Street house to inspect the damage from the raid. Wild Bill Huston was still in bed as the political dignitaries were escorted through the house. Hearing a commotion outside his door, a stark naked Wild Bill jumped up from bed and flung open the door to see what was going on, just as the starched and coiffed Feinstein went walking by. "Sorry you had to see that," Wild Bill later told Feinstein, who stayed for the commune's spaghetti dinner. "She said it was fine. She even chipped in a couple bucks for beer when we passed the hat," he recalled. "I thought that was cool."

DESPITE THE UNRELENTING POLICE harassment, Good Earth continued to thrive. The commune was built loosely around Kever's charismatic but reluctant leadership. "I never liked to call myself a leader; it was all somewhat anarchistic," Kever recalled. And yet the commune developed a strong social code and work ethic that allowed it to weather police aggression and neighborhood upheavals, while absorbing a steady influx of new members from all over the country. Everyone was expected to share household cooking and cleaning duties, while also working to help support the commune. Good Earth ran a trucking business, mechanics shop, clothes store, crafts business, recycling operation, day care center, and house-painting crew. The commune even had its own house band, Osceola, that sometimes featured ex-Monkee Peter Tork.

"The goal was to do everything ourselves," said Ferguson. "We thought, 'Screw the business world. We have to get off the grid, unplug from Babylon.'"

"I was always trying to disprove the 'lazy hippie' epithet," said Spud Moore, who took pride in his work with the paint crew, sprucing up dozens of old Victorians in the Haight. "Everybody in Good Earth had some type of skill, especially the ex-navy guys, who knew machinery, carpentry, electricity. If you didn't work hard, you'd be quickly ostracized, and you got the message. We'd call those people 'energy rip-offs.'"

Sometimes Moore's work brought unexpected benefits. When the Jefferson Airplane hired the Good Earth crew to paint their Fulton Street mansion, Moore couldn't believe his good fortune. After coming home from Vietnam, he had bought all the Airplane albums and listened to them in constant rotation. The work was hard: the crew had to strip years of paint from the mansion's big Greek columns with butane torches, sand them down, and restore the beautiful redwood underneath. But Moore still found it a joy to show up every day. "While we worked, we could hear the Airplane rehearsing inside. I thought, 'Here I am listening to Marty Balin's voice soaring out the windows.' It was something I could only dream of back in Boston."

One of Moore's fellow housepainters discovered another perk to the job. While working on the scaffold, he looked into bassist Jack Casady's second floor bedroom window and spied a big bag of weed. Climbing through the window, he helped himself to the stash.

But the work itself was surprisingly rewarding at Good Earth. "Didn't matter how laborious it was—garbage or recycling runs, moving furniture, painting, etcetera—we were doing it for ourselves," said Huston. "That in itself was a gas, and to do it with the sense of love and loyalty to one another made it much more special. Self-sufficiency running at full speed."

Despite all the hard work, Good Earth was far from a drone culture. Everyone was young, healthy, and fun loving. And all the houses were charged with sexual electricity. While sex was readily available, predatory behavior was not allowed. "Relations between the sexes were incredibly equal," said Dana Jaffe, a beautiful, self-possessed fourteen-year-old runaway who became Steve Kever's lover. "Back then, men really felt like brothers. The guys were tough—after all, some of them came out of prison, some out of the military. But there were not a lot of male conflicts and power games. It felt like a different type of society, where everything seemed possible."

The Good Earth "hippie wonderland," as one member called it, seemed robust enough to survive the 1970s, the graveyard of the 1960s.

But in the end, it was hard drugs—what else?—that brought down the saviors of the Haight.

DRUGS WERE ALWAYS CENTRAL to Good Earth's operation, since most of the commune's revenue came from dealing weed and acid. But in the early years, Good Earth banned members from using, let alone selling, anything harder. Commune members knew that smack had almost killed the community, and they were mortal enemies of the junk trade. But by 1974, cocaine was creeping into San Francisco. Good Earth vigorously debated whether "nose candy" was a hard or soft drug, but in the end, the commune's leadership made a fateful decision. "We finally decided it was a soft drug," said Jaffe.

It was a decision that she, as well as Kever, would come to deeply regret. "Drugs and money were our downfall," she said. "We became very self-indulgent; we got seduced by all the flash. There was suddenly huge amounts of money from dealing coke, and we had access to a kind of lifestyle that people can only dream of. We had been a hard-working hippie commune, and suddenly people were giving you their flashy cars when they got tired of them because they wanted something flashier."

As coke suppliers for the city's rich and famous, Good Earth's royal couple were suddenly in demand, and Kever and Jaffe began showing up at the mansions of San Francisco luminaries like celebrity lawyer Melvin Belli. Early one morning, a gaggle of Good Earthers ended up at Pam Pam's, a downtown diner favored by the late-night drug crowd. They noticed David Bowie standing in line, and one communard invited Ziggy Stardust outside for a toot, delicately putting a spoon to each one of the rock star's nostrils.

Even the grease monkeys in the Good Earth garage started snorting the stuff, and when they did, they noticed that lots of girls from the neighborhood started swarming them. "Sex turned from something intimate, from simply enjoying each other, to sex for drugs," said Huston.

One night in 1974, at an Oak Street house party, a pack of beautiful young women whom no one in the commune had ever seen before came strutting through the front door. The beauties headed straight for the long communal dining table, where a crowd was gathering around a man as he cut up generous lines of white powder on a big mirror. The glamour girls couldn't wait their turn—suddenly they began crawling over people to get to the coke. "They were like animals," said Huston. "I said to myself, 'Jesus, this is not good.'"

Along with the coke riches came even more paranoia. Even in the weed-and-acid days, there was always tension as Good Earth braced for the next raid. Commune members practiced their own version of fire drills in preparation for the police sweeps. Some of those who were assigned to the commune's pot store, which operated in a safe house behind several heavily bolted doors, cracked under the psychological pressure and asked to be reassigned. But the cocaine racket turned up the heat higher than ever. Good Earth members began walking around with guns and looking over their shoulders.

"People were afraid, burned out," said commune member Chris Wickman. "We were always fighting the cops, fighting evictions, fighting the utility companies by pouring concrete over our meters. And we were fighting more and more with each other. The Good Earth scene went from being a very mellow, gentle vibe to a hard, reality-based scene. It all had to do with drugs and money."

Wickman and other commune members began leaving the city for a more pastoral life in Oregon. Those who stayed behind in the San Francisco drug business, like Kever and Jaffe, faced a grimmer journey. Kever got caught in a US Drug Enforcement Agency coke bust in 1976 and served seventeen months in federal prison. After he was released, he became addicted to crack cocaine, and his life skidded downward until, years later, he ended up in living in a tent city in Florida. "It was disgusting," he said. "I hated to even take a shower there." He finally picked himself up, put himself through community college, graduating in 2008 on his seventieth birthday, and becoming a social worker and activist for the homeless.

Jaffe left Good Earth when she was twenty and got deeper into the cocaine trade. She was arrested for trafficking in Colombia, spending six months in prison there and another year under house arrest. She too would finally turn her life around, winding up as an executive chef at a four-star hotel in the Napa Valley wine country. And like Kever, whom she would always consider the love of her life, she looked back at the Good Earth days with a full heart.

"We saved the Haight," she reflected. "We helped create San Francisco values. We had, and still have, real convictions. We weren't nearly as laid back as we're pictured in Hollywood movies and the media. Nothing in popular culture has captured the reality of our experience. We were trying to save the world."

Kever, Jaffe, and many others from the scattered Good Earth tribe found one another decades later in an online forum, brimming over with feelings for their youthful selves. But before they could reach that serene place in their lives, they—and the utopian city they fought for—had to go into "free fall," as Jaffe put it. The freakish and the cruel, the desperate and the cracked—all of San Francisco's darker impulses began to flourish when the final community bulwarks like Good Earth came flying apart. After these neighborhood levees crumbled, anything was possible. *The blood-dimmed tide was loosed, and everywhere the ceremony of innocence was drowned.*

18

DUNGEONS AND DRAGONS

B Y THE EARLY 1970s, the revolution was over in America, and San Francisco—its fallen capital—staggered on the edge of chaos. The city was overrun with false prophets and savage messiahs, as well as double agents and police informers. Strange creeds and mysterious leaders developed overnight followings. Inexplicable communiqués were issued from the underground. The sacraments of blood and guns replaced peace and love.

A wave of bombings rocked the city, striking corporate offices, super-markets, electrical plants, and neighborhood police stations. The front of Mayor Alioto's house was torn open by an explosive device hidden inside a box of See's candy left on his family's front steps. The anarchy Alioto had witnessed growing up in North Beach in the 1920s was back in full force.

The leading players in the bombing craze called themselves the New World Liberation Front (NWLF), and the press speculated about how many secret cells and combatants were involved. One scholarly radical journal heralded the NWLF as "the most tactically advanced guerilla group in the United States" and gushed that "its record of success . . . verges on the astonishing," with nearly fifty bombings to its credit. The underground group even boasted its own magazine, *The Urban Guerrilla* (*TUG*), which featured esoteric debates about Maoism and armed struggle, and offended gays and feminists with its reactionary positions on sexual liberation.

But the New World army turned out to be nothing more than a front after all—the work of one mad bomber and his aboveground PR man. The bomber finally fell into the hands of the law after he murdered his wife in the Santa Cruz mountains. "They believed in reincarnation, and she wanted to be reborn, so he chopped off her head with an axe," explained Tony Serra, who put his services at the bomber's disposal. His defense? Insanity, what else? But it didn't work. The mad bomber died in prison.

There was only so much a lawyer could do, even a brilliant one like Serra. By then, heroic clients were in short supply. Instead there were axe murderers, terrorists, and drug dealers.

As the broader movements for peace and social justice fell into disarray, the left-wing action in the Bay Area shifted to the dark burrows of prison reform. In the early 1970s, the California penal empire had only a fraction of the staggering inmate population—170,000 souls—it has today. But it was already on its way to becoming the nation's most dysfunctional prison system, bloated by ever more draconian sentencing laws and filled with grotesquely disproportionate numbers of black and brown men. California maximum-security dungeons like San Quentin, Folsom, and Soledad were cauldrons of prisoner rage and official brutality.

It was George Jackson who came to symbolize the desperate plight of California's black prison population. Arrested at eighteen for a gas station robbery that netted $70, he spent his entire adult life behind bars: one more intelligent young black man whom the state of California could find no other use for. Jackson ensured his lifelong incarceration when he got involved in militant prison politics. As Bob Dylan, one of the many artistic and intellectual figures who came to celebrate Jackson, later sang, "He wouldn't take shit from no one, he wouldn't bow down or kneel." Jackson saw the prison system, with its cruel conditions and forced labor programs, as a modern form of American slavery. And he refused to be a broken-back field mule.

In January 1970, Jackson and two other black Soledad inmates were charged with murdering a prison guard—a vengeance killing, authorities claimed, for the deaths of three other black prisoners who had been cut down by gunfire from a guard tower. Held in solitary confinement for twenty-three hours a day as they awaited trial, Jackson and his codefendants became internationally renowned as the Soledad Brothers. While in the hole, Jackson studied Marxist theory and black liberation philosophy, and wrote a steady flow of impassioned letters about race, injustice, and prison life that were later collected into two bestselling books, *Soledad Brother* and *Blood in My Eye*.

Jackson's life now seemed on some flaming trajectory with a preordained fiery finale. In August, his seventeen-year-old brother, Jonathan—who had grown up with the legend of his brother but not his brother—burst into a Marin County courthouse, brandishing an automatic weapon. He freed three prisoners in the courtroom and took several hostages, including the judge, who was led outside with a sawed-off shotgun taped to his neck. The younger Jackson hoped to use the hostages to force the release of his brother. But as the group tried to escape from the court building in a county van, the vehicle came under a massive hail of fire from San Quentin guards and other lawmen, who clearly had no regard for the lives of anyone in the van, including the judge. Jonathan Jackson and two of the escaping prisoners were killed, as well as the judge, whose head was blown off when the shotgun discharged.

A year later, just days before he was to go on trial, George Jackson met his own violent end when he was shot down by San Quentin guards during what prison officials claimed was an attempted escape, but which Jackson supporters such as French writer Jean Genet declared "a political assassination." Jackson's death sparked a wave of furious protests and bombings in the Bay Area, and instantly wreathed him in a romantic glow. Black intellectual, unbending political prisoner, resistance fighter. Jackson became the model for would-be revolutionaries inside and outside of California's barbed-wire empire. And he became a ghostly nightmare for state law enforcement officials, who feared that his Stagger Lee Marxism would inflame the poor, black, and angry everywhere.

Bay Area radicals began looking to rally around other eloquent black prophets in California's penal hellholes. Black prisoners were championed by many on the left as the bleeding edge of the revolution. Meanwhile, police and intelligence agencies began grooming counterfeit leaders and informers to embed inside the volatile world of the prisoner rights struggle.

The FBI had been targeting a broad range of antiwar, civil rights, and black power groups throughout the 1960s and early 1970s with its counterintelligence program, Cointelpro, infiltrating the groups and using a variety of subversive measures to disrupt them. At the extreme end, this even included assassination. A charismatic, young Black Panthers leader named Fred Hampton was murdered in his bed in 1969 by Chicago police connected to Cointelpro, and Los Angeles Black Panthers Bunchy Carter and John Huggins were shot down on the UCLA campus in 1969 by members of the rival United Slaves (US) organization, a murky black nationalist group run by Ron Karenga. The FBI had incited the murderous hostilities between Karenga's group and the Panthers, and, according to one FBI informant, the US assassins were even ferried from the scene of the crime by the bureau. It was Karenga, who ruled his turf with a mixture of Afrocentrist mumbo jumbo and thuggish violence, who went on to give black America Kwanzaa. He created the holiday after being released from California prison in 1975, after serving four years for stripping and torturing two women he accused of trying to poison him with magical crystals.

FBI director J. Edgar Hoover and his secret police clearly understood the dark powers of subversion. And his agency was not alone. In 1967 the FBI was joined in its clandestine war against American activism and radicalism by the CIA, which launched a nefarious, Bondian-sounding program called Operation Chaos. A direct violation of the CIA's charter, which forbids the spy organization from engaging in domestic activities, Operation Chaos, among other things, sought to enlist "assets" in the black movement for purposes that were left unspecified. Finally, the state of California also ran its own intelligence operation aimed at black militants, prison rights crusaders, and other activists, as did the police departments in Los Angeles and other cities.

THIS WAS THE CHURNING froth of black rage and counterrevolutionary cunning from which slithered the Symbionese Liberation Army in late 1973. The group would turn San Francisco and Berkeley upside down and hijack headlines around the globe for more than two years, pitting left-wing groups against one another, tarring the prison reform movement, and generally sucking air and light out of the progressive scene.

The fantastical group, which invented a completely imaginary world of armed revolution, seemed the hideous dream child of those overheated Berkeley communes and Washington counterintelligence offices, which were the only places where something like the SLA made sense. The true symbiosis in the Symbionese Liberation Army was not between all "the oppressed peoples" it claimed to be fighting for, but between the SLA and the police agencies that hunted it.

The SLA was born in the Black Cultural Association (BCA), a behavior modification program masquerading as an African-American consciousness-raising group in Vacaville, the California prison system's medical facility. Vacaville Prison had a controversial reputation as a center of mind control experimentation. And BCA was run by a man with a shadowy intelligence background named Colton Westbrook. A pudgy, black linguistics instructor at UC Berkeley, Westbrook had served in Asia with the US military and worked in Vietnam for Pacific Architects and Engineers, a CIA-controlled firm that built the interrogation chambers for the spy agency's notorious Operation Phoenix program, which used torture and assassination to destroy suspected Vietcong cadres.

BCA won favor with prison authorities, rejecting George Jackson–style militancy and offering black inmates classes and workshops that advocated a soothing blend of racial pride and self-help. But black prisoners distrusted Westbrook. Although he tried to keep his military and intelligence backgrounds hidden, stories circulated about the brainwashing techniques he had learned in Asia and how he was applying them at Vacaville. One of the few inmates with whom Westbrook developed a close bond was Donald DeFreeze, an armed robber and gunrunner with a history as a police informer.

DeFreeze had led the charmed life of a snitch for several years, released or paroled time and again after being arrested for stealing and selling enough guns and explosives to fill an armory. In 1968 he was recruited by the Criminal Conspiracy Section, a secret intelligence unit within the Los Angeles Police Department, to supply guns and grenades to be used against the Black Panthers. There is evidence that the guns used to kill Bunchy Carter and John Huggins on the UCLA campus were delivered to Karenga's assassins by DeFreeze.

But in 1969 the LAPD's patience with DeFreeze finally ran out when he was wounded during a gun-blazing shootout after trying to cash a stolen $1,000 check at a Los Angeles bank. By the time he was imprisoned in Vacaville in December 1969, DeFreeze felt that his life had hit rock bottom. At age twenty-six, he was deeply estranged from his wife and six children, his only skill was the black-market gun trade, and he was facing a long stretch in prison. "I was slowly becoming a nothing," DeFreeze later wrote a friend.

DeFreeze found a savior in Colton Westbrook. Under the BCA overseer's tutelage, the convict developed his own prison course, which he titled Unisight, and began teaching a bootstrap philosophy lifted directly from the seven Kwanzaa principles popularized in black circles by Ron Karenga: self-determination, production, cooperation, collective work and responsibility, faith, unity, and creativity. DeFreeze later emblazoned each principle on the seven-headed cobra that became the exotic symbol of the SLA.

At Vacaville, DeFreeze reinvented himself as Cinque, taking his new name from the legendary African slave who led the 1839 rebellion on board the *Amistad*. His fellow inmates kept the odd, self-promoting Cinque at a wary distance, and Unisight failed to attract a big following. But Cinque's work did win Westbrook's admiration. "We were a hell of a team in many ways," Westbrook remarked later. "Cinque did his job . . . He wasn't brilliant, but he was smart. He was quite methodical and thorough. He had his shit together. He was the type of brother who would take a lead."

Though Cinque touted Unisight as a mind-liberating tool for the black man, it was young white men and women who filled his prison classroom. The BCA program at Vacaville had become a magnet for white radicals from nearby Berkeley. Inspired by the legend of George Jackson, they signed up as tutors in the program, hoping to become part of the prisoner rights struggle. One of the most active group of tutors came from a Maoist commune in Berkeley called Peking House, including future SLA members Russell Little and his girlfriend Robyn Steiner, and William Wolfe. Why a virulent anti-Communist like Westbrook would allow avid young followers of Chairman Mao to hijack his program is unclear. Westbrook later explained, rather weakly, that BCA "lacked the money to draw tutors other than those people at Peking House."

After a while, Westbrook claimed to be fed up with the young "self-taught commies," as he called them, and he funneled them into the

Unisight course, where he thought Cinque would keep them firmly in check. Instead Cinque's consciousness-raising class became the seedbed for the Symbionese Liberation Army: an "army" led by a sketchy black snitch with an even murkier prison patron, and made up of earnest, middle-class firebrands suffering from deep self-loathing and white guilt.

In December 1972 Cinque was suddenly transferred to Soledad Prison, in the coastal farmlands of central California. Shortly after, Westbrook followed in the path of his favorite inmate, when he was hired to teach community relations to Soledad guards. Cinque seemed to be under the wing of prison officials, and other prisoners suspected that he was an informer. In March 1973 Cinque was given a plum job as a late-night boiler attendant in a remote, unguarded section of the prison grounds. On his first night, Cinque was dropped off by a guard at the facility. As soon as the guard drove away, Cinque sprinted to the twelve-foot fence and scaled it, making his way north up Highway 101 to the Bay Area and his date with infamy. He had escaped from the same area of the prison where Colton Westbrook taught his class. Westbrook realized this seemed to implicate him in Cinque's drama, and he claimed that he looked into the strange coincidence "to see if I was being set up."

As Cinque roamed around the Bay Area, prison authorities seemed surprisingly lax about tracking him down. He approached various radical groups and offered his services as "a hit man," which the stunned activists declined. Many of them suspected that he was a provocateur. After reuniting in Berkeley with the young white militants who had filled his Unisight class at Vacaville, Cinque soon began building his own underground liberation force, which he named the Symbionese Liberation Army. The SLA leader mesmerized his followers with his revolutionary gibberish and his prison-hardened, bull-like physique. He strutted around the SLA's various safe houses buck naked and fully erect, quickly establishing sexual dominion over the women in his flock, even lesbian lovers Patricia Soltysik (Mizmoon) and Camilla Hall. He swilled plum wine and squatted on the floor, rattling a handful of small bones, mumbling voodoo incantations, and weaving a spell over his acolytes. Cinque and his women formed the power nucleus within the group. None of the men ever challenged him; his skin color and prison credentials gave him supreme status.

"I crave the power Charlie Manson had," declared Cinque, who claimed that he had met the fellow ex-con in Los Angeles. Like Manson's followers, the SLA soldiers were disillusioned children of the sixties. But in contrast to Manson's girls, they came from solid, middle-class backgrounds. Angela Atwood (formerly DeAngelis) was a high school cheerleader from a strong Catholic Italian-American family in New Jersey. Camilla Hall, the daughter of a Lutheran minister and missionary, had worked as a social worker in Minneapolis. None of them seemed destined for lives as revolutionaries. Bill Harris, a Vietnam veteran, met his wife Emily at the University of Indiana, where she was an honors student and sorority girl. While at Indiana, Emily and Bill worked for the Indiana State Police Department, setting up drug arrests, before moving to Berkeley in the spring of 1973.

They were all raised in the bosom of Middle America, and were dutifully making their way up the chutes and ladders of life, heading toward their own versions of the suburban family dream in which they had been raised. But something snapped in each of them along the way. Sincere young Americans, they were driven crazy by the 1960s—or more precisely, by what America was becoming in the sixties. There is no other way to put it.

Joe Remiro had been a "gentle boy" and a good student at San Francisco's Sacred Heart High School, according to his father, Charles. But after Remiro served two tours of duty in Vietnam as a decorated, gung-ho rifleman with the 101st Airborne Division, he was "never the same."

Nancy Ling Perry grew up in Santa Rosa, a sun-splashed, idyllic corner of small-town America eighty miles north of San Francisco. Her family, the owners of a successful furniture store, were prominent in local business circles and supporters of conservative standard-bearer Barry Goldwater. But something cracked in Nancy at age sixteen, when she watched the national nightmare in Dallas on November 22, 1963. Later, she explained the Kennedy assassination's impact on her, in a "letter to the people" that seemed more from the heart than most of the SLA's bombastic communiqués.

"When I was in high school," Nancy wrote, "I witnessed the first military coup against we the people of this country. I saw us passively sit by our TVs and unconsciously watch as the militarily armed corporate state took over the existing government and blatantly destroyed the constitution that some of us still believed in. I listened to the people around me deny that a military coup had taken place and claim that such a thing could not happen here . . . In 1964 I witnessed these and other somewhat hidden beginnings of the military/corporate state which we now live in. And I heard my teachers and the government-controlled media spread lies about what had happened. I saw the civil rights protests, the killings and bombings of my black brothers and sisters and the conditioned reactions of extreme racism in my school and home . . . I told my teachers and family and friends that I felt that we were all being used as pawns and puppets, and that those who had taken over the government were trying to keep us asleep and in a political stupor. I asked my teachers to tell me what happened in Nazi Germany; I asked them to tell me the meaning of fascism; I asked them to tell me the meaning of genocide. And when I began to hear about a war in Vietnam, I asked them to tell me the meaning of imperialism. The answer to all my questions then was either silence, or a reply filled with confusion and lies."

This is as clear and concise a summary of the radicalization process in the 1960s as you will find. We've long been conditioned to accept this grotesque sequence of events, to put it all away in a safe time capsule labeled "the Tumultuous Sixties." But for a young person at the time, one with a searching heart and mind, these traumas—assassinations of popular leaders, imperial war, and brutal acts of government repression—were crimes against the national conscience. And the longer they went unpunished, they became, to these young people, stark proof that American democracy was a fairy tale.

Many young radicals in the early 1970s, faced with the ceaseless gore of Vietnam, as well as the police-state measures employed by the Nixon administration and the FBI against the left, felt that they were engaged in a war with the government. Groups all over the Bay Area— from Berkeley to the Santa Cruz mountains—began arms training and munitions making. The looming showdown with the militarized "corporate state" might end in a suicidal inferno, but "the revolutionary vanguard" believed that it was its duty to set an example and inspire the people to rise up. A thick air of doom and drama hung over the youth ghettos of San Francisco and Berkeley. But nowhere was this atmosphere of death and glory more pungent than in the subterranean world of the SLA.

As FALL 1973 APPROACHED, Cinque huddled with his soldiers. It was time to strike. They pored over the business sections of local newspapers and trolled through business periodicals and annual reports at the public library, searching for suitable members of the corporate state to kidnap or execute. The target selection process had an absurdly macabre quality. At one point they seriously considered killing Charles O. Finley, owner of the World Champion Oakland A's, who had enraged the baseball team's blue-collar fan base by firing popular manager Dick Williams. In the end, Cinque zeroed in on Marcus A. Foster, the superintendent of the Oakland public school system. It seemed like an equally bizarre choice.

Marcus Foster was a progressive black educator who had committed himself to turning around the city's deeply troubled public school system. Teachers and students did not feel safe going to school in Oakland. Pressures mounted on Foster to increase security after a young elementary schoolteacher was raped in her classroom in front of an eight-year-old student. In response, Foster announced that he would ask Oakland police officers to patrol campuses and would issue photo identification cards to students. To Foster, creating a safe environment in which to learn was essential for the survival of Oakland's public schools. "We are going to have to get away from the rhetoric of the 1960s, where policemen were called pigs and were viewed as enemies of the people and all of that foolishness," he told a community meeting. "We are going to have to see policemen as protectors of our society."

In response to an outcry from some activist parents and Black Panthers leaders, Foster later softened his security proposal, making it clear that the campus cops would not be armed. But either the SLA news monitors weren't following the story closely enough, or they didn't feel Foster's compromises were sufficient. Cinque issued his death warrant: "We are gonna off that nigger," he told his army. "We want to show the oppressed peoples there are black pigs just as there are white pigs."

Strong black men like Marcus Foster seemed to push Cinque's buttons. One SLA chronicler speculated that authority figures put Cinque in mind of his father, a laborer who muscled his family into the middle class but took out his violent rages on his son, whom he beat regularly with his fists, and even a baseball bat and a hammer, until the boy finally fled home at age fourteen.

Thero Wheeler, another escaped black convict, and Robyn Steiner were the only SLA members who questioned Cinque's fatal selection of Marcus Foster. "If you are talking about executing a highly positioned black man in Oakland," said Steiner, "you will defeat our objectives straight away by alienating the black population." But Cinque made Wheeler feel that his life was unsafe, and he fled the group. After the Foster assassination was carried out, Steiner also ran for her life.

Foster was ambushed on the evening of November 6, 1973, as he walked with his deputy, Robert Blackburn, to the parking lot behind the school administration building. Cinque fired first, blasting both men with a sawed-off shotgun. Then Cinque's two accomplices—his "official" bedmate Patricia Soltysik and the ever-loyal Nancy Ling Perry—joined in, firing with automatic pistols. It was Nancy, the woman who decried "the killings of my black brothers and sisters," who stepped over Foster's wounded white deputy and pumped eight cyanide-filled bullets into the chest of Marcus Foster. As the SLA assassins ran for their getaway car, she was heard giggling. When Steiner asked Nancy how she felt about killing a person, she said, "He's not a person, he's a pig."

After the Foster assassination, a cloud of fear and suspicion fell over the Bay Area. Activists puzzled over the mysterious organization that claimed credit for the killing. To many, "symbionese" conjured some exotic overseas guerilla army. When it became clear that the violent group was homegrown, some radicals immediately suspected a government plot, since Foster—despite his tough security proposals—was a progressive who had shown that he was willing to negotiate with groups like the Black Panthers. The Panthers saw the Foster murder as part of a government campaign to stir up "hatred, fear, and disunity in the black community" and to inflame white paranoia. When SLA members Russ Little and Joe Remiro were caught in a police dragnet in January 1974, many on the left breathed a sigh of relief, hoping that the bizarre drama was coming to an end. It had only just begun.

19

THE REVOLUTION WILL
BE TELEVISED

D ESPITE THE POLICE noose that seemed to be tightening around
the SLA after the arrests of Little and Remiro, Cinque decided
that the group needed to strike again "to prove to the world the Foster
killing wasn't an isolated action." This time they would rivet the public's
attention by kidnapping a high-profile target and issuing demands on
behalf of the downtrodden. Cinque kept a thick, blue journal filled with
names of powerful figures in politics, business, and media who were
potential kidnap victims, including President Nixon and his daughter
Tricia, Governor Ronald Reagan, and Senator Edward Kennedy. But in
the end, the group settled on Patricia Hearst, daughter of *San Francisco
Examiner* publisher Randolph Hearst and his wife, Catherine, a Reagan appointee to the University of California Board of Regents. Patty
Hearst, a Berkeley undergraduate, conveniently lived, unguarded, just
blocks away from the SLA hideout.

Like Marcus Foster, Patty Hearst was an indefensible target, both
morally and politically. Though the nineteen-year-old coed was born into
a family that presided over a vast media empire, whose newspapers were
known for their reactionary editorial slants, she bore no responsibility
for the Hearst Corporation's hidebound conservatism. As Robyn Steiner,

who was put in charge of surveilling her, found out, Patty was no "rich bitch" but a socially conscious young woman who attended protest rallies on the Berkeley campus. She also was outspoken in her criticism of the Hearst press, including her father's own newspaper, telling him, "Dad, nobody under eighty reads the *Examiner* anymore. It has become irrelevant to the times."

For that matter, neither was Randy Hearst stamped from the same conservative mold as his father and older brothers. In fact, realizing that his daughter was right, Hearst launched an effort to liberalize and liven up the *Examiner,* hiring his young nephew Will to shake up the fusty editorial page and pushing his news editors to do a better job of covering the city's overlooked groups, including blacks, Latinos, Chinese, and the young.

But Cinque was not interested in the moral component of the kidnapping. Ever mindful of how the SLA was playing on the public stage, he was focused on the crime's potential media impact. Once the young Hearst newspaper heiress was in the SLA's hands, Cinque knew that he would become the ringmaster of a gaudy media circus. In this respect, it was a brilliant decision.

The SLA's mad dash onto the world stage began on the evening of February 4, 1974, when Cinque, Bill Harris, and Angela Atwood forced their way at gunpoint into Patty's Berkeley apartment, beat her fiancée, Steven Weed, gagged and blindfolded her, dragged her down the building's concrete stairs in her bathrobe, smashed her in the face with a rifle butt, and stuffed her in the trunk of a car. Patty was kept blindfolded in a closet in a Daly City safe house, just south of San Francisco. Her captors scorned their "prisoner of war" as "Marie Antoinette" and "a bourgeois bitch," and she was subjected to weird interrogations by Cinque, who grilled her about the stocks that her parents owned, how much money her father made, and whom he visited when he went to Washington—none of which she knew.

Later Atwood informed Patty that "Cin wants to fuck you," explaining what "a great honor" it would be for her. He entered the closet and ordered her to take off her clothes, then raped her on the floor of her stale, musty cell. "I lay there like a rag doll, my mind a million miles away," she recalled. Afterward she told herself, "Well, you're still alive." Cinque and his armed band established complete dominion over Patty's body, letting her know when she could eat and go to the bathroom, and who would rape her.

As Patty underwent her ordeal, the SLA gloried in the media explosion sparked by her kidnapping. The revolutionaries glued themselves to the TV and radio, spinning the dials and searching for the latest reports on their exploits. Cinque stoked the publicity fires with his strange, militaristic communiqués from the underground. In one taped message released in early April, he announced that "all corporate enemies of the people will be shot on sight at any time and at any place," setting off more panic in elite circles.

Colton Westbrook tried to establish contact with his former prison protégé, holding a bizarre press conference on the Berkeley campus during which he read an open letter to Cinque in "black English."

"No rich white man is going to talk to a nigga, especially a pure nigga. But maybe a bousie nigga and a pure nigga can rap a bit," declared Westbrook, standing in front of a battery of TV cameras and microphones. The portly lecturer, wearing an African cap and matching vest, then went on to compliment Cinque's "brilliant" political strategy, while cautioning restraint in handling Patty Hearst. "Dig it, Cin, I can understand your Symbionese thing and know that you will not harm Patty unless the man makes a bum move."

Westbrook then made a puzzling reference to Cinque's "leader," as if he were someone known to both men. But when asked about this by reporters, Westbrook shrugged it off, saying that he was only referring to a statement made by Cinque in one of his taped messages.

Finally, Westbrook urged Cinque to talk to him "man to man, brother to brother, nigga to nigga." He suggested that the SLA leader could relay messages to him through one of a number of convicts and ex-cons whom he listed by their "reborn," or Swahili, names.

Was it a comical sideshow in the SLA media circus, or was the former CIA spook trying to send Cinque a veiled message? If Westbrook was trying to reestablish a supervisorial role over the escaped con, it obviously didn't work. Cinque announced his break with Westbrook in typically dramatic style when he publicly called for him to be "shot on sight." On the FBI's advice, Westbrook immediately fled east with his wife and child.

As WESTBROOK NOTED IN his open letter, the most ingenious demand issued by Cinque came a week after the kidnapping, when he ordered Randy Hearst to underwrite a massive food giveaway to the poor. The demand, which came with a thinly veiled threat about Patty's "health" if it were not met, set off an extraordinary chain reaction. The food giveaway would reposition the violent gang as benefactors of the poor, pit left wing groups that cooperated with the food program against those that rejected it, drive a wedge between press mogul Hearst and his powerful friends, and create a witches' brew of political intrigue.

As Patty Hearst's desperate father scrambled to see how he could meet the SLA's food distribution scheme—which California welfare officials estimated would cost a bracing $400 million—it soon became clear that his corporate and political cronies would be of no help. Governor Reagan grimly quipped that he hoped those who took the food were stricken with botulism, and suggested in a more serious vein that anyone who did accept the handouts would have their welfare checks cut off. Ludlow Kramer, a Washington state official whom Randy Hearst appointed to direct the food effort, and the publisher's young nephew Will made an urgent call on the chairman of the Bank of America. Kramer and Will Hearst—who was long-haired, unshaven, and wearing sandals—took an elevator to the top floor of the B of A headquarters, a dark tower looming over the San Francisco financial district. "Sir," Kramer told the bank chairman, "what I want you to do is call—you're the one man who can do it that I know of—call forty of the top businessmen to meet with me for cocktails this afternoon or breakfast tomorrow morning." But instead of helping the Hearst family raise the ransom money for Patty, the Bank of America chief offered Randy Hearst a $4 million loan instead—a loan that he was in no financial position to accept.

The SLA kidnapping exposed the fact that Randy Hearst and his brothers did not have access to the vast resources of the company founded by their legendary father. In the end, he scraped together a $2 million food budget, wheedling $1.5 million from the surprisingly stingy directors of the Hearst Foundation and putting up the other $500,000—one quarter of his wealth—himself.

The Randy Hearst who emerged at regular intervals during the fifty-seven-day kidnapping drama to face the media swarm outside his home was a study in muted agony. Outside his two-story French chateau in plush, suburban Hillsborough squatted a permanent encampment of jostling TV reporters, cameramen, and newspaper scribblers from around the globe. The cacophonous scene must have struck him as some sort of hellish punishment for all those decades of Hearst yellow journalism. But in front of the cameras, tightly gripping the hand of his stricken-looking wife, he appeared resolutely composed and polite, in his thick-rimmed spectacles and tailored suits. Hearst displayed more dignified grit than one would expect from a man born into the pampered comforts of his family, with its storied castle, club memberships, and luxurious trips abroad.

Will Hearst—who went through the ordeal with his uncle, living in the Hillsborough "bunker"—pointed out that Randy had flown transport planes through enemy flak in World War II and was a "man of signature bravery." But life inside the family bunker was "a living hell for my uncle," Will recalled. "It totally devastated his life. He was never the same again. It changed what reality was to him forever. He had the strength to live through it. But it surely haunted him. Is it enough to have a quiet, comfortable life and have a bunch of sweet kids and live in a sweet place, when all that can be blown away? Maybe one has to be more armored and serious in life."

Life inside the Hillsborough mansion during the long ordeal was a nightmarish carnival. Randy and Catherine Hearst engaged in heavy drinking bouts, sometimes with Charles Bates, the FBI San Francisco bureau chief who was in charge of the SLA hunt. At the urging of Patty's four sisters, the family brought in psychics who attempted to locate the kidnap victim and her abductors with their extrasensory powers. One of the psychics—whom the Hearst girls labeled Swami Number One, Swami Number Two, and so forth—constructed a small altar on the Hearsts' dining room table to perform rituals. Meanwhile, Catherine, a devout Catholic, turned to a steady flow of priests for consolation, when she wasn't relying on the bottle. Her drinking unleashed a fiery temper, which she often directed against Patty's weaselly fiancé, whom she accused of not being man enough to die fighting her daughter's abductors.

At one point, the agile Colton Westbrook even inserted himself in the Hearst family compound, spending two late-night sessions with Randy and Catherine in Hillsborough. Hearing about Westbrook's intelligence background, the distraught parents begged him to use his connections to help track down their daughter. But Westbrook demurred, insisting, "I am no kind of a superagent." Late one night, after Catherine went to bed, Randy and Westbrook shared another round of heavy tumblers of scotch, and Randy asked the question that had long been nagging him: "Is it possible that Patty is pregnant by Cinque?" This time Westbrook could provide an answer, though it turned out to be false. "I've heard those rumors," he said with a nod.

Patty was her father's favorite daughter. He liked her feisty sense of humor and independent streak. She was known as "Randy's spoiled brat." He would do anything to save her life.

"I've never put in an honest day's work in my life," the publisher once joked. "I don't really know what it's like out there." But as the ordeal dragged on, Randy began getting a hard education about life. He drifted away from his club society and entered a world vastly different from anything he had ever known. It was a world peopled by the militants and community activists whom he recruited to implement his People in Need (PIN) food distribution program. The anguished father was convinced that somebody in this world could connect him to the underground tunnel where his daughter was hidden.

The PIN program got off to a chaotic start in February 1974. Some of the organizations that the SLA requested to coordinate the food giveaway, including the Black Panthers and the United Farm Workers union, refused to play a role, with Panthers leader Huey Newton proclaiming that he wouldn't be a party to SLA "extortion." Many of those groups that did participate used it as an opportunity to steal food and to shake down Randy Hearst for more money. Meanwhile, fewer than half of the twenty thousand people whom PIN organizers hoped to feed on the first day actually received food packages, with long lines forming outside distribution centers before daylight, made up mostly of black women, many with children in tow. The bags of food included a frozen turkey, a box of saltine crackers, a small can of tomato juice, a box of biscuit mix, and, occasionally, a quart of milk and some eggs. But as the day wore on and the food supply began running out, frustrations grew. Fights broke out at the East Oakland center, and a number of people were injured when distribution workers began throwing the frozen turkeys from the back of trucks into the crowd.

In the following days, Hearst worked frantically to improve the quality of the food and to appease the community groups involved in PIN. He ordered the *Examiner* to run flattering stories about activists who were participating in the program. He sat down for a four-hour lunch meeting at a Hilton hotel in San Francisco with suspicious American Indian Movement (AIM) leaders Russell Means and Dennis Banks, who—after first making their bodyguards taste the meal—agreed to help with PIN.

Hearst also made a series of generous gestures directly to the SLA, hiring power attorney William Coblentz to represent Little and Remiro and trying to arrange a live national telecast for the SLA's two jailed "soldiers." Hearst even contemplated turning himself into an SLA hostage to win his daughter's freedom.

The SLA drama sent Hearst tumbling down a rabbit hole into the company of vivid personalities with whom he never would have crossed paths before Cinque's gang upended his life. They circled through his executive office at the *Examiner,* with the big oil painting of his father staring down at him, Citizen Kane in his prime. He featherbedded the staff at the PIN headquarters with them; they drifted through PIN's China Basin warehouse building near the San Francisco docks, snarling at reporters, threatening the white administrators, helping themselves to food supplies, and working their shady hustles. There were ex-cons, street-tough detectives, left-wing firebrands, loopy volunteers, undercover cops, FBI informers.

Randy's most surprising new friend was Wilbert "Popeye" Jackson, the iron-pumping, forty-four-year-old black ex-con who led the radical United Prisoners' Union. Like George Jackson, who was no relation, Popeye Jackson had spent a good chunk of his life in prison for robbery, and, despite his soft Louisiana drawl, he exuded a badass charisma that white activists, especially women, found irresistible. Like Cinque, whom he had known behind bars, Popeye Jackson also had a reputation as a police snitch.

Randy brought Jackson into the PIN operation and treated him like a prized executive. He offered to underwrite a private school education for the ex-con's son. He made sure that Jackson's prison reform work got glowing coverage in the *Examiner,* and it was no surprise when the paper editorialized that Jackson should remain a free man despite a parole violation for drug selling. Two weeks later, the state parole board agreed. In return, Hearst asked that his new friend tell him anything he heard about the SLA's movements and Patty's whereabouts. They had a gentleman's agreement.

Jackson was flattered by all the attention he was getting from his Hillsborough booster. "Hearst has great respect for me as a man, and I respect him," the ex-con told friends. But the unusual relationship did nothing for Jackson's reputation on the street. When his parole was not revoked, some Bay Area militants speculated that he was an informer—not only for Hearst but, worse, also for the FBI.

In the dark, early morning of June 9, 1975, Popeye Jackson drove home from a party, pulling to the curb in front of his Albion Street apartment in the Mission. His wife, who was pregnant with his child, was inside the apartment. But Jackson, accompanied by a woman named Sally Voye, didn't want the party to end. Voye—another one of his white admirers in the United Prisoners' Union, and also an undercover narcotics agent—was burying her face in Jackson's lap when a man walked up to the car and emptied the clip of a 9-millimeter automatic pistol into the couple, killing both of them.

Popeye Jackson's murder released another poisonous plume around the SLA case. Frantic claims and counterclaims clouded the air. A letter to the underground *Berkeley Barb* speculated that he had been killed by the New World Liberation Front because he was a double agent. Jackson loyalists in the United Prisoners' Union charged that he was killed by the cops. The SFPD, in turn, zeroed in on the Tribal Thumb, yet another militant Bay Area group led by an alpha-male ex-convict, Earl Satcher. The cops arrested a Tribal Thumb member, who was tried and convicted of the murder.

ALTHOUGH IT WAS LONG kept quiet, Randy Hearst had another strange bedfellow in the PIN subculture. Her name was Sara Jane Moore. Eccentric even by the colorful standards of the SLA cast of characters, she showed up one day at the food program's warehouse headquarters and announced, "God sent me to help." The scruffy volunteers stared dumbfounded at the middle-aged woman in her preppy Peck & Peck pantsuit, pearl necklace, and tight-curled salon perm. But Moore soon wormed her way into the heart of the organization, taking over its book-keeping duties, setting herself up as its press spokeswoman, and becoming a confidante of Randy Hearst.

Moore had led several different lives before she showed up at PIN. Born in West Virginia during the Depression, she was raised in a traditional Baptist household grimly presided over by her father, the superintendent of a DuPont chemical plant, and her spic-and-span mother. Moore rebelled, running off to join the Women's Army Corps, and burning through two unhappy military marriages. She gave birth to three children, but, clearly not the mothering type, abandoned them with her own parents and disappeared. Moore popped up for a while in Hollywood as a bookkeeper at RKO Studios, where she met and married an Academy Award–winning sound technician and became pregnant with child number four. But a month after her wedding, Moore again overturned her life and headed for the Bay Area. Here she would marry husband number five, a successful doctor, and reinvent herself yet again as a gardening housewife in Danville, an exclusive East Bay enclave. For a while, she seemed to fit into her conservative surroundings, volunteering in the reelection campaign of Republican senator George Murphy, an amiable old Hollywood song-and-dance man in the Reagan political mold. But after the inevitable conclusion of her fifth marriage in 1973, the shape-shifting Moore suddenly found herself in the middle of the SLA storm.

In April 1974, as the PIN program was winding down, Moore was approached by FBI special agent Charles Bates, who was carefully monitoring the food operation and its murky undercurrents. One afternoon Bates picked up Moore on a designated San Francisco street corner and drove her to tony Pacific Heights, where he parked the car and asked her to become an informer. In the press, the fifty-four-year-old Bates came off as a lanky, genial G-man with a lazy Texas drawl, but the FBI veteran had a deep history in some of the nation's most sensitive cases, including the assassination of President Kennedy and the Watergate investigation, which he had led for the bureau. The FBI saw the Bay Area in the early 1970s as a critical battleground in its struggle with the radical left. Sitting in their car that afternoon, Bates and fellow agent Bert Worthington convinced Moore that she could play a vital role in this battle, spying on Popeye Jackson and other activists, and finding out what they knew about the whereabouts of the SLA. "These are dangerous people," Worthington told her. "They are out to destroy the country. Many of them are dupes of foreign governments, of the KGB and the Red Chinese."

It was Moore who later helped seal Popeye Jackson's fate, circulating a letter among Bay Area radicals that accused him of being an informer for Randy Hearst. *Rolling Stone* later called it Jackson's "death warrant."

The FBI men planned to keep Moore busy. They wanted her help not only in probing the Bay Area radical underground but also in keeping tabs on Randy Hearst, whom Bates suspected was running his own private investigation of the SLA. Moore agreed to work for the FBI, throwing herself into her clandestine assignments so vigorously that the bureau was soon loaning her out to other law enforcement agencies, including the San Francisco Police Department.

But when it came to infiltrating the radical underground, the FBI's judgment was often unsound. Sara Jane Moore turned out to be one of the most embarrassing informers in the bureau's history. During her brief career as an FBI snoop, the ever-surprising Moore shifted alliances a dizzying number of times, betraying her G-men controllers, and then sweet-talking her way back into their good graces—and doing the same with her radical targets.

While reporting back to the FBI about Randy Hearst, Moore was developing a close bond with the newspaper publisher. Hearst, in fact, asked Moore to develop secret lines of communication with the SLA. Neither Hearst nor Bates knew that she was acting as an informer for both of them. Meanwhile, Moore was also reporting about Hearst and the FBI to radical friends whom she had befriended while spying on *them*. The many-lived Sara Jane Moore had finally found her ideal place in life, inside an utterly bewildering hall of mirrors.

All the conflicting forces inside Sara Jane Moore exploded on the morning of September 22, 1975, when she bought a .38-caliber Smith & Wesson revolver from a Danville gun dealer and drove across the Bay Bridge to assassinate President Gerald Ford as he was leaving the St. Francis Hotel. Feeling increasingly desperate, like a spy without a country, Moore decided to choose the antigovernment side in the end, and to prove her allegiance with a dramatic act of violence.

Jerry Ford was a bland Washington hack, but he had somehow set off a perplexing firestorm of madness. Two weeks earlier, Charles Manson devotee Lynette "Squeaky" Fromme, had waved a gun in the air in a Sacramento park where Ford was speaking. Moore proved more of a threat, squeezing off a shot that ricocheted off a wall just behind Ford's head. If her revolver's sight had not been faulty, as she pointed out later, Moore might have found her target.

As she tried to adjust her aim and fire a second shot, a Vietnam veteran named Oliver Sipple knocked down Moore's arm, and a San Francisco cop pried the gun from her hand. Sipple was hailed as a national hero, but when Herb Caen revealed that he was gay, it tore apart the ex-marine's closeted life. Sometimes, when he was drinking heavily— which happened more and more frequently in his later years—Sipple would wish out loud that he'd never saved Ford's life, because of all the torment that fame had brought him. It was one more twisted footnote in these strangest of times.

Sara Jane Moore served thirty-two years of a life sentence for the attempted assassination. In 2009, after she was released from prison, she tried to make sense of what she had done. "I thought if I didn't try to kill President Ford, someone else would . . . that was the tenor of the times," she said. "I thought it would trigger a new revolution.

"We thought San Francisco was the world—and it wasn't."

BUT TO THE SLA members, it seemed that their ratty safe houses were the center of the universe.

In early March 1974 the SLA moved from Daly City to a new hideout in San Francisco, a one-bedroom apartment at 1827 Golden Gate Avenue, in a predominantly black neighborhood north of the Panhandle. Cinque and his seven soldiers transported their captive in a large plastic garbage can. It was here—in the dreary Golden Gate safe house, with a filthy Indian bedspread covering the bay windows and old mattresses crowding the floor—that Patty Hearst was transformed into Tania, the SLA's pin-up girl, the reincarnation of Che Guevara's brave companion in the Bolivian jungle. Cinque sat down at the edge of her new closet cell and put the question to his blindfolded prisoner: did she want to be released or did she want to join their revolution? She instantly knew the right answer. "He was testing me, and I must pass the test or die."

"I want to join you," Patty said into the darkness around her. "I want to fight for the people." In return, she was finally allowed to take off her blindfold and look into her captors' faces. "Oh, God," she thought, "what a bunch of ordinary-looking, unattractive little people." Somehow, after hearing only their assaultive voices for weeks, she had expected them to look "bigger, stronger, more commanding."

"Well, now that you've seen us, what do you think of us?" burbled Angela Atwood.

"Oh," said Patty, forcing a smile, "you're all so attractive!"

Cinque told his soldiers what a stunning "propaganda coup" this would be for the SLA. They dressed up Patty like a combat doll, chopping off her hair, putting a beret on her head, sticking a sawed-off M-1 carbine in her hands—and posing her in front of the serpent-covered SLA banner, they snapped the Polaroid photo of her that would forever change her image. Then they wrote the script announcing her conversion and made her read the words into a tape recorder. It was a bitter farewell to her parents. She called her father a "corporate liar" who cared more about his wealth than his daughter's life. "One thing I learned," Patty read in a grim monotone, "is that the corporate ruling class will do anything in their power in order to maintain their position of control over the masses, even if this means the sacrifice of one of their own."

The Tania communiqué, which the SLA released on April 3, set off a new round of media convulsions. It also excited the more romantic ranks of the radical left, which posted photos of the new, gun-toting Patty all over the Berkeley campus, with the gushing salutation, "We Love You Tania." Patty herself hoped that her father would see through the tape recording's stilted language and realize that it was coerced. He did. "I don't believe it," he told the press, after listening to the tape twice. "We've had her twenty years, and they've had her only sixty days, and I don't believe she's going to change her philosophy that quickly in that time."

Meanwhile, Cinque plotted an operation that would prove to the world that Patty Hearst belonged to him, not to her family. Day after day, he put his soldiers through their commando drills in their stuffy apartment—and this time Patty was included. As they ran around with their weapons, they were soon sweating and panting in the claustrophobic room, its windows shut tight and draped heavily for security. Cinque, who never joined in the exercises, swilled his plum wine on the sidelines and exhorted his troops. "Come on girls, it's hot—take your shirts off!" he would say. He loved to see his female soldiers bare breasted while they exercised.

On the bright, crisp morning of April 15, the SLA members unveiled their next act, leaving their safe house and piling into two cars. Patty felt dazed as she left the darkened apartment, feeling the sun and wind for the first time in two and a half months. Cinque's last words to her before they drove off were, "If you mess up, if you do anything different from what you're supposed to, you're dead." She felt like she was "walking to the gallows." Minutes later the group pulled up outside a branch of the Hibernia Bank—which, ironically, was owned by a friend of the Hearst family—in the quiet Sunset neighborhood. Bursting through its front doors, weapons drawn, they scooped up more than $10,000 in the heist and shot and wounded two older bank patrons before driving back to their hideout on Golden Gate. Caught on the bank security cameras, cradling her sawed off M-1 and wearing a wig, Patty Hearst seemed no longer a victim but a desperado.

Randy Hearst was stunned, but he remained convinced that his daughter was being coerced, and the *Examiner* reflected his conviction. "Patty a Puppet?" a headline in the newspaper suggested. But Hearst's friends in high places now abandoned him altogether. Evelle Younger, California's politically ambitious Republican attorney general, declared that the San Francisco police and FBI had been too timid because of concern for Patty Hearst's safety, but now she was fair game. "I think the moment of truth has long since passed for Patricia Hearst," the lawman intoned grimly. In Washington, President Nixon's attorney general, William Saxbe, weighed in, opining that Patty "was not a reluctant participant," and lumping her in with the other SLA "common criminals." Randy Hearst lashed back, denouncing the "irresponsible statements," and even the more buttoned-up Catherine got into the fray, pointing out the assumption of innocence at the heart of our judicial system. But after the Hibernia robbery, the blood was in the water.

As Mayor Alioto confidently predicted that law enforcement agencies would soon "wipe out the SLA completely," more than 125 federal agents combed the Sunset district and other neighborhoods, going door to door in their search for the outlaws. They waved around hundreds of thousands of dollars in reward money. One person thought to be connected to the SLA was shown an FBI briefcase stuffed with $50,000 in cash.

Despite the tightening dragnet, Cinque was feeling cocky. One day in late April 1974, he and Emily Harris showed up outside the Pacific Heights home of Angela Veronese, the married daughter of Mayor Alioto. While Cinque cased the house from across the street, Harris approached Veronese's two young children, who were playing outside while their mother gardened nearby. Harris asked the kids where their grandfather was. "Upstairs," they told her. The mayor, who was having marital difficulties at the time, was staying temporarily with Angela and her family. When Angela came over to ask what Harris wanted, the SLA soldier told her, "None of your business," and quickly walked away with Cinque. If the SLA had tried to kidnap the mayor, it certainly would have resulted in a bloody showdown. Alioto, the target of many threats, was being guarded round the clock by the SFPD's tough tac squad.

IN EARLY MAY RANDY Hearst offered $50,000 in reward money for the safe return of his daughter, prompting Cinque to finally decide that it was time to flee San Francisco. Although Cinque was forever reminding his white troops how fortunate they were to have him as their leader—and how he "could be leading a whole army of black soldiers" instead—the truth is that he could never win the allegiance of black followers. And Cinque feared that one of the SLA's cash-strapped black neighbors on Golden Gate Avenue, or later in the Hunters Point ghetto where they relocated briefly, would turn in his army for the tempting reward. On May 8 Cinque and his gang slipped out of San Francisco and headed south for Los Angeles. It was a fatal miscalculation. LA was not the Bay Area, with its underground networks of safe havens. And the Los Angeles Police Department was a more ruthless force than the SFPD.

On May 10, 1974, Lake Headley, a Los Angeles private investigator hired by author-activist Donald Freed to dig into Cinque's shadowy past, called a press conference in San Francisco. The SLA press pack, tipped off to some of Headley's startling inside information, jammed the event, and the private eye did not disappoint them. Headley, a former Las Vegas cop with good law enforcement connections, ran down Cinque's long rap sheet and the special treatment he had received from police and the courts as a multiple offender. He laid out evidence indicating that the escaped convict had worked as a snitch for the LAPD and later as a double agent for Colton Westbrook and the CIA, as well as the state prison system. Headley, whom Manson prosecutor Vincent Bugliosi once hailed as "the best private investigator on earth," concluded with a stark prediction about Cinque's fate.

"He'll be killed, probably in a shootout," the private eye told the press.

Headley was certain that Cinque had become a liability to his former sponsors. "He could not be allowed to live," he later observed, "any more than Lee Harvey Oswald could be allowed to survive and start talking."

One week later, on the evening of May 17, Headley was sitting down for Friday dinner at his Los Angeles home when his local TV news show cut away to live coverage of a police showdown in the black South Central part of the city. A massive law enforcement army—including 150 Los Angeles police officers, 100 FBI agents, 100 sheriff's deputies, and an assortment of motorcycle officers—had surrounded a squat yellow stucco bungalow where the SLA was holed up. Moments after issuing a perfunctory warning to surrender, the assault force let loose an awesome fusillade, pouring five thousand rounds into the little house, as well as a number of highly flammable tear gas projectiles. Only about fifty shots were fired from inside the bungalow, and no officer was hit. When Nancy Ling Perry, Angela Atwood, and Camilla Hall tried to surrender, they were driven back to the house by a hail of bullets. Nancy was later found dead in the backyard with a bullet in her back. When the house went up in flames, police blocked firefighters from putting out the blaze and continued to pour gunfire into the pyre. Clearly, no one inside was supposed to come out alive that day. As *Rolling Stone* remarked acidly, "It was not really a shootout at all; it was a police shoot-in."

Six SLA members died in the flames and the gunfire, including Cinque, who put a bullet through his head before he could be burned alive. After the Los Angeles inferno, there was a rash of press speculation about Cinque before he disappeared completely from media view. When he was buried in Cleveland, his hometown, the *New York Times* ran a story headlined, "Cinque: Still a Mystery." The *Times* reporter, interviewing a young black mourner outside the funeral home, was told, "Even his family didn't know him." One reason that Cinque might have been a mystery to his family was that his father's savage beatings drove him from home at a tender age. But none of his relatives dwelled on that.

Lake Headley probably came the closest to understanding Cinque. He was a "monster," Headley said, created in the dark criminal nether-world where police and government agencies manufacture their agents of chaos. And when their Frankenstein went rogue and began imagining that he truly was a revolutionary hero, he had to be put down.

Cinque had a gift for engineering public havoc, with the help of a panting press corps. Before it was finally extinguished, his army engaged in assassination, kidnapping, bank robbery, murder, and attempted bombings and executions of police officers. The SLA gave America the closest look it would get at the kind of bloody mayhem that the Red Army Faction was capable of producing on a grander scale in West German society during the 1970s.

The SLA stumbled on for over a year, kept alive by survivors Bill and Emily Harris and a few more recruits they scraped together in Berkeley. The Harrises, with Patty Hearst in tow, watched the fiery end of their comrades on a motel TV near Disneyland, sobbing and screaming at the television as the sickening spectacle unfolded live and in color. Bill Harris had triggered the chain of events that resulted in the SLA massacre when he shoplifted a bandolier at Mel's Sporting Goods store in the Inglewood neighborhood of LA and got into a scuffle with a store security guard. When police found the Harrises' abandoned getaway van, they discovered a parking ticket in the vehicle with the address of the SLA hideout. "It's all my fault!" wailed Harris as they watched the inferno in their Magic Kingdom hideout. "If it weren't for Mel's . . . I killed them . . . Oh, I should have been there with them, shooting it out to the end . . . I wish I were dead too."

Patty couldn't stand listening to the TV news cacophony and the Harrises' loud lamentations anymore. She crawled into the bathroom and shut the door behind her. All she could think was that she was glad Cinque and the others were dead. "They deserved to die for what they did to me," she reflected later.

She hated the Harrises too but felt that she was stuck with them. Throughout that weekend, as the press speculated about her whereabouts, Patty sobbed until her chest ached, thinking about her fate. The trigger-happy army that surrounded the SLA bungalow assumed that she was also inside, but that had not stopped the cops from torching it to the ground. She felt that her family and her old life were lost to her forever. As soon as she was spotted, she would be gunned down. "My fear of the police outweighed my hatred for the SLA," she later remarked.

Patty and the Harrises soon made their way back to the Bay Area, which they agreed was their "true territory," and the safe place they never should have left. The threesome made for an odd group marriage. They bickered constantly—arguments that would frequently end with Bill Harris slugging the women in the face and blackening their eyes. The short, vain, hot-tempered Harris was forever trying to assert his masculinity, turning whiny and wheedling when his wife denied him sex.

Rejected, he would turn to Patty, who didn't have the will to stand up to him. "There was nothing loving, romantic, or even affectionate in this," she recalled. "I had no feelings whatever. In fact, much of the time I was half drunk, feeling no pain, on mountain red wine."

The remnants of the SLA spent their first night back in San Francisco huddled in the crawl space under a dilapidated Victorian. Later they made their way to Berkeley, where they found a resurgence of support for their cause in the wake of the horrific police bonfire in LA. At a memorial rally for the SLA dead in a Berkeley park, a disguised Emily Harris heard a woman named Kathy Soliah mourn the brutal death of her friend Angela Atwood. And then Soliah bitterly announced to the crowd, "I am a soldier of the SLA." Afterward, Emily approached Soliah, who agreed to help the hotly pursued outlaws.

Soliah connected the fugitives to sports author and activist Jack Scott, who saw a bestselling book in the SLA story and agreed to find them a safe haven. Scott and his wife, Micki, transported the Harrises and Patty to a farmhouse in the rolling hills of Pennsylvania, where they spent a quiet summer. After Scott grew disillusioned with the SLA, he dropped the book project, but he arranged for the fugitives' safe passage back to Berkeley before he parted company with them. In Berkeley, the SLA trio reconnected with Soliah, who decided to join their battle, bringing several new recruits with her, including her sister, brother, and boyfriend. The group began plotting a new wave of bombings and robberies that would prove to be the last stand of the SLA.

All during this time, Patty Hearst's family continued to explore every avenue they could to find their daughter. When *Rolling Stone* reporters Howard Kohn and David Weir began digging up exclusive information about the SLA's subterranean journey, using their contacts in the radical underground, the Hearsts regarded them warily, fearing that they would portray Patty as a true convert to the SLA. But in the course of their investigation, the reporters developed a relationship with Will Hearst, swapping information with him, and they got to know Randy as well.

Weir saw how the ordeal was turning Randy Hearst's life upside down, alienating him from the authorities, who in their blood lust had been willing to incinerate his daughter along with her kidnappers—and, in the process, turning the SLA "dingbats," as he scornfully called them, into "martyrs." The Hearst family had grown deeply estranged from law enforcement officials and no longer counted on them for protection. On his lawyer's advice, Will Hearst hired a private eye to guard him, explaining, "Neither I nor my family have any faith in the FBI or the local police."

The ordeal was also driving a wedge between Randy and his more conservative wife, who infuriated him by agreeing to let Governor Reagan reappoint her to the University of California Board of Regents, even though the announcement was certain to inflame the SLA. As their torment dragged on, Randy and Catherine went increasingly separate ways.

At one point, Randy reached out to Jack Scott, asking him to dinner at a house in San Francisco, where they ate roast beef and drank vodka late into the night while the publisher pumped him for information about Patty. On another occasion, Scott met Randy and Catherine at a Mexican restaurant in Ghirardelli Square near San Francisco's Fisherman's Wharf, where he reported to them that Patty was growing increasingly disenchanted with the Harrises' macho style as she developed a feminist consciousness and was talking of secretly visiting her parents. Randy wondered if Patty might agree to return if Catherine resigned from the UC Board of Regents, but again his wife refused adamantly, saying that she didn't trust "that little weasel Scott." She was growing increasingly fed up with her husband's dalliances with the radical underground.

"Randy would meet with anybody who might help find Patty," recalled

Weir. "He struck me as a very uptight, traditional person, but sincere. When I look back at him through older eyes, the eyes of a father, I feel sorry for what he went through. He would have given away his whole fortune to get her back safely. I think the whole thing broke his heart."

THE NEW SLA TEAM was cut from the same all-American cloth as the original members. The Soliahs grew up in a Southern California high-desert town where their father, an ardent Nixon supporter, was a teacher-coach at the local high school. Their friend and fellow recruit Michael Bortin was the product of a typically liberal San Francisco family, half Jewish and half Unitarian, and he graduated from the city's most elite public high school, Lowell. Bortin grew up during simpler times in San Francisco, playing baseball day and night, and hanging around Candlestick Park to talk to his favorite Giants. Willie Mays used to give Bortin and his friends rides in his pink Thunderbird.

But Bortin was raised with a strong social conscience, accompanying his father, a capital punishment lawyer, to San Quentin as a kid. And the events of the sixties only deepened his sense of estrangement from American society. After dropping out of UC Berkeley, he hung around the Haight for a year, taking acid and working a "shitty job" at Western Union.

"I started seeing these telegrams that said, 'Your son so-and-so,' and underneath there'd be three or four boxes saying, 'You can see his remains at the airport' or 'It's a closed coffin,'" he recalled. "One of the boxes would be checked. And I thought, 'What a hell of a way to tell people that their kid has been killed in Vietnam.' I just tore them up. That's just no way to find out."

Later Bortin volunteered in Bobby Kennedy's 1968 presidential campaign, going door to door in black neighborhoods in Oakland. "The people were supernice," he said. "It seemed like half of the homes had statues of JFK. That had a big impact on me."

The night Bobby was assassinated, Bortin was celebrating his victory in the California Democratic primary by dropping acid. "You don't want to get bad news like that on acid," he said later. His fury grew in the following weeks as the Democratic Party tried to go about business as usual. "Watching the convention in Chicago just kept turning the knife in you more because Bobby wasn't there. Those assholes were trying to substitute for him."

Soon after, Bortin walked up to a Students for a Democratic Society (SDS) table on the Berkeley campus, declaring, "I'm willing to burn down ROTC buildings." It was a rage that would take him all the way to the SLA.

"After Bobby was killed, something grew inside me that has been with me ever since—it was the realization that I really hate this country. I hate it totally."

When he joined the SLA, Bortin took an immediate dislike to the Harrises. "They were like Patty's evil stepparents. One time she had a black eye. We put a stop to that. Bill was treating her like a prisoner. I think he had manhood problems. She made the SLA what it was. Everybody respected Patty. Everybody liked her. She didn't play games like the Harrises. She was a pretty together person, in my opinion."

Despite his antipathy toward the Harrises, Bortin was willing to work with them, plotting bank robberies, cop killings, and other SLA missions. In the end, the SLA was responsible for only one more death, but it haunted Bortin the rest of his life. On the morning of April 21, 1975, the SLA gang walked into a bank in a Sacramento suburb, pulled out their guns, and ordered the patrons to hit the floor. When a forty-two-year-old woman named Myrna Opsahl did not move fast enough for Emily Harris, who was leading the heist, she thrust her shotgun at her to speed her up. The gun, which Harris was warned had a hair trigger, went off, killing Opsahl instantly. The mother of four had come to the bank to deposit a collection from her church. Her husband, a surgeon, was later called to his hospital emergency room, where he found his wife dead on the table.

"It doesn't really matter," shrugged Emily Harris when she heard about Opsahl's death. "She was a bourgeois pig anyway."

Patty, who had driven the getaway van, felt sick. "I loathed the Harrises more than ever before. They were violent, evil, unpredictable, incompetent people," she later remarked. She would soon find a way to get away from them forever, moving into a second-floor apartment at 625 Morse Street in San Francisco's Outer Mission with Wendy Yoshimura, a fellow SLA feminist who shared her disgust for the Harrises.

Bortin too pulled away from the group after the bloody bank robbery.

"I still have dreams about that day," he said. "It was a sunny morning. As we were going inside the bank, there were these three women behind us. I didn't want them to get hurt, so I slowed down and held the door for these ladies. And one of them turns to me with this real nice, warm smile, like, 'Finally, a young person who has manners.' And she looked at me and said, 'Thank you.'"

He was running to the bank counter when he heard the roar of Emily Harris's shotgun. Spinning around, Bortin saw instantly that the bloodied woman on the floor was the same one who had complimented his good manners.

Bortin eventually served three years for the second-degree murder of Opsahl. At his sentencing, he took shared responsibility for the murder, even though he hadn't pulled the trigger. "By our recklessness," Bortin told the Opsahl family members gathered in the courtroom, "we killed a woman. Whatever consequences we suffer is of no consequence. I can offer nothing but apologies. I'm sorry."

ON THE AFTERNOON OF September 18, 1975, San Francisco police and the FBI finally swooped down on the Harrises, as they returned from jogging in nearby Precita Park. The couple were arrested in front of their safe house at 288 Precita Avenue, in the funky, lefty Bernal Heights neighborhood. An hour later, a San Francisco police intelligence officer named Tim Casey and an FBI agent broke through the glass-windowed back door of the house on Morse Street, and, with guns drawn, charged inside to arrest Patty Hearst and Wendy Yoshimura. Patty froze in terror, wetting her pants. She couldn't believe it when they didn't shoot her, the end she'd always expected.

"Why . . . Patty," said Casey, who was just as surprised to have finally found her. "What are you doing here?"

Returning to San Francisco from Los Angeles turned out to be one of the SLA survivors' few smart decisions. Their long run did not have a fiery finale.

Randy Hearst, now comfortable with San Francisco's left-wing milieu, hired Vincent Hallinan and his two-fisted son Terry "Kayo" Hallinan to represent his daughter. When she was driven to county jail in the police car, she was photographed raising her handcuffed right fist in a power-to-the-people salute, and when she was booked, she stated "urban guerilla" as her occupation. Reunited with her elated parents and sisters in jail, Patty felt oddly removed from them, as if she were a different person. She was exhausted and just wanted to sleep all the time.

But Patty bonded with the curly-haired, roguishly handsome Terry Hallinan. And after Yoshimura told Terry about the ordeal that Patty had undergone in the SLA closet, he began to peel away the Tania layers. Terry and his father thought that Cinque had subjected Patty to some kind of drug-induced mind control program that he had learned in Vacaville. The Hallinans wanted to build their case on an "involuntary intoxication" defense of Patty. But her parents didn't want drugs to be brought up in the trial. And Catherine in particular developed a strong repugnance to the left-wing Hallinans. "She thought of me as some kind of Russian agent," Terry said later with a smile. The Hearsts decided to replace the Hallinans with one of the biggest brand names in the legal profession, Boston criminal attorney F. Lee Bailey.

Ironically, Bailey wound up presenting a defense similar to the one proposed by the Hallinans, arguing that Patty had been "brainwashed" by the SLA. But he gave the argument a different twist, ignoring the drug and sensory deprivation methods that Cinque might have learned at Vacaville, and contending instead that the SLA leader's mind control program was modeled on insidious techniques developed in Mao's China. The author of this line of defense was none other than Dr. Louis Jolyon "Jolly" West, the CIA-sponsored psychiatrist who had studied mind-altering drugs in the Haight in the 1960s. At first Patty was repelled by the "too smooth" Jolly West, with his "creepy, hypnotic voice." But she finally opened up to him, and West became Bailey's leading expert witness. It was another strange intrusion by the psychiatrist into San Francisco's saga.

In the end, however, the jury believed the prosecution's key witness more, Harvard-trained forensic psychiatrist Harry Kozol. He looked like a "fuddy-duddy Kewpie doll," according to one court chronicler, and had a high-pitched squeak. But his testimony had a ring of truth. After interviewing Patty five times in jail, Kozol told the court, he concluded that she was a genuine convert to the SLA. Why else would she have sprayed gunfire at the windows of Mel's Sporting Goods to free Bill Harris after he was apprehended for shoplifting, he pointed out, and why else would she stay with the Harrises on their long underground journey, when she had numerous opportunities for escape? "In a sense," he testified, "she was a member of the SLA in spirit, without knowing it, for a long, long time": a "rebel in search of a cause" at the time of her kidnapping, who had grown deeply alienated from her suffocating family and fiancé. "She was ripe for the plucking," he declared, in his most memorable turn of phrase.

As Kozol testified, Patty "turned the dead white color of a fish's belly," according to an observer.

The truth about Patty Hearst was probably a complex mix of the psychiatrists' opinions. Some type of conversion did occur, but she accepted the SLA's subterranean existence only under extreme duress. At the time of her trial, the Stockholm syndrome—named after the 1973 Swedish bank robbery during which the hostages became emotionally attached to their captors—was not yet a widely accepted concept. But that explanation probably comes closest to getting at the dramatic transformation of Patty Hearst.

After a two-month trial, she was convicted of bank robbery and sentenced to seven years in prison. However, her sentence was commuted by President Jimmy Carter in 1979 after she had served nearly two years. Looking back, Patty felt that she had been victimized twice: once by the SLA and then by the court of public opinion, where she became a convenient scapegoat in the increasingly conservative pre-Reagan climate. "So much anger was directed at me," said Patty, "because of the whole sixties generation that had disappointed their parents so badly."

Patty married her bodyguard, a San Francisco cop named Bernard Shaw, after she was released, and they moved to Connecticut, where they raised two daughters. "Marrying her bodyguard? I don't think that requires Dr. Freud to figure out," remarked her cousin Will. "But I think they like each other, and they have a good relationship." Shaw found a new line of work as a Hearst Corporation security executive. And Patty ended up creating the kind of comfortable suburban family life that she had shunned as a teenager, though her irreverent, wild streak came out at times, as when she popped up in John Waters movies and other campy cameos.

Randy and Catherine Hearst divorced after the SLA ordeal. He too fled San Francisco, moving back to New York, where at the age of seventy-two he married forty-two-year-old socialite Veronica Beracasa.

Hearst resumed his life as a media tycoon, splitting his time between a Fifth Avenue penthouse apartment and a mansion in Palm Beach, Florida. The days of late-night meetings with ex-cons and left-wing militants and CIA spooks were long behind him. He led a more cautious life, surrounding himself with bodyguards until his death in 2000.

While the Hearsts found calmer lives elsewhere, San Francisco continued to be racked by demons. Contemplating the Symbionese Liberation Army's morbid legacy years later, sociologist Todd Gitlin observed that the SLA was the "graveyard" of the 1960s New Left. But after the SLA, the city continued to be haunted by ghouls and gravediggers.

20

BLACK AND WHITE
AND RED ALL OVER

O N THE EVENING of December 13, 1973, Art Agnos, an administrative aide to California assemblyman Leo McCarthy, was leaving a community meeting near his home on Potrero Hill, a racially mixed, blue-collar neighborhood overlooking the downtown San Francisco skyline. At thirty-five, Agnos retained the sense of Kennedy-era optimism that had drawn him into public service in the 1960s, first as a social worker and later as a Democratic political operative. San Francisco was still his dream city. After growing up in tradition-bound Springfield, Massachusetts, where his Greek immigrant father toiled as a shoeshine man, Agnos was eager to fill his lungs with San Francisco's bracing sea drafts when he disembarked from a Greyhound bus at Seventh and Mission Streets in 1967. The clean, chill wind smelled like freedom to him. "It immediately felt like the kind of city where you could be whatever you wanted to be," he recalled.

Agnos felt good that night as he left the meeting of predominantly black activists. He had come to reassure the neighborhood, which was a few blocks away from the bleak housing project where football star O. J. Simpson had grown up, that a long-anticipated community health clinic was finally making its way through legislative channels in Sacramento.

It was one of those golden moments when the system seemed to be working.

As he walked down the 900 block of Wisconsin Street to his parked car, Agnos was stopped by a couple of women from the meeting who wanted to follow up on an item of business. While they were chatting, Agnos suddenly saw their eyes grow wide. A split-second later, he felt two deep, dull thumps to his back, as if a boxer had delivered a one-two kidney punch. Agnos spun around to face his attacker and saw a tall, handsome, well-groomed young black man with a smoking .32 automatic pistol in his hand, and he knew that he hadn't been punched. The gunman gazed directly at Agnos, as if in a trance, and then turned and ran into the night.

The women were running in the opposite direction, screaming. Agnos, strangely calm, hurried after them, to reassure them that they would be all right. "It's not us—it's you!" they shouted, pointing at the widening red splotch on his shirt. Now Agnos was surrounded by a cluster of people from the meeting, who helped him across the street to a house, where he knocked on the front door.

"Excuse me," he told the startled middle-aged African-American man who answered, "I've been shot—can you call an ambulance?" By now Agnos was having trouble breathing, so he lay down on the man's floor. "Hey, man," said the home owner, staring down at the gravely wounded Agnos, "you're bleeding all over my rug."

Agnos was fortunate to be shot near San Francisco General Hospital, with the city's most skilled trauma unit at treating gunshot victims. The emergency medical team was waiting for him on the ambulance dock. It immediately began cutting off his suit coat and shirt. A young female resident surgeon was straddling Agnos, her dress riding up her thighs. "For someone I just met, you're getting to know me really well," said Agnos, slipping into shock. The resident laughed and told Agnos she was just trying to identify his wounds.

The bullets had ripped through his insides, damaging his spleen, kidney, lungs, and colon. But the SF General trauma team saved his life that night on the operating table. After surfacing from his chemical slumber, Agnos realized how fortunate he was. He learned that he was the sixth victim in a mysterious carnival of blood that was rolling through the city, and only the second survivor.

As Agnos recovered from surgery at Kaiser Hospital, where he was transferred, his room was guarded by San Francisco cops. One day two homicide detectives showed up to see the shooting victim: fellow Greek-Americans named Gus Coreris and John Fotinos. The inspectors, who'd been friends ever since they played football against each other in high school, were a tight team: two ethnic outsiders in a department filled with multigenerational Irish and Italian cops. "It was all Gaelic and garlic—no Greek," said Coreris. "We had to prove ourselves."

Standing over Agnos's bed, the detectives began speaking to him in Greek. What they told him was so explosive, they didn't want it to be overheard by any nurses or hospital orderlies. They informed Agnos that he was the victim of a Black Muslim death cult that was randomly shooting and slashing white men and women in the city. Agnos couldn't believe his ears. Ever the good liberal, he immediately thought that they were overplaying the race angle. "You cops are all the same," he told them. The detectives were flabbergasted by Agnos's uncooperative attitude.

But in the months to come, as the soon to be nicknamed "Zebra killers" claimed a total of twenty-three victims in 179 days, Agnos realized that Coreris and Fotinos were right. San Francisco was in the grip of a bloody nightmare that tested the very threads holding it together. Cities are frighteningly fragile social enterprises, built on the tacit compact that one racial or religious group or neighborhood won't start warring on another. Gang violence within the same community is generally shrugged off by the civic establishment as an unpleasant fact of urban life. But when blood is spilled across turf lines, an electric charge of alarm surges through a city—particularly within urban boundaries as tight as seven-mile-by-seven-mile San Francisco, where racial, class, and ethnic tribes are crowded elbow to elbow. One racially charged murder, or even hit-and-run accident, can set off a prickly panic: a flushed foreboding that the whole tinderbox could blow.

The Zebra murders—named after the Z police radio frequency that was assigned to the case—struck a drumbeat of terror, inexplicable and unrelenting, that threatened to drive the city mad. The bloodletting went on day after day. And each explosion of gunfire or grisly discovery of butchered remains took San Francisco closer to the brink of civic breakdown.

San Francisco was already on the edge. In the early months of 1974, the city was reeling from two other unsolved crime sprees in addition to the Zebra murders. While combing the city for Zebra clues, the over-burdened SFPD was also fanning out in search of Patty Hearst and the SLA, who were still hunkered down in their Spartan hideout on Golden Gate Avenue. And in January, the Zodiac serial killer—the publicity-mad psychopath who killed at least seven people in the sixties and early seventies—suddenly resurfaced after a silence of nearly three years. Zodiac again began tormenting the city with cryptic letters that he sent to the *San Francisco Chronicle.* One of the killer's creepiest mailings was a 408-symbol cryptogram that, when decoded, sent shivers throughout the city. It was a misspelled, upper-case, unpunctuated howl from some rank cave deep in the human soul:

I LIKE KILLING PEOPLE BECAUSE IT IS SO MUCH FUN IT IS MORE FUN THAN KILLING WILD GAME IN THE FORREST BECAUSE MAN IS THE MOST DANGEROUE ANAMAL OF ALL TO KILL SOMETHING GIVES ME THE MOST THRILLING EXPERIENCE IT IS EVEN BETTER THAN GETTING YOUR ROCKS OFF WITH A GIRL THE BEST PART OF IT IS THAE WHEN I DIE I WILL BE REBORN IN PARADICE AND THEI HAVE KILLED WILL BECOME MY SLAVES

By 1974, the Zodiac killer seemed more interested in staging macabre theater and toying with the police and press than in taking any more lives. In one handwritten postcard to the *Chronicle,* he engaged in some twisted humor with the newspaper's editors, complaining about the newspaper's "poor taste" in deciding to run ads for *Badlands,* Terrence Malick's controversial movie about a couple of sexy, young serial kill-ers. "In light of recent events," Zodiac wrote, with tongue grotesquely in cheek, "this kind of murder-glorification can only be deplorable at best."

Despite the Zodiac's media antics, it was the Zebra murders that unnerved San Francisco deepest of all—particularly after it became clear to the public what the police already knew: that the savagery was racially motivated. The "Zebra" code name might not have been intended to convey a racial meaning, but the city soon realized that the slaughter was a black-on-white thing. The killings were a direct assault on the city's sense of itself as an oasis of racial harmony and civility. In reality, that image was largely false, masking a city of raw racial divisions—between whites and Chinese, whites and Latinos, and especially between whites and blacks.

Prentice Earl Sanders, a black homicide cop who was forced to break down one color barrier after the next within the Irish-dominated SFPD, was keenly aware of the city's racial codes. The racism he experienced in San Francisco was not like what he encountered growing up in Jim Crow–era East Texas. But for all its softer edges, it was still deeply humiliating. "There wasn't some scowling cracker on the other end of the whip," Sanders observed. "In San Francisco, racism came at you with a smile. Like they were doing you a favor when they told you that they didn't have any jobs open after you'd seen a half dozen white guys fill out applications; or that you couldn't buy a house, when they'd just sold one to a white guy who made less money."

Rev. Amos Brown, who became a pillar of San Francisco's black community in the 1970s after moving from Mississippi to take over the Third Baptist Church in the heart of the Fillmore, was astonished by the stories he heard from older members of his congregation about the liberal Bay Area. He was told that even baseball star Willie Mays had trouble overcoming the race ban when he and his wife went looking for a house near posh St. Francis Wood in 1957, even though the Giants' move from New York after the '57 season had electrified San Francisco.

"It was a strange place back then, in the fifties and early sixties," said Rev. Brown. "There were certain areas that were off-limits, certain restaurants where if you went to eat, after you finished, the waiters would break the dish in front of you. San Francisco was only truly liberal when it came to sex. As far as race, it was a microcosm of the United States."

The demolition of the Fillmore district was the greatest source of poison in the city's black-white relations. The uprooting of the neighborhood's population not only stirred a simmering rage among those black residents who clung on but also wiped out much of the community's business bedrock and stable leadership. The subsequent vacuum—a social and economic void as desolate as the neighborhood's weed-choked vacant lots—would attract various types of mischief and madness for years to come.

Among the perverse saviors who worked their way into the Fillmore's carved-out heart in the 1970s were the Black Muslims, Elijah Muhammad's occult, white-hating sect that spread its tentacles from its Chicago headquarters into prisons, ghettos, drug dens, and other pits of African-American misery. In one of the sorrier developments of the times, the Black Muslims took over the old Fillmore Auditorium at the corner of Geary and Fillmore—the scene of so much ecstatic, black-and-white harmonic convergence—after it was abandoned by Bill Graham in 1971, and they turned the venerable building into a mosque known as Muhammad's Temple no. 26. It was this mosque that gave rise to the Zebra murder cult that terrorized San Francisco from the fall of 1973 to the spring of 1974.

The core group of killers came together at the Black Self-Help Moving & Storage Company, one of the enterprises that operated under the Nation of Islam's umbrella. Two of the Zebra murderers were college dropouts from comfortable middle-class backgrounds: Larry Green and J. C. Simon. Two were prison-hardened ex-convicts recently released from San Quentin: Jesse Lee Cooks and Manuel Moore. The moving and storage company on Market Street was owned by Tom Manney, another son of relative privilege. A graduate of elite St. Ignatius High School, Manney starred on the football field at San Francisco State College and was drafted by the Pittsburgh Steelers. But the team cut him before the start of the season, and he drifted back to San Francisco. The ex-convicts and other Black Muslim converts who found their way to Black Self-Help Moving found not only work and companionship under Manney's roof but also new meaning in their lives and an explanation for life's bitter disappointments. The machinations of the white devil—the "grafted snake"—were behind all black men's sorrows and tribulations.

A select group was invited to attend evening meetings in the second-floor loft of the moving company. They watched films about the white man's atrocities; they heard lectures about his perfidy. On special occasions, they were addressed by a distinguished official from Chicago, the Nation of Islam's "New Mecca." The white man's depraved rule was coming to an end, he told the young believers. The white devil was beyond reform or salvation. He must be killed.

"All Muslims will murder the white devil because they know he is a snake," declared the Nation of Islam official. "Each Muslim is required to kill four devils." The reward for slaying the requisite number of serpents would be admission into a rarefied knightly order of "Death Angels" and free transportation to New Mecca to see Brother Elijah Muhammad himself. Led by the minister from Chicago, the meetings climaxed in a chorus of martial chants: "Kill the grafted snakes!" "Kill the blue-eyed devils!"

Pumped up by the bloodthirsty rhetoric, the Zebra killers cruised San Francisco in search of white victims, riding in a Black Self-Help Moving van and a black Cadillac borrowed from Manney. The bloodshed began one balmy evening in October 1973 following a meeting in the loft, when Green, Cooks, and Anthony Harris, another ex-con recently released from San Quentin, began prowling the streets of the Excelsior, a drab neighborhood of stucco bungalows and lowered expectations.

They were on the lookout for white children, because killing women and kids was the quickest way to become a Death Angel. Cooks, who as a boy had tried to smother his dozing mother with a pillow, had particularly savage fantasies about white kids, telling his Muslim brothers that he wanted to pick them up by their feet and smash their brains out against a wall. On Francis Street, Cooks and Green pulled a gun on two young girls and a teenage boy and tried to hustle them into their van, but the kids broke away and saved their lives by dashing down the street.

Not to be denied their first kill, the aspiring Death Angels fled and headed north on the freeway, exiting on gaudy Broadway in North Beach. It was here they found Quita Hague, a pixie-faced twenty-eight-year-old reporter for a business newspaper, and her thirty-year-old husband, Richard, a mining engineer, as the newlyweds strolled down Telegraph Hill from their Chestnut Street apartment. The Hagues were forced at gunpoint into the back of the van, where their hands were bound behind their backs and they were pushed facedown on the floor. As Green drove back onto the freeway, heading south, Cooks and Harris began molesting Quita. When Richard objected, Cooks smashed him repeatedly in the face with a straight lug wrench, shattering his jaw and knocking him out.

Green pulled off the freeway at Pennsylvania Avenue and drove to a desolate warehouse area at the base of Potrero Hill. Here, hissing, "The white devil is mine," Green dragged Quita out of the van by her thick dark hair to a stretch of railroad tracks. Then, as she begged for her life,

Green raised a sixteen-inch machete high over her head and swooshed the blade downward against her throat with all his might, nearly decapitating her. Afterward, the elated Green snapped Polaroid pictures of his mangled victim, to make sure he got credit for his kill.

Meanwhile, as the flashbulbs ignited the darkness, Cooks pulled the unconscious Richard out of the van and, after dumping him across the tracks from his wife's body, began hacking at his face with the same long blade that had taken her life. After finishing their butchery, the men jumped back in the van and drove off.

Later that night, a married couple driving near the dark intersection of Twenty-fifth and Minnesota Streets saw a figure come stumbling out of the gloom. At first the couple thought it was a drunken tramp, but then they looked closer at the horrible specter. It was Richard Hague. The flesh on his face had been hacked into bloody strips, the wounds so deep that they exposed his skull. The couple drove Richard to a nearby police station, where he frantically told the cops about his wife. Rushed to San Francisco General, Richard miraculously survived his ordeal. But as soon as the police found Quita's body, crumpled near the train tracks, they knew she had not.

Earl Sanders, who later inspected Quita Hague's body at the morgue, thought he was prepared for anything after nearly ten years on the force. But what he saw in the autopsy room took his breath away. The deep gashes in the woman's face, head, and upper body "screamed out hate," Sanders later recalled. "Whoever cut her didn't just cut through flesh, they cut through bone. They cut *deep*." Sanders thought it was like looking at a beautiful painting that had been slashed to shreds by a madman.

Ten days later, Cooks—whose victim had not died—was eager to go out again with his devil-hating accomplices, but they told him it was too soon: the cops were on high alert after what they did to the Hagues. Cooks could not wait; the walls of his dingy little apartment off Market Street seemed to be closing in on him. That evening he began walking the streets. The University of California extension campus was only a block from where he lived. He was lurking in the shrubbery near the front gates of the campus when a twenty-eight-year-old student named Frances Rose rolled slowly up the driveway in her gold Ford Mustang, on her way to class. Cooks suddenly emerged from his lair, threw open the car's passenger door, and jumped inside. Rose had no time to even scream before he began firing point blank at her, hitting her four times in the face and chest.

Jack Cleary and his partner Frank Falzon, who were patrolling nearby when the call came in, went racing to the campus. When the detectives got there, they saw the young woman hanging out the side of her car. She died in Cleary's arms. After getting a description of the shooter from a witness, the cops jumped back into their car and began prowling the neighborhood. On Steiner Street, they spotted a muscular black man with a shaved head. It was Cooks. Cleary jumped out and cornered him in a doorway. The shooter's right hand made a twitching movement for his belt. The cops drew their service revolvers. "Just freeze, mister!" When they patted down Cooks, they found the automatic stuffed in his belt.

After he was handcuffed and installed in the backseat of the patrol car, Cooks became surprisingly cooperative. "Before I could even read him his Miranda, he was confessing," Cleary said. "He said, 'Oh yeah, I shot her, I shot her.' He had raped a woman a few days before, and he didn't want to get caught for that because he was Muslim." Killing a white devil would look much better in the eyes of his Nation of Islam death cult.

Cooks's arrest was a swift piece of police work, but it didn't stop the Zebra onslaught. A few weeks after the vicious murderer was taken off the streets, the Zebra killers' ranks were reinforced by two new recruits: a handsome, ambitious, true believer from Houston named J. C. Simon, who had found sanctuary in the Black Muslims from his failing marriage and career; and a big, genial, dull-witted ex-con named Manuel Moore, who had been taken under the Muslim wing at San Quentin. The killing resumed with a new fervor.

THE DEATH ANGELS FLOATED through San Francisco, striking randomly by day and night, shooting down the young and old, women and men, all of them white, or at least white looking. One rainy Sunday morning, Simon walked into a corner grocery store in the Civic Center area owned by a Jordanian Muslim with whom he had a friendly relationship. "Peace be with you," the two men would tell each other in Arabic when Simon went there to buy his daily apples. But this morning,

Simon pulled out a .32 after exchanging greetings, took the man into the back of the store, and shot him in the head. The store owner was a fellow Muslim. But to Simon, his lighter skin color still made him a white devil.

Some of the savagery that came out of the Black Self-Help Moving Company rivaled the baroque barbarity of the Spanish Inquisition. One night a young white man was kidnapped near Ghirardelli Square and taken back to the warehouse loft, where he was stripped naked, tied to a chair, and gagged with a dirty cloth. A line of devil slayers then took turns on him while he screamed into his gag. Using a hideous assortment of instruments—including knives, meat cleavers, and metal cutters—they clipped off parts of his body, starting with his fingers and toes, until he was disassembled like a hog in a butcher's shop.

Anthony Harris, who by then was feeling estranged from his blood-mad Black Muslim brothers, was summoned to participate in the depraved ceremony, but he arrived after it was over. "You too late," said Larry Green—a former Berkeley High School basketball star who once dreamed of playing in the NBA, a young man who had kissed his mother every day when he was growing up. "All the fun done through." Green and the others ordered Harris to dispose of the body, or at least a large chunk of it, which was wrapped in canvas and plastic. Harris drove the grisly package out to Sutro Heights, where he lugged it to the edge of the cliff and heaved it into the sea. It washed up nearby on Ocean Beach on a foggy Christmas Eve morning, where it was discovered by a woman whose dog picked up the deep biological scent.

Once again Earl Sanders had the duty of inspecting the body. The odor hit him first, and then he saw the bundle: it reminded him of the frozen turkeys the department handed out each Christmas. "It was like a fever hit me. I felt dizzy. Like there was no up or down, just gray everywhere I looked—clouds, sea, fog, everything. And right in the middle was this thing that had once been a man."

The body's head, hands, and feet had been chopped off, even its penis and scrotum. A deep hole had been gouged in the stomach, from which spilled ribbons of intestine as the plastic was peeled away. Sanders knew immediately that the same zealous rage that had taken the life of Quita Hague was responsible for the butchery before him. The police had no way of identifying the deconstructed human on the beach. They simply labeled him Unknown Body #169. Some cops called him the Christmas Turkey.

The biggest night of mayhem in the Zebra gore fest took place after Muhammad Ali's dramatic comeback victory over Joe Frazier on January 28, 1974, in the second of their three legendary heavyweight bouts. After watching the bout on closed-circuit TV at the Winterland Ballroom, Simon and Moore, high on their Black Muslim hero's triumph, pressed Harris into joining them on an extended killing spree. Gliding through the city in their black Cadillac of death with the big shark fins, the trio shot down a young woman on her way to a fabric store, a retiree whistling as he strolled home celebrating his sixty-ninth birthday, an eighty-four-year-old homeless man rummaging through a trash bin, a middle-aged woman doing her weekly load of clothes in a Laundromat, and, finally, a twenty-three-year-old mother carrying a box into her family's new apartment. She was the only one who survived, but she was paralyzed from the waist down.

The eruptions of unspeakable violence made this most beloved of cities seem like hostile territory. Suddenly Herb Caen's lovely jeweled city became strange and ominous—the way one's house feels after it's been broken into and ransacked. Whites saw blood in the eye of every able-bodied black male, and every black man saw fear and rage in white faces. Everyone scanned the streets as if on combat patrol, even when walking to the corner store. The city's very identity began to dissolve.

That cruel night in January was the final tipping point for the nerve-racked city. Panic shot through its neighborhoods before the killing was even done, while police sirens were still wailing in the distance. A young gay couple was dining at a Potrero Hill restaurant that evening when their black waiter suddenly interrupted their meal with a distraught look on his face. "You have to go home," he said. "They're killing white people."

The scream that San Francisco had been choking back for weeks finally burst from its throat. The next day's newspapers echoed with the horror. "A Night of Killing in SF." "Madmen Slay Four on City Streets." "SF Killing Spree—5 Shot on Streets." Gun applications soared. Hotels were hit by a wave of room cancellations. For the first time in San Francisco's history, the police officially warned citizens not to venture outdoors after nightfall. The streets were soon deserted, the city's raucous nightlife grew ghostly. Even Caen couldn't muster his usual moxie. "After reading about the latest wave of San Francisco killings yesterday morning," he wrote, "I walked out into the foggy street and looked both ways. Nobody was in sight. Was I the only person left alive in the city? 'The Last Time I Saw Paranoia' is not my favorite song, but I felt a chill."

Caen was not the only one on edge. Others who emerged from their homes darted their eyes nervously over their shoulders. The yellow chalk outlines on the sidewalks reminded them of the mayhem that had left its mark on nearly every district in the city. People got off the streets as quickly as they could. Shades were drawn. Kids were kept home from school. "We are very frightened," one woman told a reporter. "We do not know who they are or when they will come back."

In their agony over what their city was becoming, three women wrote a letter to Jack Valenti, president of the Motion Picture Association of America, to complain about how Hollywood had turned San Francisco into a "crime mecca," with blood-soaked movies like Clint Eastwood's *Dirty Harry* and *Magnum Force*, as well as *The Laughing Policeman*, whose deranged killer opens up with a machine gun on a crowded San Francisco bus. Meanwhile, Karl Malden and Michael Douglas were closing off city blocks so that they could be filmed shooting it out with gunmen on TV's *The Streets of San Francisco*. It was just all too much for some local residents. The gore was everywhere, on the screen as well as the streets.

Even in the midst of the madness, some San Franciscans managed to display grace and civility. While Art Agnos was recuperating from his wounds, fourteen black men of varying ages who were involved with the community health clinic campaign met to vent their anger about his shooting. They decided to take some positive action to reduce the racial tensions in their neighborhood. When Agnos returned to the block on Potrero Hill a month after he was shot to take part in another clinic meeting, he was startled to see four sturdily built black men waiting for him as he parked his car on the street. As they began to cross the street toward him, Agnos struggled to control a rising feeling of panic, telling himself that not every black man in the city was out to shoot him. One of the men walked directly up to Agnos and introduced himself. "Mr. Agnos," he said, "we're your escort."

"My escort?" stammered Agnos.

"That's right. We're going to walk around with you tonight. We want to show anybody who's looking that when you come into this neighborhood, you come as a friend. And that nobody better *ever* mess with you again . . . The hate has got to stop someplace. Maybe this will be the place."

But elsewhere in the city, tensions were rising. Sanders and his partner Rotea Gilford could feel it when they showed up at the latest Zebra murder scene—this one in the racially mixed Ingleside neighborhood, where a twenty-three-year-old man had been shot down while helping a friend move a rug. As Sanders and Gilford worked with the Greek detectives to secure the crime scene and gather evidence, the African-American inspectors noticed that white and black neighbors were standing in separate groups, eyeing each other across an eerily quiet chasm.

"I don't think either Gil or I slept that night," remembered Sanders. "We kept talking about it after we left the scene. If things were like that in Ingleside, what would happen if a crowd formed in the Fillmore, or Hunters [Point], and someone did make a move, white against black or black against white? The whole place could go up in smoke."

The specter of a race war was already looming over the city. After the mayhem on Muhammad Ali's victory night, Herb Caen got a phone call in his office at the *Chronicle* while he was sorting through items for his next day's column.

"Five white people are dead, right?" the caller asked. "I just want you to know that tonight some of us are going out and get ten blacks in trade."

"That's not very smart," replied Caen, trying to keep his voice calm.

"Smart or not, we're going to do it. Two for one is about right, don't you think?"

THE POLICE WERE UNDER withering pressure from Mayor Alioto, the press, and the public to crack the case. The SFPD Zebra unit, which was eventually put under the command of Coreris and Fotinos, worked around the clock. The Greeks staggered through the long days and nights, rarely seeing their families, fueled by cop-house coffee and late-night diner food. They took the case personally. This was their city, they were San Franciscans born and bred. And they could see what the murder wave was doing to it. The cops flooded neighborhoods with patrol cars, they slipped money to informants, they tracked every lead. But nothing paid off.

The police department was hobbled by its own racial troubles. The SFPD had few blacks in its ranks, so it had limited access to the black community. In 1973, black police officers—with Gilford and Sanders taking a leading role—filed a civil rights lawsuit in federal court against the SFPD to end age-old discriminatory practices in the department. The lawsuit triggered a savage backlash from the old-boy network of Irish cops, one of whom shouted out as Gilford and Sanders passed by, "Somebody ought to take a contract out on those two niggers!"

Coreris and Fotinos were seen by black officers as the most unbiased white detectives in homicide. "I'm not white," Fotinos used to laugh, "I'm Greek." But even the Greek partners felt frustrated as they tried to get inside information on the black community, particularly on the Black Muslim temple at Fillmore and Geary that they suspected was the sanctuary for the Zebra killers.

Coreris complained that the Nation of Islam, which had a few converts on the police force (at least one of whom seemed to take an inappropriate interest in the investigation), had more success infiltrating the SFPD than the other way around. The detective liked to drive by the Fillmore mosque at night; it made him feel he was homing in on the killers. But he knew that was as close as he would get to the temple. The Black Muslims were too careful about screening strangers to let a police informant get inside. Coreris wanted to put Temple no. 26 under full photographic surveillance, but city law prevented him from subjecting a house of worship to this type of police scrutiny. After the Zebra executioners claimed their eighteenth victim in San Francisco, state investigators finally helped Coreris circumvent the local law by putting the mosque under their own surveillance.

By the time that the Zebra victim count hit number twenty-three on April 16, 1974, city hall was frantic. Alioto made clear that he would clean house if the police department didn't come up with something fast. But Coreris and his team had no firm suspects or even strong leads. In desperation, he and Fotinos went to a police artist and had him draw a composite sketch of one Zebra shooter, based on witness descriptions. The artist came up with a generic-looking portrait of an African-

American man with a pencil mustache that vaguely resembled a significant percentage of the Bay Area's black male population. On April 17,
Alioto announced that police would resort to an "extreme" measure to
stop the reign of terror: stopping anyone they saw who resembled the
composite drawing.

The mayor knew that this kind of dragnet, the country's first official
racial profiling operation, might spark an uproar. "I want the people of
San Francisco to understand that this is not a racial issue," he told a
packed press conference, "but it is a blunt fact that the victims are white
and our description says the suspect is black."

The mayor used all his political influence, drawing on his admirable
record of minority appointments, to line up support for the police sweep.
Alioto was the first San Francisco mayor to open city hall to minorities,
naming African Americans to head the police commission, public utili-
ties commission, and BART (Bay Area Rapid Transit) board, as well as
appointing a black deputy mayor. "So there wasn't any question about
our credentials," he later remarked.

But Police Chief Donald Scott lacked the mayor's deft touch. "We're
not going to stop very young blacks or big, fat blacks," he announced
ham-handedly. "We're not going to stop seven-foot blacks or four-foot
blacks." Even worse, police officials announced that they would be
handing out a "Zebra card" to those black men who were searched and
cleared—a document, as Earl Sanders angrily declared, that brought
to mind the pass books that blacks were required to carry in apartheid
South Africa. Sanders and Gilford were so outraged by the police measure that they stood up and walked out of the department meeting where
it was explained.

Despite Alioto's best efforts, the reaction from black community leaders was equally furious. Rev. Cecil Williams accused the city of imposing
a "police state" on the black community, which he direly predicted could
set off "a racial war." Black Panther Bobby Seale charged that the SFPD
would never target white people this way, stopping "every white girl," for
instance, who resembled Patty Hearst. But as Alioto pointed out later,
San Francisco cops were doing precisely that. Even Cinque, who was
still in hiding in San Francisco at the time, waded into the Zebra storm,
denouncing the operation in a taped message as the white man's attempt
to "remove as many black males from the community as possible."

The city seemed to crackle with madness. A combustible jumble of civil rights groups and militant left-wing sects convened on the steps of city hall to protest the Zebra operation, carrying signs that read "Stop Alioto Storm Troopers" and "Smash Racism—The Rich Man's Tool to Divide and Rule." As the crowd, estimated at over one thousand, worked itself up, Alioto and two aides suddenly emerged from the building and began walking down the steps to his limousine at the curb. It was a typical act of Alioto bravado: he refused to flinch when confronting a hostile force. As the mayor and his aides made their way through the crowd, demonstrators began jostling him and spitting on him. One began whacking him on the head with a picket sign before his aides could clear a path to his car. Then the crowd surrounded the limousine, pounding on it and rocking it back and forth until the mayor's driver could finally speed away.

As the protests against Operation Zebra grew, helmeted Nazis and other white-supremacy groups mounted counterdemonstrations outside city hall, volunteering to help police round up black suspects and exchanging loud insults with the other demonstrators.

Meanwhile, the police dragnet seemed to be spiraling out of control. Within three days of its announcement, the Zebra operation had swept up more than five hundred black men of all ages, shapes, and sizes, including doctors, lawyers, and other pillars of the community. On the fourth night, the city came perilously close to the long-feared inferno when an elderly black man was accosted on a street in the Fillmore by a plainclothes cop. Instead of stopping, the pedestrian—who in the city's fetid climate of fear thought that he was being attacked by a crazed racist—pulled out a pistol and began firing at the cop. The street was thick with undercover policemen, who all pulled out their Dirty Harry .357 Magnums and unleashed a hail of fire, bringing down the old man, who, miraculously, lived despite being tattooed with six bullets.

That same night, a brawl broke out south of Market between white cops and several blacks who refused to stop. Gilford and Sanders were able to cool the situation when they arrived on the scene, but then two more white cops came roaring up in their squad car and began lashing into the subdued blacks with their billy clubs. "Gil lost it," said Sanders. The black detective began to go at it with the white patrolmen. Sanders threw himself between the fuming cops to stop the confrontation from turning even uglier. But Sanders knew how close that the highly pressurized San Francisco police force, with all its bubbling racial tensions, came to blowing up that night.

Less than a week after Operation Zebra began, a federal judge pulled the plug on it, ruling that widespread profiling of African Americans was a violation of the Constitution's Fourth Amendment ban on unfair search and seizure. The ruling left the city in a strange state of suspended animation, shamed by what it had done to many of its citizens but afraid that there now appeared to be no other options. Everyone seemed to be holding his breath, waiting for the next spasm of gunfire to crack the city's psyche.

IN THE END, IT was a kind of fluke that pulled San Francisco back from the fiery abyss. When the composite Zebra drawing was splashed across the Bay Area's front pages and TV screens, many young black men undoubtedly saw their own faces in its generic features. Among these men was Anthony Harris, who by then was deeply alienated from his fellow Death Angels. At the time, Harris was lying low in Oakland with his wife and baby, trying to pull away from his Muslim brothers without rousing their murderous ire. It was a delicate dance, and Harris knew his days might be numbered. When he saw the police sketch, he thought that the noose was tightening around his neck. Harris decided his only option was to turn himself in to the San Francisco cops and seek immunity as the prosecution's star witness.

As soon as Harris sat down in the hall of justice interrogation room on the evening of April 22 and began telling the gory tale, Coreris and Fotinos knew their long hunt was finally coming to an end. Harris provided the kind of details that only someone who had gone on the death rides could supply. But the detectives weren't done yet. They needed to keep Harris and his family safe from harm until they could negotiate a formal confession with him. Harris, his wife, and baby were checked into a Holiday Inn near the hall of justice. The next morning, a black Cadillac pulled up to the motel, and five well-groomed black men strode into the lobby, asking for Anthony Harris. The Black Muslims had found out Harris's whereabouts when his wife, lonely and distraught in police custody, phoned the wife of a minister at the Fillmore mosque. Coreris blocked the men's passage long enough to allow Fotinos, with gun drawn, to hustle Harris and his family down a fire stairwell. They escaped just as the Muslims came flying up the motel stairs.

The Black Muslims didn't give up their search for Harris. They made the rounds of other San Francisco hotels and motels, politely asking desk clerks if a man fitting Harris's description had checked in. But the most brazen attempt to locate Harris came when a black officer approached Coreris in his office and asked about the witness's whereabouts on behalf of "some friends of mine."

"Are your friends Muslims?" Coreris asked the cop.

"Yes, as a matter of fact," he replied, taken aback.

Coreris bluntly informed the cop that he would report him to Chief Scott.

Harris finally agreed to make a formal confession, but only if he could give it directly to Mayor Alioto. "He wants his promise of immunity to come straight from the horse's mouth," Harris's lawyer told Coreris. "He wants to meet with Mayor Alioto."

The cops tracked down the mayor in Los Angeles, where he was campaigning for governor, and explained the urgency of the situation. Alioto flew home after midnight and rushed to his office at city hall. It was here—after three in the morning, in the morgue-like silence of the high-domed building—that Anthony Harris brought the Angels of Death crashing down.

In the predawn hours of May 1, 1974, an army of more than one hundred law enforcement officers led by Coreris and Fotinos swept down on apartments on Fillmore Street and Grove Street, as well as the Black Self-Help Moving and Storage Company on Market, arresting seven men named by Harris, including J. C. Simon, Manuel Moore, Larry Green, and Tom Manney. An eighth suspect, Jesse Lee Cooks, was already behind bars at Folsom. In the end, they went with a whimper. "Don't shoot, don't shoot!" Simon pleaded, shivering with fear in his bed as Coreris and Fotinos burst through the door with their guns drawn.

The Zebra arrests came at the final hour, as the poison was dangerously leaching. Two nights before, an eighteen-year-old black student named Theodore Gooden was driving through the Broadway Tunnel in North Beach with his friend, James Cook, an army medic stationed at Letterman Hospital on the nearby Presidio base. Suddenly a pickup raced up alongside Gooden's car. A long-haired white man leaned out the truck's passenger window, aimed a gun at Gooden and Cook, and fired three times before the truck roared away. Gooden was wounded in the hand. His friend crumpled onto the seat beside him, where he died.

At a press conference following the arrests, Alioto fanned public fears when he announced that the seven Zebra suspects were part of a nation-wide Black Muslim cult "dedicated to the murder and mutilation of whites and dissident blacks," and insisted that unless law enforcement continued to crack down on the shadowy organization, there would be more bloodshed. Alioto said that the total Zebra victim count through-out the state might exceed eighty, not the twenty-three officially listed in San Francisco, and suggested that the mysterious disappearance of numerous hitchhikers on California roads might be tied to the group that he identified as "the Death Angels."

The information about a wider Muslim conspiracy was fed to the mayor not only by Harris but also by state investigators. There was a lurking suspicion in law enforcement circles that not all the Zebra con-spirators had been rounded up. In the end, only Green, Simon, and Moore were positively identified by witnesses at the police lineup and only they, in addition to the already incarcerated Cooks, stood trial for the Zebra mayhem. The other suspects, including former local gridiron hero Manney, went free.

The SFPD continued to stake out the Black Self-Help building. Many in the department believed that the four Zebra defendants must have had accomplices in the Muslim organization, since they had borrowed vehicles from Manney and carried out some of their goriest butchery in his moving company loft. Some frustrated cops even slashed tires on the company's trucks and torched one of the vehicles, to provoke Manney and his employees into doing something rash. But the Zebra killings stopped after the arrests, and Earl Sanders was among those who came to believe that Harris had exaggerated the dimensions of the Zebra plot and even its official connection to the Black Muslims.

Still, it was the Nation of Islam that paid for the defense of all the Zebra suspects, except for Cooks. Mosque officials cut him loose after he confessed to the murder of Frances Rose—a violation of Black Muslim code, which forbade cooperating with white authorities. The other three defendants remained defiant throughout their trial, which took longer than a year, making it the longest courtroom drama in California at the time. Gus Coreris stationed himself at the prosecution table throughout the lengthy proceedings, to make sure justice was done. Finally, on March 9, 1976, the jury found the defendants guilty of all counts. The death penalty had been suspended temporarily in California. All four Zebra killers were sentenced to life in prison, where they remain today.

After the Zebra case was cracked, San Francisco enjoyed a respite from the carnage and terror that bedeviled the city in the early seventies. The city was buoyed by a new wave of progressive activism—young men and women of all races and sexual preferences who took their fever for change into the city's cultural and political mainstream instead of underground cells. One of the new leaders who rode this ebullient groundswell was named Art Agnos. In 1987, long after the horror of Zebra had faded, Agnos won an overwhelming victory in the San Francisco mayoral race, gathering 70 percent of the vote. In 1989 his leadership of the city would be severely tested when the Bay Area was slammed by the Loma Prieta earthquake, killing sixty-three people, setting the Marina district aflame, and leaving thousands homeless. Throughout the crisis, Mayor Agnos showed the same calm serenity and self-command he had displayed on that night when a stranger walked up to him and pumped two bullets into him at point-blank range.

21

THE EMPRESS OF
CHINATOWN

L IKE WILLIE BROWN, her longtime political comrade, Rose Pak
mastered San Francisco by walking it. Young Willie, a transplant
from the sleepy East Texas railroad junction of Mineola, strolled the
streets of San Francisco all day long in the early 1950s after moving in
with his flashy, high-rolling uncle, Itsie Collins, in the Fillmore. Uncle
Itsie, who gave his nephew some pocket change every morning, advised
him to talk to as many people as he could during his daily wanderings—
a stiff challenge for a seventeen-year-old black kid from Texas, particularly in some less than hospitable neighborhoods. But it turned out to be
good training for the man who became San Francisco's most successful
African-American politician, and the city's first black mayor.

Rose Pak learned much about San Francisco politics from watching
its master, Willie Brown, at work. Pak would turn herself into Chinatown's top power broker. In the process, she was able to protect her own
community from suffering the same fate as the Fillmore district.

Pak arrived in the city as a teenager in 1967 to study at the Catholic-
run San Francisco College for Women. It was evening when she landed
at the airport after a long flight from Hong Kong. She was alone and had
no family or friends to greet her. But Pak was used to relying on herself.

In 1951, when she was three, her family fled China after the Communist takeover, but only Rose, her younger sister, and her mother made it to Hong Kong. Her father, a wealthy businessman on the Communists' blacklist, disappeared during their escape and was never seen again. At age nine, Pak was sent to a Portuguese Catholic boarding school for girls in Macao that was run by Italian nuns. There were only a few other Chinese students. She had to learn Portuguese, as well as Italian and English. The nuns liked to make her stand in front of the class and read from Western classics while the other girls roared with laughter at her accent. But Pak had a strong will. By the second year, she was running the school's boarding company.

After Hong Kong's neon blaze and hustle and bustle, the streets of San Francisco seemed so quiet and dark to Pak. She was staying with a doctor in Pacific Heights, where she received room and board in return for being his wife's companion. When Pak looked out her window, she couldn't see one person on the street. But she was enchanted by the city's fairy-tale beauty. The painted lady Victorians looked like dollhouses to her.

Chinatown had a special allure for Pak. It seemed like an old movie set, with its green pagoda buildings, strings of red lanterns, and ferocious lion statue guarding the entrance gate on Grant Avenue. But the neighborhood's quaint exterior masked a social tempest. Following the immigration reform law of 1965, which eased the longtime anti-Chinese quotas, a new wave of immigrants came flooding into San Francisco's Chinatown, West Coast capital of the Chinese diaspora. The neighborhood's dreary tenement buildings, welfare hotels, and public housing barracks were soon stuffed with families from Guangdong Province and other Asian regions that were the chief exporters of human capital to America.

By the time Pak arrived in Gold Mountain in the late sixties, the disenchantment of Chinatown's youth was spilling into the streets. "Keep Grant Avenue Narrow, Dirty, and Quaint for Tourists," read a sign carried by a droll, young protester at one Chinatown demonstration. "Preserve Chinatown's Uniqueness—Highest TB Rates, Most Suicides, Lowest Wages," read another.

The youthful rebellion in Chinatown mirrored the turmoil in the rest of the pulsating city. Like Willie Brown a decade earlier, Rose Pak trekked the hills and valleys of San Francisco, sampling all its strange and wondrous offerings. In college, she had to wear pumps and curtsy to the reverend mother. When she went downtown with her classmates, they had to wear white gloves. But in her free time, Pak was an intrepid explorer. In the Haight, she would follow hippies down the street and into their homes, as intrigued as a jungle anthropologist. They were warm and welcoming, but she was mortified by the jiggling, braless girls, and she thought that the hippies' habit of sharing wet joints was grossly unsanitary. When she began to experiment with magical smoke, she used glass water pipes.

In the Fillmore, Pak walked into churches and talked to worshippers. "I was interested in everything having to do with African Americans," she recalled. "I wanted to find out why they were rioting."

One day Pak—a lover of English poetry, particularly Keats and Shelley—saw a flyer announcing a women's poetry reading. She showed up at the address, which turned out to be a house in the Mission. There were a dozen women gathered in the living room, in jeans and flannel shirts. The women told Pak they were there to make poetry that expressed their love. "If you're expressing love, why aren't there any men here?" Pak inquired innocently.

"They looked at me like I was from Mars," she later recalled. "I had never heard the word *gay* before. Lesbianism? I mean how would you do it? I had no clue."

Rose was a crusader; she wanted to save the world. She was studying to be a journalist because she felt that would give her the best platform to speak to people. But she was a political operator at heart.

Pak started out in city politics by volunteering for Dianne Feinstein's first campaign for the board of supervisors in 1969. Feinstein was an attractive young Pacific Heights housewife with strong political ambitions, and, like Pak, the strict discipline of someone raised by nuns: in Feinstein's case, the sisters of the Convent of the Sacred Heart High School.

Pak, Feinstein, and the candidate's second husband—Dr. Bert Feinstein, a wealthy surgeon utterly devoted to his younger wife—drove all over town, climbing up ladders and nailing campaign posters to telephone poles.

"Dianne never climbed up those ladders," remembered Pak. "She was the same person she is today: very proper, never swore. The madams taught us well. If she had gone to a cocktail party, and a button had popped off her dress and it fell down to around her knees, she wouldn't have blinked an eye. She would've simply reached down, picked it up, and pinned it perfectly in place."

Pak took her growing political expertise back to Chinatown. She loved everything about the neighborhood: the strings of ducks in the store windows, the gambling joints in the back, the wheeling and dealing at the smoky Empress of China bar. It was a pushing, shoving throng of humanity—a steaming urban teapot filled with the type of people who had the moxie to uproot themselves and travel halfway around the globe so that their children could have better lives.

Pak dedicated her life to giving the Chinese of San Francisco a voice in city affairs. As late as the 1970s, Chinatown was still an insular world. She knew that its immigrant population arrived with a heavy baggage of fears and inhibitions. "We come from countries where there are no free elections. So politics is a dirty word." It wasn't until 1977 that San Francisco elected an Asian-American to the board of supervisors, and he could not manage to get reelected.

Rose Pak would become a one-woman Tammany Hall for her community, building political connections downtown, pulling strings, arranging favors, scratching for a place at San Francisco's table. She had the devotion of a nun. "It was a choice that I did not get married, that I did not have children," she said. "It would have taken time from the work I do."

By rousing Chinatown, the sleeping dragon, Pak tapped into a new vein of human energy that helped revitalize the entire city. The Chinese, confined for years in a forbidden city surrounded by downtown skyscrapers, Nob Hill hotels, and North Beach Italian hostility, began to break out and redefine San Francisco.

PAK WAS JOINED BY a rising generation of young activists. Ed Lee, a Rhodes Scholarship finalist and UC Berkeley Law School graduate, could have joined his classmates who went to work for elite corporate law firms. Most of the Chinese kids he knew in professional schools were practical; they went for the money. But Lee was too angry and rebellious to go down that path. Growing up in Seattle, one of six kids in a household that spoke Toisanese and Cantonese, he always resented the way that his father was treated. Lee's father worked as a cook in a restaurant, and toiling alongside him as a dishwasher, he saw his dad get yelled at and insulted day after day. They treated him like a coolie. The older man had to take the abuse; the family came first. But the stress took its toll, and he died too young of a heart attack. Lee, who was fifteen at the time, told himself that when he got into a position to do something about it, he would make sure that the Chinese didn't get pushed around like his father.

While still in law school in the mid-1970s, Ed Lee went to work for the Asian Law Caucus and began to organize tenants in Ping Yuen, a forbidding-looking public housing fortress that towered over Chinatown. The San Francisco Housing Authority officials who ran Ping Yuen—which means "Tranquil Garden"—treated the immigrant families stuffed into its boxy rooms like caged chickens. It was just clucking to them when the tenants complained that they had gone without heat or hot water for months, that the elevators didn't run, the lights were out in the hallways, and their families were preyed upon by thugs and thieves. Lee and the other law crusaders told the tenants that they had the right to withhold rental payments until the building was brought up to code. But a rent strike at Ping Yuen would never succeed, the activists were warned. Chinese immigrants were too quiet and submissive to put up a fight.

Then late one night in 1978, Julia Wong, a seventeen-year-old girl who worked as a seamstress in a Chinatown sweatshop, came home to Ping Yuen after her long shift. As usual, the elevator was out, and Wong began climbing the dark stairwell to her apartment. On the fifth floor, somebody tried to rape Wong and then threw her screaming off the balcony onto the pavement below. Miraculously, she survived. But her attacker was persistent. He dragged her back upstairs and again hurled her to the ground, this time killing her.

Julia Wong's hideous murder galvanized the Tranquil Garden's long-abused tenants. They told Ed Lee and his legal warriors that they were ready to fight back. Ping Yuen's outraged residents unfurled a banner over an upper-floor balcony announcing a rent strike. Housing authority bureaucrats were stunned. Chinese residents were the most dependable renters in the city's public housing system; they always paid on time.

When they started withholding their monthly payments, the housing authority immediately felt the financial pinch. After six months, housing officials caved, agreeing to make a long list of improvements at Ping Yuen.

The successful Chinatown rent strike was the beginning of Ed Lee's career as a community organizer. "You can go to law school to make money, or you can go to help the community," Lee said. "I fought landlord-tenant battles where I would face off against people I went to law school with. They were working for corporations trying to evict people, and I was trying to stop them. Landlords—many of whom were absentee, and many were Chinese—hated my guts. They saw me coming and said, 'There's that Communist Ed Lee!'"

The housing battles of the 1970s were the crucible for an entire generation of new activists in San Francisco. The city was a finite peninsula of competing dreams and ambitions. Was it to become a Manhattan of the West, whose office towers and high-rise apartment buildings overshadowed everything else, or remain an affordable, human-scale city of light nestled into the hills and hollows? The land-use war sparked a full-blown identity crisis for San Francisco, forcing the city to grapple with a range of social, economic, and aesthetic dilemmas.

Tensions exploded in 1977 during a dramatic showdown over the International Hotel, a decrepit brick building squeezed between Chinatown and the financial district that was home to nearly two hundred elderly Filipino and Chinese tenants. The residential hotel at the corner of Kearny and Jackson Streets became a symbol of resistance for a new generation of Asian activists, community organizers, and student radicals—including Ed Lee—when it was bought by developer Walter Shorenstein, who planned to raze it and build a parking lot. After Shorenstein was stymied by lawsuits and public opposition, he dumped the property, selling it to a mysterious Bangkok tycoon known as "the Godfather." The tycoon's company announced plans to build a commercial tower on the I-Hotel site and finally succeeded in ramming an eviction order through the courts.

Late one summer night, as the rest of the city slept, an army of helmeted riot cops, some on horseback, began marching on the I-Hotel. Some three thousand protesters formed a human barricade around the building and sang "We Shall Overcome," as they were eerily lit up by the midnight sun of countless TV lights. "It was like the Roman Legions coming after the Christians," one young Asian protester said later. "I could almost hear drumbeats; their batons looked like swords drawn." The riot cops bulldozed their way through the crowd, scaled the hotel's fire escapes, and began smashing through the windows with sledgeham-mers. Once inside, they dragged the terrified old tenants out of their rooms and began trashing the building, breaking toilets into pieces and knocking down walls to make sure that the I-Hotel would never again be inhabited.

The demolition of the I-Hotel was the last stand of old Manilatown, once home to thousands of Filipino farmworkers, cannery workers, houseboys, and sailors—like the hotel's elderly tenants, most of whom never married because of antimiscegenation laws and restrictive immi-gration policies. But the hotel residents' plucky fight, and their rough treatment at the hands of police, galvanized neighborhood activists throughout the city. Determined to clamp limits on the runaway cor-porate real estate machine that was plowing through the city during the Alioto era—fueled by powerful downtown business interests and labor unions—organizers put anti–high rise initiatives on city ballots and cam-paigned for sympathetic local candidates. Nowhere was this battle more urgent than in Chinatown, where some thirty thousand people—mostly Asian immigrants—were crammed into twenty-four square blocks, all in the growing shadow of a steadily encroaching financial district.

GORDON CHIN WAS ONE of the young Chinatown crusaders lit up by the I-Hotel fireworks. Chinatown was his native ground, the richly storied turf that he would dedicate his life to protecting and revital-izing. Chin was born in Chinese Hospital in the heart of Chinatown. His parents waited tables by day, but at night they went out gambling, a Chinatown passion. When his mother was young, she and her friends would dress up and go out dancing at Forbidden City, the nightclub that featured leggy Chinese showgirls and singers who belted out Broadway show tunes. The club, which opened in 1938, also advertised its "exotic Oriental dancers," nude performers who hid their female charms with nothing more than balloons and fans. Forbidden City attracted celebri-ties like Bob Hope, Duke Ellington, and Gene Kelly—the latter of whom cruised through the club searching for entertainers to cast in *Flower Drum Song,* the Rodgers and Hammerstein musical he was directing on Broadway. Behind the red door at 363 Sutter was a world that remained, well into the 1940s, truly forbidden, where white men and Asian women danced together on the ballroom floor—and sometimes, in defiance of race-mixing prohibitions, fell in love.

Chin came of age in a different San Francisco, haunting the city's jazz and soul music clubs, where he heard Miles Davis and Smokey Robinson perform. In his day, cool Chinese kids took their lead from black musicians and militants. At Merritt College in Oakland and later at San Francisco State College in the late sixties, Chin got caught up in the black power confrontations, listening to Huey Newton and Bobby Seale speak on campus and taking inspiration from their defiant swagger. But Chin and his friends were not into burning down the system, they wanted to pry it open. He interned in the San Francisco office of Congressman Phil Burton, the city's powerful Washington operator, watching rising young stars like Nancy Pelosi and Willie Brown glide past. "Willie had charisma and style," Chin recalled. "Everyone wanted to be like him; he was cool. If Miles Davis had gone into politics, he would've been Willie Brown."

When the city was convulsed by the SLA and Zebra, Chin and his fellow activists just kept their heads down. "We knew all that stuff was just a passing circus," he reflected. "We were committed activists who were in it for the long haul. We weren't out to overthrow the American government or even city hall. But we did want to force fundamental change in the system."

The long march of San Francisco crusaders such as Rose Pak, Ed Lee, and Gordon Chin eventually paid off. Years later, they could look back and marvel at what they had accomplished. There, one evening in February 2011, ensconced at a window table at North Beach Restaurant, were the two political veterans whom the *San Francisco Chronicle* anointed as the city's reigning "power couple": Willie Brown and Rose Pak. At ages seventy-six and sixty-two, respectively, they might have simply been reminiscing about old times over their Italian dinners. Instead they were feting San Francisco's new mayor: none other than Ed Lee, the man they craftily maneuvered into office after it was vacated a year early by Gavin Newsom, who won California's lieutenant governorship in 2010. Lee, the former public housing agitator, was now in charge of the city bureaucrats with whom he once clashed. Lee made history in November 2011 when he secured the office in the municipal election, becoming the first Asian American to be elected mayor in San Francisco.

Meanwhile, Gordon Chin was finishing a long and successful career as the founding executive director of the Chinatown Community Development Center, a nonprofit organization that has built more than two thousand affordable housing units in the neighborhood and rehabilitated many more. As he looked back over his accomplishments, Chin was proudest of the sixteen-floor residential hotel he built on the corner of Kearny and Jackson. The building's views of the Bay Bridge and downtown skyline were the kinds usually enjoyed by owners of luxury condos and lofts, but these hotel rooms were reserved for seniors on fixed incomes. Chin's organization built the hotel on a vacant lot; a hole in the ground that had remained an ugly scar in San Francisco for more than two decades. When the building opened in 2005, it was given the name of the old brick structure that once stood there: the International Hotel.

But all this was decades in the future. Before San Francisco could congratulate itself on its inclusive civic climate, the city had to withstand other shock waves. The biggest tremor shook San Francisco even more powerfully than the city's bulging Asian immigrant population. It was triggered by a cultural invasion as momentous as the hippie migration of the sixties.

Ever since its earliest Barbary Coast days, San Francisco had, with varying degrees of hospitality, made room for its dandy men and masculine ladies. But the gay carnival that rolled into town in the 1970s was like nothing the city had ever seen, or any other city for that matter. Like the hippies, gays arrived in San Francisco from all corners of the country and planet, on the run from brutality, boredom, and the daily tyranny of clenched minds. Once they arrived, they had no intention of leaving. They promptly began giving San Francisco a makeover in their own image. It was the closest thing to a hometown they had ever experienced. The resulting identity war embroiled the city for years to come. There would be blood, rioting, and plague before San Francisco was finally liberated.

22

SAN FRANCISCO
SATYRICON

J OE ALIOTO WAS a complex man. A lover of poetry and the arts, he
could rise to defend the authority-bedeviled Allen Ginsberg, as he
did at the Spoleto Arts Festival in July 1967, when Italian police arrested
the poet after local authorities read "Who Be Kind To," his paean to the
"orgy of our flesh." The carabinieri questioned Ginsberg, never one to
make a secret of his homoerotic appetites, about the exact nature of
some of his orgiastic verse. Perhaps the following words got lost in trans-
lation: "Desire given with meat hand and cock, desire taken with mouth
and ass, desire returned to the last sigh!" Alioto, who was on the festival's
board, introduced himself to the police as Ginsberg's $1-a-year lawyer—
certainly the lowest rate ever charged by the millionaire attorney—and
quickly managed to spring the poet.

As a poetry enthusiast, Alioto could champion the bard who wrote
lines like these:

Come beautiful boys with breasts bright gold
Lie down in bed with me ere ye grow old,
Take down your blue jeans, we'll have some raw fun
Lie down on your bellies I'll fuck your soft bun.

233

But as mayor of San Francisco, Joe Alioto was no friend of queers. In his official role, he was true to his traditional Italian upbringing when it came to policing the city's sexual frontiers. Playing to his Catholic base, Alioto oversaw one of the most severe crackdowns on gays in San Francisco history. Driven from bars by unrelenting police raids, gays were forced into city parks, but the cops pursued them there as well. By 1971, San Francisco police were busting an average of nearly three thousand gay men a year on public sex charges. The same year, by contrast, New York City police made only about sixty such arrests.

The SFPD was not as perversely clever as it was in the 1930s: when staking out one notorious Market Street theater, some undercover cops painted their cocks with Mercurochrome before allowing gay cruisers to suck them. The unsuspecting cruisers, their lips aflame with telltale red, would then be arrested as they exited through the lobby. But police entrapment was still in widespread use under Alioto. And San Francisco courts could not be counted on for leniency. In 1971 alone, over one hundred local men were sentenced to a stunning fifteen years to life for the crime of "sodomy and oral copulation."

"To tell you the truth, I don't think my father knew many gay men," said Alioto's daughter, Angela. "I think he was sheltered at the time. I was raised in a house where the word *sex* was never mentioned."

Joe Alioto's police sweeps would be the last hurrah in San Francisco City Hall's century-old, hot and cold war on homosexual freedom. By his second term, Alioto faced a mutiny in his own government when the board of supervisors voted in 1972 to prohibit city contractors from discriminating against homosexuals—a legal landmark in the long battle for gay rights. "Does this mean that contractors have to hire men who wear dresses?" asked a genuinely perplexed Supervisor Dianne Feinstein when lesbian activist Del Martin first suggested the law. But within five years, Feinstein, responding to the city's shifting mores, was hosting a lesbian wedding in the backyard of her Pacific Heights mansion.

As San Francisco's political climate became more welcoming, more and more gays flocked to the city. By 1976, the police chief estimated that more than 140,000 gays were living in San Francisco—more than one in five citizens—and nearly 100 homosexual settlers were arriving each week, figures widely considered to be conservative.

VINCE CALCAGNO WAS ONE of the young gay men who arrived in San Francisco that year. He had grown up in blue-collar Akron, Ohio, in an Italian Catholic family, and after graduating from college had found a John Waters–like bohemian niche for himself in Cleveland. Calcagno lived with his boyfriend Fred in a house owned by Paige Palmer, a local TV fitness queen with million-dollar gams who would demonstrate scissor kicks and jumping jacks in black fishnet stockings and pumps. Colorful personalities flowed through the house, including the young musicians who would later become the New Wave group Devo. But by 1976, Calcagno felt that he had done Ohio, and he and Fred headed west.

They arrived in February, rising up from underground on a BART escalator that deposited them at the downtown corner of Market and Montgomery. The temperature hovered around seventy, and they were bathed in a soft winter light. Strolling down Market to the cable car turnaround at Powell Street, Calcagno spotted a phone booth and called his mother in Akron. "Mom, you lied," he told her. "The grass *is* greener." She burst into tears. "It sounds like you're never coming home."

He never did.

That first evening, Calcagno and Fred checked into a small hotel off Polk Street, picked up a gay tourist guide, and went looking for the Castro district. Riding on a bus near the corner of Market and Duboce Streets, they knew that Oz was near when a stark naked man scampered merrily across the street, and the entire bus erupted into cheers. On Castro Street, the couple were surrounded by more gay men than they had ever seen in one place. Calcagno had a feminine halo of hair and big disco shades. But these men had a macho swagger, dressed in tight Pendleton wool plaid shirts and ass-hugging jeans or army fatigues and leather bomber jackets. "I just didn't know if I could do this," remembered Calcagno. "I grabbed on to Fred and thought, 'I'm probably going to lose my boyfriend here.' The whole thing seemed scary to me." He paused. "I got over that quick."

San Francisco in the mid-1970s was a never-ending party for gay men. Calcagno went to work in a Castro store that made T-shirts and processed film—including gay customers' X-rated pictures. He and his coworkers pored over the photos when they came back from the developer, wide eyed at the infinite ways that men could find to pleasure each other. One of the most popular T-shirts on sale in Castro shops showed Judy Garland from *The Wizard of Oz* and read, "Toto, we're not in Kansas anymore." It was a feeling that Calcagno had nearly every day.

On their first Halloween in San Francisco, he and Fred put on sailor suits and dance shoes, and tapped their way up and down Castro Street like Frank Sinatra and Gene Kelly in *Anchors Aweigh*. Halloween—the one night that San Francisco cops traditionally ceded to gays, allowing even the most dazzling creatures to flutter around town—was a high holiday in the Castro and up and down Polk Street.

Their first Gay Freedom Day Parade was even more unforgettable. Crisscrossing the city on foot and bus, they felt like they were part of a moveable orgy. "There were people having sex on the MUNI [municipal] trolleys, there were people having sex in broad daylight in the park," said Calcagno. "There were bands and music all over. It was ninety-six degrees, and everyone was stripped down and sweaty."

Gays were changing the face of San Francisco in countless ways. They bought ramshackle Victorians in the Castro from Irish-American families fleeing the homosexual invasion and turned them into postcard gems. They edged into drug- and crime-infested neighborhoods in the Mission and the Duboce Triangle and spruced them up too, opening cafes and flower shops and clothing stores.

The food revolution that is still sweeping the nation—based on locally grown organic ingredients, seasonal cycles, and the age-old wisdom of the Mediterranean—was largely the creation of female and gay foodies in the Bay Area during the 1970s. Like Alice Waters and her dashing gay chef, Jeremiah Tower—founders of Chez Panisse in Berkeley—this new culinary wave simply expected a more sensual experience than the local dining world provided.

"When I began cooking at Chez Panisse in the early seventies," recalled Tower, "I'd go to the meat markets in Oakland and see all these boxes of frozen meat marked 'Ernie's' and the names of other top San Francisco restaurants. It's hard to imagine, but you couldn't find fresh herbs, very few fresh vegetables. In California! I had to go to an Italian deli to buy good olive oil; it was the only place in the Bay Area that carried it. After we got things going, people began showing up at the back door of the restaurant with fresh mushrooms they had gathered. And it was, 'Here we go!'"

In San Francisco, the first gay-owned restaurants in the 1970s were known for their floor shows more than their food. Hamburger Mary's, at the corner of Folsom and Twelfth Streets in the heart of the leather district, was opened by a man nicknamed Trixie and his hippie friends. It was a truck-stop diner on poppers, catering to the gays and gay-friendly who worked up powerful appetites on the dance floors and in the back rooms of nearby clubs like the Stud, Febe's, and the Eagle Tavern. The carb-heavy menu was known for its greasy burgers and pillowy omelettes, but Trixie's hippie roots could be found in the mound of green sprouts atop his salads. The service, provided by distracted bare-chested men with nipple rings, was chaotic. And the décor was loopy, with a giant ruby slipper doubling as a planter, rubber-nippled baby bottles serving as creamers, and anything-goes unisex bathrooms. But Hamburger Mary's was the perfect blend of 1960s and 1970s San Francisco, an only-in-SF mix of nine-grain wholesomeness and disco mania.

It was the Zuni Café that took San Francisco cuisine to a new level. The restaurant was opened in 1979 by Billy West, a boyishly charming sprite who learned about the joys of food while traveling the world as a navy "wife" with his sailor boyfriend. Inspired by the Southwest themes popular at the time, West took over a Market Street storefront next to a cactus store, hand plastered the walls to give it an adobe look, and began serving dishes inspired by cookbook author Diana Kennedy's Mexican sojourns. Later, with the help of former Chez Panisse chef Judy Rodgers, West began working French and Italian influences into the menu, all the while developing bonds with local farmers and ranchers, and introducing diners to the new splendors of California cuisine. Succulent Tomales Bay oysters, grass-fed beef from the Niemann-Schell ranch in Bolinas, cheeses from organic Point Reyes dairy farms, arugula and escarole from Green Gulch gardens that were sprinkled by the wet sea breezes off Muir Beach. These were the ingredients of the San Francisco food revolution that would challenge the rest of the country to eat local, fresh, and organic.

Zuni quickly became the most popular watering hole for the new San Francisco, drawing a democratic clientele that included rakish gay men, Pacific Heights socialites, city hall politicos, and struggling writers and artists with their last freelance checks in their pockets. It was Jeremiah Tower's favorite late-night escape, inspiring him to open his own legendary San Francisco restaurant, Stars, in 1984. "I once figured I spent over three hundred thousand dollars eating and drinking in Zuni's," Tower said. "I'd nip over there, and if they didn't have a table, I'd just stand at the bar and have a glass of champagne and a soppressata sandwich. It had the best bar in town."

The restaurant drew the town's luminaries and those just passing through. Robin Williams, Julia Child, Mick Jagger, Hunter Thompson, Phillip Roth, Ted Kennedy. No one bothered them while they were eating. There were no celebrity photos on the walls. That was for the Fisherman's Wharf joints that served shrimp scampi.

Not long after Zuni opened, Billy West, aware of his limitations as a manager, brought in Vince Calcagno to help him run the place. "Billy was very smart, very cute, very fun—but like a lot of creative people, his head was in the clouds," said Calcagno. "He was a hippie, but he ended up with a Maserati. He liked nice things."

Calcagno, who had worked in a bank back in Ohio, proved to be a well-organized and disciplined manager. His skills were sorely tested in Zuni's early years, when he found waiters shooting up drugs and fucking in the bathroom. "In those days, even managers always had a glass of wine going; you were never stopped from drinking. So it was hard to tell the waiters they couldn't get high. It felt hypocritical."

There was a lust for life that spilled out everywhere in the city. "Everyone was sleeping with everyone, and everyone knew and no one cared," said Calcagno. "All the boundaries were being broken. It seemed there was no end to it."

The gay carnival eroticized all San Francisco. Bars like the Stud began as dark, rough-trade dens of iniquity but somehow morphed into polymorphously perverse playgrounds for men and women of all sexual tribes. Gays went carousing at the Stud with their favorite fag hags, who drew straight men into their flirtatious webs. A Freddy Mercury type shaking his ass on the dance floor would suddenly be groped from behind, and couldn't be sure if it was the man or woman dancing next to him. Most bathhouses in the city were strictly gay cruising zones, but a few—like the coed Grand Central and Sutro Baths—began catering to men and women who fantasized about public or anonymous sex.

Gay men started the party in San Francisco in the 1970s. But everyone was soon invited.

INSPIRED BY THE GAY and feminist bravado of the period, a beloved party girl named Margo St. James brought prostitution out of the closet in San Francisco, founding a hookers' liberation group in 1973 called Coyote (Call Off Your Old Tired Ethics). St. James had arrived in town in 1959, a wide-eyed farm girl from Bellingham, Washington, and soon became part of the North Beach beat scene. The parties in her upstairs apartment at the corner of Grant Avenue and Green Street, which she shared with a couple of ladies of the night, drew the likes of Lenny Bruce and Ken Kesey, as well as bartenders, 49ers football players, and off-duty cops. The colorful parade of men was drawn by the charming young women and by the fourteen-foot marijuana plant that St. James kept in a backyard shed.

Party girls like Margo St. James, with big hearts and outsized personalities, are clasped to San Francisco's bosom. Herb Caen thought San Francisco's Holly Golightly made a merry sight zooming around town in her sporty Triumph TR3 convertible, wearing an overturned salad bowl on her head for a helmet, and she popped up often in his column. St. James delighted lovers by shaving her pubic hair into a heart shape— years before actress Valerie Perrine, who played Honey Bruce in the 1974 movie *Lenny,* made headlines with her own pussy valentine.

St. James knew everyone in town. While moonlighting as a secretary at a bail bondsman's office, to pay off her own bond on a prostitution bust, St. James ate lunch across the street at the hall of justice. Her lunch companion was often a rising young attorney named Willie Brown. "Willie took a lot of hooker cases back then. We used to eat together in the cafeteria because he's black and I'm a whore, and nobody would sit with us, so we sat together."

One evening at a party in her home in woodsy Marin County, where she had moved in the early seventies, St. James accosted guest Richard Hongisto, the iconoclastic San Francisco sheriff. Hongisto, who was known as "Big Dick" by St. James's hooker friends, was a favorite of every liberal group in San Francisco. St. James thought it was time for prostitutes, still preyed upon by SFPD vice squad zealots and often abused by pimps, to stand up for their rights. She asked Sheriff Hongisto what it would take for a union of whores to win the respect of the feminist and gay rights groups that supported him. Hongisto told her that a prostitute with spunk, a working woman from the "hidden victim class," needed to speak out; that was the only way the issue would be heard. After mustering her courage, St. James decided that she would be the one.

As the founder of Coyote, St. James fought for the rights of all those she described as "sex workers"—including whores, porn film actors, strippers, and massage parlor employees. She argued that women who sold their labor in the sex industry should be granted the same rights as those who worked as secretaries or nurses. Coyote offered legal advice and referrals to sex workers and lobbied city hall to decriminalize prostitution. But St. James realized that the quickest way to San Francisco's heart was to create a spectacle.

Coyote began promoting an annual Halloween Hooker's Ball: a bawdy gathering of men and women in debauched masquerade that grew more flagrant and more popular each year. By 1978, the erotic extravaganza was drawing more than eighteen thousand to the cavernous Cow Palace arena—home to epic roller derby duels and rodeos and site of the 1964 presidential nomination of Republican Barry Goldwater.

The night began with a roaring parade of tap dancers, cheerleaders, and a squadron of Harley-straddling Dykes on Bikes. Then the curtain parted, and out came the Whore Queen herself, Margo St. James, riding on an elephant and dressed like the scourge of the San Francisco sex industry, Supervisor Dianne Feinstein. Around midnight, George Carlin made a brief appearance onstage, but the comic quickly realized that the real entertainment was happening among the carousing masses down on the floor. After shouting a string of FCC-banned words into the microphone, he quickly made an exit.

WHILE MARGO ST. JAMES was trying to revolutionize the world's oldest profession, two aspiring San Francisco porn film moguls—brothers Jim and Artie Mitchell—were striving to take X-rated movies out of the seedy, sticky-floor, stag-film era and inject them with a giddy, groovy sensibility that appealed to a new generation of men and women. The Mitchell brothers, born and raised in the Okie culture of the Sacramento Delta, escaped the drudgery of the local paper and chemical mills the same way that their cardsharp father had: by learning to hustle. They proved to be shrewd carny barkers, opening a porn theater in the early seventies in an old Pontiac showroom on the edge of the Tenderloin and screening their own film productions. Mitchell Brothers movies developed a reputation for their slicker production values and their quirky, self-mocking attitude—giving them a cool buzz among the counterculture crowd. They hired hippies and college girls instead of hookers to star in their films, and the women actually seemed to be enjoying themselves, not just laboring over their partners' towering erections.

In 1972 the brothers released their underground masterpiece, *Behind the Green Door,* which, along with *Deep Throat,* took porn into the American mainstream. *Green Door* is a hazy, druggy sex fantasy, the extended wet dream of an innocent, young woman named Gloria who gives herself over to her deepest desires. Blindfolded and carried off to a secret world, Gloria is first caressed by a troop of robed women, then ravished by a beautiful black god, and, finally, taken by a group of horned satyrs in trapeze swings. As Gloria is flooded with pleasure, she is publicly displayed before a kinky mélange of masked sybarites, who—driven mad by the wanton spectacle—fall on one another in all variations of couplings and sate their lust. The film, suffused with the wild sexual imagination of 1970s San Francisco, set a variety of porn precedents that later became standard hard-core fixtures, such as interracial and bisexual coupling.

The Mitchell brothers scored a casting coup by convincing a nineteen-year-old blonde, all-American-looking actress-model named Marilyn Briggs to take the part of Gloria. Briggs, the daughter of a Madison Avenue advertising executive, had never acted in a hard-core film before. But after shrewdly negotiating a percentage of the profits, she agreed to star in the film under the name Marilyn Chambers.

In a huge stroke of luck for the filmmakers, the manufacturers of Ivory Snow detergent released a newly designed box of soap flakes just as *Behind the Green Door* premiered. Pictured on the box was a sweet-faced Marilyn Briggs—who had done the photo shoot months before her reincarnation as a porn star—cuddling a cherubic baby. The story of the pure-as-Ivory-Snow porn queen exploded around the world, helping *Behind the Green Door* set adult film box office records. The movie, which cost $60,000 to make, eventually earned $50 million, an estimate that is probably low because of all the bootleg copies that circulated.

The Mitchells' success as mainstream pornographers—and their ballsy way of flaunting it, such as staging a Hollywood-style premiere of *Behind the Green Door* at their O'Farrell Theater—inevitably aroused the ire of prudish city officials like Feinstein and the Irish Catholics who ran the police department. It didn't help win friends downtown when the brothers released *Reckless Claudia,* which featured a scene in which the horny heroine sucks an aroused priest in a confessional and is splattered with his holy fluid. The police routinely raided the O'Farrell Theater, busting one or both brothers. During one raid, a vice cop ordered the lights turned up in the theater and proceeded to scold the unfortunate patrons like a red-faced Irish priest. "You gentlemen should be ashamed! Ashamed!" he fumed as he stalked up and down the center aisle. "It's a beautiful day outside, and you pasty-faced perverts are in here abusing yourselves! Don't you care about your health?"

But unlike old-school smut peddlers, who deflected police aggression by crawling off to the city's shadows and greasing the right palms at the hall of justice, the Mitchell brothers fought back. With the help of their attorney, Michael Kennedy, another brawling San Francisco barrister in the Hallinan mold, the brothers played hardball, filing injunctions and lawsuits and demonstrating once again that the best defense is a good offense. They also courted local reporters, politicians, and hipsters like Robert Crumb and Hunter Thompson. The upstairs room at the O'Farrell—with its massive pool table, bare-breasted dancers, and congenial flow of drugs and booze—became a popular boys club for an emerging crop of San Francisco players.

The most potent factor in the Mitchell brothers' defense, however, was the changing nature of the local porn film market. Contrary to the fulminating cop, not all of the theater's customers were pasty-faced perverts. Many were couples on adventurous dates, in search of some extra, precoital stimulation. When police officials threatened to yank the Mitchells' theater permit, a healthy cross section of the local bourgeois showed up at the public hearing to protest, including an architect who

urged the police commission to grant the permit because San Franciscans needed a nice, clean place to enjoy their porn movies.

THERE WAS A NEW San Francisco being born like a chrysalis in the
crumbling shell of the old city. And no one captured the feeling of this
butterfly world better than a young gay writer named Armistead Maupin. Like many of San Francisco's homosexual refugees, Maupin had a
deeply ironic American backstory. Raised in a wealthy conservative family in Raleigh, North Carolina, that was one step removed from the Con-
federacy, he interned at the radio station owned by the rising tribune of
white southern reaction, Jesse Helms; the future senator was a "hero
figure" to the young Maupin. Later Maupin joined the navy, serving a
tour of duty in Vietnam as an aide to legendary admiral Elmo Zumwalt.
His duties consisted primarily of escorting senators and congressmen
on thirty-minute PR tours of the war. Maupin, desperate for a combat
action ribbon to impress his flag-waving father, was glad when his base
finally came under a rocket attack, which immediately qualified him for
the commendation.

After leaving the navy, Maupin was recruited by the Nixon White
House to return to Vietnam and build houses for disabled Vietnamese
sailors—a publicity stunt meant to counter the political threat posed by
a young naval lieutenant from Massachusetts named John Kerry and the
"unpatriotic" Vietnam Veterans Against the War. Maupin—looking like
a photogenic Young Republican, with his helmet of longish blond hair,
and wearing a dark blazer and tie—was ushered into the White House
to shake hands with the president.

"Nixon was trying desperately to seem like a real guy in front of us
GIs," recalled Maupin, "and he did so by saying, 'Aren't those Vietnamese girls cute with their little pouty eyes and hair flowing behind them
like butterfly wings?' It was creepy—creepy on a level that I cannot convey to you. And he's trying this out on a closet homosexual."

In 1971, when he moved to San Francisco as a twenty-seven-year-old
Associated Press reporter, Maupin was still a southern Republican and
"gentleman racist." He expected to be shunned by the city's liberal social
world. At a party in Sea Cliff—the city's windblown balcony—in a mansion later owned by Robin Williams, Maupin was introduced as a navy

veteran just back from Vietnam. There were no antiwar lectures. Instead a man looked at Maupin, wrapped his arms around him, and said, "I'm so glad you're alive. Welcome home."

"The man was certifiably straight," said Maupin. "And I came from a place where straight men didn't hug each other. They never spit on me here."

It took three more years of living in San Francisco's warm embrace before Maupin finally mustered the courage to come out. After downing three Mai Tais, he decided to announce his sexuality to a friend named Jan Fox, showing up at her apartment as she was bathing her babies. When Maupin told her that he had something urgent to tell her, the worried Fox immediately came out of the bathroom. "I made this big weeping confession, and Jan knelt in front of me, took my hand, and said, 'Big fucking deal.' That was a big discovery for me—I had landed in a place where the heterosexuals were more comfortable with homosexuality than I was."

Bottled up his entire life, Maupin suddenly was free to express himself. Encouraged by the *Chronicle*'s crusty but literary Charles McCabe during one of the columnist's ritualistic rounds of heavy drinking at the Washington Square Bar & Grill, Maupin quit AP and began freelancing, eventually creating a new column about Bay Area manners and mores for the weekly *Pacific Sun*. McCabe became a fan. At a party, McCabe confronted Chronicle owner Charles Thieriot, telling him that most of his columnists were headed for the retirement pastures at Laguna Honda. The *Chronicle* desperately needed new talent, growled McCabe—like this kid Armistead Maupin.

"McCabe was homophobic, but if he liked you individually, he'd overlook that you were a faggot, like a parent would," Maupin said.

The *San Francisco Chronicle* launched Armistead Maupin's "Tales of the City" on May 24, 1976. The daily serial gave birth to a cast of make-believe characters who summarized seventies San Francisco, including Mary Ann Singleton, a twenty-five-year-old transplant from Cleveland, and her gay sidekick, Michael Tolliver, Maupin's alter ego. After moving into a Russian Hill apartment building at mythical 28 Barbary Lane, Singleton falls into a magical world where single gals don't just drink Tab and heat up Stouffer's TV dinners at night. They explore the city with their gay pals, going to jockey shorts dance contests at the Endup and sunning themselves at Devil's Slide, the nude gay beach south of the city. Maupin's San Francisco was part Balzac's Paris, part Lewis Carroll's Wonderland, and part Federico Fellini's *Satyricon*. Society dames slummed it with Chinese delivery boys and Samoan mechanics with big tools while their husbands dallied in the bathhouses. Party girls swallowed ludes and snorted "happy dust" and praised Jesus with the drag queens at the Reverend Willie Sessums's holy rock 'n' rolling Glibb Church (read Cecil Williams's Glide Church). Meanwhile, up above in the sky over Telegraph Hill, a raucous squadron of electric-green wild parrots went jetting through the wisps of fog on their way to the eucalyptus trees that shaded Julius' Castle, the fairytale-looking restaurant that clung to one side of the hill. The part about the feral parrots was real. Maupin lovingly colored his series with real-life local flora and fauna, like Edsel Ford Fong, the abusive "warlord turned waiter" who presided over Sam Woh's in Chinatown—or the boys in their tight Pendletons "circling the floor in predatory delight" on Gay Night at the roller skate rink as the organ merrily played "I Enjoy Being a Girl."

For all the kinky and fantastical twists and turns in "Tales of the City," Maupin's San Francisco was essentially a warm-hearted hometown where people like Mary Ann and Michael could get over their Christmastime blues when everyone else was huddled with their families, by donning their gay apparel and creating their own families. That's how Maupin saw the city: it had "a small-town vibe with cosmopolitan attitudes." He couldn't imagine any other city in the world coaxing the newspaper serial out of him day after day. San Francisco was a "waking dream," thought Maupin, a place that was as much about people's self-invention as it was about the misty, movie-set scenery.

It did not take long for "Tales of the City" to become a San Francisco institution, as avidly read at the exclusive Bohemian Club on Nob Hill as it was in Cafe Flore in the gay Duboce Triangle. *San Francisco* magazine declared that the city was embracing Maupin's serial "with a passion hitherto reserved for the Cockettes." Nurses at a private San Francisco health care agency became such big fans, reading each episode out loud over their brown bag lunches, that they named their modest medical library after Maupin.

But the serial almost did not survive its rocky takeoff. *Chronicle* publisher Charles Thieriot went bug-eyed when he began reading "Tales," with its Samoan-loving socialites and its drag queen nuns zipping through town on speed skates. "People don't act like this!" thundered Thieriot, who apparently led a sheltered life for a lifelong San Franciscan.

Gordon Pates, the paper's punctilious, mild-mannered managing editor, grew concerned about the proliferation of gay characters in the serial. He instituted a new rule, telling Maupin that homosexuals must never number more than one-third of the cast in "Tales of the City." Pates kept a chart labeled Heterosexual or Homosexual in his office, adding each new character that Maupin introduced to a column.

"I spent two weeks trying to find a way to queer this, so to speak," Maupin recalled. "I wrote an episode in which Frannie Halcyon, the Hillsborough matron, has an affair with her Great Dane. This was done very tastefully and subtly, of course. I suppose an affair would be an inaccurate way to put it. She had passed out drunk in the rose garden and woke up to find the dog on top of her, but didn't want to complain because she knew the dog didn't mean it. After I wrote this episode, I came into Gordon's office and told him the dog had to go in the heterosexual column." That was the end of Pates's quota system.

With his impeccable southern manners, twinkly eyed charm, and cavalry officer good looks, Maupin routinely outmaneuvered his *Chronicle* editors, who—in the post–Scott Newhall era—were not known for their dazzle. Constantly fretting that "Tales of the City" would offend subscribers in the sleepy Sunset district, the paper's overseers were poised to pull the plug on the serial. But its fan base was too damn big and loyal. "They stuck with me," Maupin said, "because the readers stuck with me."

Armistead Maupin not only chronicled the new San Francisco but also helped dream it to life. Fans of the serial started feeling like they were living out their own true-life tales of the city. Vince Calcagno—like Mary Ann Singleton, recently arrived from Cleveland—was far from alone when he had his "Mary Ann moments" as he navigated his way through his new city. The serial became a daily touchstone for the new San Francisco. As a neighbor told Mary Ann in one episode, "Nobody's from here." Everybody in San Francisco was making it up as he or she went along. And reading "Tales of the City" each morning told the city's newcomers they were no stranger than the next person—and San Francisco accepted them, even loved them, for who they were.

By the time "Tales of the City" debuted, everything seemed in flux in San Francisco, including the political establishment. Looking back long afterward at his tumultuous eight years in office, Joe Alioto said that his main task had been to "manage the revolution" that went roaring through the city. He was like the captain of a storm-tossed ship, presiding over a dining table whose glassware, wine carafes, and cutlery were constantly on the brink of being dashed to the floor. If Alioto tried to keep a rein on the turbulence, his successor rode the revolution into office. And he, George Moscone, would become a victim of its violent backlash.

23

CIVIC WAR

GEORGE MOSCONE, RUNNING hard to succeed Joe Alioto in San Francisco's 1975 mayoral race, swept into the hippie commune on Ashbury Street with a couple of young aides hustling beside him. Sue Bierman, the godmother of Haight-Ashbury neighborhood activism, had set up the meeting for the mayoral candidate. Bierman became a big fan of Moscone in 1964 after he cast the deciding vote on the board of supervisors against a freeway extension that would have bulldozed the Golden Gate Panhandle. An old-fashioned populist from a long line of Nebraska radicals and anti-slavery Republicans, Bierman midwived a new generation of San Francisco crusaders with her battles against downtown fat cats and developers' wrecking balls. Among her young protégés was Calvin Welch, one of the Haight community agitators whom Bierman had persuaded to meet with Moscone.

But despite Bierman's embrace of Moscone, Welch and his fellow commune members were skeptical of the mayoral candidate. Moscone was, after all, a career politician, a breed that Haight activists had come to disdain. Welch and his housemates decided that in order to win their support, Moscone would have to pass the ultimate Haight-Ashbury test.

Moscone and his hippie hosts were seated around a massive communal table. As they began to discuss neighborhood issues, one of Welch's comrades fired up a pillow-sized reefer. "We were going to pass it around the table and see if that motherfucker takes a hit or not," recalled Welch. As the smoldering joint came around to George Miller, Moscone's young aide and a future California congressman, the protective Miller tried to pass it over his boss to an aide on the other side of Moscone. "*Waaait* a minute!" the candidate exclaimed, deftly intercepting the contraband.

"Moscone grabs the joint and takes a huge fucking hit!" Welch laughed.

The whole room burst into applause. The candidate passed the test. The Haight was in his column.

George Moscone ran as the candidate of change in 1975. If Alioto was the embodiment of establishment power, Moscone presented himself as the people's champion. "It's time to take the decisions out of the secret rooms in the Fairmont, out of the secret rooms in Hillsborough, and the secret rooms in Marin County, and give them back to the people of San Francisco," he roared at one tumultuous campaign rally.

In some ways, Moscone and the outgoing mayor were strikingly similar. Both San Francisco natives were products of Italian families and Catholic schools. Both men were avid readers of literature and philosophy, and could quote the gospels and papal encyclicals in debates, although Moscone leaned more toward Saul Bellow and Bernard Malamud than to Dante. Both had a taste for good wine and food, and an eye for women.

But Moscone was more a man of the streets than Alioto. He was raised by a single mother in the Cow Hollow–Polk Gulch area, a colorfully scruffy neighborhood he later described as Runyonesque. His father was a movie-star-handsome drunk who careened from job to job as a garbageman, milk deliveryman, and San Quentin prison guard. When George was nine, Lee Moscone defied her Catholic upbringing and kicked out her roguish husband for good, going to work as a secretary at a car dealership and machine shop and finally at the Department of Motor Vehicles to support the two of them.

Lee Moscone's travails as a working mother made her son a lifelong battler for the underdog. "When I hear people today talking about single parents, women's rights, and tenants' rights, my mother did it all," he said years later. "I mean, she got chased out of one apartment house after another because she had a son. They always do it subtly by raising the rent. She worked all day and then on weekends as a clerk in a liquor store so I could have a good education. She just made every sacrifice in the world for me."

Young George learned about San Francisco by playing basketball in the city's parks. His talent on the court allowed him to cross turf lines and play with Irish, black, Chinese, and Latino kids. He was a high school basketball star at St. Ignatius, making the all-city team. Moscone worked his way through high school and college, taking jobs as a sports director at the parks. He helped pay his tuition at UC Hastings College of the Law in San Francisco by working as a school janitor alongside his friend and fellow law student Willie Brown, who dubbed the two of them "the Broom Brothers." While in law school, Moscone began dating Eugenia Bondanza, the sister of an elementary school classmate. Gina was small and delicately built, with big eyes that dominated her fine-boned features. Like Moscone, she was raised by a single mother, after her father died of cancer when she was eleven. While she was growing up, Gina planned on becoming a nun. But as soon as she started dating George, they both knew that they would marry.

Later, after two decades of marriage, Gina Moscone was asked if she had any regrets. Just one, she said. She wished that George had never gone into politics. A private woman, she resented the constant public demands on her husband. But she knew it was his calling.

Moscone was handsome and charming. Smoothly comfortable in his own skin, he had a gift for putting people at ease. "He was the most charismatic guy I've ever met," said Welch. "Guys loved him. Women loved him. I got to know people who went to school with him at S.I., when he was all-city. I remember this one guy telling me, 'Fourteen-year-old boys dream of having sex, but George *had* sex, and we all knew it. He was our god.'"

John Burton, his best friend since high school, opened the door to politics for Moscone when he introduced him to his older brother, Phil, the city's congressional power broker. Moscone became a rising star in the Burton machine, along with Willie Brown. The machine was powered by Phil's bare-knuckled ambition. But it was more about scoring victories for Burton's liberal constituencies—labor, minorities, gays, and environmentalists—than it was about delivering patronage and graft. "The Burton machine was based on ideology and public service," said

Art Agnos, who belonged to the rival Leo McCarthy machine but still admired the Burton operation's significant accomplishments. "It was all about making a difference in people's lives."

Moscone soon made it clear that his political career was rooted in deeply held progressive values. In 1965, not long after winning his first election to the board of supervisors, he announced that he was going to Mississippi with a task force of lawyers to help blacks register to vote—a mission that took physical courage in those days of bloody civil rights struggle. "If you've got to die, it's better than dying on a freeway," Moscone declared.

The following year, he was elected to the California State Senate, where his Democratic colleagues made the popular legislator their majority leader. Moscone proved himself a master vote getter, shepherd of progressive legislation, and worthy opponent of Governor Reagan—a man he loathed. While serving in Sacramento, Moscone helped create California's school lunch program. Later, with the help of Willie Brown, then the powerful Democratic whip in the state assembly, he pushed through bills that decriminalized the possession of modest amounts of marijuana and—to the everlasting gratitude of San Francisco's gay population—sex between consenting adults. Unafraid of taking controversial stands, Moscone fought to overturn the state death penalty. "I'd rather lose the damn election than twist my views to fit popular opinion," he once said.

In the spring of 1967, Moscone invited Don Peri, a teenager interested in the workings of government, to watch him in action on the Senate floor in Sacramento. The senate was hotly debating a bill to legalize abortion in California, and Peri—a fellow Catholic—was shocked to see Moscone stand up and argue for its passage. Later Moscone came over to the teenager and said quietly, "You and I know it's wrong, but that doesn't mean we can tell other people what to do."

WHEN MOSCONE ANNOUNCED HIS campaign for mayor in December 1974, he made clear that his goal was to redistribute power in the city—from downtown suites to the neighborhoods, where families were struggling to hang on against developers and real estate speculators. He also vowed to expand the democratization process that Alioto had begun at city hall, bringing gays, women, and more minorities into the halls of power once firmly controlled by the city's old Irish-Italian network.

Moscone's populist race was helped greatly by a new city law that clamped tight limits on mayoral campaign spending. In the previous mayoral race, Alioto had spent more than $600,000 to get reelected. But now each candidate was limited to $128,000, a level playing field that made it possible for Moscone to run without big corporate money and to cap individual donations at $100. The *Examiner* declared Moscone "the poorest candidate" in the crowded field, reporting that his only assets were his family home and a modest piece of rental property in suburban Antioch valued at $10,000. But in the people's election of 1975, that was no drawback.

Dianne Feinstein, running in the center as a good government candidate, was originally considered Moscone's toughest opponent because of her high political profile and the strong support she attracted from downtown business interests. But the new campaign law rendered her wealthy backers' deep pockets irrelevant. Instead Supervisor John Barbagelata, a West Portal realtor and gadfly critic of government spending, emerged on the right as Moscone's top adversary, knocking Feinstein out of the race in the November election and forcing a December runoff with his fellow Italian.

Barbagelata was the voice of old San Francisco: a conservative Catholic who was baffled and enraged by the new social currents flowing through his city. The father of eight was so devout, he remarked that "if the pope asked me to push a peanut with my nose down the middle of the street, I'd do it." He entered city politics in the 1960s to fight the spread of moral contamination in his city, and as supervisor he succeeded in banning bottomless dancing in North Beach clubs and in covering Carol Doda's blinking neon nipples on the marquee of the legendary stripper's Condor Club. In the 1970s, Barbagelata took aim at the rising gay peril. The Gay Freedom Day Parade, spilling out of the Castro and down Market Street in all its shameless exhibitionism, filled him with revulsion on behalf of his city. And when the board of supervisors proposed that city contractors open their hiring to gay job seekers, Barbagelata fumed that city hall had no right to force companies "to hire perverts."

ALARMED BY THE PROSPECT of four more years of antihomosexual fervor at city hall, gay activists rallied around Moscone, the man who had
legalized sodomy in California. Harvey Milk, a rising political star in the
Castro, urged gay voters to block Barbagelata. "I think he wants to be a
priest and not a mayor," said Milk.

The Moscone campaign was buoyed by strong support from gay, labor,
and civil rights groups, as well as neighborhood organizations fighting
the "Manhattanization" of San Francisco's skyline. But Moscone under-
estimated the lingering power of Barbagelata's traditional San Francisco.
The surprisingly tight runoff campaign divided the city down the middle: with the older, white districts west of Twin Peaks, along with the
upscale Marina and Pacific Heights firmly aligned with Barbagelata; and
the poorer, nonwhite, and newcomer neighborhoods such as Bayview–
Hunters Point, the Fillmore, the Castro, and Haight-Ashbury heavily
supporting Moscone. The race was as much a culture war as it was a
class war.

Barbagelata's campaign was fueled by a different kind of populist
rage: it was a revolt of San Francisco's middle-class home owners and
taxpayers, the city's financial bedrock. These families felt ripped off
by the city's powerful unions and the labor-friendly Burton machine,
and John Barbagelata was the voice of their resentment. San Francisco
needed a "businessman mayor" to make sure that people "get their money's worth," he told voters. And a good half of the electorate agreed.
With his blunt, no-nonsense manner and his lean, sharp-featured,
bespectacled good looks, Barbagelata resembled a trustworthy family
accountant—the kind of man who could balance the city's checkbook.

Election night on December 11 was an excruciating ordeal for
George Moscone, who was stunned that a conservative realtor had taken
him to the brink of defeat. It rattled his sense of San Francisco, a city
whose heart he thought he knew intimately. As the evening dragged on,
Moscone's early lead eroded steadily until the candidates were neck and
neck. Phil Burton, the master vote counter, was monitoring the election
results for Moscone in a boiler room at city hall, and the updates he
phoned in were filled with grim portents. As the candidate and his circle

of family, friends, and campaign aides huddled in his seventh-floor suite at the unglamorous San Franciscan Hotel on Market Street, he chain-smoked Viceroys, drank cognac, and stared at the TV while his mother rubbed the back of his neck.

Moscone was finally declared the victor late that night, squeaking by Barbagelata with a wafer-thin margin of 4,443 votes. His hotel suite erupted with cheers. "It's just like Kennedy!" one aide enthused, summoning up JFK's by-a-nose finish over Nixon in the 1960 presidential election. By then, the mayor-elect was wrung out. Minutes later, Moscone stood at the ballroom podium in front of his raucous supporters, his shirt drenched with sweat, wiping tears from his eyes.

Corey Busch, Moscone's young press aide, had been at the Ambassador Hotel in Los Angeles the night in June 1968 when Bobby Kennedy celebrated his final victory in his race for president. After Bobby was assassinated that night, Busch thought he would never work on another campaign. But Moscone breathed new life into the dispirited young politico. "He represented everything that was good about politics," said Busch.

Now, surveying the smoky, crowded ballroom at the San Franciscan, Busch marveled at the wide variety of urban energy packed into the room. "Some reporter later said it was the greatest cross section of San Franciscans ever assembled under one roof in the history of the city," he reminisced. "I was twenty-six years old, and I couldn't believe that we were actually going to be able to shape a major American city and make the changes we wanted to make."

Willie Brown had been in the political trenches much longer than Busch, but he too had a bedazzled, "pinch-me" look on his face that night. "Can you imagine George Moscone in city hall?" he kept saying out loud. "It's a whole new world."

At the victory podium, Moscone made a point of calling out to his gay supporters, who had delivered a critical block of voters in the close election. San Francisco, he proclaimed to loud cheers, is liberated territory—a haven that "allows with pleasure gay people walking the streets of the city with freedom from harassment."

But Moscone's state-of-the-art field operation could not have succeeded without two organizations that were beginning to make a major impact on San Francisco. "The two institutions that were most helpful in getting George elected were the Delancey Street Foundation and the Peoples Temple," said Richard Sklar, who became the city infrastructure's indispensable fix-it man under Moscone. "They each put hundreds of bodies on the streets during the campaign." Both organizations served society's rejects, and both were run by charismatic misfits. Delancey Street, a self-help community of addicts and ex-convicts, was founded by John Maher, a Bronx grade school dropout and ex-junkie with a Tammany Hall gift for street politics. The Peoples Temple, a renegade church that ministered to a flock of mostly black lost souls, was run by a more mysterious man, the Reverend Jim Jones.

John Maher and George Moscone had a genuine affection for each other, based on their shared values and spirited love of politics. In the end, Maher and his partner Mimi Silbert helped resurrect thousands of lives and enriched the city's soul. The only person Maher irreparably harmed was himself, when he fell back into addiction and could not pull himself back to shore. Moscone's relationship with Jim Jones was a much different story. What began as a political marriage of convenience ended in unspeakable horror.

Even in the midst of all the jubilation that election night in December, a sad note played somewhere in Moscone's heart. A physically affectionate father, Moscone clasped the face of his fourteen-year-old son Christopher in his hands and made the boy look directly at him, the way he always did when he had something important to say to his kids. "Promise me one thing," Moscone said, peering into Christopher's eyes.

"I'm thinking, 'Anything—just let me go,'" remembered Christopher Moscone years later.

"Promise me you'll never go into politics," Moscone told his son on the night of his greatest political triumph.

It wasn't until he was older that Christopher fully understood. Because for people like his father, politics demands everything. "Because you're all in. And it eventually killed him."

HERB CAEN CALLED MOSCONE'S populist victory a "bloodless civil war." Dick Nolan, the *Examiner's* political columnist, wrote that "a bell tolls for [San Francisco's] Tories," declaring the election "a turning point between the old 'in's' and the newly awakened neighborhood 'out's.'"

Moscone, caught up in the excitement of the moment, announced that he had a sweeping ambition for San Francisco: to make it a beacon of tolerance and enlightenment to the world. "I will only be satisfied," he said, "if in four—or hopefully eight—years, I can not only change the face of San Francisco, but change the soul of San Francisco, and, with its extraordinary international authority, [make it] a catalyst for conversion for the rest of the country, if not the world."

At his inauguration in the city hall rotunda—a ceremony stripped of the pomp and circumstance of Alioto's ascension—Moscone dedicated his administration to serving the public instead of private interests. "My door will be open, and, more importantly, I will be inside," he said, a line that electrified the audience but was greeted grim faced by the outgoing mayor, who was known for his back-door deals and his jaunts around the state and country in search of higher office. As if to underline the upstairs-downstairs transition, Alioto stripped the mayor's office of the Louis XIV treaty table and high-backed chair, the gold candelabrums, and other decorative finery that he had installed, leaving Moscone to scavenge for old furniture from the city hall basement.

A new era of "small is beautiful" government was dawning in California, with conservative tax revolts like Proposition 13 placing strict curbs on government spending and a rising generation of Democratic leaders led by recently elected governor Jerry Brown trying to balance social needs with fiscal realities. Moscone immediately signaled that his administration, like Brown's, would be "lean and mean."

At forty-six, the tanned, trim six-foot-one mayor projected an energetic image. He dispensed with Alioto's official limousine and chauffeur and zipped around town in his aging maroon Alfa Romeo, waving to startled citizens at stoplights. Sometimes he imposed on staff members, many of them young and long haired, to drive him to civic events in their even more battered cars. The young aides prized their time with their affable, quick-witted boss. But sometimes they prayed that it wasn't him calling when their home phones rang on Sundays.

"It was not unusual for me to get a call from George on Sunday to play some basketball on the courts at Nineteenth and Vicente," Busch recalled. "Even if I didn't want to, hey, he was the boss. He'd show up down there in a T-shirt and shorts, and we'd start playing a pickup game with some guys. He was a competitive guy, so he's backing into guys and playing hard. He was in his forties, definitely the oldest guy there, but that didn't stop him. One day this young guy looks at him and says, 'Man, you play some rough ball. And, hey, you look a lot like our mayor.' George says, 'I am.'"

Moscone always carried around "a little bit of that street thing," said Busch, even as mayor. Aides had to stop him from getting into fistfights in restaurants when drunken customers' taunting grew too personal. Before his election, Moscone got into a brawl at a party when someone called Willie Brown a "nigger." On another occasion, Moscone and his police bodyguard Jim Molinari were having drinks late one night in a North Beach restaurant when two yahoos from Los Angeles began heckling the mayor, berating him for coddling gays and accusing him of being gay himself. The mayor jumped up and, moving toward the two men, prepared to explain San Francisco values to them. "Sit down, Mayor!" Molinari barked, with visions of ugly headlines looming before him. The cop calmed the situation by telling the two men, "Keep your mouths shut or you're going to jail."

Moscone recognized that he was operating in a new era of Spartan political life, but he lacked Jerry Brown's monastic temperament. A San Francisco sensualist, he gloried in the bounties of his city, roaming the town nearly every night—seldom with his wife, who hid at home from the clatter of social functions—and often in the company of Willie Brown, who played Sammy Davis Jr. to his Frank Sinatra in their version of the Rat Pack. Moscone loved jazz, he loved scotch, he loved North Beach restaurants. There was no more satisfying meal in life, he said, than Dungeness crab with a mayonnaise-mustard dip, a plate of fettuccine, and a good bottle of chilled wine. He couldn't quit his cigarettes, and he couldn't give up the black women. And although he never managed to save any money from his public salaries, he always found a way to dress elegantly, drinking scotch in the dressing rooms at Wilkes Bashford while the exclusive clothier displayed his hand-sewn Italian wares.

"Every day of his mayorship, George told me, 'Man, you gotta be mayor. This is like being king.' And we really had a ball," recalled Willie Brown, who was a rising power in Sacramento during Moscone's city hall tenure but still found time to enjoy the San Francisco nightlife with his friend. "He loved everything about this city. He was indigenous. He *was* the city."

While Moscone immediately took to the job he called the greatest in the world—running the city he loved—his administration was embattled from the very start. John Barbagelata proved a bitter loser, charging voter fraud after his narrow defeat and sending 150 of his supporters marching into the voter registrar's office to inspect ballots. Barbagelata demanded a recount, and a stormy air hung over the city as the tedious process unfolded. The recount awarded Barbagelata only seventy-three more votes, not enough to bring him victory. But even after Moscone was sworn in as mayor, his resentful opponent refused to give up.

Barbagelata thought that Moscone was delivering San Francisco to a horde of barbarians: outsiders who did not share the city's traditional values. And his feverish suspicions focused on the heavily poor and black congregation of Peoples Temple, which was shifting its base from rural Redwood Valley to San Francisco at the time of the election. Barbagelata was convinced that the sketchy church had stolen the election for Moscone by busing in nonresidents and driving them from precinct to precinct to vote. As Peoples Temple cast a long shadow over San Francisco, it became clear that Barbagelata had good reason to be suspicious.

The Moscone administration found itself ensnared in a culture war that pitted it against not only relentless political foes like Barbagelata but also the old-boy power structure of the San Francisco Police Department. The SFPD grudge against Moscone was personal. "George and I grew up with a lot of guys who became cops," recalled John Burton, "and later on they'd say shit like, 'You two guys are nigger lovers,' or 'You two guys are fags.' They were kind of old-fashioned." The force was full of cops who thought Moscone was a traitor; that he'd sold out their city to the freaks and fairies who were driving out families like their own.

San Francisco's new mayor made it as clear as a blazing siren light that he was going to shake up the police department when he hired Charles Gain as his police chief. The soft-spoken Texan, who called himself a "sociological cop," was known as one of the most liberal law enforcement officials in the country. As chief of Oakland's historically redneck police force, he eased the city's explosive racial tensions by reaching out to the black community. Later he served as a deputy to innovative, gay-friendly San Francisco sheriff Richard Hongisto, who was more interested in rehabilitating his prisoners than breaking them.

Gain wasted no time in challenging the SFPD's rosary-and-billy-club culture. He outraged veteran cops by taking down the big American flag in the chief's office, explaining that it was an overly zealous display of patriotism, and replacing the flag with a potted plant. He banned drinking on the job, a longtime tradition on the force that reinforced its brawling Irish image. He announced his support for District Attorney Joseph Freitas Jr.'s hands-off policy on streetwalkers, effectively decriminalizing prostitution in the city—a policy that had been lobbied for by the chief's ally Margo St. James. Gain also encouraged gay cops on the force to come out, insisting that such honesty "will help everyone." And he ordered the SFPD's black-and-white patrol cars to be repainted powder blue—a move that he thought would soften the department's authoritarian image.

The police force reeled under Gain's social experimentation. Cops muttered that their new leader was a flaming queen. They called him "Gloria Gain" behind his back. They took their complaints to the *Examiner,* long known as the cops' newspaper. "It's disgusting," one anonymous officer told the paper. "First Gain called us alcoholics, and now he's calling us fruits," said another.

Gain refused to ease up, even after senior police officials began resigning in protest. "I don't look for controversy," he said, "but change has to come."

As word spread that San Francisco was a wide-open town, hookers began flooding downtown streets. Hoteliers and convention bureau officials lobbied for a police crackdown—an ironic turn of events, since it was a wide-open secret that San Francisco's tourism business was boosted greatly by the local sex trade. But the new wave of prostitutes was apparently not up to the local convention industry's standards. "If she is black or if she is garishly dressed, she is more likely to be stopped than if she is elegantly dressed," explained a local prostitute-rights activist who worked with Margo St. James.

Moscone finally caved to the downtown business pressure and ordered Gain to reverse his tolerant policy on prostitution. But for the most part, the mayor stood squarely by his beleaguered police chief. This became particularly difficult in the fall of 1977, when Gain became embroiled in another only-in-San-Francisco tempest. On the evening of October 28, Chief Gain, caught up in the festive spirit of the Hooker's

Ball, showed up at the libidinous event, which drew ten thousand people that year to the Civic Auditorium. To compound his sin, Gain—who had the long, somber face and plastered-down hair of a country undertaker—was photographed at the ball by the *Examiner,* wedged between a madly grinning St. James and a woman identified only as "Wonder Whore," who displayed a dildo instead of a laser gun on her belt.

As the police commission later determined, Chief Gain had admirably maintained "officer-like conduct" throughout the evening. But this was of little consolation to the Barbagelata crowd, which saw it as one more sign that its city was going to hell in black lace panties. Quentin Kopp, a curmudgeonly lawyer following in Barbagelata's footsteps on the board of supervisors, demanded that Moscone fire Gain. The police chief's appearance at the Hooker's Ball, Supervisor Kopp huffed, was "too much even for a tolerant city like San Francisco . . . What a spectacle for the children of San Francisco: their police chief reveling with self-professed whores and their associates." But Moscone shrugged off the sound and fury. Gain's track record as a crime fighter "is a far better barometer of the chief's performance," he said, "than a photograph at a social event."

Moscone further antagonized the police force by pushing hard for an out-of-court settlement of the long, bitter civil rights lawsuit against the department. And in February 1978 the mayor again riled the SFPD by ordering a halt to its racial profiling practices. "Stopping and frisking people because they are black in a white neighborhood is simply not going to be tolerated," he announced, calling such "police state" tactics "unconstitutional." Moscone's order followed an ugly incident in the Richmond district when police pulled over a successful realtor named Paul Sing after apparently deciding that a Chinese-American had no right to drive a Mercedes sports coupe. Sing was frisked twice, with a gun pointed to his head, before the cops finally let him go.

THE SNARLING ABOUT MOSCONE grew louder in police stations. Cops passed around eyebrow-raising stories about him. Not only was the mayor soft on crime, they said, but he himself was an outlaw. They talked about weed, cocaine, black hookers. The stories went back a long time, and they had popped up during the campaign. On the eve of his inauguration, Moscone had sat down with a *Chronicle* reporter, telling him that he was finally "ready to talk about my personal weaknesses." But all he was willing to reveal was that he had sampled pot before introducing the state bill to decriminalize it, because "I wanted to be an authority to some extent"—an explanation undoubtedly greeted with hilarity by anyone who knew Moscone's deep knowledge of cannabis. As mayor, he pledged, scotch and soda would be "good enough for me."

Moscone swerved sharply in the interview to avoid any discussion of his extramarital life. But the *Chronicle* helpfully reminded readers in a sidebar about an "unhappy incident in Moscone's past" when he collided with another car in the parking lot outside a Chinese restaurant in Sacramento called Frank Fat's. Police reported that Moscone smelled like a bar and was accompanied by a young black woman whom the politician had kindly agreed to drive home.

The restaurateurs and bartenders who presided over the city's nightlife knew that Moscone kept the party going as mayor, often sharing the fun with Willie Brown. "The two of them were with a black woman in an alley at two in the morning at some restaurant in North Beach," said Ed Moose, the legendary proprietor of the Washington Square Bar & Grill, the most popular watering hole in the city for the political and literary crowds. "That whole gang of people, when they got together, they felt pretty hip. John Burton was part of that gang too. They were all using marijuana and cocaine."

Herb Caen snickered that Moscone meant "Big Fly" in Italian, making it all a matter of ribald fun rather than career-ending tragedy. Moscone knew his city well enough to tell one press conference that rumors about his personal life "won't rattle San Francisco's teacups." As he reminded the *Chronicle* reporter, "All of us, we're all so terribly human." He was not the only good Catholic in town with a Madonna at home and whores on the side.

In the end, most San Franciscans with an opinion on the subject thought that the mayor's personal life was between him and his family. George and Gina had worked out some kind of church-and-state separation. The family was holy ground, and Moscone was utterly devoted to his four children, showing up for their games and performances, spoiling his two daughters and straightening out his two sons. The two boys, Christopher and Jonathan, never forgot the morning ritual when their father came into their room before school and brushed their unruly hair, breathing hard through his nose as he flattened the every-which-way sprouts. Once Archbishop Joe McGucken was called in to help the Moscone marriage through an especially stressful period. But the couple managed the rough strife of marriage largely on their own, behind closed doors.

What George did outside the home was his business. But Gina was adamant that it never interfere with the family. "Saying that everything about him is public is something I can't buy," she said in one of her rare interviews. "Not when the family is involved."

Moscone came to feel he was invisible in his late-night romps through the city. And he largely was—exposing and shaming was just not part of San Francisco's culture, even as city politics grew more bitterly partisan. But there was one group that kept a close eye on the mayor: the city's cops, centurions of the embattled moral order. They watched the mayor at play, and they filed it all away for the right time. Moscone's antics made some of them sick, like vice cop Joe Ryan. "He's so high and mighty," sneered Ryan, "and he's pulling these capers and getting away with it."

Some cops had urged Barbagelata to use Moscone's sexual escapades against him during the campaign, but he refused out of concern for Moscone's family. Barbagelata grew to despise Moscone, but the men's families went way back together. Barbagelata's brother attended St. Ignatius with Moscone. One of Moscone's daughters dated one of Barbagelata's sons. Barbagelata was old school, and he believed you don't do certain things to another man's family, no matter how passionate the feud.

"My dad knew everything about George Moscone: the prostitutes, the drugs," said son Paul Barbagelata, who today runs the family realty business. "And he was told to bring it out, but he didn't. He was just being a stand-up guy for Gina's sake. In his mind, George was dirty, but he would never say that in public."

WHILE HE STEERED CLEAR of Moscone's personal life, John Barbagelata remained a constant political thorn in the mayor's side, using his platform on the board of supervisors to bottle up Moscone's initiatives and frustrate his efforts to guide the city in a new direction. Moscone was worn down by the raw grind of city politics, which struck him as much pettier than the legislative give-and-take in Sacramento. "He had guys like Kopp and Barbagelata who every morning couldn't wait to figure out how to set the next bonfire," said Busch. "They harassed us on everything we did."

In the spring of 1977, Barbagelata's protracted guerilla war on the Moscone administration escalated into a bold frontal assault. Moscone's implacable foe succeeded in putting an initiative on the local ballot that would force the mayor, the DA, and the sheriff—San Francisco's liberal triumvirate—to run for office all over again in November, two years before their terms expired. It was a deft saber thrust on the part of Barbagelata, who had never accepted his defeat.

The campaign to fight Barbagelata's Proposition B, however, had an electrifying effect on the listless Moscone administration. The humiliating prospect of a recall brought the mayor to life. "Nobody cuts short my term," an infuriated Moscone told his staff, finally showing the sharp-elbowed drive he'd learned on the city's basketball courts. Moscone's activist base rallied to his side, and he stockpiled a $150,000 campaign war chest with the help of Democratic millionaires like developer Walter Shorenstein and Levi Strauss & Co. board chairman Walter Haas Jr. The solicitation of downtown support was a surprising move for the populist Moscone. But when downtown power brokers tried to extract a quid pro quo for their financial support, Moscone rebuffed them.

One day during the Proposition B campaign, Moscone was summoned to lunch in the Bank of America's downtown black tower to meet with chief executive A. W. "Tom" Clausen. Moscone brought along his young, bearded, long-haired aide Josh Getlin, who was outfitted in a rumpled sport coat and clashing tie that could only have dismayed the stylish mayor. The two were ushered into the private dining room on the top floor of the bank's headquarters, where, over drinks, Clausen and his men quickly got to the point. They knew that Moscone was on the ropes. If the bankers came to his rescue, could they count on him to block rent control in the city? It was a battle that the San Francisco business community had made a top priority.

"I could never promise you that," said Moscone, who never forgot how his mother had been treated by landlords. "There are a lot of people who have to be heard from. They're the people who rent homes and work in this city." It was the kind of stand that made young aides like Getlin fall all over again for their boss.

On August 2, 1977, Moscone rolled to a crushing victory, beating Proposition B by a two-to-one margin. It was a huge turning point in his mayoral reign. He finally cast off the shadow that had been hanging over his administration ever since his squeaky victory over Barbagelata in 1975. "I think George took that close election in '75 personally," said John Burton. "It came as a real shock to him." But now he had swamped his nemesis. Moscone celebrated that night by taking his family out to dine on roast duck at elegant Fleur de Lys: the first time he had eaten with them since the frantic recall battle started three months earlier.

The 1977 election was a major turning point for San Francisco in another key way. Voters approved a new way of electing supervisors: by district instead of citywide. District elections for supervisors—long a dream of neighborhood activists—brought in a new, more grassroots board in November, since candidates did not have to raise as much money as they did when they had to campaign throughout the city. The most dynamic player on the new board was the Castro district's new representative, Harvey Milk.

Milk, a glad-handing, New York Jewish force of nature, had turned his funky Castro Street camera store into the boiling eye of the city's gay hurricane. Until the 1977 election, Milk had lost so many campaigns for office that he joked he was the gay Harold Stassen, the sad-sack Republican who couldn't stop himself from running for president every four years. But district elections, which allowed Milk to wave his rainbow flag high, finally opened the door for him to city hall. He won office by beating a rival gay candidate—an establishment-backed goody-goody named Rick Stokes—and none other than Terry "Kayo" Hallinan.

Hallinan, whose father, Vince, had instilled in his sons enlightened views about homosexuality, found himself utterly charmed by his ebullient opponent. "Harvey wasn't easy to run against because there wasn't much we didn't agree on," recalled Hallinan. "As the campaign went on, we ended up becoming friends."

Michael Stepanian, who served as Hallinan's campaign manager, also wound up falling for Milk. "Early in the campaign, Terry and I decided we'd better check out this guy Harvey," recalled Stepanian. "So we go to this event where he and Stokes are giving speeches. Stokes is gay, but a very straight guy. He gets up and says, 'I'm very concerned about Harvey Milk. One time I was outside his camera shop, and a man and woman walked by with their child, and Harvey used a profane word.' Then Stokes says, 'I don't want to be referred to as the gay candidate for supervisor. I want to be known as the candidate who happens to be gay.' Polite clapping ensues. Then Harvey gets up. 'Fuck that shit, mother-fucker! I'm gay!' The place went wild with screaming. I looked over at Terry and said, 'How the hell we gonna beat this guy?' I loved Harvey from the start, just loved him."

Moscone, who had his political ups and downs with Milk in the past, also ended up embracing the new supervisor. The mayor and Milk—who saw his gay rights crusade as part of a much broader progressive agenda—formed a powerful duo. With Milk shaking up the board of supervisors and taking on Moscone enemies like Quentin Kopp, the mayor seemed newly energized. In April 1978 Moscone signed a land-mark gay rights law that had been pushed through the board by Milk. The two beaming men were pictured in the next day's newspapers shak-ing hands at the signing ceremony.

As Moscone settled into his new groove as mayor, he began winning over some staunch critics. *Examiner* columnist Kevin Starr sat down with Moscone at a restaurant for a three-hour interview and made the extraordinary gesture of apologizing to the mayor for being too hard on him. Moscone, in an expansive mood after a round of vodka on the rocks and Chardonnay with dinner, gave his most heartfelt defense of the changes he was bringing to city hall. "Believe me, I'm no leftish ideologue," he told Starr. "Like you, I was raised in the Catholic school system in this city. From both the Gospel and papal encyclicals on social and economic justice, weren't we both taught that people who were bit-terly antiblack or anti-Chicano or antipoor were jerks, just plain jerks? I never could stand racism or indifference to poverty. That doesn't make me a lefty ideologue. It makes me an ordinary American.

"When I first tried to break into politics in this city," he continued, "it was the dispossessed who welcomed me. They were getting short shrift from a lot of the fat cats in office. I'm not going to abandon the poor now that it has suddenly become fashionable to sound hard-line and ultrarealistic about social goals. That would make a farce of my previous beliefs.

"Sure, I brought new sorts of people into city government—blacks, Asians, Chicanos, gays. But look around you: I brought them into government because they constitute a significant portion of the people who are now here, committed to making San Francisco a decent, viable place. What would you have a mayor to do, suppress the new San Francisco to satisfy the old?"

It was a remarkable expression of Moscone's core values, and it could have served as an eloquent basis for his reelection campaign. As Moscone neared the last year of his term, it seemed liked the political momentum had shifted his way. But the forces unleashed by the Moscone and Milk revolution were waiting to devour them.

Legendary San Francisco attorney Vincent Hallinan—flanked in this 1932 news photo by his beautiful future spouse, Vivian (left), and the wife of his notorious client Frank Egan—epitomized the city's world of Hammett-like criminal intrigue and brawling politics.

By the 1960s, thanks to the pugilism of pioneering progressives like the Hallinans, San Franciso's old Irish-Catholic order began to give way to a new spirit of sublime anarchy. In January 1967, Allen Ginsberg—a combination of holy man and Jewish mother for the new cultural movement—celebrated the dawn of the future at the Human Be-In festival in Golden Gate Park. *Steve Rees/Associated Press 1967.*

Radical hippie attorney Tony Serra learned his combative courtroom style from the master, Vincent Hallinan. Floating in an acid reverie, Serra enjoyed the vibes at a city hall rally held to promote his 1971 mayoral campaign on the Platypus Party ticket. *Copyright © Michael Zagaris.*

The Diggers, fronted by the roguish Emmett Grogan (flashing the peace sign), wanted to turn San Francisco into a "free city," unplugged from the capitalist grid of 9-to-5 serfdom. *"Diggers,"* GAP0073, *photographer Gene Anthony, © www.wolfgangsvault.com.*

While the Diggers tried to care for the runaway teens flooding the city during the 1967 Summer of Love, it was a renegade minister named Edward "Larry" Beggs (wearing eyeglasses) who defied the law by setting up a shelter for the young refugees from middle America. *Photo courtesy of Edward Beggs.*

Dr. David Smith realized that his neighborhood, the Haight-Ashbury, was becoming ground zero for the youth revolution. But until he opened a free clinic in 1967 for the street children, San Francisco's medical establishment turned a cold shoulder to their suffering. *Copyright © Liz Hafalia/San Francisco Chronicle/Corbis.*

The *San Francisco Chronicle*'s beloved columnist Herb Caen weaved a fantasy city in which all San Franciscans wanted to live. According to Caen, those locals who turned up their noses at the hippie invasion were guilty of the ultimate San Francisco sin: they were "bores." *Copyright © Brant Ward/San Francisco Chronicle/Corbis.*

Before she rocketed to rock stardom in 1967, Janis Joplin belonged to the Haight-Ashbury. Everyone knew her, or knew someone who had slept with her. *Photo copyright © Baron Wolman.*

Fueled by the rising power of rock music, a new San Francisco social support system emerged. In 1975, rock impresario Bill Graham (far right) called on friends like Francis Ford Coppola and Marlon Brando to stage a benefit concert for the city's after-school programs. *Copyright © Michael Zagaris.*

The wild, gender-contorting Cockettes burst onto the San Francisco stage on New Year's Eve 1970. "We're just chicks with cocks," explained one troupe member to the press. *Copyright © Michael Zagaris.*

For a soaring moment, Moby Grape was San Francisco's most powerful band. The group's tumultuous decline mirrored the city's own growing turmoil. *Courtesy of Sony Music Entertainment.*

Anton LaVey, high priest of the Church of Satan (shown here in an occult ceremony with his wife, Diane), held a strange allure for women, including actress Jayne Mansfield and future Manson follower Susan "Sexy Sadie" Atkins. LaVey was just a carny showman at heart, but his gothic cult reflected the dark side of the City of Love. *Copyright © Bettmann/Corbis.*

By the mid-1970s, Lucifer was rising in San Francisco as the city fell under the spell of hard drugs, guns, and radical violence. Kidnapped in 1974 by the SLA, an underground gang with delusions of revolutionary grandeur, young socialite Patty Hearst became the eye of a boiling media storm as she seemed to join forces with her captors. After she was finally arrested, Hearst went on trial for her complicity with the group in 1976. *Associated Press.*

Mayor Joseph Alioto—who struggled to "manage the revolution" roaring through San Francisco in the 1960s and '70s—fielded questions from the press after a pre-dawn police raid on May 1, 1974, finally ended the reign of racial terror known as the Zebra murders. *Copyright © Bettmann/Corbis.*

In 1977, George Moscone (right), the city's new, progressive mayor, rewarded Peoples Temple leader Jim Jones (left) for his decisive help in winning the mayoral race by appointing him to the city's housing commission. It was a pact with the devil that would later haunt Moscone. *Copyright © Clem Albers/San Francisco Chronicle/Corbis.*

Inspired by the militancy of the black power movement, a new wave of young Chinese activists such as Rose Pak, pictured here in 1977, began to demand a place at the head table for their long ignored community. Over three decades later, Pak and Brown helped engineer the ascension of San Francisco's first Chinese-American mayor, Ed Lee. *Copyright © Joseph Rosenthal/ San Francisco Chronicle/Corbis.*

After George Moscone took over city hall, a diverse generation of new leaders began to challenge San Francisco's Irish-Catholic hierarchy. Willie Brown, who rose from the streets of the Fillmore district to become California's powerful speaker of the assembly, high-stepped it at a 1978 fashion show put on by his clothier friend Wilkes Bashford. *Copyright © John O'Hara/San Francisco Chronicle/Corbis.*

Supervisor Harvey Milk (wearing tie), the whirl-wind behind the city's gay revolution, celebrated the twenty-fourth birthday of his aide Cleve Jones (wearing eyeglasses) in October 1978. Weeks later, Milk was dead. *Copyright © Rink Foto 1978.*

Supervisor Dan White is taken into custody after assassinating Mayor George Moscone and Supervisor Harvey Milk in city hall on November 27, 1978. White, a former cop who seethed with the bitter resentments felt by many traditional San Franciscans, was greeted like a hero by some members of the police department. *Copyright © John Storey/San Francisco Chronicle/Corbis.*

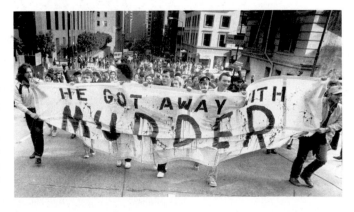

Dianne Feinstein (left), at a press conference following the assassinations, took over as mayor during the city's darkest days since the Great Earthquake of 1906. Though she lacked Moscone and Milk's progressive spark, Feinstein gave the shaken city the stable leadership it needed to absorb the tumultuous changes. *Copyright © Bettmann/Corbis.*

Fiery rioting erupted after Dan White received a shockingly lenient manslaughter verdict in 1979. When he was released from prison in January 1984, after serving just five years for the carnage at city hall, White again sparked angry protests like this one. *Copyright © Susan Gilbert/San Francisco Chronicle/Corbis.*

In the 1980s, the San Francisco 49ers' legendary duo—coach Bill Walsh and quarterback Joe Montana—brought a blaze of glory to a city in desperate need of resurrection. *Copyright © Michael Zagaris.*

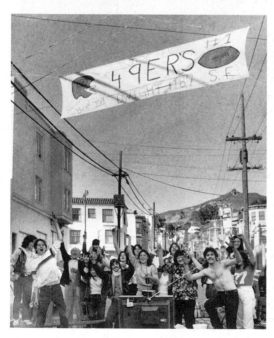

Fans poured into the streets on January 25, 1982—still celebrating the day after the 49ers won their first Super Bowl. As Mayor Feinstein rode in the raucous victory parade, she felt the shroud finally begin to lift: "I saw with my own eyes what a team can do for a city." *Copyright © John O'Hara/San Francisco Chronicle/Corbis.*

The terrifying AIDS epidemic that began scything its way through San Francisco in the early 1980s could have sparked a new wave of civic panic and fury. Instead—led by gay activists and by courageous health workers like Dr. Paul Volberding, cofounder of San Francisco General Hospital's pioneering AIDS ward—San Francisco became a model of compassion. *Copyright © Roger Ressmeyer/Corbis.*

24

INSIDE MAN

DAVID REUBEN—A SHORT, scrappy investigator with the kind of commanding beak that looked like he enjoyed sticking it in people's business—leaned back in his chair in the district attorney's office, nursing a cup of jailhouse java. Reuben listened with growing intensity as a middle-aged couple named Al and Jeannie Mills unraveled a jaw-dropping story about their lives in Jim Jones's peculiar church. The Millses were the kind of homespun, *American Gothic*–looking people you wouldn't glance at twice on the streets. But if 10 percent of what they were saying was true, Reuben figured, this case was going to rock the city—and the tremors would radiate far and wide.

Reuben had been recruited by Joe Freitas after he took over the DA's office in the 1975 liberal electoral sweep. Like Moscone, Freitas was a Kennedyesque Catholic politician with wavy-haired, Mediterranean good looks. Raised in a Portuguese family in the Central Valley, Freitas had served in all the stations of the liberal cross, including the National Urban League and Common Cause, before running for San Francisco DA at the age of thirty-six. Brimming with youthful self-confidence and political ambition, the new district attorney created a special prosecutions unit, filling it with young "red hots"—as Reuben described himself and his gung-ho colleagues. Freitas promised his mod squad a free hand in going after city corruption. "He told us there were no holds barred:

dirty cops, dirty politicians, payoffs," recalled Reuben. "Joe said, 'I don't care who it is, you go after them.'"

Freitas recruited crusading lawyers and investigators from all over the country for his new unit. Reuben and his crew came in with guns blazing, targeting the deep corruption in the San Francisco police force, including payoffs to cops by the skin trade moguls in North Beach. But Reuben soon found that the San Francisco justice establishment was more impregnable than he had imagined.

Coming from Chicago, where he had broken in as an investigator for the state attorney's office, pursuing corruption in Mayor Richard Daley's permanent regime, Reuben thought he had seen it all. But the San Francisco cop culture proved an even tougher nut to crack. "I thought that coming from Chicago, I knew old-boy's networks," he said, "but this was really something out here. It's a true old-boy's network. All the cops and prosecutors know each other, they're all friends and family, they all went to the same parochial schools. And here we all come into the DA's office: we were all in our twenties, and we're all ballbusters. I mean, I took on the Daley machine. We didn't care, we were going to investigate every-body. Well, it turns out that you don't do that in San Francisco—not unless you have the inside support. And I'm Jewish, from Chicago. So I was more outside than you can ever imagine."

By the time that Al and Jeannie Mills walked into his small office at the hall of justice in early 1977, Reuben and his team were beginning to feel demoralized. They had won some minor victories in their campaign against police corruption, but they were feeling increasingly isolated—not just within the hall of justice, where police inspectors feared and hated them, but within the DA's office itself, which was bitterly divided over Freitas's progressive reign. But the Peoples Temple investigation could make up for all the frustrations, Reuben realized. It was the kind of case that could make an investigator's career.

The Millses, who defected from the Peoples Temple in 1976, told Reuben and his team that Jim Jones was a violent, drug-crazed des-pot. They accused him of ordering the murders of disaffected members and subjecting others to savage beatings, including their sixteen-year-old daughter, who was whipped so severely, according to Al, "her butt looked like hamburger." The couple—who had changed their names from Elmer and Deanna Mertle to evade temple enforcers—told the investigators that Jones forced members to turn over their property and possessions to the church and confiscated their welfare and Social Security checks. They said Jones had also built his organization into a potent political machine, manipulating elections and politicians and working his way into the inner circles of power in San Francisco.

Reuben and his colleagues immediately recognized how explosive the Millses' charges were. "At the time, Jim Jones was an acknowledged civic leader," recalled Reuben. "I mean, he was the Second Coming in this city, bringing together black and white, rich and poor. He had presidents and governors and congressmen kissing his ring. And Joe Freitas was one of those people."

Reuben and the chief of the special prosecutions unit, a former US prosecutor named Bob Graham, girded their loins and walked into their boss's office to present the accusations against the Peoples Temple. As Reuben and Graham itemized the charges to Freitas and his number two man, Danny Weinstein, the room grew tense. "We lay it all out, and you could've heard a pin drop," Reuben said. "And then Joe looks at us and says, 'What, are you guys nuts?'"

Freitas heatedly pointed out to his special prosecutions team that people walked into the DA's office all the time with wild charges and personal grudges. "You guys can't just buy this stuff," Freitas admonished them.

Reuben and Graham were incensed. The hard-charging, windmill-tilting DA who had hired them—and told them they had carte blanche—was now suggesting that they back off what could be the hottest case they'd ever worked. They immediately knew what was going down. They'd read the newspapers and knew all about the furious allegations from the Barbagelata camp: that Jim Jones and his zombie flock had stolen the election for Moscone, and had worked hard for Freitas too.

"We were pissed," Reuben recalled later. "It was too dynamic for us not to dig into. All the names mentioned—Willie Brown, Dianne Feinstein, George Moscone—the whole gang was in there, I'm sure. And, of course, it was obvious to us—we're not idiots—Joe was in the middle of the thing. He knew that if we started doing this thing, *his* career might be affected."

Freitas was too politically savvy to simply shut down the Peoples Temple investigation. He knew that his angry investigators' suspicions could wind up in the press. So he gave his special team just enough leash to quietly look into the Millses' accusations. And to make sure that Reuben and Graham did not dig too deeply, Freitas appointed a young deputy named Tim Stoen as his liaison on the case.

REUBEN DID NOT KNOW much about Stoen. The deputy DA, who wore horn-rimmed glasses and three-piece suits, was a straitlaced loner. "He was a nerdy kind of guy," Reuben recalled. "Very bright, well spoken. We thought he was one of us, a reformer. But we joked about it, because he seemed *too* idealistic. He really wasn't friendly with anybody, just did his own thing."

As Reuben and his team dug deeper into the Millses' hair-raising stories about the Peoples Temple, the allegations were checking out. Interviewing other defectors and anxious relatives of temple members, the investigators soon learned how fearful these people were of reprisals from Jones's security guards—all of whom, Reuben discovered, had long rap sheets. Reuben promised his witnesses that he would protect their anonymity. But when he and his colleagues casually referred to their partner on the case, Deputy District Attorney Tim Stoen, the witnesses looked stunned. "*Tim Stoen?*" said one defector to Reuben, with panic in his eyes. "He's Jim Jones's top legal advisor."

A chill ran up Reuben's spine when he heard this. Afterward he and Bob Graham stumbled in a daze over to a cop bar across the street from the hall of justice, to compare notes. What the hell was going on? The question hung over them like a noose as they hunched over their drinks. "So now we're figuring, Is Stoen a plant? Does Freitas know who he is, or did this guy just weasel his way in? Does this all go back to Jones? Even before this, we didn't know who to trust in the office. But now we're really paranoid, because we don't know who's calling the shots."

The two investigators marched into Freitas's office to confront their boss. "We blew up," recalled Reuben. "We said, 'What's going on here? Are we being made patsies in this whole thing?'"

Freitas acted surprised. "He said, 'Are you guys sure?' And this and that, like he didn't know anything about Stoen." But the investigators realized that Stoen was far too cozy with their boss for him not to have known.

Joe Freitas would later tell the press he had no idea that Tim Stoen was Jones's right-hand man when he hired him; that he had simply plucked his resumé out of the slush pile. But in truth, the Peoples Temple, which had contributed money and campaigned for Freitas, engineered Stoen's insertion into the DA's office as a political reward for its efforts. And in a brazen move to cover up the voter fraud committed by the temple during the 1975 election, Freitas put the temple's lawyer in charge of the investigation. In doing so, he ensured that San Francisco would never find out who'd really won the mayoral election. Stoen brought in Peoples Temple clerical volunteers to help with his politically sensitive probe. The foxes had free run of the henhouse, and they left only feathers.

Three years later, after the name Jim Jones had gone down in infamy, state and federal investigators finally began looking into the shady election. When they asked for all the rosters showing who voted, the city's deputy registrar of voters went searching for the records in three locked vaults where they were kept. All the records were missing.

After they found out about Stoen, Reuben and Graham began taking their files home at night, no longer sure that they could protect the confidentiality of their Peoples Temple witnesses, some of whom feared for their lives. The investigators' suspicions were well founded. Stoen, it turned out, was literally a sleeper in the DA's office. He often spent the night there, though he had a residence on Page Street, giving him free access to the office's most sensitive documents for almost a year. Stoen and his wife, Grace, whom he had brought into the temple, enjoyed "a free romp through the place after hours," one source reported. Freitas later shrugged off his deputy's after-hours routine. "He was a hard worker," the DA explained, and after toiling late into the night he often needed to avail himself of his office couch.

Freitas accommodated Stoen in other ways as well. When citizen complaints about temple criminality came into the office, Freitas made sure that Jones's lieutenant was brought into the loop. Hannibal Williams, a charismatic Fillmore leader who fought a brave but losing battle against the razing of his neighborhood, was one of the few black pastors who dared to criticize Jones's operation. When Williams was threatened by Peoples Temple thugs, he went to the DA, only to be turned over to Tim Stoen.

If Tim Stoen confounded his colleagues in the DA's office, he was also a mystery to some members of Jones's inner circle. A deeply religious Republican attorney with political ambitions when he discovered Peoples Temple, Stoen soon became a true believer and a man so trusted by Jones that the temple leader delegated much of the organization's legal and financial affairs to him and his wife. Despite Stoen's middle-American upbringing and early anticommunism, he declared himself a disciple of Jones's oddball socialism. "Tim Stoen was so close to my dad; I think he was Dad's real true friend," said Jim Jones Jr., the cult leader's adopted son.

Nonetheless, Jones, easily threatened by accomplished men like the Stanford-educated lawyer, put Stoen through the same bizarre loyalty tests and sexual humiliations to which he subjected other temple members. Jones toyed perversely with the Stoens' marriage, wheedling Tim into having affairs with other women in the church and then planting doubts in Grace about her husband's loyalty and sexual orientation.

Jones—whose sexual appetites were imperial, establishing rapacious dominion over men and women alike—was of the eccentric opinion that he was the only true heterosexual male in the temple. All the other men around him secretly harbored lusts for their fellow man, Jones insisted, and he was in the habit of offering to relieve various fellows of their illicit desires by buggering them. Jones once finagled Stoen into going out shopping for a bra and panties, and then used the female frillies to convince Grace that her husband was a closet drag queen. The preacher also tried to get Tim to confess in front of a church assembly that he was gay, but the buttoned-down lawyer refused.

Other times Stoen seemed recklessly willing to prostrate himself before his master's will. In February 1972—after Grace gave birth to a baby boy named John Stoen—Tim agreed to sign a document stating, "I entreated my beloved pastor, James W. Jones, to sire a child by my wife [because I] was unable after extensive attempts to sire one myself. My reason for requesting James W. Jones to do this is that I wanted my child to be fathered, if not by me, by the most compassionate, honest, and courageous human being the world contains." This wanton act of self-abasement would come back to haunt the Stoens.

Despite the many mortifications of serving Jim Jones, Tim Stoen remained zealously steadfast. One member of the temple's inner circle was amazed to see the lawyer go along with some of Jones's most violent fantasies without objection. "Jim started turning crazier by the day in San Francisco," said the temple insider. "I knew he was going over the edge when he ordered a woman named Maria Katsaris to start taking flying lessons. He wanted her to learn how to fly so they could fill a plane with temple members and then crash it, in an act of 'revolutionary suicide,' as he called it. Maria went to flight school, but she hated it. Stoen knew about Maria's flight training. He was in the room when it was discussed. It was talked about a number of times."

On another occasion, Stoen told a temple insider to get a gun, in case Jones was harmed by outside enemies and the organization needed to strike back. The lawyer also talked about putting plutonium in the Washington, DC, water supply. One of Stoen's ideas, according to the insider, apparently surprised even Jones. "He ordered a couple of us to set up a bomb factory in San Francisco. I went to Jim and told him. He said he knew nothing about it, and he told me not to do anything."

The insider came to believe that Stoen was an agent provocateur. Later, after Jones began shifting his operation to Guyana, other members of the temple's leadership circle, including Jones himself, also concluded that Stoen was a government agent. While rummaging through Stoen's briefcase in Guyana, Jones's lieutenants found a newspaper clipping about his arrest in East Berlin when he was an overseas college student, as well as a diary from this period, full of strong anti-Communist sentiments. They also discovered a second passport. In the febrile and suspicious atmosphere of the Peoples Temple, this seemed to prove that Stoen had some sort of intelligence background.

While Stoen was working in the San Francisco District Attorney's Office, however, he did nothing to inflame Jones's paranoia. As far as Dave Reuben could tell, he was a temple loyalist, Jim Jones's man inside the hall of justice. "I didn't talk to Stoen after we found out about him," said Reuben. "I probably wanted to shoot him. We may have even tailed him at some point."

Stoen always denied he was aware of the Peoples Temple voter fraud and its coverup, despite the key positions he held within the church and the San Francisco DA's office. "Jim Jones kept a lot of things from me," he later told the *New York Times*. Years after the Peoples Temple saga, Stoen went full circle, returning to the north California coast region where he had joined Jones's church and resuming his career as a respected prosecutor and Republican Party politician in Humboldt and Mendocino counties. Stoen declined to comment for this book on his years with Jones.

Jim Jones proved a master at politically wiring San Francisco in the midseventies. Planting Stoen in the DA's office was just one of his successful maneuvers. Considering the criminal underside of his operation, it was also one of the most useful. *Sun Reporter* publisher Dr. Carlton Goodlett, one of the pillars of the black community to be seduced by Jones, marveled at his ally's manipulation of the civic power structure. "You always got a man pretty close to a law enforcement agency in a town, don't you?" Goodlett once observed.

"You're very perceptive," chuckled Jones.

Later, after Jonestown became an international symbol of mass lunacy, it was widely assumed to be one more outgrowth of "San Fransicko." But, in fact, Jim Jones was a God-fearing product of the American heartland.

25

SLOUCHING TOWARD
SAN FRANCISCO

J IM JONES WAS raised by a mother whose dreams were too big for the
Indiana farm town where they lived. "Don't be nothing like your dad,"
Lynetta Jones drummed into her boy, while Big Jim rocked forlornly in
his armchair, his lungs so badly scarred by mustard gas in the First World
War that he couldn't wheeze his way through a full day's work. The boy
developed a messianic complex at an early age, killing a cat so he could
try raising it from the dead. One day he marched into the drowsy, God-
fearing town wearing a makeshift white robe to confront the sinners in
the pool hall—including his own sad, hard-drinking father. "You're all
going to hell," the boy preacher proclaimed sternly.

Jones became a rising young Pentecostal preacher in Indianapolis,
building a mixed-race congregation—a daring move in 1950s Middle
America—and starting a rainbow family of his own with his wife, Marceline. Soon after Marceline gave birth to their first son, Stephan, the
couple adopted a girl from a Korean orphanage and an African-American
infant whom Jim anointed with his own name—only the beginning of
what would become a multiracial brood.

A cloud of menace hung over Jones's racially advanced church.
The preacher and his wife received late-night crank phone calls, and

a dead cat was thrown at their house. Someone painted a swastika on the church door, and Jones once found glass in his Sunday potluck dinner. But some members of the church wondered if the hostile acts were staged by Jones himself.

In July 1965 Jones convinced 140 members of his congregation to abandon their lives in Indiana and move westward with him to the California promised land: a valley in Mendocino County where Jones said they would be safe from redneck tormentors and from the nuclear doomsday that he predicted would reduce most of America to poisonous smoke and ash. It was the first exodus engineered by Jones, who was always trying to outrun his own demons. His followers headed west in a dusty caravan of pickup trucks, vans, and cars.

As the Peoples Temple established itself in Redwood Valley— recruiting new members, many of them black and poor, from the Bay Area, Los Angeles, and other cities—Jones set about infiltrating the local power structure. Though Jones told his flock that the one true God was socialism, the church worked hard to win over the Republican establishment that controlled Ukiah, the county seat. The Peoples Temple bought tickets to local Republican fund-raisers, bombarded GOP politicians with flattering letters, and contributed to their campaigns. Jones announced that he was a registered Republican and was supporting Nixon for president in 1968, and even befriended the head of the local John Birch Society. Meanwhile, the church infiltrated members into the sheriff's department and the county social services department, and Tim Stoen went to work in the Mendocino County District Attorney's Office as the county counsel. The same political strategy that would work so effectively in liberal San Francisco was first tested in conservative Ukiah.

It did not take long for Jones, always looking for the big stage that his mother envisioned for him, to outgrow the Redwood Valley. He began extending feelers into San Francisco, leading weekly services at a junior high school auditorium in the Fillmore as early as 1970. Long before George Moscone came into their sights, temple officials wooed Mayor Alioto, buying one hundred tickets to a breakfast fund-raiser for Alioto in 1973 and sending him a box of homemade candy in 1975.

That year, the Peoples Temple moved its headquarters to San Francisco, taking over an old Jewish synagogue next to the Black Muslim mosque on Geary Boulevard once occupied by the Fillmore Auditorium. It was an eerie synchronicity—the building once a haven for the Zebra butchers sitting side by side with the temple that would become infamous as the headquarters of the deadliest cult in US history.

Using the same bag of tricks he used on politicians—including donations, bouquets of flattery, and his considerable personal charm—Jim Jones won over key black church leaders in the Bay Area, including activist pastors Cecil Williams of Glide Memorial in the Tenderloin and J. Alfred Smith of the Allen Temple Baptist Church in Oakland. With Jones's impassioned pulpit performances and his organization's social outreach programs, including a free medical clinic and food and clothing donations, the Peoples Temple soon established firm roots in the devastated Fillmore neighborhood. Traditional black churches—whose pastors "preached the sweet by-and-by," in Rev. Smith's words, and limited their social services to Christmas basket giveaways—found it hard to compete with Jones's theatrical evangelism. The white preacher began luring away hundreds of black worshippers; massive "sheep stealing" that rival black ministers grumbled about but did little to counteract.

Jones moved into the Fillmore at its most vulnerable moment. Urban renewal czar Justin Herman had "literally destroyed the neighborhood," observed neighborhood activist Hannibal Williams, "[and] people were desperate for solutions, something to follow. Jim Jones was another solution. He had a charismatic personality that won the hearts and souls of people. And people followed him to hell. That's where Jim Jones went. That's where he took the people who followed him."

In the beginning, Jones was greeted as a "godsend" in the black community, remarked Rev. Smith. Here was a white pastor who "had the gift of communicating with black people. He didn't communicate in the sterile way of the seminary. No, if you listen to Jones's sermons, you can hear him following the rhythms and cadences to match the beating of the human heart."

And his flock, ignored and scorned by society, was electrified by Jones's vision of a new Eden. Everybody was exalted in his services, even the lowliest recovering drunks and addicts. "He made us feel special, like something bigger than ourselves," said one temple member. "Total equality, no rich or poor, no races," said another. "We were alive in those services," testified one more. "They had life, soul power."

Jones—an oddball and renegade his entire life, someone who never felt at home in his own skin—had found his identity by taking on a black persona. He saw himself following in the footsteps of Malcolm and Martin, leading "his" people out of bondage and into the promised land.

In reality, Jones maintained a racial hierarchy within the organization. While church membership was primarily black, the thirty-seven-member planning commission, as Jones called his leadership council, was dominated by white women—at least six of whom were his sexual conquests and firmly under his sway. "When people talk about my father manipulating black people, that's true," said Jim Jones Jr., the preacher's black adopted son. "It was politically advantageous for him to give me his name."

There was something exhibitionistic about the way that Jones and his wife treated their black son. "I was the chosen one," he said. "I was more loved in my family than the other kids, even their biological son, Stephan. I remember Mom wiping charcoal off a dirty pot one day and rubbing it all over her face—to show that we were all black."

JONES SOON LEARNED THAT his control over a well-organized, mixed-race army of some eight thousand dedicated followers gave him major stature with San Francisco's liberal elite. Redevelopment had bulldozed the Fillmore's political power into the ground. But now this strange white man with the hipster shades, Indian-black hair, and cadences of a black Bible-thumper seemed to be erecting a new political power line into the rubble-strewn, crime-ridden no-man's-land. Jones could be counted on to deliver busloads of obedient, well-dressed disciples to demonstrations, campaign rallies, and political precincts. The city's liberal Burton machine quickly identified the Peoples Temple juggernaut as a potentially game-changing ally in its long battle to take over city hall.

It was Willie Brown who first recognized that Jones's organization could play a pivotal role in his friend George Moscone's run for mayor. A meeting was set up between Jones and Moscone in the office of Don Bradley, the candidate's veteran campaign manager. Bradley was initially cautious. "I was a little leery we were getting into something like the Moonies," he later recalled. But after he looked into the temple's campaign history in Mendocino and saw how effective it was in delivering victories there, Bradley enthusiastically embraced Jones's volunteer army. Nearly two hundred temple members showed up at Moscone headquarters, fanning out to campaign in some of the city's toughest neighborhoods, and helping the candidate finish first in the November election.

In the December runoff between Moscone and Barbagelata, Peoples Temple went even further to secure victory for its candidate. On the eve of the election, Jones filled buses with temple members in Redwood Valley and Los Angeles and shuttled them to San Francisco. Security at polling places was lax on Election Day, and many nonresidents were able to cast their ballots for Moscone, some more than once. "You could have run around to twelve hundred precincts and voted twelve hundred times," said a bitter Barbagelata later, after losing by a whisper of a margin. But he was not the only one who claimed that the Peoples Temple stole the election for George Moscone. Temple leaders also claimed credit.

"We loaded up all thirteen of our buses with maybe seventy people on each bus, and we had those buses rolling nonstop up and down the coast into San Francisco the day before the election," recalled Jim Jones Jr. "We had people going from precinct to precinct to vote. So could we have been the force that tipped the election to Moscone? Absolutely! Slam dunk. He only won by four thousand votes. I'm sorry, but I've got to give my father credit for that. I think he did the right thing. George Moscone was a good person; he wanted what was best for San Francisco."

Jim Jones made sure that George Moscone never forgot his political debt to Peoples Temple. The man who began his term in city hall with a ringing promise to make San Francisco a beacon of enlightenment would start off his administration with a wretched burden on his back. The mayor could never rid himself of the stench of contagion that Jones brought with him, and as time went by, the power-hungry preacher only sunk his fangs in deeper. The pastor was a wickedly smart reader of a politician's character, and he knew that the way to enchant Moscone was with young women, not money. When it came to bribing politicians, the temple leader had ample supplies of both. Jones bragged of supplying Moscone with black female members of his congregation. Jim Jones Jr. remembered the mayor as "a party guy. He'd always be there at temple parties with a cocktail in his hand and doing some ass grabbing."

Temple insiders talked about how Mayor Moscone was one of the politicians under the control of "Father." They gossiped about the night that the mayor had fallen into Jones's hands. "Moscone was known to be a boozer; he liked to drink at parties," recalled temple member Hue Fortson, now a pastor in Southern California. "One night there was some sort of temple event that the mayor attended. The next morning I heard that Jones phoned Moscone and told him it was a pleasure to see him the night before and to see him having such a good time. 'But I want to let you know that the young lady you went off with is underage,' Jones told him. 'Now don't worry, Mayor, we'll take care of you—because we know that you'll take care of us.'"

Jones might have made up the stories of sexual blackmail. He was known to concoct outlandish tales. "Jim was always bragging that he had sexually compromising information about politicians," remembered Terri Buford, an on-again, off-again mistress of Jones who belonged to the temple's inner circle. "But you never knew if what he said was true. He once told me that Willie Brown was sexually attracted to him. He just made stuff up."

Whether or not Moscone was sexually compromised by Jones, he was certainly politically ensnared. The mayor initially resisted the temple's efforts to insert its members throughout city government. And when Jones himself pushed for a high-level appointment, Moscone at first tried to appease him with a harmless post on the human rights commission. But the temple leader insisted on a position that had more clout, and the mayor decided he was in no position to alienate Jones. In October 1976 Moscone announced that he was naming Jones to the San Francisco Housing Authority, which oversees the operation of the city's public housing. The agency, the largest landlord in the city, was a notorious maze of corruption, and it provided Jones's organization with ample opportunity for shady self-dealing. A few months later, Moscone pulled strings to promote Jones, making him chairman.

Jones swept into the normally tedious meetings of the housing commission like a banana republic despot, surrounded by an entourage of aides and grim-faced security guards. Looking stern and inscrutable behind his aviator sunglasses, Jones ran the meetings with scripted precision while sipping a frothy white drink brought to him by a hovering retainer. The audience, packed with elderly black temple worshippers, erupted into wild cheers at his most routine pronouncements. Temple enforcers roamed through the meetings, keeping a watchful vigil, and even blocking people from entering the bathroom while Jones was inside.

Jones used his position to take possession of public housing units and install temple members in them, and he put other followers on the housing authority payroll. The preacher was building his own power base within city government. "He was using his power to recruit members and to put the hammer on people," said Dave Reuben. "He had a lot of authority."

"Jim Jones helped George Moscone run this city," said Jim Jones Jr., a chillingly matter-of-fact assessment of the temple leader's creeping encroachment in San Francisco.

Political leaders, aware of Jones's ability to deliver—or manufacture—votes, lined up to pay tribute to the preacher. He worked his way into the good graces of officials high and low—most of them Democrats, since that was the party in power in California and San Francisco in the mid-1970s. But Jones was also happy to exchange mutually complimentary correspondence with the offices of Ronald Reagan and statesman Henry Kissinger.

During the 1976 presidential campaign, Jones wangled a private meeting with Jimmy Carter's wife, Rosalynn, at the elegant Stanford Court Hotel on Nob Hill, arriving with a security contingent that was larger than her Secret Service squad. Later Jones accompanied Moscone and a group of Democratic dignitaries who climbed aboard vice presidential candidate Walter Mondale's private jet when it touched down at San Francisco International Airport.

Governor Jerry Brown sang the preacher's praises. Congressman John Burton lobbied the governor to appoint Jones to the high-profile board of regents, which oversaw California's sprawling public university system. Supervisor Dianne Feinstein accepted an invitation to lunch with Jones and to tour Peoples Temple.

But no political figures were more gushing in their praise of Jones than Harvey Milk and Willie Brown. Milk, a perennial candidate for office until he finally won a supervisor's seat in 1977, aggressively sought Jones's political blessing. "Our paths have crossed," Milk wrote Jones during an earlier campaign for supervisor, in a letter filled with the kind of awed reverence that the cult leader demanded from his followers. "They will stay crossed. It is a fight that I will walk with you into . . . The first time I heard you, you made a statement: 'Take one of us, and you must take all of us.' Please add my name."

Not content to hear dignitaries whisper flatteries into his ear, Jones staged a testimonial banquet in his own honor and demanded that politicians in his debt offer him public tribute. On the evening of September 25, 1976, the temple on Geary Boulevard was converted into a formal dining hall with linen tablecloths and floral arrangements. At the head table sat Mayor Moscone, District Attorney Freitas, and Assemblyman Willie Brown, who acted as the evening's exuberant master of ceremonies. As he introduced the man of the hour to the overflow audience, Brown reached new heights of shameless, ass-kissing puffery. "Let me present to you," Brown roared, "a combination of Martin King, Angela Davis, Albert Einstein . . . Chairman Mao." By the time Jones rose to tumultuous applause, he seemed likely to walk on water.

Privately, San Francisco political leaders expressed doubts about Jones and his strange church. One day a friend of Milk's named Tory Hartmann dropped off some boxes of campaign brochures at Peoples Temple, so that Jones's army could distribute them. Hartmann was immediately creeped out by the uptight, high-security atmosphere inside the temple, where sentries stood at attention outside each room, like the palace guards in the Wicked Witch's castle. "This is a church?" Hartmann said to herself. Later, after she sped back to the Castro and told Milk about her bizarre experience, the naturally cheery politician turned deadly serious.

"Make sure you're always nice to the Peoples Temple," he told her. "They're weird and they're dangerous, and you never want to be on their bad side."

Cleve Jones, a young Milk aide, accompanied him to Peoples Temple for a couple of Sunday services. "Harvey told me, 'Be careful, they tape everything.' Everyone knew Jim Jones was creepy, everyone knew he was a megalomaniac. But everybody also saw this church full of black and white people—black people from the Fillmore who had been subjected to apartheid-like policies and seemed to finally be getting some respect."

Members of Moscone's staff were also beginning to hear troubling reports about Peoples Temple. One day mayoral aide Dick Sklar suggested to his family maid—an African-American woman who had followed the Sklars to San Francisco from Ohio—that she attend a Sunday service at Peoples Temple. "I didn't know anything about it," Sklar said, "but she was a churchgoing woman, and I thought she might like it. Afterward she came back and said it was the scariest place she'd ever been. They searched her, asked her questions. I had no idea."

Moscone himself could not ignore how peculiar his political ally was. "I was at every meeting that Jim Jones ever attended with the mayor," said Corey Busch. "I can tell you that after every one of those meetings, the reaction was, 'This is one weird bird.' He always wore the dark glasses. You couldn't predict Jonestown, but he was definitely weird. In retrospect, maybe we should have seen that, but we didn't."

As city hall looked the other way, Jones quietly consolidated his power in San Francisco, extending his influence in political, religious, and media circles. The temple worked its mojo on dozens of community organizations, from small groups like the Telegraph Hill Neighborhood Association to higher-profile ones like the American Civil Liberties Union, the National Association for the Advancement of Colored People, and the United Farm Workers. Jones won their gratitude by donating money and flooding their rallies and events with vocal supporters.

By early 1977, it seemed that Jim Jones had conquered San Francisco. He had the mayor in his pocket and commanded the fawning loyalty of power brokers such as Willie Brown and rising stars like Harvey Milk. Using San Francisco as its power base, the Peoples Temple was ready to expand its operations in Los Angeles, Seattle, and other cities where it had already sunk roots.

There was only one politician who seemed willing to confront the powerful cult: cantankerous John Barbagelata, the fading voice of San Francisco conservatism.

26

PROPHET OF DOOM

J OHN BARBAGELATA, WHO'D never stopped fuming about his shady mayoral defeat, kept banging the drum about Jim Jones's political machine and its insidious influence in city hall. During the Proposition B recall campaign, the supervisor charged loudly that San Francisco was being taken over by extremists and kooks—and the Peoples Temple was the most dangerous element of this new coalition. Moscone angrily rejected Barbagelata's accusation. "There's no radical plot in San Francisco," the mayor declared. "There's no one I've appointed to any city position whom I regard as radical or extremist."

Meanwhile, Joe Freitas bluntly dismissed Barbagelata's voter fraud charges. In March 1977 the DA wrote Barbagelata, assuring him that his deputy Tim Stoen had investigated the fraud allegations and had determined "that there was not sufficient evidence" to pursue the case. An outraged Barbagelata, now finally aware of Stoen's blatant conflict of interest, circled Tim Stoen's name in red on the Freitas letter and scrawled, "President Peoples Temple."

By then Stoen had disappeared from the DA's office and had flown to Guyana, where Jones was already preparing his next refuge in a remote jungle. But Barbagelata kept after the Peoples Temple, which he suspected of getting its hands on foster children and kids deemed "incorrigible" by courts, and spiriting them off to Guyana, along with the public funds attached to the children. The anxieties of Peoples Temple relatives were beginning to rise as members began vanishing from San Francisco and Oakland. The conservative supervisor was the only city official who seemed to be making inquiries about the fate of children in Jones's control. San Francisco's welfare chief reacted huffily that Barbagelata would even propose such an investigation.

It took courage to confront Jones's maniacal organization. Barbagelata was barraged with scornful letters from a phalanx of well-positioned Peoples Temple supporters such as the Reverend Norman E. Leach, executive director of the San Francisco Council of Churches, who condemned the supervisor's talk of a "radical takeover" of the city as "merely sour grapes."

Leach then went on to offer pious counsel to Barbagelata: "Have you ever discussed with the Reverend Jim Jones your views as to his belonging to some sort of 'coalition' which is eroding the 'balance of power in San Francisco' and 'attempting to control everything'? I know Jim and know him to be an independent person, a man of strong values and convictions, and a man not beholden to any organization or group or individual . . . Build your own coalition, if you wish. But don't find secret coalitions in existence which are not there." Jones was sending his number one political enemy a message: if Barbagelata sat down and came to terms with him, maybe he too could reap the benefits enjoyed by San Francisco's political winners.

Rev. Leach had been arrested in 1974 and convicted of "contributing to the delinquency of a minor twelve or younger" in Napa, California, but if temple officials knew about the Presbyterian minister's legal record, they apparently did not use it to manipulate him. "They were simply very good at co-opting people," Leach said later.

Other letters that Barbagelata received from temple members felt more ominous. "We got letters from Jones's followers saying, 'We hear you've been saying these things about Father, and we want you to stop saying these things about Father.' And then there were subtle threats," recalled Barbagelata's son Paul.

The Peoples Temple letters came during a very disturbing period for the Barbagelata family, which had been subjected to a terror campaign for months, beginning during the 1975 mayoral race. To serve in San Francisco politics during the 1970s was to sign up for war duty. Many local officials—especially high-profile ones such as Mayor Alioto and Supervisor Feinstein—were subjected to death threats and bombing attempts. But Barbagelata, the city's leading conservative, was a particular obsession of the radical underground.

The Barbagelata home in quiet, leafy St. Francis Wood, was the target of more than one bombing attempt; strangers showed up at St. Brendan's, the family's church, saying they'd been asked to drive the Barbagelata kids home; bricks, beer cans, and other projectiles were thrown through Barbagelata's real estate office and campaign headquarters; and cars belonging to campaign volunteers were firebombed and vandalized.

THE NEW WORLD LIBERATION Front, San Francisco's leading mad bombers, were Barbagelata's principal tormentors. One day in January 1976, the underground group delivered a box of See's candy—the supervisor's favorite—to the family residence. His kids were eager to open it, but Barbagelata's wife told them they had to wait until their father came home. At one point, two of his daughters playfully tossed around the unopened package. Early that evening, a frantic Supervisor Quentin Kopp, who had received a similar package and figured out it was wired to explode, called the Barbagelata home, warning the family in time.

The NWLF bombed dozens of targets in the Bay Area, including corporate buildings, Pacific Gas and Electric Company power stations, and even luxury cars and homes owned by rich businessmen. The public face for the NWLF was a tall, lean, mustachioed man in his early thirties who called himself Jacques Rogiers (real name: Jack Rogers). Rogiers, operating out of an Oak Street flat, churned out threatening communiqués on his Poor People's Press. When Rogiers—the son of a Minnesota Twins baseball scout who'd once played professionally—was finally arrested, the group launched a campaign to release him, accusing Barbagelata of squelching his freedom of speech. Leaflets depicting Barbagelata as a bloody-fanged rat were brazenly stuck to the marble walls inside city hall.

Early one evening in March 1977, the mad bombers took more direct action against Barbagelata, tossing an explosive at the family home.

The device fell short, exploding in the yard next door, minutes after the neighbor's young boy had stopped playing there. Barbagelata never liked to show that he was rattled by the radical elements trying to drive him and his family from his hometown. But this time he let his temper fly. "These people have twisted and depraved minds," he exploded in the *Examiner*. "Had their little game been played fifteen minutes earlier, they would have blown that little boy away. Here's a message for them. If that ever happens, then a few of them are going to be blown apart by people who refuse to be intimidated."

A heavy smoker who had suffered a heart attack in 1970, Barbagelata showed signs of the strain, collapsing one day on his way to mass at St. Brendan's. But the crusty conservative refused to give in. Barbagelata—not trusting the SFPD, which he felt had fallen apart under liberal Chief Gain—armed himself and his oldest son and installed floodlights in his backyard.

On some occasions, the family would be wakened by phone calls from the police in the middle of the night, warning them to leave the house immediately. Barbagelata quickly packed his family into their station wagon, and they sped away, driving to a walnut grove near Stockton where Mrs. Barbagelata's relatives lived.

In the middle of the terror campaign against the Barbagelatas, Jim Jones suddenly appeared at the supervisor's city hall office to offer him Peoples Temple security guards as protection. It was a surreal moment. Barbagelata considered Jones's organization an even bigger threat to San Francisco than Jacques Rogiers's mad bombers. He declined Jones's offer. The temple enforcers were just as likely to shoot him, thought Barbagelata, as protect him.

John Barbagelata was finally driven out of politics—not by terrorists or mad cultists, but by the voters of San Francisco, who rejected his warnings about a radical takeover and defeated his attempted recall of the city's liberal leaders by a lopsided margin. "This is the last hurrah for conservatives in San Francisco," he bitterly told an *Examiner* reporter on the night that Proposition B went down to defeat. "I've done everything I can to expose the deceit, deception, and dishonesty in city government. Maybe the people will wake up someday, but I'm going back to my family and business."

As he announced his retirement from politics, Barbagelata issued a dire prophetic warning to his fellow San Franciscans: "In the next few months, the people are going to go through an emotional experience when they find out who's running the city."

JOHN BARBAGELATA DID NOT understand the heart of San Francisco the way George Moscone did. He was so flustered by homosexuals that he choked on the word *gay,* and the city's cultural revolution just seemed coarse and offensive to the old-fashioned Italian Catholic who had a hard time pronouncing intimate body parts. San Francisco's powerful unions, he believed, were not a vehicle for middle-class prosperity and social decency, as most of the city regarded them. In Barbagelata's mind, they were leeches on the public treasury. And the city government was not a guardian of the poor, the nonwhite, and the dispossessed. It was the bully that had taken his family home under the brute authority of eminent domain when he was boy growing up on verdant Lombard Street, because the cottage stood in the way of the expanded, new thoroughfare to the Golden Gate Bridge. To Barbagelata, government would always be the enemy of decent home owners and taxpayers.

But Barbagelata was not simply a curmudgeonly skinflint. He was the kind of man who would take homeless people off the street and put them to work painting a back room at his real estate office. Some colleagues suspected that was the sole purpose of the room. Later he would bring the hard-luck fellows home for a hearty Italian dinner, just as good families took care of hoboes during the Depression.

"I would say, 'Mom, who is that guy?' and she would say, 'One of your father's friends,'" remembered Paul Barbagelata. "My father was tough, inflexible, and a hard-ass. But the other side of him was quite compassionate. As long as you were not lazy, he could like you. He truly cared about this city and its residents from all walks of life."

Barbagelata never stopped caring about San Francisco. And if he didn't understand how the city was changing, the way that Moscone and Milk did, he was more aware than his rivals were of the sinister elements in their new coalition. Barbagelata was the only one to confront the serpents in the garden. And it galled him that others didn't take the threat as seriously as he did.

As he faded from the political stage, the crusty Cassandra lit a fire under the local newspapers, which had shown little interest in the slithery maneuvers of Jim Jones as he wrapped his coils around the city. "I think the media has to get off its goddam ass and find what's going on in this city," Barbagelata growled as he made his exit.

The *Chronicle* blithely dismissed Barbagelata's fulminations. "This newspaper is accused by Barbagelata of having complacently ignored his warnings of evil doings in San Francisco politics," the newspaper editorialized in August 1977. "In truth, his theory of some gigantic conspiracy against the public interest and weal in city hall is a theory we don't understand and have never found any evidence for."

The more conservative *Examiner* fretted that Barbagelata might be on to something, but simply hoped for the best. "It's true Barbagelata's imagination is overactive," the newspaper opined, "but he was right when he said the city must not be turned over to leftists and kooks. Let's hope his prophecies of doom are off the mark."

The men who ran San Francisco's influential dailies would soon learn that Barbagelata's prophecies were hideously accurate. But by then it was too late. The city's watchdogs did nothing to alert the public to Jim Jones's growing menace. The cult leader won the local media's silence with the same artful combination of seduction and intimidation that he had used on San Francisco's political caste.

Later, after the horror of Jonestown was reverberating around the world, a reporter for a neighborhood newspaper found Barbagelata at home on a rainy afternoon, where they talked over a lunch of chicken sandwiches and beer. The retired politician was recovering from a recent stroke, and from the calamities of his service in San Francisco public life. He still seemed stunned by it all: the evil machinations of Peoples Temple, the complicity of city hall, the stubborn refusal of the press to investigate the "growing train wreck" that was San Francisco. He was not a naïve person, he had seen some dark and vicious things in his life of nearly six decades. "But that was nothing," he said, "compared to San Francisco politics."

27

EXODUS

J IM JONES'S MOST ardent supporter in San Francisco press circles
was Steve Gavin, the *Chronicle*'s city editor. A Baltimore native, he
joined the *Chronicle* in 1969. Life in San Francisco agreed with Gavin,
a gay man in his thirties who loved theater, baseball, and a well-mixed
Manhattan. The socially aware newspaperman was delighted when he
discovered Peoples Temple and its racially mixed, politically energized
congregation. His increasingly warm relationship with Jones made
Gavin feel connected to the kind of constituency that newspapers usually overlooked: the black, poor, and religious. Jones and his slick media
strategist—a handsome, former local TV newsman named Michael
Prokes—made sure that Gavin felt the temple's love.

"Jones took Gavin under his wing and made a big fuss over him,"
said *Chronicle* reporter Marshall Kilduff. "It was very flattering. And I
think there was a degree of social usefulness in the relationship. Jones
handed him a chunk of the city that wasn't a big *Chronicle* franchise.
Gavin liked that."

Gavin began exchanging heartfelt letters with Jones in 1976. In July
the city editor wrote to the preacher, thanking him for serving him lunch
and taking him on a tour of the temple. "I enjoyed our discussion," Gavin
wrote. "As I told you, I look for small victories [in life]. You have accomplished major ones. I know the feeling of getting discouraged. There is

so much to do. It helps, periodically, I think, to count our blessings and to look back, to see how far we've come. To this outsider's eye, you have done a tremendous job . . . Thank you for what you are contributing to my city."

A few days later, Gavin sent the cult leader a wryly charming homily from Irish writer Brendan Behan. Jones, communicating through Prokes, responded that he was "delighted" by the quote and urged the newspaper editor to call on him for assistance if he ever needed it.

That fall, Gavin did call on Jones for help, asking him to support four *Fresno Bee* reporters who had been jailed for refusing to reveal the names of confidential sources. Jones dispatched busloads of temple members to Fresno to demonstrate on their behalf.

Around the same time, the temple deluged the *Chronicle* city editor, who was suffering from a persistent cold, with a pile of get-well letters. Gavin, touched by the congregation's generosity, responded with another fervent letter, telling Jones that he wished the press could be as compassionate as the temple was toward "the multiplicity of people that make up our community . . . Caring is all."

Jones was a master at drawing liberals and idealists who yearned for a better world into his web. He could smell the feverish longing for deliverance that wafted off them, and he made them believe he was their salvation. Jones offered a vision of heaven on earth that made even the most secular suspend rational judgment and take a leap of faith. It was all for show, but people like Gavin longed to embrace the Peoples Temple pageant: black and white, rich and poor, gay and straight, all joining hands in blissful communion.

"I was always wary of being manipulated by [temple officials] and conscious of the possibility, but I don't think I was," Gavin later insisted. "I think all my decisions about Peoples Temple stories were made on a professional basis." But the record shows a newsman who was utterly in thrall to Jones.

The Peoples Temple skillfully courted other journalists too, including Herb Caen, who enjoyed two long, chatty lunches with the cult leader. "I found him appealing—soft-spoken, modest, talking earnestly of helping people," Caen wrote later. "If he was a con man, he was masterful at it." Jones continued to get good play in Caen's column even after the bloom was fading from the temple's rose.

But no one in the San Francisco media world proved more useful to Jones than Steve Gavin, who single-handedly made sure that the city's leading newspaper did not shine a harsh spotlight on the cult leader. When *Chronicle* reporter Julie Smith began working on a story about the temple in the spring of 1976, Jones somehow learned the exact contents of the story draft while it still sat in her newsroom desk. Later Marshall Kilduff, who had a prickly experience with Jones while covering his strange performance on the housing commission, decided to write a profile of him. Showing up at the temple on a Sunday in January 1977 to interview church officials, the *Chronicle* reporter was taken on a long tour that ended in the main auditorium, where a service was in progress. As Kilduff was escorted to his seat near the front of the congregation, he was stunned to see his boss, Steve Gavin, sitting among the worshippers.

The next morning, Kilduff gingerly approached Gavin in the *Chronicle* newsroom. "Quite a show," said the reporter. "Don't you think we should do a story about this guy? I hear he's powerful politically."

But the city editor cut him off. "We've already done it," said Gavin, referring to the bland, carefully managed article produced earlier by Julie Smith.

Blocked by his own newspaper, the dogged Kilduff continued to work the Peoples Temple story on his own time, while searching for a magazine to publish it. As he tracked down sources, temple members kept close watch on him, digging through his garbage and reporting his every move to Gavin, their friend at the *Chronicle*. In March, Kilduff finally got a freelance assignment from *New West,* a regional magazine owned by Rupert Murdoch. But when a temple delegation called on its editor, Kevin Starr, and explained that the article would harm its humanitarian work, he killed the piece. Only after Starr was replaced by a more enterprising editor, Rosalie Wright, did *New West* revive Kilduff's assignment.

WHEN THE STORY, "INSIDE Peoples Temple," was finally published, it marked the beginning of the end for Jones's sinister reign in San Francisco. The article, written by Kilduff and *New West* reporter Phil Tracy, was based on the disturbing accounts of many of the same defectors who had taken their complaints to the San Francisco DA's office, only to

see them bottled up. They told of the beatings, the bizarre temple ceremonies, the confiscation of members' money and assets, and the political empire building throughout the state. Among the reporters' sources
was Grace Stoen, who had been forced to leave behind her five-year-old
son, John, when she fled the temple. To his mother's anguish, the boy
had been taken away to the temple's Guyana retreat.

While the reporters were still working on their exposé of Peoples
Temple, Tim Stoen also defected, disappearing from the temple's command post in Georgetown, the capital of Guyana, in June 1977. The
defection of Stoen, who joined his wife in an increasingly desperate custody battle for John, was a particularly grievous blow for Jones. Stoen
knew all the organization's legal and financial secrets. His betrayal sent
Jones spiraling downward into a whirlpool of panic. Battle-mode fever
gripped the temple.

Before the *New West* article hit the newsstands in late July, Jim
Jones ran off to Guyana, leaving his stunned liberal supporters in San
Francisco to make sense of it all. Moscone was privately rattled by the
magazine's charges, but he and the rest of the city's liberal elite publicly closed ranks behind the temple leader. After Jones took flight, the
temple officials who were still in San Francisco organized a rally in their
Geary Boulevard citadel to show support for their embattled leader. Willie Brown was still willing to shill for Jones, blaming his flight on his
political enemies. "When somebody like Jim Jones comes on the scene,"
Brown told the gathering, "that absolutely scares the hell out of most
everybody occupying positions of power in the system." The assembly
then listened raptly as Jones himself ranted over a long-distance radio
hookup, denouncing his tormentors as "bitches" and "bastards," sounding more like a tantrum-throwing brat than an esteemed religious leader.

Assemblyman Art Agnos, another benefactor of Jones's support, was
visiting the temple for the first time, sitting next to Harvey Milk in the
audience. Listening to the frantic, disembodied voice from Guyana,
Agnos turned to Milk and said, "Harvey, that guy is really wild."

Milk, who was still standing by Jones, replied weakly, "Yeah, he's different, all right."

As the political fallout from the *New West* article grew, some San
Francisco officials began running for cover. In late August Joe Freitas
ordered investigator Bob Graham to write a memo stating that the DA's

office looked into the charges leveled by the magazine and found no basis for legal action. Graham's memo also gave Tim Stoen a pass, stating, "So far, no evidence has surfaced that would link Stoen with any criminal activity in San Francisco." The memo was one more humiliation for Freitas's gung-ho investigators. They had tried hard to dig to the bottom of the Peoples Temple swamp, only to be roped in by their boss. Now Freitas was making them concoct a cover story for him.

"It was an ass-covering memo," said David Reuben. "It gave Freitas the ability to talk to the press and say, 'Yes, we looked into the charges and couldn't find anything.' But the truth is, we kept investigating after that memo. Bob Graham would not have taken a dive, and I certainly wouldn't. We were too invested in the case."

The problem, however, was that Jim Jones, the chief target of their probe, was now in Guyana, far from the reach of San Francisco investigators. And no officials—federal, state, or local—seemed interested in pursuing Jones into the jungle.

Reuben and his team were stunned by Jones's sudden flight. They thought the timing of his escape was suspicious, prompted not just by the imminent publication of the *New West* exposé but also by their own investigation. Somebody in the hall of justice had clearly tipped off the temple. "We were ready for grand jury indictments; we were *this* close," said Reuben. "And Freitas would've had to go along with it, because he had no other choice. The next thing I know, I get a phone call in the middle of the night. 'Guess what, he's gone.' Jones is gone, and the temple is packing up and getting ready to join him. I remember, we had a meeting in the office, and we said, 'Somebody snitched us off.'"

In the fall of 1977, as Jim Jones hunkered down in Guyana's steaming tropical wilderness with his flock of more than one thousand souls, disturbing reports about the "utopian" community began filtering back to the Bay Area. But political supporters like Harvey Milk, newly elected to the board of supervisors, stuck by the increasingly fanatical leader, out of fear, expedience, or stubborn loyalty. In December 1977 Milk wrote to Joseph Califano, President Carter's secretary of health, education, and welfare, protesting HEW's decision to stop forwarding Social Security checks to elderly temple members in Guyana—a key financial pipeline for Jones. "Peoples Temple," Milk informed Califano, "[has] established a beautiful retirement community in Guyana, the type of which people of means would pay thousands of dollars to patronize."

In February 1978 Milk intervened on Jones's behalf in the raging custody battle over young John Stoen, writing to President Carter himself in support of the cult leader. "Rev. Jones," Milk told Carter, "is widely known in the minority communities here and elsewhere as a man of the highest character, who has undertaken constructive remedies for social problems which have been amazing in their scope and effectiveness." Milk complained that Tim and Grace Stoen were trying to get the State Department to help win the return of their son—a move, he warned, that could create an international incident. "Not only is the life of a child at stake, who presently has loving protective parents in Rev. and Mrs. Jones," Milk wrote, "but our official relations with Guyana could stand to be jeopardized."

Jones was maniacally obsessive about hanging on to little John Stoen. Keeping custody of the boy was a way to continue control over Tim Stoen, ensuring that the high-level defector kept silent about temple secrets. The long-running furor over the case was also a way for Jones to keep his followers in a constant state of fear and embattlement, always on the lookout for the helicopters carrying US agents or Guyanese soldiers that might swoop down on them to seize the boy and destroy their last refuge.

As he whipped his followers into frenzies of fear, Jones called on fellow revolutionaries back home to demonstrate their support. Radical celebrity Angela Davis—a charismatic Marxist scholar who had been tried and acquitted of aiding Jonathan Jackson in his doomed attempt to free his brother George—was a die-hard temple defender. She sent heartfelt greetings by radio to the emotionally wrung-out community, her voice booming out to a temple assembly over loudspeakers. "I know you're in a very difficult situation right now, and there is a conspiracy," Davis declared. "A very profound conspiracy designed to destroy the contributions which you have made to the struggle." But Davis assured her "brothers and sisters" in the temple that "we will do everything in our power to ensure your safety."

The temple assembly also heard Huey Newton via a crackling phone patch from Cuba, where the Black Panthers leader was in exile: "I want the Guyanese government to know that you're not to be messed around with. Keep strong, and we're pulling for you."

Longtime Black Panthers attorney Charles Garry, a lion of the Bay Area left, agreed to represent Jones in his legal battles. Garry became an aggressive mouthpiece for the temple back in the United States, telling the press, "There is a conspiracy by government agencies to destroy the Peoples Temple." Garry began to question Jones's mental stability, but he kept his doubts to himself. After visiting Jonestown in October 1977, the radical lawyer announced, "I have seen paradise."

IN REALITY, THE JONESTOWN "paradise" was a nightmarish Third World police state. Everyone but the youngest and oldest were forced to work like mules from dawn to dusk in the sweltering fields, scratching out a living from the wild jungle terrain. Chronically short of food, residents struggled to keep their weight up with starchy meals like cassava bread drenched in brown syrup and rice soaked with gravy. Families and lovers were forced to live apart, relatives were pitted against one another, neighbors were ordered to inform on each other.

After dinner, the exhausted community was forced to assemble for interminable "emergency meetings" and listen to Jones's increasingly mad ravings late into the night. Punishment was swift for those who nodded off. One evening a sixty-year-old father of five named Charlie, worn out from fieldwork, slumped to the ground. An incensed Jones commanded Charlie's son to wrap a boa constrictor around his father's neck, releasing him only after the poor man's face was turning red and he had humiliated himself by pissing his pants.

Jones and his heavily armed security team kept the community in a state of terrorized obedience. Minor infractions could send malefactors of all ages, even children, to the dreaded Box, a stuffy underground cubicle where they could be held for days. Those who dared to dissent were dispatched to the medical unit, where they were forcibly drugged and kept in a zombified state indefinitely.

While his followers lived hungry, spartan lives, Emperor Jones resided in relative splendor in a cottage well stocked with electric appliances, delicacies like hard-boiled eggs, snacks, and soft drinks, and a cache of medications that he had expropriated from his aging and feeble residents. His drug supplies were endless.

The temple leader had been dependent on amphetamines, sedatives, and other drugs for years. Jim Jones Jr. remembered that as far back as the family's days in Redwood Valley, his father kept a tray of white liquid in the refrigerator and would fix syringes with the fluid and inject himself. One time he overdosed, flailing around on the floor, and the worried kids were told that their father had suffered a heart attack. But years later, after working in a hospital, the younger Jones came to realize his father had displayed the symptoms of a speed addict.

In the glorious isolation of Jonestown, under his tropical canopy, Jones surrendered fully to his drug-fueled manias. He created an Orwellian dystopia and forced his captive followers to live in it. The nights were the worst, as the jungle's dark silence was broken by a ghastly soundtrack of howler monkeys' screechings and Jones's sudden eruptions over the loudspeakers. Father's voice was everywhere: in the huts, outhouses, fields. There was no getting away from his sleepless rants.

"White Night!" Father would yell in the deepest black of night, jolting his followers from their exhausted slumber. "White Night!" Residents were rushed toward the glaring lights of the pavilion, the elderly shuffling along in a daze, the children crying. When they were all gathered there, Jones—spazzy and hot-wired on speed—told them that the US government was about to pounce. They had to act quickly.

"Hear that sound?" Father told them. "The mercenaries are coming. The end has come. Time is up. Children . . . line up into two queues, one on either side of me."

The guards stood solemn vigil over a large vat next to Jones.

"It tastes like fruit juice, children. It will not be hard to swallow."

The White Night drill. It was terrifying but not real. Until the day it was.

28

RAPTURE IN THE JUNGLE

BACK IN THE United States, relatives of Jim Jones's terrorized flock grew increasingly desperate as they tried to arouse the interest of public officials. Democratic congressman Leo Ryan, who represented a suburban district south of San Francisco, was the only one who took their concerns seriously. The State Department shrugged off Ryan's inquiries, assuring him that all was well in Guyana. He held a hearing on Jonestown, inviting defectors and worried relatives to testify before a congressional panel, but his colleagues were distracted and uninformed, and the witnesses' testimony drew little media coverage.

Ryan was the kind of congressional lone ranger who tackled issues in dramatic ways. He once traveled to Prince Edward Island off Newfoundland to confront fur hunters who were killing baby harp seals. He decided to fly down to Guyana and inspect Jonestown firsthand. Ryan invited other members of the Bay Area congressional delegation to accompany him, but they all turned him down. The congressman knew the risk. David Reuben warned him not to go. Before he left Washington, Ryan gave his will to an aide for safekeeping.

"I think he was afraid," said his daughter Pat Ryan. "But he also believed that, goddammit, somebody's got to do something."

As Ryan walked out of the family's Bay Area home on the way to catch his plane to Guyana, his daughter hugged him for the last time. "Don't let anybody shoot you," she joked anxiously.

"Don't worry," her father assured her. "I'll be fine."

Ryan and his entourage, which included two San Francisco newspaper reporters, a *Washington Post* reporter, and an NBC news team, hoped there would be safety in numbers. Everything seemed calm during the delegation's visit to Jonestown, as the cult leader managed to shake off his drug haze and keep his congregation in line. But when the visitors prepared to leave, one resident after the next came forward nervously and begged to go with them. The defections, sixteen in all, cracked the hellish community's carefully constructed façade, and the madness began sluicing out.

As Ryan was politely taking his leave, one of Jones's loyalists rushed forward and threw his arms around the congressman. "Congressman Ryan, you motherfucker!" he spat out, jabbing at Ryan's jugular with a homemade knife. Others lunged for the attacker, and after a frantic scuffle on the ground, he was disarmed. Ryan was not hurt, but as he jumped aboard the truck taking the delegation and the defectors to the nearby landing strip, a thick air of menace hung over the group. It was suddenly, terribly clear that nothing—not Ryan's congressional status, not the presence of a media pack—protected them here in the blazing, humid middle of nowhere, in Jim Jones's remote empire.

While the group was boarding two small planes, a Peoples Temple tractor-trailer rolled onto the runway carrying several armed men. They opened fire on Ryan's delegation with rifles and shotguns. When the explosion of gunfire stopped, five people were dead, including the congressman, and ten were wounded.

As word got back to Jonestown about the massacre at the airstrip, the congregation was gathered in the pavilion, in the midst of another White Night drill. But Jones knew this was no drill, it was his final stand. A congressman had been murdered. This time they really would be coming after him.

Always looking for a wider audience, the megalomaniacal preacher taped his last sermon—a rambling, self-pitying, insidiously seductive performance that is deeply disturbing to hear. Jones addressed his distraught flock from his usual throne, a wooden garden chair on the stage. Assembled before him were over nine hundred men, women, and children who had followed him into the wilderness and would soon be told to join him in oblivion. Many had been outcasts: welfare mothers, convicts, and addicts. But most were solidly working-class people. They were former factory workers, nurses, teachers, longshoremen, and field hands. Around 70 percent were black, and women outnumbered men nearly two to one. Later they would be portrayed as figures of pathos, but there was nothing pathetic about their dreams of a better world— dreams that Jones manipulated brilliantly.

Now he played on those deep aspirations one last time, in his lulling voice, trying to convince them that the promised land could not be found in this life, it awaited them in death.

"It's all over," Jones told the assembly. "The congressman has been murdered." Troops would soon overrun Jonestown, he said, and horribly torture them; even the children and old people would not be safe. They must avoid this terrible fate by taking control of their destinies and committing "revolutionary suicide."

"My opinion is that we be kind to the children and be kind to the seniors and take the potion like they used to take in ancient Greece, and step over quietly," he explained to them, with the patience of a schoolteacher. "Because we are not committing suicide. It's a revolutionary act."

ONLY ONE MEMBER OF the assembly dared to stand up and disagree with Jones that day as the setting sun began to burn itself out and Jonestown prepared to sear itself into history. Not surprisingly, it was an outspoken, middle-aged woman from Los Angeles named Christine Miller—an African-American "church lady" who had repeatedly demonstrated that she was not afraid to speak her mind to Jim Jones, even at great risk. Miller's brave argument with death is that grotesque spectacle's only redeeming act of humanity.

Miller had fought her way through life, picking cotton in the scorching Texas fields as a young girl and eventually finding work as a county clerk in Los Angeles. "I pulled myself up by my bootstraps," she used to say. After a lifetime of hard work, Miller was able to buy a home and a Pontiac Grand Prix, and could afford some of the finer things: furs, jewelry, and travel. But she was the kind of woman who wanted to be of service. When she discovered the Peoples Temple, its social mission struck her as a truer manifestation of Christ's teachings than what she found in the sweet-by-and-by churches. She began to give away her hard-earned possessions to Jones's organization and moved to San Francisco to join a temple commune. But even after she made the trek to the Guyana wilderness, Miller kept a few articles of fancy clothing and some jewelry pieces as totems of her past accomplishments—and Jones knew well enough not to collectivize the proud woman's last items of distinction.

Miller was not happy in Jonestown, where the sweltering agricultural compound brought back harsh childhood memories of the Texas cotton fields. She wrote letters to Jones, complaining that she had worked too hard in life to be pushed so hard in Jonestown. During one pavilion assembly, Jones grew fed up with Miller's vocal independence. "Shut up, woman!" he barked at her.

"You can't talk to me that way," Miller replied.

"I'll talk to you any way that I like, I'm the leader," Jones shot back.

But Miller stood her ground. "Oh, no, you won't."

Outraged to have his authority challenged so brazenly in front of the entire congregation, Jones picked up the gun he often brought to meetings and pointed it directly at Miller. He could shoot her right there, he shouted, and have her body dragged out to the jungle, and nobody would ever find out.

The entire assembly held its breath.

"You can do that," she said, "but you are going to have to respect me first."

Jones scrambled to his feet and waded into the gathering. He walked right up to Miller and pointed the gun at her head. "Woman, I will blow your motherfucking brains out right now!"

Miller didn't flinch. She looked directly into his face with a gaze fierce enough to pierce his sunglasses. "You can do that," she repeated, "but you have to respect me first."

Hue Fortson, who was at the meeting that day, remembered the stunned silence. "We all felt he was about to shoot her. He could easily have done it and gotten away with it. But slowly he put down his gun and walked back to his chair. He tried to gloss it over, saying it showed that he was such a loving person because he didn't take her life, and what a strong leader he was. But we all knew he had backed down. Later people were afraid to talk about it. But you held it inside yourself and treasured it."

On November 18, 1978, Christine Miller lost her final argument with Jim Jones. But she put everything she could muster into the fight, combating the preacher's slippery logic with reason, using old sermons of his to counter his march toward death, and passionately defending the right of people to live, including those whose lives had just begun. Miller knew that this time it was not just her life at stake, but those of 913 people, among them more than 300 children.

It's a chilling duel. Even today, listening to recordings of Miller making her argument against mass extermination, while she is heckled by frenzied Jones loyalists, one still hopes that she can prevail. Miller's voice is clear and strong as a bell, with a slight Texas drawl. Jones's tongue is thick, and at times he seems lost in a stupor. But his powerful, dominating will is still there, and he still unleashes flashes of eloquence as he herds his flock toward its doom. Miller is the last obstacle in his way, and he alternately patronizes her ("Christine, you've always been a very good agitator . . . I personally like you very much") and heatedly rebuts her.

"I'm not afraid to die," Miller says at one point. "But I look about at the babies, and I think they deserve to live, you know."

"But don't they also deserve much more?" replies Jones sweetly, lovingly. "They deserve peace."

Miller tries a different tack, trying to appeal to the sense of defiance that Jones had instilled in his followers over the years. "When you—" she begins, catching herself before continuing. "When we destroy ourselves, we're defeated. We let them, the enemies, defeat us."

Jones responds by quoting Chief Joseph's eloquent surrender speech, after the US cavalry had tracked down the remains of his suffering Nez Perce tribe. "I am tired; my heart is sick and sad. From where the sun now stands, I will fight no more forever."

Miller lacks Jones's education and his ability to invoke history and scripture. But she has one last line of defense, and it's the most powerful of all. She has a right to choose her fate, she tells Jones, and the others do too. "As an individual, I have a right to say what I think, what I feel. And I think we all have a right to our own destiny as individuals. And I have a right to choose mine, and everybody has a right to choose theirs."

Other women in the audience seem to shift toward Miller, murmuring assent. And for once, Jones is tongue-tied.

"I have a right to my opinion," Miller insists, echoing the words of every strong black woman in American history, from nineteenth-century evangelist Sojourner Truth on. ("And ain't I a woman?") All Jones can mumble in reply is, "I'm not taking it from you."

For a brief, heart-stopping moment, it seems that Miller might win the day—as she did when she stared down the barrel of Jones's gun and made him blink. But suddenly Jim McElvane, one of the most respected black members of Jones's inner circle, jumps in. McElvane, who once had a brief relationship with Miller, silences her by reminding her that individual rights are not relevant in a socialist paradise.

"Christine, you're only standing here because *he* was here in the first place," he chides his former lover, reminding her of their leader's sacrifices. "So I don't know what you're talking about, having an individual life. Your life has been extended to the day that you're standing there, because of him."

Then the tide rushes back against Christine Miller, as the anguished and tormented congregants bow and scrape once more to Father. "You've saved so many people!" shouts a female worshipper. Once again, collective madness reigns.

Jones regains his morbid rhythm. "I've saved them, I've saved them," he agrees. But now "the best testimony we can make is to leave this goddam world."

NO ONE CAN STOP Jim Jones now. The big aluminum vat is brought out. This time, the grape Flavor Aid is laced with potassium cyanide. In his eerie singsong voice, Jones urges his flock to take their final communion—babies and children first. Ghostly church music plays in the background.

It scars the soul to listen to the infants' screaming and crying. As the children begin their death throes—vomiting and bleeding through their noses and gasping for breath—Jones urges them to stay quiet. "Look children, it's just something to put you to rest."

Many parents are now hysterical, watching their children die, and

Jones scolds them. "We must die with some dignity." But one mother can't stop wailing.

"Mother, Mother, Mother, Mother, Mother, please," croons Jones, whose own hysteria seems held down only by sedatives. "Mother, please, please, please. Don't—don't do this. Lay down your life with your child. But don't do this."

Jones seems offended that people are not dying according to his choreography. "Keep your emotions down," he commands. "I don't care how many screams you hear, I don't care how many anguished cries, death is a million times preferable to ten more days of this life."

Many Jonestown residents did not agree with their raving leader that day. But there was no escape. The pavilion was surrounded by armed security guards, including some of the murderers who had returned from the airstrip. One survivor saw dozens of people being dragged to the tub of purple-colored poison and estimated that about sixty adults were forcibly injected with the potion. By some accounts, one of those who went down resisting was Christine Miller.

Jonestown has become widely known as the biggest mass suicide in history. But with so many adult members of the community strong-armed to their doom, hundreds of children murdered, and many parents so anguished that they could not help but join their little ones in death, it is more appropriate to call Jonestown a slaughter. Even those who went to their deaths singing Jones's praises were victims of his con. Incarcerated in a jungle concentration camp and robbed of their free will, they were programmed to follow their leader to the gates of hell.

"Free at last," moans Jim Jones near the end, before someone puts a bullet in his head, his preferred method of exit. The invocation of Martin Luther King was one last sacrilege by the man who had wrapped himself in the glorious rhetoric of suffering and resistance.

When Jones staged his grand escape, he did not simply destroy over nine hundred lives and plunge thousands more into bottomless grief. He poisoned a language of social justice. Everyone who had joined hands with his crusade, whether for opportunistic or idealistic reasons, was now contaminated by Jonestown. As the news images of bloated corpses sprawled in the dust were beamed back to San Francisco, the city shuddered. The same free air that had nurtured the beats, hippies, gays, and a growing garden of the imagination had given birth to a monster.

29

THE RECKONING

AS THE GRISLY spectacle in Guyana was revealed, the Fillmore neighborhood was filled with wailing and tears. Ravaged by redevelopment, poverty, drugs, and crime, San Francisco's black heartland reeled once more. Nearly every family in the neighborhood was touched by the loss of someone in Jonestown.

Shrieking relatives and frenzied reporters and TV crews besieged the Peoples Temple building on Geary. Family members, uncertain about the fates of their loved ones, demanded information. Inside the barricaded church, the remnants of Jones's holy army—the ones who had been left behind to take care of temple business in San Francisco—wandered in a daze, trying to figure out what to do. A few spluttered with rage, frustrated that they had not been included in Jones's Rapture. Others railed against the enemy: the faceless government agents whom they were convinced had wiped out Jonestown.

Rev. Norman Leach, Jim Jones's outspoken defender in the local National Council of Churches chapter, slipped into the back of the temple on a rainy night to console the survivors. As people wept and crowded around the shortwave radio for information from Guyana, Leach walked into another room, where Angela Davis and some cohorts were holding an intense strategy meeting. Davis was using the occasion to politically vent—"her usual anti-American shtick"—and Leach couldn't take it. "These people need to be comforted, not agitated," he told her. When the Davis contingent reacted heatedly, Leach got up and left. "I was not there to argue politics," he said.

Jonestown was a hideous stain on all those in the Bay Area left who had been taken in by Jim Jones, including attorney Charles Garry. The aging lawyer was forced to flee for his life during the Jonestown blood-bath, huffing and puffing through the Guyanese jungle alongside Mark Lane—another celebrity attorney who had shared Garry's rosy view of Jones's "paradise." Garry forced Lane to carry his suitcase as they sweated their way through the thick, tropical greenery. Lane griped about his burden, but suspecting that the heavy case was stuffed with money, he kept carrying it. The suitcase was actually filled with the toi-letries and grooming equipment that the notoriously vain Garry found indispensable, including the hair blower he used to perfect his comb-over. Back home in San Francisco, Garry struggled to make sense of the debacle. "Jim Jones created one of the most beautiful dreams in the world and then destroyed it," said the still-confused attorney.

Jonestown struck George Moscone in the gut. He vomited and broke down crying when he heard the news. The mayor spent much of the next few days—what turned out be the last days of his life—consoling those who had lost loved ones in Guyana, including the family of Leo Ryan.

Moscone knew that Ryan, who had risen with him in local Demo-cratic politics, was one of the few heroes in the grotesque Jim Jones drama: the only political leader who had the courage to investigate the demonic preacher in his jungle lair. Ryan's death was particularly trou-bling to him. "I don't know how to cope with anyone being killed or assassinated," the mayor said mournfully after he was told about Ryan. Moscone wrote a heartfelt letter to Ryan's ex-wife Margaret, the mother of his five children, adding in his own handwriting, "He was a very good friend of mine, and I am without words to express my grief."

At Ryan's funeral ceremony in All Souls Church in South San Fran-cisco, Moscone again broke down in tears. House Majority Leader Jim Wright's eulogy must have been particularly painful for Moscone, the progressive politician who prided himself on comforting the poor and afflicted. Ryan, Wright told the overflowing church, had a "readiness to go where suffering was. When relatives and friends came to him with a story of abounding horror, inhumanity, and bizarre brutalities, Leo Ryan went to see and serve. And it was while helping to free captives that he met his death. Greater love has no man than this."

Moscone and San Francisco's liberal leadership had aided and abetted Jones's reign of "horror, inhumanity, and bizarre brutalities." And the press immediately clamored for an explanation. The mayor was the only political ally of Jones to admit any error of judgment, conceding that he had been "taken in" by the powerful preacher. The *Examiner* gave Moscone credit for his admission: "At least Mayor George Moscone is willing to admit he made a mistake in sizing up the charismatic leader of the Peoples Temple . . . He had the decency to admit it. Not so with some of our other politicians in this city and in the state."

While Moscone was clearly deeply shaken by Jonestown, however, he couldn't bring himself to fully acknowledge his role in empowering the cult leader. "It's clear that if there was a sinister plan, then we were taken in," he told reporters. "But I'm not taking any responsibility. It's not mine to shoulder." When a reporter pressed him, asking the mayor if he felt "culpable" for helping to politically legitimize Jones, a distraught Moscone responded heatedly, "I deeply resent that. You're reaching far out." Then he shuddered visibly and added, "It's all too bizarre for me."

Willie Brown was even more defiant, proclaiming nervily that he had no "regrets" about his close political alliance with Jones and scorching other politicians who were now running for cover. "They all like to say, 'Forgive me, I was wrong,' but that's bullshit. It doesn't mean a thing now, it just isn't relevant."

Some of Jones's useful acolytes never stopped justifying their promotion of Peoples Temple, even many years later. Norman Leach is now retired from the church and living in Nebraska, after again being convicted of pederasty, this time with a member of a Boy Scout troop he started. The judge at Leach's trial called him "dangerous" and said that he had "sexually assaulted juvenile males in every area of the country he has lived in during the last forty years of his life." Looking back at his days in San Francisco, the former reverend denied sharing any guilt for Jim Jones's reign of horror. "I feel no remorse or responsibility," said Leach, whom Jones continued to court even after fleeing to Guyana, bombarding him with dozens of obviously scripted letters from temple children inviting him to visit Jonestown. "I turned him down—it made me uneasy," he declared.

Leach concedes there were many "red flags" about the Peoples Temple. "But there's no way that I could've had insight into the depth of his evil," he insisted. "I still think the goal of Peoples Temple was beautiful: black and white, gay and straight, rich and poor, all coming together. That's Christianity right there—or Judaism, or whatever great faith you name."

The San Francisco press was as reluctant as local political and religious leaders to take responsibility for Jones's ascension. The *Chronicle,* which had chastised John Barbagelata for his strident warnings about Jones and shut down its own enterprising reporter, never acknowledged its mistakes in covering the media-savvy preacher. Herb Caen could not bring himself to do anything more than offer the city bland condolences in his daily column: "Gray skies dripped sadness and sorrow over San Francisco yesterday," wrote Jones's former booster. "Headlines told of tragedy and madness in steaming jungles . . . how to judge the insanity surrounding the end of Rev. Jim Jones . . . Who would have expected *this?*"

David Reuben, for one. The DA's investigator saw the nightmare coming, but, hobbled by city politics, could not stop it in time. After the news flashes from Guyana, a disgusted Reuben accosted his boss. *"Now* do you think we had something there, Joe?" he asked Freitas.

The district attorney, still in ass-covering mode, dodged any responsibility for bringing Peoples Temple agents into his office and impeding his own investigators' inquiry. "In the period I had contact," Freitas lamely told the press, "it was an activist church, and Jim Jones seemed a pretty okay fellow."

Reuben, one of the few people in San Francisco city government who tried to bring down Jones, still feels guilty that he failed. "Peoples Temple was the highlight and lowlight of my career. I kind of peaked and died with that investigation," said Reuben, who left government service after Jonestown and is now a private eye.

JONESTOWN RELEASED A POISON cloud over San Francisco. There was blood and terror in the air. Even those who loudly denied any guilt were running scared. City leaders were convinced that Jonestown hit squads were on the loose and were gunning for them. The district attorney's office fielded panicky phone calls from politicians who had been entangled with Jones, even taking a call from the White House. One call came from a hysterical Willie Brown, who tearfully pleaded, "What do I do?"

The Jonestown survivors who trickled back to the Bay Area had more reason to fear for their lives than the politicians did. The survivors had to confront the turbulent grief and rage of people who lost relatives in Guyana.

On the final White Night, Jim Jones Jr. was in Georgetown, where he, his brother Stephan, and the rest of the Jonestown basketball team had gone to play in a tournament. Over the radio, Jones Sr. ordered his two sons to get knives, scissors, and wire and kill themselves too, but they didn't comply with their father's final command. Others in the Guyana capital did obey, however. Jim Jr. was in the temple headquarters in Georgetown when Sharon Amos, one of his father's most zealous lieutenants, unleashed an orgy of blood. Taking her three young children into the bathroom, she began slicing their throats with a butcher knife before ordering another child to cut her own jugular. One of Jim Jr.'s teammates, Calvin Douglas, raced down the hall, threw open the door, and was able to rescue one of Amos's daughters. Jim Jr. can still remember the torrent of blood pouring out of the bathroom.

After he was flown back to the Bay Area, Jim Jr., who was eighteen at the time, moved into his sister Suzanne's house in Daly City. Everywhere he went in San Francisco, he saw the ghosts of people he once knew. He attended memorial services for people who died in Jonestown—there were many of them. One day, after the service for a woman named Valerie, Jim Jr. was sitting with the bereaved relatives and friends in the living room of Valerie's mother. Suddenly the mother appeared in the room with a gun, which she pointed directly at Jim Jr., the Peoples Temple's chosen one. "Why are you alive and my daughter is gone?" the woman asked young Jones. He looked at her and said simply, "I'm already dead."

Other mourners quickly took the gun away. Jones stopped going to the family memorials.

San Francisco crackled with a strange electricity, as if a massive thunderstorm was building offshore, out beyond the fog bank, and it was all about to burst. "Earthquake weather," they called it in San Francisco. Political leaders were hunkering down, frantically heading off investigations. But there was a powerful feeling in the city that there would be a reckoning, a growing sense that there must be blood.

30

A TALE OF TWO CITIES

EVEN BEFORE JONESTOWN, San Francisco seemed headed for a violent cataclysm. By the late 1970s, the sexual revolution centered in San Francisco had sparked a vehement backlash from defenders of traditional morality, in the city itself and throughout the country. Family values demagogues like politically ambitious California state senator John Briggs and Anita Bryant—a former beauty queen and singer who was the pitchwoman for the Florida orange juice industry—tapped into a growing pool of antigay fear and revulsion. San Francisco, which in the blink of an eye had become the ballroom for America's coming out party, was targeted by conservative crusaders as a modern Sodom.

Briggs, denouncing San Francisco as "the moral garbage dump of homosexuality in this country," kicked off a carnivalesque, moral-revival campaign for governor. The obscure politician grabbed the media spotlight by scapegoating gay teachers. Portraying them in the same lurid ways that McCarthyites once vilified Communists in the classroom—as vicious predators threatening the purity of America's children—Briggs campaigned for a 1978 state initiative to ban homosexual teachers from California schools.

Bryant also cast her holy march as a battle to "save our children," leading a successful campaign in 1977 to repeal a gay rights law in

Florida's Dade County, which inspired a wave of similar antihomosexual uprisings around the country.

Meanwhile, in San Francisco's Visitacion Valley—a secluded hollow of white, Catholic, working-class families fighting a losing battle against the encroaching black Sunnydale housing project—a former altar boy and cop named Dan White was kicking off his own moral restoration campaign. In 1977 White announced his bid for the board of supervisors in the new district elections, declaring himself the champion of all those frustrated, longtime San Franciscans who no longer recognized their city. Echoing Briggs, White lashed out at the "social malignancies" and "cesspool of perversion" that were contaminating his hometown. "I am not going to be forced out of San Francisco by splinter groups of radicals, social deviates, and incorrigibles," vowed White. "Believe me, there are tens of thousands who are just as determined to legally fight to protect and defend our conservative values." White struck a chord in his embattled district, sweeping into office along with Harvey Milk, the flag bearer for the city's "social deviates."

The escalating culture war inflamed the city's humors. Violent attacks on gays spiked in San Francisco. Roaming packs of teenagers and young men sprang on gays with fists and knives. Many of the attackers were from the heavily Latino Mission district that abutted the Castro—a neighborhood that had shared the Mission's Catholic family values until gays displaced the Irish. Some of the young thugs were wrestling with their own sexual confusions. In June 1977, on the first warm night of summer, Robert Hillsborough, a thirty-one-year-old city gardener known as Mr. Greenjeans to the kids at the park where he worked, was jumped by four young men as he walked to his apartment with his boyfriend. A nineteen-year-old Latino named John Cordova pinned Hillsborough to the ground and plunged a fishing knife repeatedly into his chest and face, screaming, "Faggot, faggot, faggot!" It was an intensely personal and physical way to kill a man. Cordova, it was later revealed, led his own secret homosexual life.

The savage murder of Robert Hillsborough set off new emotional eruptions in the city. The victim's mother blamed antigay crusaders like Anita Bryant, who was busy telling America that one homosexual act should land offenders in prison for at least twenty years—as a grim warning to young men who were contemplating the gay lifestyle. "My son's blood is on her hands," said Hillsborough's grieving mother.

Mayor Moscone agreed, attributing the rise of antigay violence in San Francisco to the "climate of hate and bigotry" fomented by Bryant and Briggs. Moscone ordered flags at city hall and other municipal buildings to be flown at half staff in honor of the murdered city gardener. The mayor's decision set off a backlash of complaints from citizens who thought it was an improper civic display.

Feeling unsafe in their own neighborhood, gays in the Castro began carrying whistles to sound the alarm if they came under attack. Some of the district's more butch residents formed street patrols, surrounding neighborhood invaders until the police showed up. An editorial in the police-oriented *Examiner* denounced the "semi-vigilante" tactic and admonished gays not to "get hysterical" and interfere with police business. But when cops did respond to attacks on gays, they often ended up arresting the victims instead of the assailants.

One evening Harvey Milk and a friend heard a whistle and ran to the scene of the crime. Milk, a navy veteran who believed in aggressive self-defense, chased down and tackled the thug, who begged Milk not to beat him. When the victim, more afraid of the police than he was of the attacker, said he wouldn't press charges, Milk was forced to let the gay basher go. But as he released the thug, Milk warned, "Tell all your friends we're down here waiting for them."

HARVEY MILK, THE STREET-SMART ex–New Yorker, often drew historical comparisons between the treatment of Jews and gays. He vowed that homosexuals would fight back against their tormentors to their dying breath. "Do you think gay people are going to go with their heads bowed into the gas chambers?" he asked an *Examiner* reporter one day, in an impassioned tone that made clear his answer. "I mean, I'll go kicking and screaming before I go with my head bowed."

As a San Francisco supervisor, Milk brought the same combative spirit to city hall. But he was also a master at the sweet and gentle art of politics, reaching out to groups that normally had no use for faggots and sodomites, from teamsters to black church groups.

"Get a load of this fruit. He ain't half bad," growled a tough old labor guy in a union hall where Milk had gone for a meeting. That's when Cleve Jones, Milk's political protégé, began to realize it: *Everybody* liked Harvey. And the feeling was mutual.

"He really loved lots of people; he was a natural politician," Jones said. "He wasn't just deploying the significant eye contact. And it was more than simply caring about people—he *enjoyed* them. The best evidence of that is the kids. At a time when gays were being demonized as child molesters, kids just *adored* him, they flocked to his camera store. He was always surrounded by gay kids, straight kids, boys, girls. I was hardly the only young person he mentored. He just had a gift for making people feel good. He would hear that a woman in the neighborhood had a miscarriage, and he would go out and buy a bouquet of flowers and go visit her. I had been bullied all through my childhood, and I hated straight people out of fear. But to see Harvey fearlessly crossing all these boundaries, going into union halls and all these ethnic and racial communities—it made us all braver."

"Milk has something for everybody." That was Harvey's first campaign slogan, lifted from the dairy industry's billboards. The sentiment was a sharp contrast to White's rallying cry of resentment, "Unite and fight with Dan White." But Milk believed that he could even win over White. After both men won seats on the board of supervisors, the odd couple began making joint appearances on local talk shows, warmly praising each other. White claimed that he was referring to junkies, not gays, when he condemned "social deviates." The two men began having coffee every Thursday morning at a café in the Castro.

A friend of Milk said it sickened him to see the two political opposites schmoozing that way. "Harvey, that guy's a pig," he said. "He's never gonna be different. He's a cop." But Milk strongly disagreed. "Dan White is just stupid. He's working class, a Catholic, been brought up with all those prejudices. I'm gonna sit next to him every day and let him know we're not all those bad things he thinks we are . . . Everyone can be reached. *You* think people are hopeless—not me."

Milk's attitude—ebullient, embracing, and more than a little patronizing—both charmed and enraged White. The gay leader would come to realize how tough a challenge Dan White was, even for someone with his dazzling political and personal skills.

Warm, wickedly funny, and flirtatious, Harvey Milk was the opposite of Dan White in more ways than one. White was the son of heroic fireman Charlie White, who worked himself into an early grave trying to feed ten hungry mouths. Grim and devout, White spent his entire life trying to live up to his father's life of service. In Catholic school, Danny White became known for being good with his fists, mixing it up with the black kids whose families were pressing in on the old Irish neighborhoods. He was also good at sports, captaining his high school football and baseball teams, and heading for the New York Yankees farm system until an injury ruined his playing career.

White's life never measured up. He served in Vietnam but saw no action, and army officials called his record undistinguished. A self-described "romantic," he grew a beard and ran off to Alaska to write stories like Jack London, but he had no literary talent. He joined the SFPD, but, disappointed that it did not offer the heroic opportunities in his imagination, he quit and became a fireman. He finally matched his father's heroism one day, rescuing a mother and baby from the seventeenth floor of a blazing fire at Geneva Towers—ironically, the crime-infested housing project in Visitacion Valley that symbolized to many in White's neighborhood the end of their way of life. It was a daring act, rushing through the flames and out onto the balcony where the woman was screaming, with her baby cradled in her arms, and then sweeping them both to safety. But the next morning, the *Chronicle* buried the story about the courageous fireman who was also running for supervisor on page six. His late father's heroics had made the front page.

The handsome, square-jawed White married the woman he was supposed to: a pretty Catholic-reared schoolteacher named Mary Ann Burns, whose father was the commander of White's firehouse. Mary Ann reminded White of his own sainted mother. In the beginning, the young couple seemed happy enough, and Mary Ann bore Dan a son. But the passion seemed to leak from the marriage too soon. White seemed happiest when playing shortstop on the police softball team, where he attacked every game with the spikes-flying zeal of Pete Rose. He stayed in athletic condition into his thirties, sculpting his body with weight lifting and exercise.

One day the board of supervisors organized a softball game against Mayor Moscone's staff. Milk asked White what he should wear on the field, and White told him whatever he wanted to. "Well, I've got a brand-new print dress," flounced Harvey. "Would that be okay?"

"Dan went nuts," Moscone aide Dick Sklar recalled. "He hated being taunted. And Harvey was always taunting Dan."

White was flustered by the witty and nimble Milk. He found his gay colleague alternately captivating and exasperating. Milk thought his political opposite was just as vexing. White invited Milk to his son's christening—an invitation he extended to only one other colleague on the board of supervisors. But while fraternizing with the country's only openly gay elected official, White also railed against the disgusting carnival of male flesh he saw on display whenever he drove through the Castro. "They're screwing around right out in the streets," White fumed to his equally censorious friend, a Visitacion Valley parish priest named Father Tom Lacey. White was also disturbed when he squeezed among the throngs lining Market Street to watch the raucous and shameless Gay Freedom Day Parade go strutting by.

Milk told Cleve Jones that he thought White was secretly gay. And the more he got to know White, he became convinced that the former altar boy was a cauldron of bubbling emotions that could boil over at any time. "Dan White is a closet case," Milk confided to a boyfriend one day. "And he's dangerous."

HARVEY MILK AND GEORGE Moscone were everything that Dan White was not: charming, politically shrewd, sexually rambunctious, and comfortable in their own skins. The cool, athletic Moscone sometimes acted like a suave father for White, who had lost his own workhorse dad at age seventeen. And Milk was like a wild older brother to White: sometimes adorable, often maddening. But in truth, Dan White was a stranger, utterly lost in these two men's world.

Moscone and Milk were the dynamic duo of San Francisco's progressive revolution. They never forgot what they were elected to do: to fight for the burdened and afflicted, for those whose voices were never heard in the halls of power. They fought for the rights of workers, minorities, gays, and renters. And they made the same enemies: the chamber of commerce, developers, realtors, the SFPD.

Moscone and Milk both loved politics, and they loved the city they served. They roamed its streets, savoring its rich brew, always ready to plunge in. Christopher Moscone remembers going with his family to a North Beach restaurant, and when they emerged after dinner, his father spotted some people down the street picketing and chanting for higher wages. "My dad just joined right in, walking the picket line. We all stood there waiting for him, and my mom's like, 'Any time now, George.'"

Harvey Milk liked to ride the MUNI to city hall so that he could overhear San Francisco talking. He never got over the ornate beauty of his workplace, the temple of gold, marble, and carved wood dedicated to the people of San Francisco. He liked to give friends tours of the building, explaining the intricate friezes that illuminated the interior of the grand rotunda and urging them to pretend they were stars of a Cecil B. DeMille spectacle and go sweeping down the epic marble staircase in the colonnaded lobby. "Never take the elevator when you're in city hall," Milk advised. "Always take that stairway. You can make such an entrance—take it slowly." In his own dreams, Milk wasn't Gloria Swanson but the mayor of San Francisco. He had dreamed of becoming mayor from the time he first set foot in this jewel box of a city. There were some city hall observers who believed that Milk was indeed Moscone's logical successor. He would make history again when he was elected as the country's first openly gay mayor.

In the meantime, the city's current mayor was already championing gay liberation. George Moscone was as much a product of the San Francisco parishes and parochial school sports as Dan White. But he embraced all of San Francisco. He looked as comfortable in Amelia's, the divey lesbian bar on Valencia Street, as he did in the dining room at North Beach Restaurant.

Moscone shared Milk's mischievous sense of humor. One day Milk told the mayor that he had been picked up on a Castro street corner that morning while waiting for a bus by fellow supervisor Quentin Kopp, who gave him a ride to city hall in his official car. Kopp was the perfect foil for the two fun-loving liberals: a tall, gawky, balding, bespectacled bean counter. "You've got to do me a favor," Moscone told Milk. "Next time

Kopp picks you up, reach over and grab the inside of his thigh." Milk exploded in laughter and promised the mayor he would do just that.

IN THE FALL OF 1978, Moscone joined Milk in the campaign to defeat Proposition 6, the antigay Briggs initiative. The two men made regular Saturday morning visits to the San Franciscans Against Prop 6 head-quarters. In the closing days of the campaign, the momentum swung against Briggs as a phalanx of political leaders took a stand against the nasty piece of legislative intolerance, including President Carter and Governor Jerry Brown.

Desperate to create a media spectacle to turn the tide in his favor, Briggs—a dreary little man with thinning hair and baggy, brown suits from an equally dreary Southern California suburb—phoned the SFPD and announced that he would be showing up that night at the Hallow-een festival on Polk Street. Anything could happen if Briggs waded into the annual street carnival, which had long been a gay high holiday in San Francisco. The ruthless politician was clearly hoping for the worst. As Briggs headed for Polk Street, surrounded by a media swarm eager to capture his confrontation with San Francisco's leather boys, he pro-claimed righteously, "I'm going because this is a children's night, and I'm interested in children."

But San Francisco was Moscone's and Milk's town, not John Briggs's—and they had a surprise for him. The police car carrying Briggs did not stop at Polk Street but instead dropped him a few blocks away, where an official delegation including Moscone, Milk, and pro-gay police chief Gain welcomed him to San Francisco. Moscone then informed the trou-blemaking state senator that it would not be in the best interests of law and order for him to roam Polk Street that night, which was choked with some eighty thousand party maniacs. Chief Gain, flanked by twenty-five cops, firmly agreed. Briggs spluttered with rage, but he had no choice. Outwitted by San Francisco's politicians, he was packed into his car and driven back to Sacramento.

Just a few years before, the SFPD happily billy-clubbed any flagrantly costumed Halloween revelers who made the mistake of wandering off Polk Street. But with Moscone and Milk in city hall, times had changed.

Now the cops were being used on Halloween to run the state's leading gay basher out of town.

The following week, Briggs's attempted pogrom against California's gay teachers was crushed by a two-to-one landslide at the polls. In San Francisco, the vote was even more lopsided, with Proposition 6 losing by a three-to-one margin. At the ecstatic celebration in the Castro that night, a brass band marched into the hall blaring "San Francisco," the Judy Garland show tune that gays had revived as the city anthem ("San Francisco, open your golden gate / You let no stranger wait outside your door"). Joining Milk onstage, Moscone was greeted by a thunderous ovation. The exuberant mayor declared the night a Waterloo for all those bigots and blowhards who'd tried "to make political advances on the backs of those who are at the bottom of the spectrum."

"This is your night!" Moscone shouted to the crowd of activists who had appealed to California's better angels and won big. "No-on-six will be emblazoned upon the principles of San Francisco—liberty and freedom for all, forever!"

But not all of San Francisco was celebrating. The Briggs initiative won a majority vote in Dan White's District 8, where crucifixes and saints under glass protected homes from the devilry over the hills. And the same old values held sway at the hall of justice and the precinct stations. Most San Francisco cops would have preferred to run Moscone and Milk out of town that Halloween night instead of Briggs.

By November 1978, the rage in police ranks against the mayor and his liberal police chief was white hot. Moscone was close to winning the board of supervisors' approval for a resolution to the civil rights lawsuit against the SFPD that would make the department's old-boy culture extinct. Meanwhile, Chief Gain was continuing to reengineer the force, recruiting gays, promoting women and minorities, and driving out the drunks, burnouts, and bullies long coddled by the department.

The veterans felt betrayed by Moscone. When he was running for mayor in 1975, he'd met with the bureau of inspectors, the core group of detectives that traditionally provided the SFPD's leadership. As he looked at the stone-faced cops gathered in the fifth-floor auditorium at the hall of justice, the liberal candidate knew what he needed to promise them to get their support.

"Let me tell you something: when I'm mayor, the chief of police will come from this room," Moscone declared. "In fact, I'm looking right at the man I'm going to appoint: Captain Ray Canepa."

"Boom—that's what we wanted to hear," recalled veteran homicide inspector Frank Falzon. "Canepa was the most popular guy in the room, liked by all the cops. So when George Moscone leaves the room that day, every inspector stood up and gave him a round of applause."

But after he was elected, Moscone picked maverick outsider Charley Gain instead. "He was our worst nightmare," said Falzon. The veteran cops felt stabbed in the back by Moscone.

It got worse as the police watched Moscone and Gain preside over what they saw as a morally lax regime. "We had some serious problems, and now they're not being dealt with correctly," said Falzon. "Things you were told were against the law were suddenly no longer against the law." Gay bathhouses, for instance, were off-limits to the cops in the new San Francisco. And the permissive climate only seemed to draw more homosexuals. "They were migrating from everywhere," Falzon remarked. "A lot of cops felt it was the liberal attitudes—the anything-goes atmosphere—that was attracting them here." Soon there would be nothing left of the San Francisco that they had grown up in, the San Francisco that Dan White kept warning was dying.

The resentment in the ranks was so palpable that a police beat reporter wasn't surprised when he saw this graffiti on a police station bathroom wall one day: "Who's going to get the mayor?"

Rumors began flying around the city in 1978. The cops were going to kill Moscone, or Gain, or both. As San Francisco's most high-profile hooker, Margo St. James heard a lot of the murderous chatter, passed along from cops she knew. One day a cop who was one of her clients phoned her, and, knowing that she was friendly with the police chief, warned her to stop Gain from going out at night. St. James tracked down the chief at a local college where he was giving a speech and told him to go home. "The cops are going to bump you off," she said.

The cops messed with Gain. One time officers showed up at the chief's house and told him that his car in the driveway had a bomb planted in it. "It was a lie," said St. James. "They just hated him. They thought he was handing the city to the dogs."

The streets buzzed with assassination talk. One day an ex-con who had served in Vietnam and was known for his lethal skills was approached by someone claiming to represent a prominent San Franciscan. He promised the ex-con a big reward for killing Mayor Moscone.

Milk also received death threats, including a flurry in advance of the 1978 Gay Freedom Day Parade, where he was scheduled to speak. "You get the first bullet the minute you stand at the microphone," read one neatly typed postcard.

Milk spoke often about his premonitions of a violent death. "I'll get it from a closet queen," he predicted. Cleve Jones grew tired of his mentor's morbid talk. "Who do you think you are?" mocked Jones. "Martin Luther King? Gandhi? You're not on anybody's radar, you're just a gay shopkeeper."

"I was wrong," Jones said years later.

31

DAY OF THE GUN

I T WAS DAN White who became the missile of old San Francisco's rage. The pressures had been building inside him ever since he took his supervisor's seat at city hall. John Barbagelata had warned White not to get involved in San Francisco politics when the young fireman came to the retired supervisor for his blessing. Barbagelata, whose health was still damaged by his municipal battles, didn't think that White had the temperament for the San Francisco arena. Some of White's old friends on the police force, such as Frank Falzon and Jack Cleary, also worried about him. They thought he was too much of a Boy Scout for the city hall snake pit. "Why do you want to go down to city hall and get caught up in all that bullshit?" Cleary remarked to him. "You're a good fireman."

After White took his seat on the board—at age thirty-two, the city's youngest supervisor—it soon became clear he was out of his depth. He was outmaneuvered by his nimble adversaries on the left, Milk and Carol Ruth Silver. And even allies like Quentin Kopp seemed more interested in manipulating the political novice for their own purposes than in grooming him as a civic leader. The only supervisor who seemed to take White under her wing was Dianne Feinstein, but she was often distracted by her own personal and political burdens, including the wrenching illness of her beloved husband, neurosurgeon Bert Feinstein, who died in 1978 after a long bout with cancer.

Meanwhile, White was under growing financial pressures at home, having given up his $18,000 fireman's salary for a role in city government that paid only $9,600 a year. To supplement the family's income, he put in long hours with Mary Ann at the Hot Potato, a struggling French fry and baked potato concession that the couple had opened on touristy Pier 39. Ever since he was a boy, White daydreamed of being the kind of man, like his dad, who would take care of his loved ones and rescue people. But now—sinking in debt and flailing to support his family and take care of his constituents—it was Dan White who needed to be rescued.

On November 10, 1978, White stunned the San Francisco political community—including his own supporters—by announcing that he was resigning from the board of supervisors, explaining, "I didn't have any time to be both a good husband, father, and supervisor."

Moscone, long troubled by the toll that politics had taken on his own family life, responded with feeling to White's announcement. Expressing sympathy for White's decision, the mayor told reporters, "I've always harbored strong admiration for someone who can push aside the vanity of public service and gauge his life accordingly."

But White's biggest backers were not as understanding. The cops and the downtown business establishment were increasingly frantic about San Francisco's leftward direction. They knew that political control of the board of supervisors was hanging in the balance. As soon as Moscone filled White's seat with a political ally, the mayor would finally have a liberal six-to-five margin on the board, and there would be no stopping his progressive legislative agenda. The board of realtors was particularly concerned, because Harvey Milk had already announced his plan to slap controls on soaring rents in the city. And the police union knew that by replacing White on the board, Moscone could finally settle the civil rights lawsuit and repaint the heavily white SFPD with all the colors of the San Francisco rainbow.

White's supporters descended on him and began twisting his arms. They told him he needed to be a man and do his job; they worked on his fears of being a quitter. They reminded him that San Francisco was becoming a cesspool, and he was the only one who could rescue the city. And they sweetened the deal: real estate developers offered to bail out the cash-strapped family man with long-term, low-interest loans.

Five days later, White reversed himself, telling the mayor that he was taking back his resignation letter. At a press conference outside his old city hall office, White made no attempt to camouflage the powerful interests behind his change of heart. Addressing reporters, he was flanked by police union officials and representatives of the real estate industry.

Once again, Moscone responded to White's flip-flop with fatherly forgiveness, telling the press, "As far as I'm concerned Dan White is the supervisor from District Eight . . . A man has a right to change his mind."

But now it was Moscone's turn to feel the political heat. Liberal supporters, including Milk, began working the mayor hard, telling him that this was a golden opportunity to finally achieve his legislative goals; that he would be crazy to throw it away. Dan White had to go, they told him.

As the backroom drama over White embroiled city hall, spilling into the weekend of November 18, the chilling reports from Guyana began filtering back home. Now there was a grisly and surreal backdrop to all the political machinations in San Francisco. Moscone's enemies quickly made it clear that they were going to hang Jonestown around his neck, with Quentin Kopp charging that the mayor had rebuffed his demands for an investigation into Peoples Temple.

Meanwhile, Harvey Milk began using Jonestown to pressure Moscone from the left, telling the mayor that he was now going to need the gay vote more than ever to get reelected the following year. "You reappoint Dan White to the board, and you won't get elected dogcatcher," Milk told Moscone—a political threat loaded with chutzpah, considering Milk's own Jonestown vulnerabilities. On Monday, November 21, Moscone signaled that he was backing away from reappointing White.

THAT WEEK, AS THE maneuvers over San Francisco's political future grew more heated, politicians also wrestled with their guilt and fear about Jonestown. Responding to the rumors about Peoples Temple hit squads, Moscone ordered tightened security at city hall. Police guards were added at both main doors to the building, where all visitors were required to walk through metal detectors. More officers were assigned to the mayor's security team.

Moscone was worried not just about fallout from Jonestown. Dan

White, whose efforts to reclaim his job were growing increasingly frantic, was also adding to the strange and jumpy atmosphere at city hall. White continued to haunt the corridors of city hall, a phantom of increasing pathos, even after it became painfully clear that he was not going to get back his old office. He began threatening the mayor with legal action, and he huddled over the city hall copy machines, cranking out "unsolicited" letters of support for his crusade that were obviously written by himself.

"I'm worried about Dan White," Moscone confided to his wife, Gina. "He's taking this hard. He's acting sort of flakey."

It was no secret to White who was working against him: the same liberal cabal that was turning his hometown into a freak show. And Harvey Milk was at the center of all the intrigue. Wandering around city hall one day, White overheard Milk on the phone, vigorously lobbying the city attorney to reject White's legal bid for his old office. Milk had pretended to be his friend, but now he was showing his true colors. He was the enemy.

On Monday, November 27, Moscone was scheduled to make it official, announcing his replacement for Dan White on the board of supervisors: a liberal federal housing official who would give the mayor his swing vote. White had spent another sleepless night in the basement of his stucco bungalow in the Outer Mission, pacing back and forth, and poring over a scrapbook filled with family clippings and photos. There was nothing in the book of mementoes about his own achievements: his heroic feat at blazing Geneva Towers, or the state softball championship that he and Frank Falzon had helped win for their police all-stars team. The scrapbook was all about his dad's bravery; about the time Charlie White had rescued a minister's suicidal son off a high tower. Dan White had made up his mind. This was the day he was going to rescue San Francisco. He showered and shaved and dressed for his mission.

An aide dropped off White at city hall around ten thirty that morning. He told her he was going to give Moscone and Milk "a piece of his mind." His .38 Smith & Wesson police revolver was tucked into a soft leather holster clipped onto the back of his belt, hidden by his suit jacket. He had loaded the gun with hollow-point bullets, to make sure the physical damage would be explosive. In order to avoid the metal detector at the front door, White went around to the side of the building and crawled through an open basement window. He then climbed the back stairs, heading for room 200, the mayor's second-floor suite.

White knew that Jim Molinari, the mayor's police bodyguard, would be in the reception area, so he entered the mayor's suite through a side door. As White walked into Moscone's office, Willie Brown was leaving. Brown had been shooting the breeze with his old friend about football, politics, and their annual plans to go Christmas shopping in the Wolf's Den, a lingerie shop where women modeled silky garments for male customers. As Brown left Moscone's office, White went gliding past him. "He always had the same blank look on his face," Brown said later.

Moscone was not happy to hear that Dan White was waiting to see him that morning. "Shit," he told his secretary when she announced that White was outside. "How come he's doing this?" But Moscone greeted White graciously, closing the door behind them so that he could give White the bad news in private. The mayor wrapped a consoling arm around his shoulders, and took the distraught young man into a private nook in the back of his office, where he kept a bottle of White Horse whisky. That's the way men like Moscone did these things. "What're you gonna do now? You thinking about being a fireman again? Maybe we can help out." Moscone was all sympathy, but his words just sounded slick and syrupy to White, who was exploding inside.

Suddenly White reached behind his back, ripped the .38 out of his holster, and began firing point-blank at Moscone. As the first two hollow-points tore through Moscone's chest and shoulder, he toppled onto the floor, blood drenching his white shirt. White was not finished. He stood over the mayor's body like an executioner, and, sticking the barrel of his gun almost directly against his victim's ear, pumped two more exploding bullets into Moscone's brain.

Jim Molinari, the mayor's thin blue line, heard nothing as White carried out his mission. While the gunfire erupted in the mayor's office, his bodyguard sat in the reception area, reading the Green Sheet—the *Chronicle* sports section—and chatting with a city hall official. "You don't hear anything in city hall, with all the marble and woodwork," Molinari explained later.

Meanwhile, White reloaded his gun with five more hollow-points and headed for Harvey Milk's office. Dianne Feinstein—who was on the lookout for White that day, worried that he would cause a scene when the new supervisor was sworn in—cried out to him as he passed her office. "Dan!" She knew that she was the only one who might be able to talk some sense into him.

"It'll have to wait, Dianne," White told her, moving with a laser intensity to his next target.

White found Milk in his office. "Harvey, can I see you for a minute?" Milk was surprised to see White. But he agreed to follow the man whom he had called "dangerous," as White led him into his old office, now nearly bare of furniture and equipment.

"What the hell are you doing to me?" White began shouting at Milk after closing the door behind them. "Why do you want to hurt my name, my family? You *cheated* me!" It was the pleading voice of a boy who had never grown up, who had never lived up to his own standards of manhood. And then he was firing his gun at Milk, one, two, three, four times. The fourth bullet slammed into Milk's skull, spraying blood and brain tissue all over the wall. But White wanted to make sure that his tormentor was obliterated. He stood directly over him and fired one more time at point-blank range into Milk's already shattered skull.

Feinstein heard the shots from her office, and immediately thought Dan White had killed himself. She moved toward White's office as if in a trance, shoved open the door, and saw Milk's body splayed on the floor in a glistening pool of blood. Feinstein, whose father and second husband had been doctors, immediately went into emergency mode, kneeling next to Milk and picking up his wrist to feel for a pulse. Her finger slipped into a bullet hole, and was coated with blood and slime when she pulled it out.

One of Milk's aides had followed Feinstein into the room, and she told him to call the police chief's office. But he was sobbing so uncontrollably that he couldn't dial the number. "Here, let me," said Feinstein, gently taking the phone out of his hand. The aide ran out of the room to a water fountain and gulped down two Valiums.

As frantic whispers about the shootings floated through city hall, the cavernous building grew small and quiet. But when word reached the hall of justice, the reaction was different. Scattered cheers broke out on the fourth floor, among the police inspectors who had felt betrayed by Moscone. The jubilation soon spread throughout the SFPD network. Moscone and Milk were dead, and a member of the cops' family, Danny

White, had done the job. The Notre Dame Fighting Irish song crackled on the police radio, then "Danny Boy." The jokes immediately began making the rounds of the precincts. "What did Mary Ann tell Dan after she heard about the shootings? 'No, Dan, I said to get milk and macaroni, not Milk and Moscone.'"

The San Francisco police force was deeply implicated in the murders of Moscone and Milk. Dan White was not carrying out SFPD orders that morning in city hall, but he was carrying out the department's will. He was no longer on the force, but he was one of them: their star ballplayer, their political representative, their brother. He knew all about the cops' murderous feelings toward the city's liberal leadership. He felt the same way. They had the will, he had the willpower.

All the cops knew Danny White. Jim Molinari grew up in the same neighborhood with him, and Molinari's brother was a close friend. Frank Falzon was a few years ahead of White at St. Elizabeth's Grammar School. Danny used to shag balls for Falzon at the park as a kid and later became the star player on Falzon's police softball team. White played shortstop, Falzon was on second. They were wizards at turning a double play. He was like a kid brother to Falzon.

When the alert went out from city hall that morning, Falzon and Jack Cleary rushed to city hall. It was Molinari who told them that Dan White was the shooter. "I felt sucker-punched," said Falzon. "He was one of my best friends." Cleary said, "Check the shithouse. Dan's gonna blow his brains out."

Instead White had slipped out of city hall just as easily as he had entered and gone to St. Mary's, the nearby cathedral that soared, gleaming and white, like a giant sailboat in the San Francisco sky. He met Mary Ann inside. He wanted to make her understand. Mary Ann convinced her husband to turn himself in, and as they walked down Cathedral Hill to Northern Station, she clutched him tightly so that he couldn't use the gun on himself. When he entered the police station, White nodded toward the .38 in his holster and held his hands away from his body to show he was going easy. But when he was led into the cramped interrogation room, the assassin had nothing to say about the mayhem he had left behind in city hall.

It was Frank Falzon who got White talking. When the homicide cop walked into the room, he played it exactly the way he felt it: like Dan

White's stunned, outraged older brother. "It hit me in the fucking throat, seeing him there," Falzon said later.

"Why?" Falzon shouted at his friend. "What's wrong with you?"

Tears were streaming down White's face. "I want to tell you about it," he told Falzon. And he began to talk. He was under so much pressure, said White. "They put a lot of pressure on me and my family." As White mentioned his family, he began sobbing, and Falzon reached out and squeezed his forearm. "Can you relate these pressures you've been under, Dan?" the cop asked softly. And then the floodgates opened: how he was trying to take care of his family and serve the people of his district and keep the potato stand going. "My wife's got to work, long hours, fifty and sixty hours, never see my family." He was crying so hard he was choking on the words now. How he was forced to give up his job as supervisor for the good of his family. How supporters rallied around him and he tried to get his job back and Moscone promised the seat was still his. But then they betrayed him: Moscone, Milk, and the others. When the mayor told him he was going back on his word, was not going to reappoint him, "I got kind of fuzzy . . . my head didn't feel right." He didn't go to city hall that morning intending to kill anyone. But something just cracked inside him, and he shot the mayor. After that, he walked down the hall to talk to Harvey. "Maybe he'll be honest with me," White thought. He told Harvey what the supervisor's job meant to him and his family, and how important his reputation as a hard-working public servant was. But "he just kind of smirked at me, as if to say, 'Too bad,' and then I just got all flushed, an', an' hot, and I shot him." Then he phoned Mary Ann and met her at the cathedral. He wanted her to understand "how the pressure hit me, just, my head's all flushed, and it's like my skull's gonna crack." She slumped when he told her—another crushing blow to the woman who was so good-hearted and giving. Mary Ann begged him not to harm himself, promised that she would stand by him, and they walked down the hill together, arm in arm to Northern Station.

It felt good to tell Falzon everything. Confession was good for the soul. But Falzon felt like hell when he walked out of the room. "I thought I was sending my friend to the gas chamber. I had a confession on two murders, had the murder weapon, had witnesses. To me it was an open-and-shut first-degree-murder case."

Jack Cleary had a different feeling when he listened to the tape recording of White's confession. "When I heard that confession, I said, 'This better be tried right in the courtroom, because if not, he'll walk.'" Cleary knew that White's emotional narrative, the story of a good family man who was finally pushed beyond his limits, could make a jury of Dan White's peers weep for his mortifications. Falzon's gentle questioning had produced the ideal psychological defense.

Later Falzon would be widely excoriated for his kid-gloves handling of White. Critics said that the veteran homicide cop should never have interrogated him—the men were too close, it was a glaring conflict of interest. Falzon strongly denied that he had compromised his professionalism. "They would say, 'You were Dan White's friend, you buddied up.' And I'd say, 'Bullshit, I did my job. I got a confession.'" But looking back on it years later, Falzon wished he never had done it. "Because I had a remarkable career." The kind of career a cop could always be proud of, could tell his grandkids about. All of it except Dan White.

White, exquisitely in touch with his own pain, showed no remorse or sympathy for his victims or their loved ones. After his interrogation, the assassin was driven to the hall of justice to be jailed. Jack Cleary rode in the elevator with White to the jailhouse floor. "As we're riding in the elevator, Dan says, 'Wasn't that a bad ball game between USC and Notre Dame?' I said, 'Holy Christ, Dan, you just killed a couple people, and you're telling me about a ball game!'"

But White knew he was among his people at the hall of justice. As he was being fingerprinted, a crowd of sheriff's deputies gathered around him. A few had fury in their eyes, but most were smiling at him. One deputy walked over to White and patted him on the ass, like a coach in the dugout greeting a player who'd just scored.

WHILE SAN FRANCISCO'S MEN in uniform greeted their hero, the citizenry was informed of the latest calamities to strike their city. It fell to Dianne Feinstein to deliver the unspeakable news. A horde of city hall reporters surged around her as she stood at the top of the marble staircase that Milk loved to sweep up and down. Feinstein's face was gaunt, and her eyes shimmered with tears. She was flanked closely by Chief Gain and by one of her aides, who seemed to be holding up her tall frame as she spoke. She later said that she had stopped herself from breaking down by focusing on a familiar face, *Chronicle* reporter Duffy Jennings.

"As president of the board of supervisors, it is my duty to make this announcement," she began with a trembling voice. Then, pausing for a deep breath, she continued. "Both Mayor Moscone and Supervisor Harvey Milk have been shot and killed." The press pack gasped and cried out, and visibly recoiled—"as if to pull away from the story," one newspaper reporter later recalled, "as if it were too much, as if this couldn't be true or that they didn't want it to be true. We're human beings first." Then came the final blow. "The suspect . . . is Supervisor Dan White."

City hall was a small world, and the reporters who covered the mayor took it hard. Jennings, born and raised a few blocks from where Moscone grew up, couldn't help but like the guy. He enjoyed being around him. Moscone was always smiling, but he didn't seem like a phony. He was streetwise and politically shrewd, and fun to chew the fat with. At the end of the day, the mayor would sometimes invite Jennings and other city hall reporters for drinks in his private back room—the dark, intimate chamber where his life had just ended.

Harvey was always good copy too, a rubber-faced clown one minute and the city's conscience the next. He turned city hall into his opera house. Even tedious supervisor meetings seemed stage-lit when Milk took the floor.

Now the enormous and beautiful old building suddenly felt like a mausoleum.

As the news sped around the city, reaching those who knew and loved the two men, the ripples of pain widened. Cleve Jones was putting in a few minutes on a hotel workers union picket line in the Castro when a bus wheezed to a stop and someone shouted that the mayor had been shot. Jones had a frantic feeling about Milk and grabbed a taxi to city hall, arriving in time to see a dazed Feinstein walk by, her hands stained with Milk's blood. There was a gaggle of cops gathered around Dan White's old office. Jones saw a pair of feet in scuffed-up wingtips sticking out the door, and he knew it was Harvey. It was the only pair of shoes Milk owned. Jones pushed his way into the room and saw Harvey's blue face and his thick, blood-clotted hair. "I had never seen a dead person before," he recalled. "I think I was in shock for a long time after that."

Milk was the first person other than his parents who had seen something in Jones. Recognizing his potential as a leader, Milk had given the young man one of his most prized possessions: his bullhorn. Jones promptly put it to good use, rallying dozens of protest marches around the city. But now, Jones thought, that was all finished.

"When I saw his body there on the floor, I said to myself, 'It's all over now.' I felt it was the end of the gay liberation movement, the end of the city. I couldn't imagine how San Francisco could ever come back from this."

It also seemed like the end of days for the Moscone family. A fireman picked up Christopher, then sixteen, and Jonathan, fourteen, at St. Ignatius and drove them home. The boys knew something terrible had happened but didn't know what until Christopher finally asked. "Your father has expired," the fireman told them. Everything seemed wavy to Christopher. He barely made it to his room. He remembers a "numbness" settling over him for a long time after that. "My mom let us do what we wanted for a while. If we wanted to go to school, we did. If we wanted to watch television until three in the morning, we could. I became very introverted."

Rebecca Moscone, an eighteen-year-old student at UC Berkeley, was pulled out of class by campus policemen the day her father was killed. Her boyfriend gave her the news. "I flipped out, started sobbing. I kind of collapsed," Rebecca recalled. "Up until then, life was great. After that was a big emptiness . . . My father taught me to play basketball. I remember driving to Tahoe with my dad in his Alfa Romeo . . . Afterward I was in this fog for a year, trapped."

Gina Moscone withdrew entirely from her husband's world, the arena that had taken so much of him and now had taken all of him. She never spoke in public about his murder. A newspaper photo of the mourning family captured Gina Moscone's fathomless grief, picturing her bent over, with her face buried in her hands, as her children tried desperately to comfort her. "I felt pretty helpless," said Christopher years later. "What could I do? She's alone, she doesn't have her partner, and nothing can replace that."

When Moscone and Milk died, they were both nearly broke. Milk was deeply in debt, and Moscone had only a few hundred dollars in his savings account. They left nothing for their families and friends. But the two men bequeathed something invaluable to San Francisco. They presided over the modernization of the city. Under their leadership, city hall was finally opened to all of those who made San Francisco their home. Milk said in his final days that San Francisco was the home that he and thousands of other gay men had been searching for their entire lives. It was a haven for dreamers and outcasts and wandering souls. Both men gave their lives for this oasis of freedom; the city where no stranger was kept outside its golden gate.

In the days after Jonestown and the city hall assassinations, San Francisco sleepwalked under a dark canopy of clouds that seemed like it would never lift. The city was racked with despair. The San Francisco Suicide Prevention center received twice its normal number of phone calls. Rev. Cecil Williams fielded a flood of calls at his Tenderloin church from distraught people who feared that they, and the city itself, would never recover from the multiple traumas. The *Examiner's* Washington, DC, bureau reported that San Franciscans visiting the nation's capital were bombarded by questions about their dark-starred city. "There must be something evil out there," one San Francisco visitor was told. "It's crazy, it's sick . . . I'm glad I'm here," another San Franciscan was informed.

Some media commentators in the local press picked up the "sick San Francisco theme," conveniently overlooking that Dan White was no denizen of the city's wacky fringe but a wholesome-looking product of the Catholic Church, US Army, and San Francisco police and fire departments. San Francisco had become "Aberration City," wrote conservative *Examiner* columnist Guy Wright, sounding like White himself. "A fermentation vat for oddball notions. A haven for all sorts of kook cults . . . A city where tolerance deteriorates into license. A town without a norm."

The defenders of a wide-open San Francisco rallied around their wounded city. Lawrence Ferlinghetti published "An Elegy to Dispel Gloom" in the *Examiner,* writing, "It's poor vanity / to think that all humanity / is bathed in red / because one young mad man / one so bad man / lost his head." Meanwhile, Reverend Williams held a special evening service at Glide Memorial Church to soothe his suffering rainbow

flock. Williams reminded worshippers why San Francisco—their spar-
kling, sea-glass city that now seemed so damned—was actually blessed.
"San Francisco is the most tolerant city in the world. Harvey Milk and
George Moscone gave their lives for that idea."

Cleve Jones soon realized that he was wrong: that it was not all over,
that George's and Harvey's San Francisco lived on. He saw it that Monday evening, just hours after the assassinations. Jones was an expert
at working phone trees whenever Harvey and he decided that people
needed to be mobilized in the streets. But that evening, it wasn't necessary. "People just knew, everybody knew what to do," said Jones.

As the sun dipped below Twin Peaks, Jones wandered toward Castro and Market and saw the huge crowd starting to gather. "It was the
most amazingly beautiful, heart-wrenchingly sad, magnificent example
of what San Francisco is. It was gay people, straight people, white people, Filipinos, Chinese, African Americans, men and women of all ages,
children, the poor and well dressed, people in fur coats next to people in
rags. We estimated there were between thirty thousand and forty thousand people. We marched in almost total silence down Market Street to
city hall and filled Civic Center Plaza, a sea of people holding candles.
I remember standing there and thinking, 'This isn't the end of anything.
This is the beginning.' And I was right.

"I think every city has a soul, every city is unique and special. But
for San Franciscans, I don't think there could ever be another place to
call home. And a lot of it has to do with what I saw that night: with this
ability to suffer horrible and dreadful events, earthquakes, civil turmoil,
assassinations, and to not only endure but to create something beautiful
from it."

Crowding into the plaza, people listened in a church-like hush as
Joan Baez sang "Amazing Grace" on the city hall steps. After she finished, Dianne Feinstein stood up and began to address the vast throng.
Hours earlier, her arms were bathed in Harvey Milk's blood. Facing the
press, she could barely choke out the announcement about the city hall
murders. The explosion of violence had caught Feinstein in a delicate
midlife moment. At forty-five, the recently widowed mother of a teenage
daughter was grappling with her future. Before Dan White overturned
San Francisco's political order, Feinstein's political career was all but
finished. She had been rejected twice by the city's voters in her quest

for the mayor's office. It seemed clear to her that she was not the leader
that San Francisco wanted—too starched, too middle of the road, too
goody-goody.

In the weeks before the assassinations, Feinstein had gone trekking
in the mountains of Nepal to ponder her next steps. "I need to get my
life together," she had said. While hiking in the Himalayas, she came
down with an intestinal illness. By the time she recovered from her nausea and fever, she had decided to announce her resignation from politics
when she returned home.

But now Dianne Feinstein was acting mayor. And as the tall, lean,
attractive woman with the bonnet of dark hair and piercing green eyes
stood before her fellow San Franciscans that candlelit evening, there
was something different about her. In the course of that terrible day,
Feinstein had become the leader that the city needed. As she began
to speak, she found the right words to express San Francisco's howling
pain and to make people believe that the broken city could be put back
together. As long as she had anything to say about it, Feinstein told the
crowd, she would make sure that San Francisco continued to follow the
path of human rights, love, and understanding. No bullets could stop
that forward march. The people gave her the kind of heartfelt ovation
she had never heard in her political career.

Two days later, at the city hall memorial service for Moscone and
Milk, Feinstein was even more eloquent. Standing once again on the
city halls steps, on a stage draped with black bunting, the acting mayor
pledged to honor the two men's sacrifice by bringing together the deeply
divided city. "Neither of the two men we mourn today were bitter or
vengeful. Their deaths should not engender feeling alien to their natures
or to the nature of this beautiful city . . . If there has been rancor between
the neighborhoods and downtown, between our different races, and
between our different lifestyles, let us put it aside. Let us join together
in a spirit of unity and reconciliation. Let us take pride in the memory of
George Moscone and Harvey Milk, for the San Francisco we all love."

It has become fashionable in recent decades to disparage public service. The political profession is widely scorned and reviled. But there are
times when political leadership seems like a blessing. San Francisco in
November 1978 was a broken vessel on a dark sea. The city had endured
so many blows and afflictions that it seemed cursed. When deliverance

finally came, San Francisco owed it in large part to an unlikely leader. Though she was a homegrown native, she seemed miscast for the role. San Franciscans had a fondness for lovable rogues and other colorful characters. But in a city of Marx brothers, Feinstein was Margaret Dumont, forever distressed and befuddled by the antics around her. Not only was she the grownup in the room, it seemed like she had always been a grownup.

Feinstein was well grounded, resolute, firm, managerial. Even her eccentricities, like her love of uniforms and ceremonial displays of military power, seemed weirdly un–San Franciscan. Yet she turned out to be precisely the right leader for the time. While she shifted the city back toward the center, she stabilized it enough to allow many of the revolutionary changes that preceded her to become fully absorbed by the body politic. Though she herself was not in harmony with all of these "San Francisco values," they became enshrined under her leadership.

PART THREE

DELIVERANCE

One way or another, this darkness got to give.

32

FIRE BY TRIAL

Looking back at the harrowing period when she became mayor of San Francisco, Dianne Feinstein said, "I found out one thing about myself. When I am really in crisis, things are much clearer to me. I move in a regular way and can just sustain myself through the crisis. And it's always been that way in my life. I just can't explain it, but it is. I needed that ability when I became mayor, because the city was falling apart."

Feinstein developed the ability to navigate her way through traumas at an early age. The oldest of three daughters, she was raised in an elegantly appointed San Francisco home that from the outside looked picture perfect. Her beloved father, Dr. Leon Goldman, was a highly respected surgeon and professor at the University of California, San Francisco, medical complex. Her mother, Betty, was a beautiful and exotic Russian émigré, the daughter of a czarist general forced to flee the Bolshevik Revolution. But Betty Goldman, who was later revealed to have been brain damaged by a childhood case of encephalitis, was prone to terrifying and unpredictable rages. She once chased Dianne around the dining room with a knife, and she often locked her out of the house at night. Dianne was forced to study for her high-stakes Scholastic Aptitude Test in the shelter of her parents' car. Feinstein idolized her father but discovered early on that he could not protect his children from their volatile mother.

Feinstein said later that she learned leadership at home by figuring out how to manage her mother's eruptions and to shield her younger sisters. "It is fair to say we lived in a great deal of fear," Feinstein recalled. "The part that was hard was the unpredictability. My mother was capable of great hostility. I mean terrible things . . . It was brutal."

Young Dianne found comfort in the clubby, male world of San Francisco politics, following her colorful uncle, Morris Goldman, a coat manufacturer and Democratic Party wheeler-dealer, as he made his rounds through the city. In 1945, when she was twelve, Dianne was taken to her first city hall meeting by Uncle Morris, who offered running commentary on "the board of stupidvisors" and pointed out how the flick of a portly city boss's stogie could change the vote count.

Feinstein, who was raised Jewish, also gained insight into the Catholic core of San Francisco politics by going to high school at the exclusive Convent of the Sacred Heart. The school, housed in the historic, white-marble Flood Mansion overlooking the San Francisco Bay, imbued in Feinstein a lifelong respect for Catholic ritual and order. Sometimes she would slip into a nun's habit when the sisters weren't looking. But when the young woman saw some of the church's deeper reactionary principles on unvarnished display during a trip to Spain, she decided she could never convert.

After studying political science at Stanford in the 1950s, Feinstein was selected as a Coro Fellow, a program started by two wealthy San Franciscans to train future government leaders. She entered city politics reeking of squeaky-clean, good-government elitism instead of the usual smoky, backroom funk. She won her first race for the board of supervisors in 1969 as a moderate Democrat without the help of any of the local machines. At thirty-six, she was the mother of a twelve-year-old girl and married to her second husband, brain surgeon Bert Feinstein, and living happily with her family in a Pacific Heights mansion. But, compelled by a restless ambition, she already had her eye on the mayor's office. And Dr. Feinstein, two decades older, was wholeheartedly dedicated to his wife's happiness, helping with all the campaign chores, the way her father had when she ran for student office in high school.

Though she had grown up in the city and had reaped the benefits of her uncle's street-savvy wisdom, Feinstein seemed painfully cloistered when she first jumped into San Francisco politics. To her credit, she felt a need to venture into pockets of the city that had always been terra incognita to her. "I wasn't ever afraid of going places or looking at new things or opening my mind," she said.

But Feinstein's fact-finding missions often verged on the ludicrous. An ardent opponent of the city's growing porn industry, Feinstein decided she should go to an adult movie to see for herself what she was up against, dragging along another nice Jewish girl, *Chronicle* society columnist Merla Zellerbach, to a seedy theater. Predictably, Feinstein and her friend were horrified. On another occasion, Feinstein—determined to clean up the Tenderloin, the city's drugged-out red-light district—put on a blond wig and stood on a street corner for three hours to learn more about the raunchy neighborhood.

The earnest supervisor once stood in front of a Glide Memorial Church congregation and lectured the downtrodden Tenderloin worshippers about the importance of good hygiene and hard work. "Good citizens," she enlightened them, "are people who keep themselves clean." Her perky sermon was met with scattered boos. Cecil Williams, sitting behind Feinstein, was tempted to pull on her coattails to stop her. "Dianne," the minister later scolded her, "you don't talk that way to these folks. If they had a place to get cleaned up, most of them would get cleaned up. If they could get a job, they'd get a job."

But over time, as Feinstein explored her city, she grew more understanding about San Francisco's changing social currents. She still tended to be stiff—as if "her feelings were wrapped in wax," as one reporter put it. And she never would be the kind of rakish politician who'd take a deep hit off a joint if it were offered. But she became more comfortable with the city's colorful cast of characters. And when Pacific Heights residents lobbied the board of supervisors to evict the Delancey Street halfway house from their tony neighborhood, Feinstein broke with her own neighbors and supported the ex-cons and recovering addicts.

"Quentin Kopp led the campaign against us," said Bill Maher, the Delancey Street founder's younger brother and political sidekick. "Kopp suggested that we move to a neighborhood more appropriate to our social stature. Dianne was our main supporter, even though she lived nearby. She was great—vibrant and young, and very progressive. She has always worn sensible shoes, and she has always been a formidable woman."

Despite the hands-on intensity that she brought to her job as a supervisor and her keen intelligence, Feinstein hit a political ceiling after losing her second bid for mayor in 1975. San Francisco respected her but didn't love her. She simply seemed too sensible, too measured for a city that fell for brawling, brash, leading men.

By the time she returned to San Francisco in November 1978—after a life-challenging trek through the Himalayas with her new friend, investment banker Dick Blum—Feinstein thought her political career was over. "I was firmly convinced that I was not electable as mayor," she said in hindsight.

Feinstein's life had been racked by grief and turmoil. Her husband Bert—the love of her life, the man who had filled her with the confidence to pursue her ambitions—had died after a long and agonizing battle with colon cancer. While he was dying, Feinstein became a target of the New World Liberation Front. One night after her deeply ill husband was brought back from the hospital, the terrorists planted a bomb on the windowsill of their Pacific Heights home, immediately underneath her daughter's bedroom. If the bomb had not misfired, the house—which was being painted at the time and was surrounded by scaffolding—could have exploded in flames. On another occasion, the underground radicals shot out the windows of her weekend beach house in Pajaro Dunes, on Monterey Bay, which Feinstein thought of as her only refuge. "It was a terrible, terrible time."

IN SPITE OF ALL this, Feinstein did not hesitate when duty called on the morning of November 27, 1978. The job that she had pursued for nearly a decade was suddenly hers, under the most hideous of circumstances. San Francisco was torn and bleeding. Her predecessor and one of her colleagues lay dead in city hall, and another colleague was under arrest for the murders. Rage and suspicion ruled the city of love. Already the target of political violence herself, Feinstein knew that her new position would make her even more vulnerable to the dangerous passions swirling through the city. But like a nun or nurse in a battlefield hospital, it never occurred to Feinstein to turn down the job when it was presented to her.

The morning following the assassinations, Feinstein awoke after a restless night in the same state of shock as the rest of the city. "I had hoped to wake up and find it was a nightmare," she said. But then she simply drove to city hall and went to work. "This will not be a rudderless city," she told the shell-shocked public. As the president of the board of supervisors, Feinstein automatically had become San Francisco's acting mayor. A week later, she outmaneuvered rival Quentin Kopp and was elected by her fellow supervisors to officially fill out the remaining year of Moscone's term.

The traumatic events surrounding her political ascension filled her with "a feeling of destiny." She had been groomed for the embattled leadership role ever since her childhood. Feinstein always steeled herself for the worst, from the time she was a bobbed-hair little girl, smiling gamely for a family photo while her demon-possessed mother looked on balefully. And now, in the worst of times, Dianne Feinstein was mayor of San Francisco.

She wisely chose to retain Moscone's staff—even his controversial police chief, Charles Gain—and to steer a similar administrative course during her first few months in office. This was primarily smart politics. Quentin Kopp had already made it clear that he would be challenging her from the right in the mayoral election the following year. Keeping the Moscone constituency happy was a matter of political survival.

Just to make sure that Feinstein realized this, Willie Brown spelled it out for her in a *New York Times* interview: "If she starts making all those changes, maybe some of us liberals—either Phil or John Burton, now in Congress, or myself—will have to take her on in the election next year. Kopp's got the right, and there is no middle. If one of us enters the race, she'll run third. One way or another, we're going to fight to keep the gains we made under George." Feinstein had already seen the way this campaign movie turned out, and she did not care to repeat it.

But honoring the Moscone and Milk legacy for the remainder of these slain officials' terms was also a matter of principle to Dianne Feinstein. This became clear as she pondered her choice to fill Milk's seat on the board of supervisors. The establishment gay Democrats in the Alice B. Toklas Democratic Club—whom Milk had reviled—were lobbying strongly for one of their own to be chosen. Feinstein, closely aligned with these mainstream activists, could have ensured that the board would be more manageable by doing so. But she had listened to the tape-recorded will that Milk had left behind in the full expectation that he would be assassinated, naming four potential successors whom he trusted to carry on his progressive mission. Feinstein simply couldn't violate her former colleague's dying wishes. She filled Milk's seat with one of the left-wing gay activists on his list: Harry Britt, a former Methodist minister and Milk protégé.

Britt, painfully shy and a novice in the world of city politics, at first resisted the call to duty. But feeling that he owed it to Harvey and the liberation politics they both espoused, the soft-spoken Texan finally agreed. It was the beginning of an often prickly relationship between Britt and Feinstein. But Harvey Milk's successor always respected the courage and integrity that Feinstein showed by appointing him.

"Dianne never had a good relationship with Harvey Milk—they weren't kindred spirits," Britt recalled. "*Her* homosexuals were not *his* homosexuals. But very much to her credit, she put all that aside when she appointed me. Because she really, passionately did not want Dan White's bullets to be the end of the Harvey Milk story. She took Harvey's will extraordinarily seriously. She deeply *hated* what Dan White had done."

The new mayor, who was concerned about rebuilding police department morale, hoped that Britt would vote her way on his first major test as a supervisor: the hotly debated settlement of the civil rights lawsuit against the SFPD. Feinstein wanted to block the settlement that Moscone had worked out. But instead Britt joined with the black police officers group and other minority plaintiffs against the department and voted for the settlement. The affirmative action deal that was finally brokered by the supervisors began to open up the white, tradition-bound force.

Feinstein's driving goal as the city's new mayor was to restore a sense of civic normality. In March 1979 she pep-talked the San Francisco business community at a luncheon held in the Sheraton Palace, the ornate grande dame of San Francisco hotels. "San Francisco is now in the process of rising once again," she assured the downtown crowd. "It's not the kook capital of the world; it's a beautiful, diverse, open, tolerant city." To help restore the corporate diners' confidence in San Francisco, the mayor announced that she was increasing the police department budget and putting more cops on the streets than ever before.

It was a balancing act that defined San Francisco's new leader: celebrate the city's bright galaxy of queer and colorful planets, and simultaneously affirm the primacy of law and order. "I believe safety is the first thing you need to guarantee as mayor," she said, looking back at her years in city hall.

The problem for Feinstein was that many San Franciscans—particularly its "diverse" citizenry—felt threatened, not protected, by the city's police force. There were strong suspicions in the Castro that the city hall assassinations were an inside job, and that Moscone and Milk were both victims of "law and order." The outrage in the gay community was stoked hotter when it was reported that police and firemen had raised $100,000 for Dan White's defense fund, and that White's jailers were allowing him special privileges behind bars, including meals from his favorite restaurants and chocolate cakes baked by admirers. These churning feelings of rancor and distrust exploded on the night of May 21, 1979.

THE WHITE TRIAL, WHICH sparked the first major crisis of Feinstein's administration, was a pageant tableaux of San Francisco's civil war. The city's deepest discords were on vivid display in department 21, the third-floor courtroom in the hall of justice.

In his opening argument, White's lawyer—a rising young criminal attorney named Doug Schmidt, who zoomed around town in a Corvette and owned six hundred acres in Mendocino County—made it clear that he was putting San Francisco values on trial. The jury, which Schmidt carefully cleansed of gays and other new San Franciscans, was told that White was "an idealistic, young, working-class man—the voice of the family" in city hall. White had been taken advantage of by scheming politicians, the same ones responsible for bringing Peoples Temple and other alien elements into a city once known for its hard-working, family values. Overwhelmed by the growing pressures in his life, and binging on Twinkies and other junk food as he fell deeper into depression, Dan White finally cracked. The story that Schmidt unfolded clearly struck a nerve with the jury, which was dominated by working-class Catholics.

Several jurors wept openly when the recording of White's teary confession was played in the courtroom.

Frank Falzon, still the chief investigator for the prosecution despite his longtime friendship with the defendant, reinforced the sympathetic portrait of White when he took the witness stand. The "shattered" figure of a man who faced him in the police interrogation room that terrible day was "totally unlike" the Dan White he had known nearly his entire life. *That* Dan White, testified Falzon, "was a man among men."

Prosecutor Tommy Norman was caught flat-footed by his investigator's testimony. Falzon was supposed to be *his* witness, but instead he came across as Dan White's most effective character witness. Falzon, who was sharply criticized for his performance on the stand, still defends himself. "I played it straight," said Falzon. "Do you deny your friendship? All I said to the jury was the man I knew was a man's man. The man fought for his country. He was a good police officer. Up until the day he walked into city hall with a gun, Dan White was my friend. All his other friends—Quentin Kopp, Dianne Feinstein—they all turned their backs on him after the shooting. I couldn't do that. This kid was too close to me."

It was Tommy Norman, a smooth hall of justice veteran who waltzed into the courtroom in sleek suits and a twinkle in his eye, who was primarily to blame for the inept prosecution of White. He and his boss in the DA's office, Joe Freitas, were utterly unprepared for Schmidt's aggressive political strategy. Because Freitas, facing reelection that year, had been deeply tainted by the Peoples Temple scandal, his prosecutors were tongue-tied when it came to countering Schmidt's charges that White was a victim of the city's snake-pit politics. Freitas and Norman made no effort to explore the hate-filled culture of the San Francisco Police Department that had spawned Dan White.

The prosecution had a slam-dunk case. The defendant was a scheming killer who cold-bloodedly plotted the assassinations of his political enemies, equipped himself with enough extralethal ammunition to do the job, and crawled through a basement window to avoid detection. But by the end of his trial, White had emerged as a broken-winged angel. And on the afternoon of May 21, the jury delivered a stunningly sympathetic verdict, finding the double assassin guilty not of murder but of manslaughter.

The rumblings began rolling through the city as soon as the verdict was announced, like the roar from a distant flash flood. City leaders, fearing the worst, rushed to denounce the jury's decision. She had found Harvey Milk's body, Mayor Feinstein told the press with tears in her eyes. She knew what the verdict should have been: "These were two murders . . . We've gone through a physical bloodbath, and now we are going through a mental one." Supervisor Carol Ruth Silver, one of White's intended victims, remarked bitterly, "Dan White has gotten away with murder. It's as simple as that."

Gina Moscone, grieving once again in private, remained silent about the verdict. But her children were in turmoil. "I remember thinking I had to go the trial because I was the oldest man in the family," recalled Christopher, who was still a teenager at the time. "I told my mom, and she talked me down from that. I wanted revenge."

The Castro did exact its revenge that night. "This means that in America, it's all right to kill faggots," a furious Cleve Jones told a radio reporter. Minutes later, Jones ran into the streets, carrying the banged-up bullhorn that Harvey had given him, and began to rally the crowd that was already forming at the corner of Castro and Market. This time there would be no candles or mournful gospel songs. This time there would be fire and rage.

By the time the crowd reached city hall, it was more than five thousand strong and screaming for blood. "Dan White was a cop!" "Avenge Harvey Milk!" "Kill Dan White!" The thin blue line on the city hall steps, shocked by the fury of men they'd long dismissed as pansies, quickly retreated inside the building. As the night wore on, the protesters lay wild siege to city hall, smashing windows and torching a row of police cars. Meanwhile, Police Chief Gain—hunkered down inside the mayor's glass-strewn second-floor office with Feinstein and her fiancée, Dick Blum—tried to keep a rein on his notoriously violent riot squad. Christopher Moscone, watching the mayhem at home on TV, was lit up with the rioters' burning rage. "I was like, 'Yeah, I get it.' I was with the rioters in spirit."

As the police tac squad finally drove away the army of night from city hall, many cops broke free from their chief's control and pursued protesters all the way back to the Castro. Now it was time for a police riot. Roving bands of cops hunted down gays on the street and invaded bars, cracking skulls with their nightsticks and screaming, "Sick cocksuckers!" Not until Gain and Harry Britt appeared on the scene and ordered a stop to the violence did the cops finally withdraw.

The poisonous feelings between cops and gays lingered long after "White Night," as the night of flames came to be called, eerily echoing Jim Jones's death drills. In the post–Dan White period, antigay street violence spiked again. And gays accused the police of standing by and letting the blood flow in their neighborhoods.

ONE OF THE STRANGER crimes involving a gay victim occurred in July 1979, when a gay artist-propagandist named Robert Opel was shot and killed in his erotic gallery in the SOMA leather district. Opel, who was known for his provocative stunts, achieved fleeting notoriety during the 1974 Academy Awards ceremony when he streaked naked past Oscar presenter David Niven. Opel later moved from Los Angeles to San Francisco, where he plunged into the sadomasochistic underground, hosting fist-fucking parties and gallery openings featuring the notoriously butch art of Tom of Finland and the early work of a young photographer named Robert Mapplethorpe.

Opel became increasingly involved in gay politics in San Francisco, investigating the Milk assassination and staging a mock execution of Dan White near the Civic Center. During the execution ceremony, Opel handed out pamphlets that read: "What would happen if a gay cocksucking faggot killed an ex-cop? Would *he* get away with murder?" Robert Opel was precisely the kind of perverse troublemaker San Francisco cops wanted out of their city.

Ten days after Opel acted out his Dan White "execution," the artist's Fey-Way Studio on Howard Street was invaded by a couple of thugs demanding money and drugs. These were not the boys in leather masks who came to Opel's parties, but *real* rough trade. One of the bandits, a scruffy, twenty-eight-year-old hustler named Maurice Keenan, stuck an automatic pistol at Opel's head and said, "I'm gonna blow your head off." The artist replied, "You're going to have to. There's no money here."

They were Robert Opel's last words. Keenan made good on this threat and blew his brains out. The thugs fled with $5 in cash, a camera, and a backpack.

When Opel's sister went to the hall of justice to meet with homicide detectives, she saw that someone had written *Homocide* on her dead brother's evidence box. After he was arrested, Keenan walked out of his unlocked jail cell at the hall of justice and disappeared. Jail officials were at a loss to explain the bizarre getaway. Recaptured, the murderer repeated his disappearing act until officials finally found a way to keep him behind bars.

Opel's friends and family speculated that he might have been set up by drug dealers or other sleazy elements connected to the police force. After his murder, other gay agitprop artists went into hiding, fearing that brazen performance pieces like Opel's execution of Dan White could put a man's life in danger in San Francisco's volatile climate.

In the raw-nerved period after the White verdict, San Francisco could have easily spun violently off its axis. But Feinstein became increasingly assertive, shedding any lingering feelings that she was merely a caretaker mayor, and taking command of the city. "This city has to be managed," Feinstein reflected later. "If you don't manage, it falls apart."

33

THE CENTER HOLDS

A S THE NOVEMBER 1979 mayoral election loomed, Dianne Feinstein hit the streets, popping up all over town—from a Tenderloin residential hotel, where she was photographed laying hands on the crippled leg of an eighty-nine-year-old tenant, to a streetcar in the Sunset, where she discussed the finer points of MUNI commuting with the vocal passengers. If she seemed painfully earnest at times, she also came across as being thoroughly on top of the city's operations.

In September the city was forced to shut down its storied but aging cable car system for long-overdue repairs. It was a potential public relations disaster, with the *New York Times* announcing, "No longer do 'little cable cars climb halfway to the stars' over San Francisco's hills." But Feinstein pushed repair crews to work eighteen-hour days and began raising a $10 million private fund to upgrade the quaint transit system, shaking down wealthy supporters and visiting celebrities such as Mick Jagger. The day before the election, the sound of clanging cable car bells was heard once more on Nob Hill.

As she threw herself into the campaign, Feinstein exposed herself to the madness that still crackled in San Francisco. While going door to door in the rough and unpredictable Fillmore district, the mayor was suddenly approached by a man who pointed a silver pistol directly at her head. The mayor and her entourage froze as the man pulled the trigger.

A butane flame came hissing from the gun instead of a bullet. "There was no time to duck or react. Sure, I was scared," Feinstein later told reporters. But she immediately gathered herself and continued campaigning.

Feinstein was no shoo-in. Her main opponent, Quentin Kopp, rallied John Barbagelata's angry taxpayer crowd, running as a fiscally responsible fix-it man, and painting Feinstein as a captive of the downtown elite and limousine liberals. Kopp tried to broaden the Barbagelata coalition by making a strong appeal to gay voters, promising them equal police protection and freedom from harassment. Feinstein's challenger won the endorsement of the *Chronicle* and the support of key political establishment figures like Joe Alioto as well as neighborhood activists such as Calvin Welch, who appreciated Kopp's endorsement of a ballot initiative to limit high-rise construction in the city.

Forced into a runoff, Feinstein fought back hard, drawing on Moscone's campaign staff and his grassroots playbook. In the end, she won a decisive victory over Kopp by holding on to much of Moscone's coalition of gays, union members, and progressives. Embracing Gina Moscone onstage at her victory party, Feinstein paid tribute to the man whose shoes she was filling. "We carry with us the heritage of a fallen leader," she told the emotional crowd. "We will not forsake that heritage."

The Moscone team never warmed up to Feinstein's centrist, downtown-oriented politics or her Big Nurse personality. As Moscone himself had put it coarsely in his Rat Pack way, Feinstein was a "stiff bitch. Her problem is that she needs a good fuck." But they knew that she was a better option than Kopp. "All of George's people helped her get elected," said Dick Sklar. "Kopp would have desecrated George's chair."

Finally elected mayor by the people of San Francisco, Feinstein quickly began putting her own moderate stamp on city hall. While keeping some of Moscone's former aides and making sure that the Moscone family was taken care of financially, the new mayor made it clear that she would lead San Francisco in her own way.

Feinstein appeased police department veterans by firing Chief Gain and by fighting the establishment of a civilian review board that would have investigated the gay community's charges of police brutality. But she also made it clear to the SFPD that the old days of fraternity mayhem were over. Under Feinstein, the department became more professional and diverse. Stories about the new police force began appearing in the newspapers, with headlines like "A Gay Cop Talks" and "Changing Times for S.F. Police"—an article featuring Heather Fong, a Chinese-American female patrol cop who years later would become chief of the SFPD. The gay cop, Woody Tennant, insisted that attitudes were rapidly changing inside the force: "You end up boring straight officers out of being uptight. Once they find out you don't want to have sex in the patrol car and that you're as boring as they are, everything's fine."

The mayor also pulled off the same balancing act with the gay community, making it clear that antigay violence was not going to be tolerated and appointing gays to prominent city hall positions, while at the same time clamping firm limits on the gay revolution in the city.

Even though she had hosted the wedding of lesbian friends in her own backyard, Feinstein vetoed a law introduced by Supervisor Britt that would have extended health insurance benefits to the live-in partners of gay city employees. Her veto of the domestic partners legislation set off a round of angry "Dump Dianne" protests, but she weathered the storm. For the rest of her days in city hall, Feinstein and San Francisco's gay community endured a rocky marriage, in which bitter recriminations alternated with outbursts of genuine affection. Feinstein could lecture gays one day about their wanton exhibitionism at Gay Freedom Day Parades, and the next day approve S&M sex safety workshops taught by the city coroner.

The mayor had a more consistently adversarial relationship with neighborhood activists, who—enraged by the downtown building boom she green-lighted—accused her of selling out the city to big developers and construction unions. She countered that in a Reagan era of diminishing public resources, she was doing what she must to bring revenue and jobs to the city. The surviving Moscone appointees on the city planning commission fought a rearguard battle with Feinstein against the high-rise proliferation, forcing developers to contribute funds for parks, sewage facilities, public transportation, and housing. In the end, the mayor succeeded in massively changing the San Francisco skyline, but her progressive opponents forced the city to concede that there were social costs to development and to take steps to help address them.

Feinstein and progressive activists also fought a seesaw battle throughout her tenure over rent control, with Harry Britt championing the city's hard-squeezed tenants. Feinstein, who herself was a landlord, would veto rent control bills passed by the board of supervisors, only to have persistent housing activists rebound by placing pro-renter initiatives on the ballot.

Despite her running battles with San Francisco activists, many progressives harbored a grudging respect for Feinstein's managerial skills. With her firm hand on the city's rudder, she managed to steer a middle course that gradually brought stability back to the city. "She ran the city with an iron fist," recalled Mike Hennessy, a former prisoner rights lawyer whose long reign as San Francisco's sheriff began the year that Feinstein was elected mayor. "Of all the mayors I've worked with, she was the best," he said. "That's because she took responsibility for this city. San Francisco is a very hard city to run. It's very politically fractious. It takes a lot of work to hold it together. And that's what Feinstein did."

EVERY MONDAY MORNING, MAYOR Feinstein briskly presided over a meeting of elected officials and department heads that evaluated the state of the city. If an official did not seem on top of his fiefdom, the mayor could be merciless. She was particularly tough on her new police chief, Cornelius Murphy, if crime stats were up in any part of the city. At one meeting, the mayor—who was in the habit of listening in on the police radio as she was driven around town in her limousine—badgered Murphy about a crime spike that she had heard about over the radio. "What do you propose I do about this, Chief?" she pressed Murphy. "Stop listening to the radio," the exasperated cop told her.

Feinstein became known as the most hands-on manager in San Francisco's history. One day, while being driven to city hall, she saw an elderly man collapse on the sidewalk. Ordering her chauffeur to stop, the mayor jumped out and rushed to the man. Rose Pak, who was riding with her at the time, was amazed to see the mayor kneel over the man, wipe foam from his lips, and give him mouth-to-mouth resuscitation.

"People later pointed to this and said, 'See, she's not a cold fish, she has a heart.' But I didn't see it that way," said Pak. "I saw her as a doctor's daughter and a doctor's widow, doing the proper clinical thing."

Jim Molinari, the police bodyguard whom Feinstein inherited from Mayor Moscone, learned that riding through the streets of San Francisco with her could be an adventure. One day Molinari saw someone burglarizing a car. Feinstein ordered Molinari to cut off the thief's escape with her limousine while she radioed for police backup. Another time, the mayor overheard a report about a Hunters Point fire on her limousine radio and ordered Molinari to race to the scene of the blaze. When they arrived, Feinstein threw on a fire coat and helped lug a fire hose toward the flames.

Hadley Roff—the lovable bear who had helped guide the Alioto administration through the political shoals and was brought back to city hall by Feinstein as her deputy mayor—thought she was the "perfect mayor for the time. She was a nurturing, tough, thoughtful person, which is exactly what the city needed. She hated to leave the city, even for important political trips, for fear that something would happen, like a mother."

Feinstein once flew home early from Washington, DC, after a gas pipe ruptured near the Embarcadero, spewing a fine mist over the city. On another occasion, she took the next flight home from Los Angeles when a fireworks factory in the Bayview exploded. Deeply sensitive about the traumas that had ravaged her city, Feinstein was on constant alert against any new calamities.

Despite Roff's respect for his boss's managerial skills, there was not a lot of fun to be found in the Feinstein administration for the roly-poly politico. The mayor seemed as constitutionally barren of a sense of humor as an undertaker. One day Feinstein and Roff met with her gay task force at a restaurant in the Castro. Among the diners was Jim Foster, Feinstein's longtime gay ally, a nattily dressed, balding man with a twitching mustache who put Roff in mind of the old Andy Gump cartoon character. During the meeting, Feinstein—a big fan of military displays and ceremonies—brought up a subject near to her heart. "By the way," she told the group, "next week is Fleet Week, and the bay is going to be filled with aircraft carriers, and there are going to be at least fifteen thousand sailors in town. I hope they're going to be given a warm welcome."

Foster wiggled his brushy upper lip and replied with queenly certitude, "Oh, they will be."

"The whole table broke out in laughter—except for one person," recalled Roff. "She just didn't get it."

Feinstein had a way of bringing out the naughty side of the men around her. Some of it was obvious sexism, the resentful response of politicos whose all-male club was finally invaded by a formidable woman. But much of it was due to her prim and proper attitude. In her role as San Francisco's straight woman, she was simply too tempting a target. At the Monday morning meetings in city hall, as Feinstein drilled down on civic issues, the Irish old boys would roll their eyes while her head was turned and make obscene gestures. Gays loved to slip into Dianne drag on Halloween, wearing Snow White wigs and her trademark suits with floppy bows.

Sister Boom Boom—a half-Catholic, half-Jewish drag queen named Jack Fertig, who wore a whore's makeup and a nun's habit and vamped it up with the other political pranksters in the Sisters of Perpetual Indulgence—was an especially aggravating thorn in Feinstein's side. Boom Boom ran a remarkably aggressive campaign against Feinstein during her 1983 reelection bid, under the slogan "Nun of the Above," eventually winning twenty-three thousand votes.

During the campaign, Boom Boom would pop up in full nun's regalia at Feinstein events—to the obvious annoyance of the Catholic-educated mayor. "Haven't we met before?" Feinstein asked Boom Boom at one function, trying to remain polite as the media gathered around. "No, darling, that was Sister Vicious Power Hungry Bitch," Boom Boom replied, taking the opportunity to pin a "Dump Dianne" campaign pin on her blouse as news photographers' snapped away.

At his own rallies, Boom Boom would provoke howls of laughter by cat-fighting with a Dianne-look-alike drag queen, finally overcoming the lioness mayor by throwing her kicking and screaming over his shoulder and hauling her offstage.

Feinstein was forever being bedeviled and bewildered by San Francisco's more colorful elements. During her mayoral campaign four years earlier, she was challenged by Dennis Peron, the city's leading crusader for legal marijuana, and Jello Biafra, the politically rambunctious lead singer of the San Francisco punk band the Dead Kennedys. Peron, a pixie-like Vietnam veteran and former Milk activist, argued that San Francisco was indeed the kook capital, and that all the kooks should vote for him. Biafra enlivened the campaign by calling for the erection of Dan White statues all over the city, from which the parks and rec department would generate revenue by selling eggs and tomatoes to hurl at them.

The shameless antics of the Mitchell brothers drove Feinstein to distraction, provoking her to launch a ceaseless wave of police assaults on the porn nickelodeon. The brothers responded in typical ballsy style by slapping a big, bold message on their marquee: "Want a Good Time? Call Dianne," followed by the mayor's unlisted home phone number. No sooner would Feinstein switch numbers than her new number would pop up on the theater sign. It turned out that the Mitchell brothers had moles inside the phone company, who in return for supplying Feinstein's private numbers were rewarded with free passes to the nudie theater.

Warren Hinckle—who was keeping alive the old Scott Newhall tradition of provocative, carny-barker journalism as a *Chronicle* columnist—also had a knack for irritating the mayor. Hinckle, a crony of the Mitchells, regularly lampooned her porn obsession. But it was a Hinckle column about rent gouging at the Hotel Carlton, the residential hotel owned by Feinstein, that finally tipped her over the edge. Spying the portly, eye-patched, often sodden scribe at a party in the decorum-conscious Presidio Officers' Club, as he predictably perched himself at the bar, the mayor strode briskly over and tried to dump a drink on top of Hinckle's head. Herb Caen, delighted by the rare flash of mayoral intemperance, later saluted Feinstein in his column. "According to less than reliable two-eyed witnesses, the drink was an Old Fashioned, that being the kind of girl Dianne Feinstein is. Or was."

By making herself the target of the city's demonic energy, Feinstein rendered it fun and largely harmless. She was the firm but fair mother figure that the city ridiculed but needed. She was unable to grab all of the city's wildness and slam it through the swinging saloon doors. But she let everyone know—cops, queers, clowns, con artists—that the party had its limits, and that the city had to get up in the morning and go to work.

In any other city in America, Dianne Feinstein would have been considered a raving liberal. She pushed through the toughest antigun ordinance in the country, banning nearly all residents from owning handguns. She supported gay rights, labor unions, strong environmental protections, and the feminist Equal Rights Amendment. She believed that government should play a nurturing role in the lives of its citizens.

Nationally, her governmental philosophy was distinctly out of step in the era of Ronald Reagan, the man who had ridden the backlash against Bay Area utopianism all the way to the White House.

But in San Francisco, it was a different story. In San Francisco, after the short-lived reign of progressive hero George Moscone and the joyful radicalism of Harvey Milk, the Feinstein administration struck the city's surging left as a false interregnum. The dreamers and firebrands driving San Francisco politics in the late 1970s and 1980s would forever have gnarled and complicated feelings about Dianne Feinstein.

"Dianne was a very gracious person," said Harry Britt, her frequent foe and sometimes admirer. "My grandmother in Georgia was gracious. But when graciousness is a central part of your philosophy, it's limiting. Because grassroots politics ain't gracious, there's a roughness about it. And the gays and lefties in San Francisco—my people—are not always well behaved. Dianne was very much in favor of good behavior.

"She wasn't a social-change person. She didn't want to be the trail-blazer on city ordinances. Her attitude was, 'Don't ask me to do something that nobody has done anywhere else before.' Still, she was a very compassionate human being, on a lot of issues. She was extremely liberal in that old-fashioned sense, meaning giving. And in a world of Ronald Reagan—or Glenn Beck—that is a very welcome sort of decency."

Feinstein gave San Francisco back its solid center, without sacrificing its core values of tolerance and adventure. She made life in the city seem normal again—a significant accomplishment after the macabre events that preceded her rule. But there was something she could never bring to the city: a sense of ecstatic communion. She was smart enough, however, to realize that a sports team could. Feinstein's efforts to bring together San Francisco were about to be boosted greatly by that magical, unifying force that only a championship team can bring to the daily chaos of a city.

34

STRANGE ANGELS

I N THE FALL of 1978, during San Francisco's darkest days, the city's lowly spirit was matched by the dismal play of its beloved football team, the 49ers. Despite their gold rush name, the Niners had never struck fortune. Each year brought their long-suffering fans new heartaches. But by the late seventies, the 49ers had sunk to the most wretched state in team history. And still the 49er Faithful—as the team's largely blue-collar diehards were known—clung on. "Wait 'til next year" became 49ers fans' increasingly worn-out mantra.

The Faithful tried to keep up their spirits with bitter jokes: "Why do they call them '49ers?' Because they never cross the forty-nine-yard line." "What do the 49ers and Billy Graham have in common? They can both fill a stadium and within two minutes have everyone throwing their hands in the air and screaming 'Jesus Christ!'"

The Niners had deep roots in the loam and life of the city. Founded in 1946 by Tony Morabito, a local Italian-American lumber salesman, the 49ers were the only homegrown professional team in San Francisco. Willie Mays and the Giants were imported from New York in 1958, while basketball star Wilt Chamberlain and the Warriors came from Philadelphia in 1962.

Until 1971, the 49ers played in the heart of the city in rough and rowdy Kezar Stadium, a neighborhood arena squeezed between Golden

Gate Park and the Haight. Going to games at Kezar was not for the faint of heart. Fans often arrived drunk and braced themselves further against the sobering ocean drafts by continuing to drink throughout the afternoon. By the end of the game, the crowd was generally in a foul mood, its temper frayed by yet another 49ers loss, the raw weather, and the steady intake of alcohol. As the Niners fled the field into the dark, dirt-floored tunnel that led to their locker rooms, they were often bombarded with beer and whisky—some of it still in cans and bottles. Visiting teams could expect the same salutation. Wise players kept their helmets on as they headed toward the tunnel of doom.

Life in the Kezar bleachers was nasty, brutish, and not short enough. The wood benches were hard on the ass—and since it was easy to sneak into the stadium, there were usually too many asses jammed together. Screeching seagulls swooped overhead, splattering fans below with their foul white glop. Over the years, the benches became so saturated with seagull droppings that you couldn't help but take the stench home with you on the seat of your pants. It was impossible to buy a hotdog without a dozen other grubby hands passing it down the row to you, and the change from vendors often disappeared on the way back. Brawls were a common occurrence, making the stands more dangerous than the field.

There were fleeting glory days for the 49ers. In the 1950s, legendary players like Y. A. Tittle, Joe Perry, and Hugh McElhenny brought the team tantalizingly close to a championship. A 49ers team led by quarterback John Brodie took another run at the gold ring in the early seventies. But Niners hopes were always dashed by rival teams during the playoffs—especially by the hated Dallas Cowboys, who scored three consecutive, dagger-in-the-heart victories over San Francisco in 1970, '71, and '72. When beloved team owner Tony Morabito dropped dead of a heart attack during a game at Kezar, it seemed to sum up the fate of his team.

In 1977 the Morabito family sold the 49ers for $17 million to Edward DeBartolo Sr., a self-made billionaire in Youngstown, Ohio, who had amassed his fortune from building shopping malls. DeBartolo, whose real estate empire included three racetracks, had long wanted to buy a major league baseball team, but he was blocked by league officials, who explained that the horse racing connection would bring an unsavory odor to America's national pastime. The DeBartolo family knew what that was code for. "Mr. DeBartolo happens to be of Italian descent," a family spokesman observed dryly. But the Morabito family had no problem with the Italian heritage of the DeBartolos, who edged out comedian Bob Hope and real estate mogul and future San Diego Chargers owner Alex Spanos for the Niners.

DeBartolo bought the 49ers for his son, Eddie Jr., who at thirty years old became the youngest owner of an NFL team. The short, brash junior DeBartolo immediately alienated the San Francisco sports press and 49ers fan base, coming off as a cocky outsider from a fading smokestack town who had been given a shiny new toy by his daddy. DeBartolo Jr. breezed in and out of San Francisco, commuting from Ohio in the family Learjet, and casually referring to the Niners' hometown as "Frisco"— a violation of local custom that, as Herb Caen had impatiently explained for many years, was committed only by clueless rubes.

Fans grew increasingly sour on the team's new ownership, as Joe Thomas, the general manager installed by DeBartolo, began running the franchise into the ground. Thomas cut stars in their prime such as quarterback Jim Plunkett, who went on to become the most valuable player in the Oakland Raiders' 1981 Super Bowl victory, and traded away valuable draft picks for broken-down veterans like gimpy running back O. J. Simpson.

As the losses piled up and team attendance plummeted, Thomas grew increasingly unhinged. He would show up in the locker room to give the players' rambling pep talks after their defeats, fortified by a drink or three. As the team spiraled downward, the general manager's postgame speeches grew more threatening than inspirational. "If I go down the fucking tubes," he railed at players after another demoralizing loss, "I'm going to take all of you with me!"

The team's thoroughly fed-up fans took out their frustration on DeBartolo whenever he showed up for games at Candlestick Park—the cavernous stadium on a bleak, wind-whipped stretch of the bay where the 49ers had moved after finally abandoning Kezar. DeBartolo took his life into his hands whenever he left the security of his private box to relieve himself in the stadium's public urinals. The young owner was subjected to fusillades of verbal abuse and occasionally to censure of a blunter variety. He was once plunked by a full can of beer.

"I began wondering what I had got myself into," said DeBartolo years later. "I was very happy in my little cocoon doing real estate in a large family company in Youngstown, Ohio. And here I am suddenly in the public eye, getting spit on and battered by cans of beer. That was a tough time."

The lowest point for the 49ers came late in their 1978 season. "We were so bad it was embarrassing," recalled guard Randy Cross. "We were about to go 2–14, and I'll tell you, we weren't nearly that good. I was surprised we won any games at all." On the night of November 27, the Niners were scheduled to play the fearsome Pittsburgh Steelers—the team of the 1970s—in a nationally televised *Monday Night Football* game in Candlestick Park. That morning Dan White crawled through the basement window at city hall with his Smith & Wesson.

A panicky Joe Thomas begged NFL commissioner Pete Rozelle to cancel the game. Thomas was not thinking about the grieving citizens of San Francisco. He was worried about himself, convinced that the killings weren't over yet, and someone might be gunning for him.

"Joe just totally lost it," remembered Carmen Policy, DeBartolo's lawyer, and later president of the team. "He thought there might be some sort of conspiracy. Joe was doing all sorts of crazy things by the end. Eddie was fed up. He told Joe, 'I'm going to the game. If you don't want to come, Joe, stay home.' It was just a terrible situation."

After the 49ers were predictably humiliated by the Steelers, 24–7, DeBartolo finally fired Thomas. It was at this dark hour for San Francisco and its football franchise that DeBartolo began seeking a savior for the team.

THE YOUNG OWNER ZEROED in on Stanford University's maverick coach, forty-seven-year-old Bill Walsh, who had knocked around college and professional football for decades without ever winning a top coaching spot in the NFL. Among the old guard of owners and head coaches who dominated the NFL, Walsh had a reputation as a brilliant but emotionally fragile offensive strategist—a man not built for a commanding role in the brutally competitive world of professional football. He was too sensitive, he became too entwined with his players. He broke down after losing games, he even choked up before every kickoff when "The Star-Spangled Banner" was played. He was a poet in a Stone Age world. Only an NFL owner as young and frantic as DeBartolo would have taken a risk on someone as intriguingly eccentric as Walsh.

Bill Walsh grew up in Southern California and later the Bay Area, the son of a hard-drinking, hard-working man who juggled a job on a Chrysler assembly line with his own auto body shop. Walsh was a moody, indifferent student. "He didn't see the benefit of being a great student, so he wasn't," said Craig Walsh, his son. "He didn't fit into any of the high school cliques; he was always an outsider."

But Walsh had a passion for sports, particularly football and boxing. He began his football career as a high school coach in blue-collar Fremont, California, turning around a losing team with a sophisticated passing game that left opponents dumbstruck. He developed a mathematician's love of diagramming plays, sometimes absentmindedly tracing Xs and Os on the back of his wife Geri when his arm was wrapped around her.

"Everyone [else] was running three yards and a cloud of dust," one of Walsh's high school players recalled. "Under him we ran three wide receivers, a lot of motion and sprint-out pass patterns. Most teams we played only had two receivers in the pass patterns. We had three to five in every play. He'd say [to the quarterback], 'This is your primary receiver, then I want you to look here, then here.' At that time, everybody played a three-deep zone defense. He really attacked that area. He'd flood the zones with two or three receivers."

It was the beginning of Bill Walsh's "West Coast offense," a delicate and brutal ballet whose intricacy would revolutionize professional football. Walsh began to perfect his multidimensional attack while working as an offensive coach for Paul Brown, the legendary head coach of the Cincinnati Bengals. Brown was a stern traditionalist whose teams were noted, as Walsh later observed, for "their almost mechanical, error-free precision." But Walsh was not afraid to challenge his boss, and gradually he began working a more complex architecture into the Bengals' game, with increasingly successful results.

Brown and Walsh had a complicated and troubled relationship. A remote father figure, Brown appreciated his protégé's brilliance while at the same time resenting how he was modernizing the game. Brown dropped hints to Walsh that he was his heir, while doing the same to another assistant coach, Bill Johnson.

But when the day arrived for the aging Brown to hand over the reins of the team, at the end of the 1975 season, the coach devastated Walsh by choosing Johnson instead. Walsh, who learned of Brown's decision from a sports reporter, immediately told his wife, "We've got to get out of here." Walsh uprooted his family from Cincinnati, where Geri and the kids had made a happy life for themselves, and began wandering around the football world in search of a new job—as his itinerant father had done when he was growing up. He was a dazzling football tactician who had devoted his life to the game, but in middle age, he found himself jobless, starting all over again.

Though Paul Brown had bequeathed his estate to someone else, like a spiteful father, he expected Walsh to stick around and still work on it. Walsh applied for head coaching positions with the Seattle Seahawks and the New York Jets, but neither team hired him. He later found out that Brown was poisoning the waters for him, spreading word throughout the league that he was "too soft" to lead an NFL team.

Finally, Walsh managed to land an assistant coach position with the Chargers, despite Brown's efforts to sabotage that opportunity as well. A year later he accepted an offer to coach football at Stanford, leaping at the chance to finally run a team himself. It was here—after working his magic for the Stanford Cardinal, capped by a dramatic comeback victory over Georgia in the 1978 Bluebonnet Bowl—that Walsh came to Eddie DeBartolo's attention.

DeBartolo and Walsh met in the 49ers owner's suite at the Fairmont Hotel to complete the deal. DeBartolo's father was skeptical about Walsh after having phoned around the league and hearing the negative, Brown-inspired chatter about him. Eddie Jr. was not inclined to listen to the old guard's take on Walsh. But before the Fairmont meeting, the elder DeBartolo took aside family attorney Carmen Policy and instructed him to sign Walsh at the lowest possible salary, "so that when we fire him, he won't cost us that much."

The tall, white-haired, professorial Walsh and the squat, dark-mopped, ebullient DeBartolo made an odd pair. But the young owner sensed within the first ten minutes of the meeting that Walsh was his man. Walsh proved to be a shrewd negotiator, wrangling out of DeBartolo an impressive $160,000 starting salary and a generous array of benefits, including a membership in the local country club—a princely package that left Policy to face the old man's wrath back in Youngstown. But in return, the younger DeBartolo made his own stiff demand. "I want a championship," he told Walsh flatly. "Don't take the job if you can't deliver that." There was a long pause. At last, Walsh said softly, "You have my word."

Bill Walsh faced a deeply discouraging task when he took over the 49ers in January 1979. Not only was the team widely considered the worst in the NFL—with less talent and experience than any other franchise—it also had the dimmest prospects for improvement, since Joe Thomas had traded away many of its future draft picks. "It was like raising the *Titanic*. I thought it might be impossible," the coach said later.

Walsh, who had felt disrespected by his colleagues throughout his career, constantly worried that DeBartolo would run out of patience before he could complete the Niners' turnaround. During Walsh's first season, the team ended with the same abysmal 2–14 record that it had the year before. His second season began more brightly, with the team winning three games in a row. But then the Niners went into a tailspin, losing eight straight games, including a spirit-crushing 59–14 blowout by their longtime tormentors, the Cowboys.

After a frustrating loss to the Dolphins, Walsh broke down sobbing on the long flight home from Miami. His assistant coaches formed a circle around him, eating peanuts and pretending to be chatting with the head coach, so the players couldn't witness his breakdown. Walsh was "an emotional basket case," he confessed later. "I felt like a casualty of war being airlifted away from the battlefield."

He had poured all of himself into rebuilding the team, working around the clock, abandoning his family, and drawing on all of his hard-won wisdom to revitalize the lowly Niners. But nothing seemed to be working. Maybe his critics were right; he lacked what it took to succeed in the NFL. He decided to quit when he got home. It took him the rest of the flight, sitting alone in the dark cabin, to pull himself back from the brink.

Throughout his years with the 49ers, Bill Walsh was a tormented soul, constantly racked by self-doubts. He carried within him a Platonic ideal of athletic achievement, a standard of physical and intellectual perfection that always loomed maddeningly beyond his reach. Everything had to be just right; he even carefully selected the paint colors for the Niners' new training facility. He would wander the hallways of the building straightening pictures. DeBartolo used to plague him by tipping them to the side. "He never knew who did it," said the team owner years later.

DeBartolo's mercurial temperament did little to reassure the fragile Walsh. During the decadelong partnership between the owner and coach, Eddie Jr. ordered Policy to fire Walsh "about four or five times," according to the team executive. "Part of my job was to keep those two stable when things were bad, so as not to cause irreparable harm."

Walsh frequently broke down in tears after team setbacks. He would lock himself in his office and listen to mournful Willie Nelson tunes. He asked the team's trainer for medication to help him sleep. "Bill was sensitive about everything," said Policy. "In some way, he was a terrible pain in the neck, a deeply insecure man. He measured everything in terms of money, and he wondered why a star player like Joe Montana made more than him. I'm not saying it was motivated by greed. I think it was a sense of insecurity. How am I viewed, how am I valued? But all this sensitivity was tied to his genius; this almost artistic way that he managed the football field."

ALTHOUGH NO ONE KNEW it at the time, the turning point for Walsh and the 49ers had come in a New York City hotel ballroom in May 1979, when the coach, brilliantly working the NFL draft, selected two players who would change the dark-starred team's history: Notre Dame quarterback Joe Montana, and a little-known Clemson University wide end named Dwight Clark, who would become Montana's favorite receiver.

Joe Montana, the eighty-second choice in that year's draft, did not strike most NFL experts as starting quarterback material. Coltish and spindly legged, at six feet two and 185 pounds, he seemed too fragile for pro football's clash of behemoths. The buzz on Montana was that he was a big-play QB but also erratic and weak armed.

Like Walsh, Joe Montana had to fight his whole life for the top spot. From age eight, when he played midget football in Monongahela— a blue-collar town in western Pennsylvania, cradle of legendary quarterbacks—Montana always started out on teams as the unappreciated backup. The scrawny athlete began his college career at Notre Dame lost in a pack of quarterbacks. He seemed destined to never break out, hobbled by injuries and disregarded by coach Dan Devine. Even after leading the team to the greatest comeback victory in Fighting Irish history, in a game with the University of North Carolina during his sophomore season, Montana continued to ride the bench.

At the start of his junior year, Montana was still listed as Notre Dame's third quarterback. "If I ever thought sincerely about quitting football, it was then," he said later. It was not until the third game of his season, against Purdue, when Montana finally secured the starting position. With just eleven minutes left in the game and Notre Dame trailing, 24–14, Devine inserted him out of desperation. Montana led three scoring drives, and Notre Dame stunned Purdue, 31–24.

It was the beginning of Joe Montana's "Comeback Kid" legend. Again and again, for the rest of his football career, the skinny-legged quarterback would demonstrate a gift for winning under the direst of circumstances. When all seemed lost, when fans were heading for the gates, the Comeback Kid would begin to work his magic, guiding his team to victory through all the mayhem swirling around him with a trance-like calm.

Montana capped his college career with his greatest comeback of all, on a freakishly cold and snowy day at the 1979 Cotton Bowl in Dallas. Suffering from flu and hypothermia, he was pumped full of bouillon at halftime. When Montana ran back onto the field in the third quarter, he had no feeling in his hands, and his team had fallen behind the University of Houston, 34–12. But Montana brought his team back to within striking distance, and with two seconds left in the game, he threw a miracle pass—a low bullet to the right corner of the end zone—and Notre Dame won, 35–34.

During their rookie years as 49ers, Montana and his friendly, shaggily handsome southern roommate, Dwight Clark, seemed dazzled just to be in the NFL. Montana, taking the field during training camp, couldn't believe that he was handing off the ball to O. J. Simpson. Clark, fully expecting to be cut, never unpacked his bags.

Walsh took his time with his young QB, slowly working him into action behind starting quarterback Steve DeBerg. During the 49ers' punishing, lopsided loss to Dallas in Montana's second year, the coach periodically turned toward the bench, as if to decide whether he should throw his young QB into the meat grinder. "I must admit, I was scared," Montana said later. "I didn't want to go in, so every time he looked around, I turned my back on him."

The coach knew that the Niners' offensive line was weak and Montana would be vulnerable, so he took pity on him. Walsh realized that a rookie could be physically and mentally scarred by being thrown too early against the speed and force of NFL opponents.

But by the end of Montana's second season, the coach—certain that his young second-string QB had learned his labyrinthine system—made it clear that he was the franchise's future. Before the start of the 1981 season, Walsh traded DeBerg. It was a major confidence booster for Montana, who had been pitted against rivals throughout his career. Now everything was on the young quarterback's shoulders.

THE 49ERS BEGAN THE 1981 season with low expectations. Ira Miller, the *Chronicle*'s 49ers beat reporter, told fans that "the most they should hope for is a .500 finish, but they shouldn't expect it." Miller predicted that the Atlanta Falcons would win the 49ers' conference and quite possibly the Super Bowl as well. When Atlanta blew the Niners off the field, 34–17, early in the season, it confirmed for many in the local sports media that San Francisco was simply not in the same league as its top rivals.

After the 49ers lost two of their first three games, fans were gripped by the same old sinking feeling. Walsh became obsessed with the idea that the press was out for his scalp, and he later claimed that one publication began running a series on the imminent demise of his 49ers career, although no such articles ever appeared in print. Offensive tackle Keith Fahnhorst, who had weathered the grim Joe Thomas years, decided he couldn't take it anymore and asked the team to trade him. "'Oh hell, here we go again'—that's what I was thinking after those first few games," recalled Fahnhorst. "Thank God the front office didn't listen to me."

Finally, in week four, all of Bill Walsh's sweat and inspiration started to pay off, as the 49ers beat New Orleans and went on to win eleven of their twelve remaining games. The elegant game that he had been designing in his head ever since he was a boy began to materialize on the field. It was a game that relied as much on mental nimbleness as it did on brute force.

"Bill didn't see football as a contest over who was the tougher man," said 49ers linebacker Keena Turner. "His game had to do with quickness of mind and body, and outthinking the opponent. It was more of a chess game than a wrestling match. That's the way he approached it, and he always wanted to be two moves ahead."

Walsh used clever strategies to mask the team's weaknesses, developing a short passing attack to augment the Niners' mediocre running game. He carefully choreographed the opening twenty-five plays of each game, hoping to seize the momentum early and control the direction of the contest. Opponents dismissed the Walsh style as "finesse football" or "swish and sway," stopping just short of calling San Francisco's team "flaming queers."

The coach did not believe in punishing practices. He was not a screamer. He came across more as a professor than a drill sergeant, teaching rather than terrorizing, and invoking epic battles and heroic feats from history to inspire his players. He told the team to call him Bill instead of Coach. But he had learned to keep his emotional distance from players, steeling himself for the day when they would inevitably break down and be cut. He was neither a friend nor a fatherly figure, but players worked hard for his respect. A smile from Walsh on the sidelines was a cherished trophy.

On paper, the 49ers were not a team that should have gone to the playoffs that year. It was a grab bag of promising but still green players, NFL castoffs, and battered veterans. "We were a no-name team," said Turner. But Walsh identified each player's potential before he himself saw it. And he made each of them believe that if they embraced his system, the 49ers could go all the way to the top. Under his leadership, the team at last found that rare chemistry that distinguishes champions, becoming more than the sum of its parts.

The 1981 team was an eccentric collection of athletes. The defense was anchored by two oddball veterans, maniacal linebacker Jack "Hacksaw" Reynolds and future Hall of Fame defensive end Fred Dean. Hacksaw Reynolds set a level of intensity for the team that lit a fire under the younger players. At the beginning of every season, Reynolds dispatched his wife to the Bahamas, knowing that he was not fit to be around while he was in warrior mode. On Sunday mornings, Reynolds rose early, dressed in full battle gear—including his pads and black eyeglare war paint—and ate breakfast in the hotel restaurant, already exuding a game-ready ferocity.

Fred Dean, who was picked up from San Diego midway through the 1981 season, was immediately credited with giving the 49ers the final spark they needed. Dean, a lightning-quick pass rusher, could create chaos in an opponent's backfield. The Pro Bowl player was stung when he found out that the Chargers were paying him less than his brother-in-law made as a truck driver, and he threatened to sit out the next two seasons if he wasn't given a raise. The Chargers decided to dump their disgruntled player instead, and Walsh was only too happy to grab him.

Dean had suffered from crippling migraine headaches after running into a massive TV camera cart on the sidelines during a 1976 game, hitting the metal cart so hard with his head that his helmet cracked. He showed up for his first 49ers meeting pulling a canister of oxygen and sucking from it with a mask. A country boy from Louisiana, where he developed an impressively muscular build in the hay fields, Dean was convinced that he did not need to work out. "Whenever I feel like exercising," he told reporters, "I lie down until the feeling goes away." Dean walked through the 49ers locker room puffing on menthol cigarettes. Walsh finally told him that if he was going to keep on smoking, he had to do it in a training room closet, away from the rest of the team.

The son of a dairy farmworker, Dean was raised to appreciate the rich language of the Bible and Shakespeare. "My parents always read us stories," he explained. "Finding the true meaning of Shakespeare under all those flowery words was always a mind twister for me." Dean was fond of quoting inspirational lines from Shakespeare in the 49ers locker room. One of his favorites was, "Cowards die many times before their deaths. The valiant never taste of death but once." He also recited his own poetry.

Walsh was well equipped to work with idiosyncratic personalities because he was one of them. Out of step his whole career with the NFL mainstream, he knew how to handle the peculiarities of his players. Differences didn't threaten him; he didn't see rebelliousness as an affront.

AFTER TAKING OVER THE Niners, Walsh hired a head athletic trainer named Lindsy McLean, whom he later discovered was gay when McLean brought his partner to a 49ers Christmas party. "I was forty, and I wasn't a player, so I couldn't understand why I had to hide," said McLean. The revelation did nothing to affect Walsh's attitude toward McLean, whom the coach deeply respected for his professional skill. When players learned that McLean was gay, however, a few freaked out. One defensive back refused to let the trainer tape a pulled groin muscle. But most players continued to treat McLean like one of the 49ers family.

Joe Montana, who brought a playground sense of fun to the game, didn't seem to give a damn about McLean's sexuality. "I never heard anything bad from Joe," McLean recalled. "He was just there to play football." Some of the toughest stars on the team, like future Hall of Fame defensive back Ronnie Lott, developed a particularly trusting relationship with McLean. Lott, who subjected his body and those of his opponents to severe punishment, relied on McLean's healing powers.

Even permanently cranky Hacksaw Reynolds warmed up to the Tennessee-born McLean, who shared Reynolds's affection for the player's college team, the University of Tennessee Volunteers.

Despite the occasional ugly remark in the locker room, the trainer continued to care for his players' battered and bruised bodies throughout the Walsh years and beyond. "On the road, I'd go to their rooms and give them their pillow fluff, and I'd give them a little massage or something." If anyone had insulted McLean in his presence, star running back Roger Craig said years later, he or Lott would've "kicked his ass."

When he finally retired from the San Francisco 49ers in 2004 after his sixth-fifth birthday, Lindsy McLean was still the only openly gay trainer in the NFL.

Bill Walsh was also ahead of his time when it came to race relations in the NFL. Concerned about the lack of coaching opportunities for African Americans, he created a Minority Coaches Fellowship Program and invited talented minority coaches to the 49ers headquarters to observe him at work. The league eventually modeled its own minority program on the coach's initiative. Walsh, the perennial outsider, knew what it felt like to be rebuffed and ignored.

The coach also brought in UC Berkeley sociologist Harry Edwards, a black liberation firebrand in the 1960s, to serve as a mentor to African-American athletes on the team. No other NFL coach would have inserted a man with Edwards's outspoken reputation into his organization, and some of Walsh's own staff expressed grave doubts about the decision.

Harry Edwards had drawn the violent wrath of the FBI and white supremacists when he tried to organize a black athlete boycott of the 1968 Summer Olympics. He was denounced by politicians like Ronald Reagan and sports broadcasters like Brent Musburger, who compared him to Hitler; his classes at San Jose State College, where he worked as a sociology instructor, were infiltrated by undercover FBI agents, and he was later fired by the administration; his off-campus apartment was broken into and his dogs were killed; his car was vandalized and repeatedly ticketed by policemen; he was warned by CBS news producer Louis Lomax that he would be targeted by government authorities for assassination if he attended the Olympic Games in Mexico City.

When track star Tommie Smith, who had taken classes from Edwards at San Jose State, raised his clenched fist along with John Carlos on the victory stand in Mexico City, they created an iconic image of black power defiance. Smith, and his mentor Edwards, also won the lasting enmity of the athletic establishment.

By the time Smith returned home with his gold medal, he was an outcast. Nobody would hire him, callers threatened to kill him. "One rock came through our front window in our living room, where we had the crib," Smith recalled. "It seemed like everybody hated me. I had no food. My baby was hungry. My wife had no dresses."

Only one coach in the country was willing to hire Tommie Smith: Bill Walsh. When he was coaching for the Bengals, Walsh tried out Smith as a wide receiver—"just to give Tommie an NFL payday," said Harry Edwards. Smith stayed with the team for three seasons, but never really succeeded in football.

Walsh brought Edwards to the 49ers as an advisor after the two men exchanged a series of letters on race, drugs, and other social aspects of professional sports. Invited to lunch at the 49ers training facility, Edwards ended up spending the night and signing on with the team. It was the beginning of a long conversation about sports, society, and life that did not end until Walsh died in 2007.

"Bill was not just a reader and a thinker," said Edwards, still an imposing edifice of a man at a solid six foot eight and wearing the wraparound shades of his Black Panthers days. "He was the greatest teacher that I had ever been around. He was analytical to the point of understanding how the flap of a butterfly's wing can cause a hurricane. In other words, he understood details and how everything mattered. He was always looking for the missing piece that would put his world together.

"He understood that the demographics of the locker room were changing. He told me that with the exception of Montana, who as the quarterback was really more like a coach, all his leaders on the team were black: Ronnie Lott, Jerry Rice, Roger Craig. He understood that these young black athletes needed to be integrated into the 49ers system. He knew what it was like to be excluded. It was written in his Irish soul. He understood what it meant as a boy when he heard the jokes— you know, like God was kind, he invented wheelbarrows and the Irish to push them."

Walsh knew that his eclectic team mirrored San Francisco itself. And he was well aware that the rest of the league regarded both the team and the city as somehow deviant. The coach used this us-against-the-world feeling to motivate the team. No one in the sports establishment believed in them, he told his players, so they had to believe in themselves.

In the sixth game of the 1981 season, a matchup with the dreaded Cowboys, the 49ers exploded on the field, avenging their lopsided defeat a year earlier and crushing Dallas, 45–14. But on ABC's *Monday Night Football* the following evening, the network did not include any footage of the overwhelming Niners victory in its halftime highlights reel. Walsh, suspecting that ABC was protecting "America's Team" from national humiliation at his own team's expense, erupted at his weekly press conference. "We're not accepted nationally, obviously," he fumed to reporters. "The jockstrap elitists don't consider us in their comfort zone. There are power sources, influence sources in the National Football League, forty-five-year-old men who are football groupies who prefer that we not exist so they can hold on to their football contracts and associations or power groups."

BUT IF THE NATIONAL sports establishment still snubbed the surging 49ers, the team's hometown was starting to glow with the unfamiliar sensation of victory. As the 49ers vanquished one team after the next, including powerhouses like the Steelers and longtime rivals like the Los Angeles Rams, the excitement steadily mounted in the city. It was too soon for euphoria. Wounded by one civic trauma after the next—and long used to the dreariness of defeat on its athletic fields—San Francisco was not quite ready to give itself over to 49ers fever. But the numbness from all those years of grisly headlines slowly began to lift from the city. The glow was spreading, like the first fingers of light over Twin Peaks, after an endless shroud of gloom.

The 49er Faithful in blue-collar San Francisco grew more celebratory each week. Even Eddie Jr. was now greeted warmly in the Candlestick bathrooms as he stood in line to take a piss. Hard-core fans were starting to love the young owner for the passion he brought to the team. "To me, the 49ers is not just a job, it's very personal," he told the press that season. "The team has become my wife." And the Faithful knew exactly what he meant.

After games at Candlestick, George Seifert, the 49ers' up-and-coming defensive coach, would drive to his in-laws' house in the working-class Mission-Geneva district to pick up his kids. As the Niners inched closer to the playoffs, the cheering and car-horn blasting that greeted him in his family's neighborhood grew louder each week.

But the 49ers were no longer the exclusive property of the Faithful. The team was starting to be embraced in every corner of the city. There was something about brainy, brooding Coach Walsh and his band of misfits that struck a chord with the city. Walsh's 49ers seemed like an only-in-San-Francisco phenomenon, but in the best possible way.

The crowds started to squeeze into bars all over the city on Sunday afternoons—from Ed Moose's Washington Square watering hole for literary folk, politicos, and Pacific Heights party drinkers, to Maud's, a flannel-and-blue-jeans lesbian bar in the Haight where the bartender wore a "Don't Fuck with the 49ers" T-shirt.

San Francisco desperately needed to enjoy itself again, and even in the Castro, the suddenly victorious 49ers seemed as good an excuse as any. "You couldn't help get caught up in the excitement even if you weren't a sports fan," said Tom Ammiano, a gay schoolteacher inspired by Harvey Milk to go into city politics. "The team began to bring the city together. I think there was a nude photo of Joe Montana that was being secreted around the Castro. Of course, there was a lot of photo trickery then, so who knows."

"There were a lot of gay folk who knew they should be happy, but weren't quite sure why," said Harry Britt, a hard-core football fan ever since his Texas childhood. "It was more like, 'Why don't they have boy cheerleaders too?'"

San Francisco cineastes were flocking that season to the War Memorial Opera House to watch Abel Gance's *Napoleon,* the 1927 silent classic lovingly restored by director Francis Ford Coppola. At one Sunday screening of the movie, the elegant Beaux Arts temple suddenly erupted in raucous cheers. Touchdown, 49ers! Dozens of the movie fans had come equipped with transistor radios and earphones.

Celebrities began gracing the beer-soaked aisles of Candlestick, where a recently freed Patty Hearst and her bodyguard husband were seen making their way through the crowds. Ferlinghetti pronounced the Niners the city's new gods, while San Francisco old gods Jerry Garcia and Bob Weir paid homage to the football deities at Candlestick. Michael Zagaris, the wild and woolly team photographer better known as "Z-Man," began bringing friends from his other life as a rock 'n' roll shooter to 49ers games, and suddenly psychedelic cowboys like Ramrod—a legendary Grateful Dead roadie and former Merry Prankster—began wandering the sidelines. When a young band from Ireland called U2 showed up in San Francisco on its first tour of America, the four members wisely took the stage at the Old Waldorf wearing Niners' red and gold.

Mayor Feinstein, who didn't know a tight end from a tight ass, suddenly developed a case of 49er fever, demanding that Willie Brown return the mayoral box seats at Candlestick that she had given him in return for securing a $25 million state bailout for the city.

Herb Caen spotted Gina Moscone at Candlestick late in the '81 season. Three years had passed since her husband's murder. The late mayor's widow was still rarely seen in public. But there she was in the stands as the home team trotted off the field to a chorus of cheers after defeating the New York Giants. "We won! We won!" she shouted, her big eyes glimmering in the late afternoon light.

As the excitement grew, San Francisco seemed closer and closer to exorcising its demons—at least those that could be expelled by dancing in the streets and kissing strangers on the lips. All that stood in the way of the city's deliverance was the grim-faced executioner Tom Landry and his horsemen of the apocalypse known as the Dallas Cowboys.

35

PLAYING AGAINST GOD

T HE DALLAS COWBOYS organization was the brutal antithesis of San Francisco finesse. The team had become an NFL juggernaut under the ownership of right-wing oilman Clint Murchison Jr. and coach Tom Landry, a God-fearing evangelical from deep in the heart of the Rio Grande Valley who turned the Cowboys into a religion in Texas. Under Landry, the Cowboys became not only America's Team but God's team. Along with two or three other dynasties like the Green Bay Packers and Pittsburgh Steelers, Landry's Cowboys seemed to have a divine calling to rule the NFL year in and year out.

Landry carved out his iconic position in pro football—alongside the likes of Vince Lombardi, George Halas, and Paul Brown—in an era when coaches ruled their empires with omnipotent authority. A chill fear filled the locker room whenever he entered. He stalked the sidelines every Sunday with a stone face, wearing a G-man's brimmed hat and overcoat. He never seemed to flinch under the pressure of combat, not even during the Cowboys' Super Bowl showdowns. "Once you commit yourself to Christ," he explained, "it's in God's hands."

When it came to religion and football, Landry believed in the fundamentals. "The best offense," his NFL mentor taught him, "can be built around ten basic plays, the best defense on two. All the rest is razzle-dazzle, egomania, and box office." The Dallas coach clearly thought that

Bill Walsh's West Coast offense was nothing but fancy-pants gimmickry, as sinuous and vaguely sinister as San Francisco itself.

Walsh and Landry were a clashing contrast in nearly every way. The former approached football like an artistic challenge, the latter like the World War II bombardier that he once was. While Walsh followed a frustrating, circuitous route to the top, Landry had marched up football's chain of command with a military-like precision. Starting as a cocaptain on the University of Texas team, he went on to become a Pro Bowl player and then coach with the New York Giants before finally coming home to take over the new expansion team in Dallas in 1960.

The Cowboys' corporate culture was light years removed from San Francisco values. Clint Murchison, a crony of reactionary FBI czar J. Edgar Hoover and a business partner of Mafia godfathers such as Carlos Marcello, was Richard Nixon's biggest financial supporter during the 1960 presidential race. Some Kennedy assassination researchers have alleged that Murchison played a key role in the plot against JFK. On the afternoon of November 22, 1963, after he was told about the president's assassination, Landry kept on running the Cowboys' practice drills as if nothing had happened just miles away in Dealey Plaza.

Many black players on the Cowboys felt the team was run like a plantation, with white athletes getting preferential treatment. Duane Thomas, a Cowboys running back in the early seventies, later wrote an exposé of the team, lambasting Landry as a "plastic man [with] a John Bircher . . . white supremacist mentality. His philosophy was intimidation, intimidation, intimidation, of the mind and body."

As the 49ers swept to a miraculous 13–3 record in 1981, they headed for the inevitable showdown with the Cowboys, the last obstacle between San Francisco and the Super Bowl. Bitterness and humiliation were built into these Cowboys playoff contests for Niners fans. The feelings were buried as gloomily in San Franciscans' genes as Jews' revulsion for Cossacks. Every time the 49ers seemed to be soaring toward a Super Bowl, the Cowboys would crush their hopes. The fact that Dallas seemed to take a holy warrior's joy in vanquishing "Sin Funcisco," as Herb Caen tongue-in-cheeked it, made the chronic defeats all the more bitter. Caen insisted that he actually didn't mind Dallas calling itself America's Team—but the God's Team business sent him, and the rest of San Francisco, screaming around the bend.

As if there weren't enough reasons to hate the Cowboys, Caen deadpanned as the hour of doom approached, "They have a quarterback named Dan White and a running back named Jim Jones." And QB Danny White was in a typically swaggering Cowboy mood despite the 49ers' upset victory over Dallas earlier in the season. "We don't have much fear of them," White drawled to the press.

Ed "Too Tall" Jones, the giant pass rusher who anchored Dallas's "Doomsday Defense," was even more dismissive. The earlier 49ers victory was a fluke, he informed reporters. "I didn't have a whole lot of respect for the 49ers before that game—I didn't know half the names of the team." And, Jones made clear, his opinion had not improved much since.

Caen, always quick to comfort and tickle his city through its bleak days, tried to prepare San Francisco for the worst. "If Dallas wins today," he wrote on the morning of the epic battle, "it will not be the end of the world—just the end of a very successful season—and San Francisco will continue to be the greatest city in the world, and don't you forget it, buddy."

But the whole city knew how devastating another loss would be. "It would be Jim Jones and the purple Kool-Aid all over again," thought 49ers team photographer Michael Zagaris.

A few days before the Dallas game, Mayor Feinstein invited DeBartolo, Walsh, and a few 49ers executives to dinner at Ernie's, one of the city's most illustrious dining spots, though it looked like a classy Barbary Coast whorehouse. "I don't know if you realize it," Feinstein told the men who held the morale of her city in their hands, "but San Francisco needs this team."

As the 49ers practiced for the big game, Walsh tried to fire up his players with the same underdog resentment he had employed earlier in the season. It was not simply a coaching ploy. He felt it in his guts. Walsh told his men how he felt about the Cowboys. "Their press releases are all about how they are going to kick ass. They're so arrogant down there in the sports empire of the world . . . I'm sick of them. I hope you guys feel the same way I do."

Throughout his career, the Tom Landrys of the league had regarded him with contempt. Now, on the eve of the biggest game of Walsh's life, he still didn't command any respect. Giants coach Ray Perkins, defeated

by Walsh in the previous playoff round, summed up the prevailing sentiment in the NFL when he predicted a decisive Dallas victory over San
Francisco, flatly declaring the Cowboys the "better football team."

WHEN GAME DAY ARRIVED on January 10, 1982, Walsh was in a meditative frame of mind. There were no pep talks in the locker room. He
simply made his way around the room, shaking hands with his players
and offering each man a few words of personal encouragement.

By this stage of the season, the 49ers were a wounded and weary
army. Fred Dean's sternum was so badly bruised that it hurt him to bend
over. Trainers heavily padded his chest to protect it, but Dean knew that
the first hit he took would be torment. Keena Turner had come down
with chicken pox, and the maddening sores had erupted all over his
body, including his mouth and his ass crack. He was slathered in cala-
mine lotion and wrapped in plastic in hopes that the pustules would not
burst in the heat and friction of the game. "I was completely miserable,"
Turner recalled. "But come on, how do you not play in a game like that?"

Many of the players had come down with the flu during the week
before the game—some with a respiratory virus, others with a stomach infection. Keith Fahnhorst, who was hacking and coughing during
practice, remembered being harnessed to an experimental device in
the training room that was supposed to loosen up the congestion in his
chest. "There were these strange prods, like a sci-fi movie. It was bizarre.
I'm not sure if it had any scientific backing." When they ran onto the
field, some players—including Dwight Clark and Randy Cross—already
felt depleted. Cross was puking on the sidelines before the game even
began.

Candlestick Park, crammed to capacity with more than sixty-five
thousand fans, was humming with an unbearable tension. Fans had
lined up for days in the stadium ticket line, braving howling wind and
rain and even hail. They wrapped themselves in plastic, they huddled
together drinking whisky and smoking weed, they slept in soggy sleeping bags. Nothing was going to stop the Faithful from witnessing this
moment of truth.

On the Thursday before the game, the storm that had been besieging
the Bay Area all week became so savage that President Reagan declared

Northern California a disaster area—which is exactly the way he had viewed the San Francisco area ever since he was governor. There were no good wishes extended to the home state team from the White House. San Franciscans assumed that the president would be rooting for Dallas.

On Sunday the clouds finally parted, and as the game began, Candlestick Park was bathed in a cathedral light. Guided by Walsh's opening script, the 49ers got off to a fast start. Driving down the field, Montana threw a fake on Too Tall Jones that sent the monster hurtling into the turf, allowing the QB to hit his favorite receiver, Dwight Clark, with a 30-yard pass that set up a touchdown. As Jones picked himself off the ground, a pumped-up Montana, losing his famous cool, screamed at him, "Respect *that,* motherfucker!"

But the Cowboys quickly responded with their own touchdown, and the game turned into one of the most excruciating seesaw battles ever played on the gridiron. Too Tall Jones and the other Doomsday Defenders subjected Montana to withering pressure throughout the afternoon, forcing the quarterback to constantly dance out of trouble. Montana seemed to play most of the game with one or two defenders hanging on to his arms and legs. Off balance much of the day, he threw three interceptions.

As the teams trotted off the field at halftime, Dallas led, 17–14 and Montana felt lucky the game was that close. In the locker room, Walsh maintained his meditative calm. The 49ers were on a level of combat where a coach's rah-rah rhetoric made no difference anymore. It was now a matter of how deeply the players could plumb their exhausted bodies and spirits.

The game continued to swing back and forth in the second half. The Niners, not used to the high-wire tension of a playoff game, seemed wound too tight, and they kept turning over the ball. As the fourth quarter began, San Francisco was clinging by its fingertips to a 21–20 lead. Then the 49ers fumbled away the ball again near the 50-yard line. Danny White drove the Cowboys for a touchdown, and Dallas retook the lead, 27–21. At that point, as Charle Young—the Niners' eloquent tight end—observed, "A big hush came over the crowd, as if a coffin had closed on our season."

The conclusion seemed preordained. San Francisco fans had suffered through this familiar ending again and again. "You can almost close your eyes and see what happens [next]," CBS football announcer Pat Summerall told the TV audience. "The Cowboys have done it so many times."

When they got the ball back on their own 11-yard line, Montana and the 49ers had less than five minutes to reach the distant goal line. As the young quarterback huddled with his team to begin the most important drive of his career, he went into that deeply calm place where his greatest gifts always awaited him. "I felt numb," Montana said later. "I heard no noise. I didn't know where I was or who I was playing. All I saw was eighty-nine yards between us and the end zone."

Montana immediately recognized that Dallas had dropped into a pass-stopping defense, with six defensive backs and only one linebacker. He knew this left the Cowboys vulnerable to a running game, and he knew that Walsh would grasp this immediately too.

At the most demanding moment in his career, Walsh abandoned his pass-centered West Coast offense and began "shoving the ball down Doomsday's throat," as Montana later put it. Walsh turned to his no-name running back, Lenvil Elliott, who had just been activated for the game after missing the entire season with a damaged knee. Elliot carried the 49ers' season on his back as he ran four of the first eight plays of the drive, baffling the pass-prevent Dallas defense and chewing up the yardage.

With Dallas on its heels from the surprise running attack, Walsh knew that he could now go back to the pass. Montana began to pepper the field with passes to Dwight Clark and Freddie Solomon, another NFL reject who had found new life in Walsh's offense.

As they fought their way down the field, the 49ers were on their last legs. Randy Cross kept vomiting in the huddle, forcing his teammates to move a few yards away to escape the mess. "Aw, man, R.C.," they recoiled, "what's wrong with you?" With 1:15 left in the game, Montana had driven the 49ers to the Dallas doorstep, on their opponents' 13-yard line. As Walsh called a time-out, the ailing Clark fell to one knee, utterly drained.

When action resumed, Elliot took the ball again, grinding his way to the Dallas 6-yard line. Now it was third down and three. San Francisco was tantalizingly close to the end zone, with less than a minute remaining in the game. Walsh took advantage of a Dallas time-out to confer with Montana one last time on the sidelines. The coach chose a play that required his QB to roll to his right and hit Solomon in the end zone, with Clark as a secondary target if his first receiver was covered.

"Joe, be very cautious," Walsh told him. "It's only third down. If we miss on this one, we still have another shot at putting it in."

"Bill, don't worry," replied Montana, still in his deeply tranquil zone. "If it's not there, I'll put it up so no one will catch the ball."

WHEN MONTANA RAN BACK onto the field, it was twilight. The crowd seemed lost in a dream that was sure to end terribly.

Montana's teammates were deeply familiar with the play that he called in the huddle. They had rehearsed it so often in practice that they were sick of it. But as soon as the ball was snapped, the team's choreography began to break down. Solomon slipped and fell on the soggy Candlestick turf, and as Montana rolled to his right, there was no receiver to hit in the end zone. Too Tall Jones and a couple of other Dallas defenders were now in hot pursuit of the quarterback, and Montana pump-faked the ball twice to slow them down. Colors—each player a bright and vivid shape—and silence. That's what it was like for Montana in these moments of frenzied urgency on the field. Suddenly Clark emerged in the end zone, running along the back line toward the right corner. By now, Jones—Montana's brutal shadow all day long—was nearly on top of him. There was no more time. Backpedaling awkwardly, Montana threw off-balance in Clark's direction.

As the high, soft pass arced into the air, it looked like a prayer. Montana himself thought it was uncatchable. "I thought it was an arm's length above his head." But Clark was in the air, soaring higher than he had ever been, his body at full extension. With his fingertips, the receiver somehow gripped the ball in midflight, juggled it briefly, and then brought it with him to the ground.

The moment Clark's feet hit the turf, the crowd exploded as if it had been holding its breath for years. Montana, sprawled on the ground and surrounded by huge bodies, couldn't see anything, but his silent bell jar was suddenly shattered by the cacophonous roar, and he knew that Clark had completed the miracle. Michael Zagaris, crouched in the far corner of the end zone with his camera, took a shot of the euphoric moment as the referees flung their arms in the air to signal touchdown, and a sea of fans leaped into the air, nearly as high as Clark. This was the exact instant of San Francisco's salvation.

The terror was not quite over for San Francisco. Cornerback Eric Wright, part of the 49ers' brilliant young defensive backfield, had to save the day by making a desperate, clawing tackle from behind on Dallas receiver Drew Pearson as the Cowboys tried their own comeback in the final seconds of the game. Then Danny White fumbled away the ball, and the game at last belonged to San Francisco by a wafer-thin 28–27.

The 49ers-Cowboy game would be immortalized as one of the greatest battles in NFL history, and Dwight Clark's heroic leap into the ages would forever be known as "The Catch." The game marked the beginning of one sports dynasty and the fall of another.

A bitter Tom Landry insisted that Dallas was still the better team, except for Joe Montana's black magic. "Montana has to be the key," brooded the Cowboys coach after the game. "There's nothing else there except him." Landry, whose coaching fortunes went into decline, later said that he never recovered from the defeat.

After leaving every ounce of himself on the field, Montana stumbled off in "a dazed dream" and immediately collapsed in the locker room. Eddie DeBartolo, whose view of the Catch had been blocked by the ass of a police horse on the sidelines, came bursting into the locker room to share his effusive joy. "I'm so proud," he said, throwing his arms around the giants who towered over him. "I don't think anything can top this in my life. I love you all."

Thousands of ecstatic fans stormed the field, cutting squares out of Candlestick's sodden turf for souvenirs. But many of the Faithful simply remained in their seats long after the game was over, some in tears, letting all the tragedies of the past come spilling out of them.

Meanwhile, bedlam reigned in the city. As he drove home from Candlestick, through Hunters Point, down Army Street, and into Noe Valley, one long-suffering fan screamed out the window of his car the whole way—and every neighborhood answered his wail. It reminded him of the day that the Japanese surrendered and the whole city went mad, in anguished celebration.

Back in the Haight, the dykes at Maud's came careening out of the bar and into the street. They cheered as a trio of middle-aged black women, who had slipped into their old high-school cheerleader skirts and sweaters, paid hip-shaking tribute to the triumphant Niners. Hordes of other fans—including long-haired veterans of Haight-Ashbury's glory days and the tough Irish families who had long been the neighborhood's backbone—snarled traffic, embracing one another in the street like survivors of a terrible siege. Some particularly nimble celebrants climbed onto the roofs of stalled buses and dazzled the crowd below with acrobatic cartwheels.

"It was like somebody had sprinkled fairy dust on the whole city," said Cheryl Bertelli, one of Maud's delirious patrons. "People were hugging strangers, laughing, singing. It was the Summer of Love all over again."

The next morning, Herb Caen spoke for the entire city, as usual, when he wrote: "Oh, I wanted the Niners to win! I especially wanted them to beat Dallas, which exalts itself as 'God's Team.' Lordy knows the God-fearing folk in that sector have long derided Sin Funcisco as Sodom West, overdue for obliteration by fire, brimstone, and earthquake. One wonders what tortures they are now going through, now that 'America's Team' is God-forsaken and the scarlet-clad representatives of Babylon by the Bay are on their way to the Super Bowl."

After the emotional whirligig of the Dallas game, the 49ers' Super Bowl battle with the Cincinnati Bengals two weeks later seemed almost anticlimactic. It was enlivened, however, by the underlying Oedipal drama pitting Bill Walsh against his former Bengals' mentor Paul Brown, who was now president of the team. Though Walsh insisted that revenge was not a motivating factor for him, his players knew how sweet the victory was for their coach when they beat the Bengals, 26–21. For the first time in football history, the San Francisco 49ers were champions.

Two days later, the 49ers returned home from the Silverdome in Pontiac, Michigan, for a Super Bowl victory parade through downtown San Francisco. As the team set out along the Embarcadero on its way to Civic Center, riding in motorized cable cars and vintage convertibles festooned with red and gold balloons, the city seemed strangely empty. Mayor Feinstein, squeezed between Walsh and DeBartolo in an open car, voiced the fear that was starting to grip all three of them. "What do we do if nobody comes?" she said. A familiar gloom was creeping over

Walsh. He was certain that the parade would be a terrible humiliation for his team.

Then the fleet of vehicles turned onto Market Street, the city's main commercial artery, and the team was greeted by an explosion of cheering, screaming, horn-blowing humanity. The boulevard was jammed with more than a half million ecstatic 49ers lovers, the biggest celebration in San Francisco's history since the end of World War II. People were clinging to light poles, jumping up and down on top of cars, and hanging out of office tower windows. The sky was a blizzard of confetti.

Tears flooded Walsh's eyes. It was at that moment when he finally felt in his heart what his team's amazing odyssey had done for the beleaguered people of San Francisco. "I saw every cross section of people, all standing in unison, from the executives who came out of the office buildings to the people who clean the streets, right next to each other, screaming. It was just the most electrifying moment I've ever had.

"Seeing that outpouring of emotion that day, I realized what an historic moment it was, not just for the team, but for the entire city. We were salving wounds and lifting spirits that had been very low for a long time."

Feinstein too felt the veil begin to finally lift that afternoon. "I saw with my own eyes what a team can do for a city."

The parade was a uniquely San Franciscan celebration. As the players chugged along on the cable cars, swarmed by fans reaching out to touch them, Eric Wright, one of the heroes of the Dallas game, turned to Zagaris. "Hey, Z-man, some motherfucker's been chasing the car yelling your name." Zagaris scanned the vast throng and saw a familiar face: Dennis Peron, the city's pixie-ish pied piper of marijuana. Peron had decided that grass could save humanity ever since it helped him survive the war in Vietnam, where he was forced to bag dead soldiers as punishment after refusing to leave his job as an air force postal clerk and shoot at Vietcong soldiers during the Tet offensive of 1968.

Zagaris, who had once been busted during a raid on Peron's marijuana supermarket, peered down at the Johnny Appleseed of cannabis as he ran alongside the cable cars. "Thank you, thank you for winning the Super Bowl!" Peron trilled, digging into a shopping bag filled with joints and flinging them to the players.

"Actually, they weren't just joints, they were bombers," recalled

Zagaris. "Ronnie Lott was saying, 'Hey, Z, I got three under my foot.' Wright was going, 'I got two!' The players wanted to know if the weed was any good. I said, 'Trust me, it's good.'"

Games are just games. No team, no matter how heroic, can undo tragedies or erase history. Life is what it is. And yet there are moments when a team seems to come to the salvation of its wounded fans. When *their* victories seem *our* victories. Victories that we can savor for a lifetime, whenever we need to be reminded that life is not just a losing battle against disappointment and defeat.

Walsh himself, the chronic worrier and self-doubter, would, in the end, psyche himself out of his job. In 1989, after winning his third Super Bowl victory, an emotionally exhausted Walsh called it quits. But by then, the 49ers had done their job for San Francisco, helping reverse the city's fate.

Cities, like people, have souls. And they can be broken by terrible events, but they can also be healed. It was just a game. It was just one catch. But sometimes that's enough.

36

THE CITY OF
SAINT FRANCIS

I N JANUARY 1984 San Francisco suffered a disturbing flashback
when Dan White was released from Soledad Prison after serving little more than five years for the carnage at city hall. His release reignited
a spasm of fury, with protests breaking out in the Castro—where nine
thousand gathered and chanted "Kill Dan White"—and Union Square,
where some demonstrators wore buttons declaring themselves members
of the "Dan White Hit Squad."

To avoid violence, authorities paroled White to Los Angeles, where
he changed his name, grew a beard, and worked out obsessively. One
day White invited his old friend Frank Falzon to visit him. White, barred
from driving, took the San Francisco cop on a long trek through the San
Fernando Valley, where he lived. While they were walking, White made
a second confession to his friend that left Falzon feeling "like I had been
hit by a sledgehammer."

"I was on a mission," White told Falzon. "I wanted four of them.
Carol Ruth Silver, she was the biggest snake of the bunch. And Willie
Brown, he was masterminding the whole thing."

White's eruption that day in November 1978 had not been tempo-
rary insanity, Falzon realized. It was premeditated murder. The enraged

former supervisor had planned to decapitate San Francisco's liberal leadership.

He was trying to rescue San Francisco, the city he loved, White told Falzon. He expected his old friend to sympathize. But Falzon was already starting to realize that the San Francisco that White was trying to protect—the one where they had both grown up—was just make-believe. "What did we really know?" said Falzon years later. "Afterward we found out that Catholic priests were having sex with boys. We were living in a fantasy world." White was trying to save a world that never existed.

After finishing his yearlong parole, White headed back to San Francisco in 1985, despite Mayor Feinstein's pleas for him to stay away from the city. He moved back into his old Excelsior home with his wife and two young sons, one of whom had been born with Down syndrome while White was in prison. Death threats were slipped under White's door. But Dan White was already a ghost. He rarely went outside; the front yard was choked with weeds. He grew estranged from Mary Ann, who was forced to support the family with her schoolteacher's salary.

One day John Barbagelata, long retired from San Francisco's political wars, was walking in St. Francis Wood. As he passed the Moscone family home, he was shocked to see Dan White come riding by on a bicycle. White had never expressed remorse or apologized to the families of his victims. But that day the assassin was clearly wrestling with a need for absolution. White stopped to talk with Barbagelata, but he found little comfort there. He had warned him, Barbagelata reminded White, not to get involved in San Francisco politics. "But you didn't listen," said Barbagelata.

On the afternoon of October 21, 1985, Dan White's body was found by his brother inside a white Buick sedan parked inside his garage. White, whose lifeless hands were clutching photographs of his family, had run a garden hose from the exhaust pipe into a partially opened car window. He left four suicide notes to family members. None of the letters mentioned George Moscone or Harvey Milk.

There was no celebration in the gay community over White's suicide. Newspaper reporters searching for searing quotes in the Castro found only weary emotions. "I'm glad his conscience caught up with him," one

Castro resident told the *Los Angeles Times*. It was the strongest feeling anyone seemed capable of mustering.

By the time White died, a phantom from another era slipping into the gray mists, the Castro itself seemed like a ghost town.

"The whole [Dan White] story had dangled like a sentence without a period. And now we have that period," said the *San Francisco Chronicle*'s Randy Shilts, the only daily newspaper reporter in the country assigned to cover gay issues. Shilts's coverage of the Harvey Milk political drama had become a compelling book, *The Mayor of Castro Street*. Now Shilts was deeply immersed in another epic story—about a scourge that threatened to destroy the gay community.

The AIDS (acquired immunodeficiency syndrome) virus slipped stealthily into San Francisco's bloodstream during the wild bacchanalia of the late 1970s. By the time the epidemic reached its fever pitch in the mideighties, more than half of the city's gay population was infected. So many young men were suffering and dying, it seemed like San Francisco was at war. Men in the prime of life crept through the city streets with sunken faces and withered legs, hobbling along on canes and walkers. Men hideously disfigured by florid lesions all over their faces, necks, and arms were greeted by appalled and awestruck reactions everywhere they ventured. The first case of Kaposi's sarcoma (KS) in San Francisco, a rare skin cancer that usually struck middle-aged men of Mediterranean and Jewish descent, was reported in April 1981. By then young gay men were also falling sick with a virulent type of pneumonia and exotic afflictions found only in people with ravaged immune systems.

Bobbi Campbell—a boyishly handsome hospital nurse who led a second life as a drag queen nun (Sister Florence Nightmare) in the Sisters of Perpetual Indulgence—was one of the first people diagnosed with KS. He noticed the purple blotches on his feet after hiking with his boyfriend in Big Sur, and at first he assumed they were blood blisters. But when they got bigger, Campbell went to Dr. Marcus Conant, a dermatologist at the UC San Francisco medical complex overlooking Golden Gate Park, and Conant recognized it as one more strange occurrence of KS. Campbell immediately went public with his diagnosis, writing a story about his "gay cancer" in the *Sentinel*, a local gay newspaper, and persuading a drugstore in the Castro to post photos of Kaposi victims in its window as a warning to the community.

A political comrade of Cleve Jones's urged the activist to meet with Campbell, who showed him the lesions on his feet and told him about his plans to start a gay cancer support group. Later, over dinner, Marc Conant filled Jones in on what he was learning about the mysterious new plague. Jones turned pale and ordered a stiff drink. He was thinking about all the young men with whom he had juicily joined flesh, and about how the Castro had turned itself into one big bed. "We're all dead," Jones muttered.

THE NONSTOP PARTY THAT was San Francisco seemed to end almost overnight. Paul Volberding, a young oncology doctor from the Midwest who worked late hours at the San Francisco campus of the University of California, used to peer wide-eyed at the wild celebrations that poured out of the bars and bathhouses in the Castro no matter what hour he drove through the neighborhood on his way to work or back home. "Suddenly it just all disappeared," he recalled.

Joel Selvin, the night-crawling rock critic for the *Chronicle*, immediately noticed the change. "In the old days, fully a third of every restaurant crowd, every nightclub, every parking lot was homosexuals. They spent more, they yelled more, they had more fun—and they were the best dressed. They were the cheerleaders of our culture. Then, poof, they were gone. The restaurants were half-empty, the clubs weren't as jammed. A light was turned off in this town. Because if you left the straights to handle the party, it just wasn't going to happen. One day it was just, 'Hey, where did the gay guys go?' You'd walk around town and see all these garage sales on the street. They were gone—only their stuff was left behind."

In the early days of the plague, when nobody knew for certain how the infection was spread, a shudder went through the entire city. Customers avoided restaurants run by gays and even shunned Castro clothing stores, not wanting to try on shirts or pants that might have been worn by a victim of the disease. When Zuni Café founder Billy West fell sick, his business partners decided to keep his illness quiet. "No one knew anything—there wasn't even a name for AIDS then," said Vince Calcagno. "We kept Billy's condition a secret for a good five years. We knew it would ruin the restaurant. People thought it could be foodborne."

As the panic spread, sick men were fired from their jobs and evicted from their apartments—sometimes by fellow gay employers and land-lords. Once, after Dr. Volberding and an AIDS patient were invited to appear on a local TV show, the sound technician refused to put a micro-phone on the sick man.

The medical workers on the front lines of fighting the epidemic were not immune to the rising panic. Volberding, who had begun treating the first wave of AIDS patients at San Francisco General Hospital, was starting a family with his wife, Molly, around the same time. In the early days of the epidemic, he frequently woke up in a cold sweat after hav-ing nightmares that he had infected his two young children. One day Molly, also a physician, noticed a little red mark on the ear of their son Alex. "Anybody else—a grandmother in Iowa—would've said, 'That's just a stork bite.' But I remember looking at that and saying, 'Could that be Kaposi's?'" Volberding and his wife were so frightened of what the plague could do to their family, they had to agree not to talk about it with each other.

Volberding, who cofounded the world's first AIDS clinic at San Fran-cisco General in January 1983, sometimes had difficulty staffing ward 5B. Once he hired a data processor to work in the clinic's computer room, but when he showed up for work, the new employee insisted that the room be disinfected from top to bottom with bleach. "We told him, 'This job is not for you,'" said Volberding. On other occasions, new employees would disappear after their first or second day on the job, when their spouses became hysterical about where they were working.

But ward 5B soon developed a highly dedicated core team of doctors, nurses, and orderlies. Dr. Constance Wofsy, a cofounder of the clinic, had a simple reply for anyone who questioned her choice of workplaces. It was a doctor's job to take care of the sick, even if that put you at risk. Period.

Volberding knew that frontline AIDS work was above and beyond the call of duty for most health workers. But the ward 5B staff was an unusual crew. As a boy, Volberding—who grew up on a dairy farm near Rochester, Minnesota, the son of German-American Lutherans—often heard about people who had "a calling" in life. "The people who worked in ward 5B clearly had that sense of calling. We worked long hours and took the job home with us. We became friends with the patients. They were our same age, they listened to the same music, they ate at the same restaurants. Some of the clinic workers' friends and lovers were patients. And some of the clinic workers became patients themselves. You're trained as a doctor to separate yourself from those whom you're treating. But we couldn't possibly do that."

One day, Lisa Capaldini, a young intern in the AIDS ward, was saying good-bye to a patient named Gordon with whom she had grown close. Gordon was about to be discharged, but he was blind and dying, and Capaldini knew that she would never see him again. While she hovered over his bed, the intern began to cry. "And I thought, 'That's okay, he won't know.' Then I realized that my tears were dropping on his face. And I thought, 'Busted.'"

Gordon reversed roles with Capaldini and began to comfort the young doctor. By the time she fled the room, Capaldini was sobbing uncontrollably. A nurse named Diane Jones, one of the tough angels who were the clinic's heart and soul, took Capaldini aside and told her she should be proud of everything she had done for Gordon. "That was one of the best moments in my medical training," recalled Capaldini years later. "To have a medical professional say it's okay to have feelings. It made me a better doctor and, I think, a better person."

San Francisco General's ward 5B became a model for AIDS care throughout the world. The clinic staff quickly realized that it had to adapt to the harrowing new medical world in which it found itself, battling an incurable and lethal disease that was devastating a unique part of the population. Ward 5B pioneered the development of what later became known as patient-centered care.

"Back then it meant that a lot of hospital rules just had to go out the window," said Diane Jones. "Such as visiting hours. People were sick and many were dying. They needed people with them, and they needed to decide who was going to be with them. Not just a father or mother or legal spouse. We said patient-centered care means you get to decide who comes into your room and who gets to be with you when you're dying."

The AIDS ward began to take on the flavor of the predominantly gay patient base that it was serving. Volunteers began flocking to the clinic, bringing bouquets and toiletries and fashionable-looking bathrobes, because no patient still in his right mind wanted to be caught dead in a hospital gown. Gay nightclub diva Sharon McNight rolled her piano into the ward and belted out songs like "Stand By Your Man" as the patients sipped champagne and screamed encouragement. For many in the audience, it would be the last show they ever saw. Rita Rockett brought her tap-dancing act, along with baskets of food, to the hospital so often that a lounge in ward 5B was named after her.

Meanwhile, another beloved San Francisco institution, Mary Jane Rathbun—aka Brownie Mary—dispensed her magical cannabis-laced cookies and brownies to ward 5B patients. The elderly Brownie Mary, a former pancake house waitress forced into retirement by a back injury, had turned to the marijuana bakery business after finding that smoking weed helped alleviate her pain. Brownie Mary was convinced it could do the same for AIDS patients, and she inspired one clinic researcher to undertake his own scientific studies of medical marijuana.

THE AIDS PLAGUE COULD have tipped San Francisco back into the bubbling cauldron from which it had just emerged. Terror and hatred could have torn apart the city, with opponents of the gay revolution condemning it for breeding the contagion and using it to inflame anti-homosexual passions. In fact, this was happening at the national level, as conservative crusaders like Patrick Buchanan flayed the suffering gay population with their hellfire rhetoric. "The poor homosexuals," remarked Buchanan, his voice dripping with scorn. "They have declared war upon nature, and now nature is exacting an awful retribution."

Instead the epidemic brought out the best in San Francisco. The city's response became a model for the nation. Inspired by the heroic efforts of the staff and volunteers at the AIDS clinic—who calmed San Francisco by talking openly and rationally about the epidemic in the media and public forums—the city as a whole began to rally around its stricken brothers.

In 1985 a retired grandmother named Ruth Brinker, alarmed to hear that AIDS patients were dying at home of malnutrition, began cooking hot meals in her kitchen and delivering them to the sick. Brinker had little money, and her only business experience was running her own antique shop. But she knew how to cook, and within three years she was serving five hundred nutritious meals a day to AIDS patients. Project

Open Hand, whose motto was "Meals with Love for People with AIDS," outgrew Brinker's kitchen, moving into a church basement, and then into its own headquarters, where it inspired similar groups all over the world.

Other volunteer groups also sprang into action, like community firefighters rushing to the scene of a blaze or people filling sandbags on a crumbling levee. "I look back on those days," said Tom Nolan, executive director of Project Open Hand, "and if you were a gay man or almost anybody [living in San Francisco] and you're seeing the suffering on the streets, the KS lesions all over people's faces, and you saw all that, how could you *not* do something . . . There was something for everybody to do."

The San Francisco AIDS Foundation, jump-started by Cleve Jones, lobbied for government funding for research and education. Project Inform educated those infected with HIV (human immunodeficiency virus), the virus that causes AIDS, about the latest medical therapies. Shanti Project offered emotional solace and practical support to people with AIDS, and the Coming Home Hospice was founded to help those who were dying. The Sisters of Perpetual Indulgence began working like real nuns, raising money for the sick at church bingos and organizing a charity dog show featuring Shirley MacLaine as emcee.

The Sisters, long estranged from the Catholic Church, began to find a surprising amount of sympathy in church circles. For a long time, the Most Holy Redeemer parish in the heart of the Castro provided the San Francisco police force with many of its toughest Irish cops. The church was a target for gay protesters after the Anita Bryant ordinance passed in Florida and after the Milk and Moscone assassinations. But the parish began to change with the times, and in 1985 some church members started an AIDS support group. John Quinn, San Francisco's enlightened archbishop, regularly visited Most Holy Redeemer throughout the 1980s to demonstrate his support for AIDS patients and their caregivers. When the church began reaching out to suffering gay men, it was the clearest sign that the savage epidemic also had a strange power to heal. These acts of human grace, in the midst of unspeakable anguish, began to help close San Francisco's deepest wounds.

Even the Mitchell brothers jumped into the AIDS battle, producing a safe-sex remake of *Behind the Green Door*. The film's leading lady—

Elisa Florez, aka Missy Manners—had grown up in a conservative Catholic family and was a former intern for Utah Republican senator Orrin Hatch and the daughter of a Reagan administration official. But the buxom, golden-skinned Florez saw her porn debut as God's work. "This film is putting an important message out there. You have to have a social conscience when it comes to having sex. We made condoms exciting. After this film, I can put condoms on a man better than anybody. I can slip them on with my mouth, and a man would never even know it."

Early in the epidemic, members of ACT-UP—the militant group formed by gay playwright Larry Kramer to agitate for a stronger government response to AIDS—showed up at the opulent opening night of the San Francisco Opera season to disrupt the festivities. As the activists ran screaming up and down the aisles of the opera house, some wealthy patrons groused that they should be arrested. But Angela Alioto—who was in the audience with her father, whom she would follow into city politics—cheered on the activists. "I thought it was pretty cool," she recalled. "I'm thinking these are human beings who want to be treated like human beings."

ACT-UP played an important role in focusing public attention on the epidemic, particularly in New York and Washington, DC. But in San Francisco, the group seemed largely unnecessary.

Under Mayor Feinstein, San Francisco mounted the most aggressive campaign in the country to confront the health crisis. In 1984 alone, San Francisco poured $7.6 million of scarce city funds into AIDS programs, while New York, with triple the caseload, was spending little over $1 million. In the mid-1980s, San Francisco spent more on AIDS than the entire federal government under President Reagan. When Supervisor Harry Britt brought Feinstein the first AIDS funding proposal in 1982, the mayor simply told him, "Fund everything."

Feinstein was not only familiar with medical crises and protocol, she had friends who were sick with the virus. She proved to be the best possible civic leader for the crisis. "Dianne spent more time visiting AIDS patients in hospitals than I did," said Britt. "She was a giver, she was a very compassionate person. I don't want to say 'queenly,' because that sounds negative, but she was a good queen."

"My staff and budget at the AIDS clinic doubled every year," recalled

Volberding, "and Feinstein didn't blink an eye. She was completely responsive to whatever I asked from her."

Other metropolitan areas with big gay populations lagged far behind San Francisco. Some cities tried to dump their AIDS patients on San Francisco. In one notorious incident in 1983, a hospital in Gainesville, Florida, put a seriously ill patient on a plane and deposited him at San Francisco General—a maneuver that Feinstein denounced as "outrageous and inhumane." When the twenty-seven-year-old AIDS patient died in ward 5B two weeks later, thousands of miles from home, Feinstein commented, "It is sad that a young man had to spend his final days as a medical outcast." Florida health officials admitted that they were having difficulty finding medical professionals who were willing to treat AIDS patients. "We are seeing people take any opportunity within the law to avoid providing care," said a Florida Health Department spokesman.

FEINSTEIN TRIED TO SPARK a nationally coordinated response to the epidemic, pushing the US Conference of Mayors to establish an AIDS task force in 1984. The federal government should have played that role. But the Reagan administration turned a blind eye to the rapidly spreading disease. The White House was under the sway of its Christian right supporters—many of whom, like Moral Majority leader Rev. Jerry Falwell, viewed the plague as "the wrath of God upon homosexuals." Even though the Reagans were friends with a number of Hollywood entertainers afflicted by AIDS, including actor Rock Hudson, the president refused to even utter the name of the disease in public. In 1985, as the contagion spread like wildfire across America and around the globe, Reagan slashed AIDS funding in his annual health budget, at the same time his health secretary was calling the disease her "number one health priority."

If Dianne Feinstein was the best possible local leader in the war on AIDS, Ronald Reagan was the most disastrous leader for the country to have sitting in the Oval Office. The demon virus took root in the population at the worst possible political moment. "The AIDS story is the purest illustration of how this administration deals with health concerns," said Stanley Matek, former president of the American Public Health

Association, during the height of the plague. "They tend to see health in the same way that John Calvin saw wealth: it's your own responsibility, and you should damn well take care of yourself. This epidemic, however, has tested the limits of that philosophy."

At a time when the American public desperately needed reliable medical straight talk about AIDS, Reagan blocked his widely respected surgeon general, Dr. C. Everett Koop, from delivering speeches or talking with the media about the disease. "For an astonishing five and a half years," Koop recalled later, "I was completely cut off from AIDS." White House advisors, he said, dismissed the epidemic as a problem for gays, junkies, and other social undesirables. The president's aides, according to Koop, "took the stand, 'They are only getting what they justly deserve.'"

Ron Reagan became so upset with his father's lack of leadership on AIDS that he intervened with his parents. "I went to my mom, because I knew she was ahead of him on that curve. She was a doctor's daughter, and all that. And I knew they had gay friends. I remember parties at our house when I was growing up where at least one gay couple was there. Patti's godmothers were a lesbian couple. And Cesar Romero was one of my mom's gay escorts when my dad was out of town. Patti would get all mad about it, like my mom was cheating on my dad somehow. But *hello!* Later, in the White House, [gay New York society fixture] Jerry Zipkin was one of my mom's walkers."

Young Reagan pleaded with his mother to get the White House moving on AIDS. "I just knew that people were suffering and dying," he said, "and the government had to move more quickly. If for no other reason than it was terrible PR to just stand there. When people they knew started dying, like Rock Hudson, it finally came home for them."

But President Reagan waited nearly two years after Hudson died before he at long last addressed the raging epidemic in public, speaking at the Third International AIDS Conference in Washington, DC, in May 1987, with actress Elizabeth Taylor urging him on from the wing of the stage. Reagan's public remarks, which came near the end of his presidency, did not lead to a late-hour burst of leadership on AIDS. To the very end, his administration remained politically incapable of mounting a full public health campaign. "In the history of the AIDS epidemic, President Reagan's legacy is one of silence," later remarked Michael Cover, the former public affairs director of the capital's leading AIDS clinic—a facility just a few blocks from the White House that was never visited by the president or first lady.

THE PEOPLE OF SAN Francisco realized early in the plague that Washington was not going to help them. They had to look out for themselves. So San Francisco took care of its own sick and dying, its own scorned brothers. The city had learned to embrace these men when they were young and wild, fleeing Kansas and Wyoming and Alabama for San Francisco's frontier freedom. Now, as they lay in sweat-soaked sheets, closer to death than life, these young men were once again wrapped in San Francisco's arms.

By taking care of these suffering men, San Francisco finally became a united city. "The city learned to behave like one organism, to fight against the disease," observed Volberding. This was the true birth of San Francisco values. The plague burned down to the city's core, where one simple truth was revealed: we must take care of each other. No matter how sick or helpless or untouchable people are.

Some said that this fundamental sense of human solidarity was wired into the very origins of the city, into San Francisco's namesake, Saint Francis—the wandering friar who renounced his family's wealth for a life of humble service, calling all creatures his brothers and sisters, and devoting himself to the poor and wretched. But it was not until the epidemic invaded the city that San Francisco truly became worthy of the saint's name.

As the years went by and AIDS researchers still struggled to find a cure, the disease came closer to home for many San Franciscans. In 1988 Bill Walsh's oldest son, Steve, was diagnosed with the infection. The coach, who had long neglected his family for football, was overcome with feelings of guilt. He tried to reach out to his son, but it was difficult. Steve Walsh, who had left home early and made a separate life for himself in Colorado as a TV and radio reporter, had been estranged from his father for so long that conversation did not come easily.

A deeply private man, Bill Walsh couldn't bring himself to talk about his son's disease in public, always referring to it as "leukemia." But after

Steve died in 2002, Walsh finally spoke the truth in a conversation with the veteran 49ers trainer Lindsy McLean.

At McLean's retirement party in 2004, Walsh told the trainer that he wanted to give a gift to him and his "pal," as he always called McLean's longtime lover, George Paiva: a trip for two to Hawaii. It was a poignant gesture. Back in 1983, Walsh had sent his staff and their spouses to Hawaii as a reward for their hard work that season. But Walsh made it clear that it would be impolitic for McLean to bring George.

"It wasn't meant to condemn me," said McLean. "Bill was only concerned with the image of the 49ers in the eyes of the rest of the league . . . Bill was accepting of my lifestyle. I never felt judged by him . . . There was no homophobic bone in his body."

Still, Walsh knew that excluding McLean's partner was wrong. Now, more than twenty years later, he was making amends. As Walsh and McLean discussed logistics for the Hawaii vacation at the party, the trainer mentioned that George was not always up for the hardships of travel. His partner had been infected with HIV years before, McLean told Walsh, and he had his good days and bad days. "Well," said Walsh, "we'd better schedule it now, while he can enjoy it."

Then Walsh stunned McLean by talking about his late son. "You know, Lindsy, my son had AIDS." McLean had heard the rumors but was too respectful of the coach's privacy to ever bring it up. Now Walsh was telling his gay colleague, a man who had shared so much of his warrior life, that they shared this wound too.

The plague kept scything through San Francisco's gay population well into the 1990s. Some of the city's brightest lights were snuffed out. Men who had breathed new life into local democracy with their passionate activism; men who had enriched the city with their artistic, theatrical, culinary, fashion, and design skills. Hibiscus, the glorious ringleader of the Cockettes, was among the first wave to die, in 1982. As the years went by, other members of the legendary troupe succumbed, one by one. Sylvester, the fabulous disco diva who had debuted with the Cockettes, fell ill in 1988. He was too sick to attend that year's Castro Street Fair, where he had performed nearly every year, a black goddess in sequins and feathers. But as he lay dying in the bedroom of his Collingwood Street apartment, the beloved entertainer could hear the crowd chanting his name two blocks away: "Sylvester! Sylvester! Sylvester!"

So many of his friends died, recalled Armistead Maupin, that he threw away an entire address book. The obituary columns grew engorged with the names of the young and vital. Award-winning documentary filmmakers Peter Adair and Marlon Riggs. Gay politico Bill Kraus, a leading crusader in the battle for more AIDS funding. Intrepid journalist Randy Shilts, whose book *And the Band Played On* would stand as the epic chronicle of the plague years, and the era's heroes and villains. Shilts, suffering from both KS and pneumocystis pneumonia, told the *New York Times* in the final months of his life, "HIV is certainly character building. It's made me see all of the shallow things we cling to, like ego and vanity. Of course I'd rather have a few more T-cells and a little less character."

Bobbi Campbell's death came as a particularly strong blow. Sister Florence Nightmare had turned himself into the "AIDS Poster Boy," charming and agitating his way into the public's heart. Campbell was a force of inextinguishable life. Adopting Gloria Gaynor's disco masterpiece as his theme song, he wore a button proclaiming "I Will Survive" and vowed to outlive the epidemic. At a rally in front of San Francisco's Moscone Center, where the Democratic National Convention was being held in July 1984, a thin but still impassioned Campbell told the country, "We're not victims—we are your children, and your mothers and fathers, and your sisters and brothers . . . It's still business as usual in Reagan's Washington while we are dying."

Soon after, Bobbi Campbell was admitted to ward 5B, where he continued to fight his illness until his last breath. "I was at his bedside when he died," recalled Paul Volberding. "I don't know many people who accept death easily, and Bobbi certainly did not. A young body is an amazingly vigorous thing. It does not want to die. People go through amazing ordeals and still cling to life. Those scenes in movies where people die gently and nobly sure don't ring true for me."

Cleve Jones organized a memorial rally for Bobbi. Jones knew how to close down Castro Street, he knew where to plug in the sound equipment: in the ever-amenable neighborhood pizza joint the Sausage Factory. Bobbi's father, a graying man in a three-piece suit, spoke to the crowd. He had struggled with his son's homosexuality, and now he struggled with his emotions. "We didn't see eye to eye," Bobbi's father told the mourners. "But my advice to parents is to give your kids support. They want your love and understanding."

CLEVE JONES HAD BEEN a human rights agitator for nearly his entire life, but these days his activism seemed to be mainly on behalf of the dead and dying. On a cold, wet Thanksgiving night in November 1985, as Jones led the annual parade to commemorate the deaths of Milk and Moscone, the gay leader asked marchers to take Magic Marker pens and posters and write down the names of friends and lovers who had died of AIDS. When the marchers arrived at the old federal building near Civic Center, Jones—addressing them with the same bullhorn that Harvey Milk gave him years before—told the demonstrators to tape the posters to the wall of the building. Soon the peeling, gray wall was covered with a blanket of colorfully drawn names.

A hush fell over the crowd as people stared at the wall of death. "I went to school with him," somebody said, pointing at one poster. "I used to dance with him every Sunday at the I-Beam," said another marcher. As he looked at their collective handiwork, Jones said to himself, 'It looks like a quilt.' It was the genesis of the AIDS Memorial Quilt, Jones's brilliant brainstorm to turn the private pain felt by thousands upon thousands of Americans into a stunning national tapestry of remembrance.

That night's march gave Jones the courage to finally take the HIV-antibody test, which he had been putting off for more than a year. He knew all along what the results would be. When he was told, he felt "absolute nothingness." The words of the lab social worker kept repeating in his head: "Sorry, Mr. Jones."

It took several years for the virus to start making him sick. During that shadowy period, he kept up a frantic pace, overseeing the AIDS Quilt as it continued to grow and displaying the billowing expanse of hand-sewn folk art all over the country. But by the spring of 1993, Jones's body was breaking down. After collapsing in the San Francisco airport on his way back home from a quilt event, he checked into a hospital suffering from pneumocystis pneumonia. He quickly went downhill after that, running fevers, fighting nausea and diarrhea, and losing so much weight that he had to sit on cushions to protect his increasingly bony ass.

There was something particularly sad about Cleve Jones falling sick. Everyone in San Francisco who knew his name, gay and straight, felt a special attachment to him. For many, he was the living spirit of Harvey Milk, and now that spirit was dying all over again.

Jones began to teeter around the Castro on a cane, like all the other wasted men he had seen over the years. Once upon a time, they had fought with cops and danced in the streets. Now they were shadows. One day he saw someone collapse and die on the sidewalk in front of Cafe Flore. Jones thought he was an old man. He turned out to be thirty.

Jones didn't want to die that way. His family scraped together $10,000, and he bought a bungalow in a hamlet on the Russian River, north of the city. He was getting sicker by the day, and he didn't want anyone to see him. He was going there to die. His aging parents came from Phoenix now and then to look after him. But it hurt Jones to see his seventy-five-year-old mother take on one more burden. He had never seen such deep sadness in her eyes.

Jones was losing his fingernails, his eyesight. He was afflicted with rashes in his throat and mouth. He couldn't keep any food in his stomach. He spent so much time emptying himself into the toilet bowl that he kept a pile of blankets and pillows in the bathroom. One day his neighbor Marigold found Jones in a half-conscious stupor. "Cleve, you've given up," she told him in her deep, firm voice. "You got to change and fight back."

Not long after that, in October 1993, Marcus Conant phoned Jones from the city. The doctor had seen encouraging results from a new combination of drugs. Jones, loath to add to his suffering with any more painful side effects, was worried about trying this latest pharmaceutical cocktail, but Conant persuaded him. An old friend named Shep, who had lost his partner to the plague, showed up to help, knowing Jones was worried about a negative reaction to the experimental drugs.

When Jones took the first handful of antiviral pills, he began puking his guts out late that night. Shep rushed into the bathroom, rolling a joint. "Smoke this," he told Jones. The sick man waved him away—he hadn't smoked pot in years and, in his miserable state, wasn't remotely interested in getting high now.

But Shep was insistent. "Smoke this or you're dead," he said. He knew it was the only way that Jones could keep down the pills.

Jones took one puff and stopped vomiting. He took a few more, and his stomach settled down enough for him to pick himself off the floor and walk out of the bathroom.

Over the next few days, Conant's elixir began to work its magic on Jones. "About a week later," he recalled, "I woke up one morning, [and] I could feel the coolness of the sheets, hear the birds out the window. To my astonishment, I had an erection. I hadn't seen one of those in a year. And I was hungry."

Cleve Jones got out of bed, put on his bathrobe and rubber boots, and stepped outside, where a light rain washed over his face. There was a small market a block and a half away. He couldn't remember the last time he had felt strong enough to walk there. He began to make his way down the winding lane to the store. He could smell the wet redwoods and ferns. When he got to the village market, he bought eggs and bacon and bread and butter and marmalade. Back home, he made himself a greasy feast and devoured it all.

Later he sat in his cottage and watched as a pale light broke through the clouds and glittered on the river.

I'm going to live, thought Cleve Jones.

I'm going to live.

EPILOGUE

WHEN VINCENT HALLINAN DIED in October 1992 at the venerable age of ninety-five, he was not memorialized in the Catholic Church, which he reviled until the end as a citadel of medieval values. He was sent off into the great unknown by a thousand mourners who gathered, appropriately, at the Longshoremen's Hall, where they sang the labor anthem "Joe Hill" and told fond stories of the invincible warrior. The audience was filled with many of the San Francisco liberation fighters whose causes Hallinan had championed during his seventy-three-year courtroom career, including labor, civil rights, antiwar, and AIDS activists. But perhaps the most eloquent tribute came from one of his old foes, former mayor Joe Alioto.

"If his duels and tilts were with God, at least he was picking on someone his own size," eulogized Alioto. "Vincent Hallinan was the social conscience of San Francisco. He was in many respects the heart of San Francisco."

Vince left behind five of his six sons and the love of his life, Vivian. Terry Hallinan had visited with his father the night he died. By then the younger Hallinan was a San Francisco supervisor, on his way to becoming the city's district attorney. The old man couldn't believe that his second son had become a member of the political establishment, but Vince heartily approved. Kayo still had the brawling, underdog instincts that his father and mother had instilled in him.

"My father was lying in his bed with a wide smile on his face," Terry recalled. "He said all his old friends 'are waiting outside for me.' Then he sang 'The Best Things in Life Are Free.' I kissed him on the forehead, and then I left."

Two hours later, Vivian called her sons to tell them their father had died in his sleep. "There were many ups, and there were many downs, but it was exciting all the way," she told the memorial gathering at Longshoremen's Hall.

Before the decade was over, Viv joined her husband, as did Joe Alioto. Many other San Francisco legends also died during the decade, including Herb Caen, Bill Graham, Allen Ginsberg, Jerry Garcia, Scott Newhall, and Artie Mitchell. It was the end of a rough and gaudy and fearless epoch. San Francisco was the greater for these knights' mighty exertions. They had tilted with God, and sometimes they had won.

SEASON OF THE WITCH PLAYLIST

The Best Songs Recorded by San Francisco Bands, 1965–1985

The Ace of Cups
 "Circles"

The Beau Brummels
 "Just a Little"
 "Laugh Laugh"
 "Sometime at Night"

Big Brother and the Holding Company
 "Call on Me"
 "Combination of the Two"
 "Farewell Song"
 "Piece of My Heart"

Creedence Clearwater Revival
 "As Long as I Can See the Light"
 "Fortunate Son"
 "Walk on the Water"

The Dead Kennedys
 "Holiday in Cambodia"

The Flamin' Groovies
 "Shake Some Action"
 "Slow Death"

The Grateful Dead
 "Box of Rain"
 "The Golden Road (To Unlimited Devotion)"
 "New Speedway Boogie"
 "Ripple"
 "Uncle John's Band"

The Great Society
 "Grimly Forming"

Kak
 "Trieulogy"

The Jefferson Airplane
 "It's No Secret"
 "Lather"
 "Law Man"
 "Somebody to Love"
 "Today"
 "White Rabbit"

Jorma Kaukonen
 "Genesis"

Lee Michaels
 "Heighty Hi"
 "What Now America"

Moby Grape
 "8:05"
 "Going Nowhere"
 "I Am Not Willing"
 "Naked, If I Want To"
 "Omaha"
 "Sitting by the Window"

The Mojo Men
 "Sit Down, I Think I Love You"

Romeo Void
 "Never Say Never"

Santana
 "Samba Pa Ti"

Skip Spence
 "Diana"

Tracy Nelson and Mother Earth
 "Down So Low"
 "Seven Bridges Road"

Translator
 "Everywhere That I'm Not"

The Vejtables
 "I Still Love You"

The Youngbloods
 "Darkness, Darkness"
 "Get Together"

For more about San Francisco history and music, go to www.talbotplayers.com

SOURCES

INTRODUCTION

Books:

Asbury, Herbert, *The Barbary Coast: An Informal History of the San Francisco Underworld*. New York: Thunder's Mouth Press, 2002.

Boyd, Nan Alamilla, *Wide Open Town: A History of Queer San Francisco to 1965*. Berkeley, CA: University of California Press, Berkeley, 2003.

Brechin, Gray, *Imperial San Francisco: Urban Power, Earthly Ruin*. Berkeley, CA: University of California Press, Berkeley, 2006.

Hammett, Dashiell, *Nightmare Town: Stories*. New York: Vintage Books, 1999.

Layman, Richard, *Discovering the Maltese Falcon and Sam Spade: The Evolution of Dashiell Hammett's Masterpiece*. San Francisco: Vince Emery Productions, 2005.

Layman, Richard, *Shadow Man: The Life of Dashiell Hammett*. San Diego: Harvest/HBJ, 1981.

Maravelis, Peter, editor, *San Francisco Noir 2: The Classics*. New York: Akashic Books, 2009.

Hammett, Dashiell, "The Scorched Face"

London, Jack, "South of the Slot"

Norris, Frank "The Third Circle."

Morgan, Bill, editor, *Howl on Trial: The Battle for Free Expression*. San Francisco: City Lights Publishers, 2006.

Sides, Josh, *Erotic City: Sexual Revolutions and the Making of Modern San Francisco*. New York: Oxford University Press, 2009.

Solnit, Rebecca, *A Paradise Built in Hell: The Extraordinary Communities That Arise in Disaster*. New York: Viking, 2009.

PROLOGUE: WILD IRISH ROGUES

Interviews:

Hallinan, Patrick
Hallinan, Terence

Newspapers and Magazines:

San Francisco Chronicle, May–June 1932; Oct. 3,1992; Dec. 6, 1995; May 13,1996; Mar. 2, 2003, Mar. 9, 2003.

San Francisco Examiner Image magazine, Feb. 22, 1987, "Hallinans Against the World," Steve Chapple.

San Francisco magazine, Nov. 1997, "Sex, Drugs and Political Paranoia," Nina Schuyler.

Books:

Hallinan, Vincent, *A Lion in Court.* New York: G.P. Putnam's Sons, 1963.
Hallinan, Vivian, *My Wild Irish Rogues.* Garden City, NY: Doubleday and Co., 1952.
Walsh, James P., *San Francisco's Hallinan: Toughest Lawyer in Town.* Novato, CA: Presidio Press, 1982.

PART ONE: ENCHANTMENT
1: SATURDAY AFTERNOON

Interviews:

Beggs, Edward   Rohan, Brian
Ferlinghetti, Lawrence   Stepanian, Michael
Kantner, Paul

Documents:

Human Be-In press release, Jan. 12, 1967, "Hippie Collection," San Francisco Public Library History Center.
"Huckleberry House and the Summer of Love," essay, courtesy Edward Beggs.

Newspapers and Magazines:

San Francisco Chronicle, Jan. 16, 1967, May 13, 1967.

Books:

Kandel, Lenore, *The Love Book.* San Francisco: Superstition Street Press, 2003.
Morgan, Bill, *I Celebrate Myself: The Somewhat Private Life of Allen Ginsberg.* New York: Penguin Books, 2006.
Perry, Charles, *The Haight Ashbury.* New York: Wenner Books, 2005.

2: DEAD MEN DANCING

Interviews:

Ferlinghetti, Lawrence   Stepanian, Michael
Hart, Mickey   Valentino, Sal
Kriegel, Marilyn (Harris) Welch, Calvin

Newspapers and Magazines:

San Francisco Chronicle, October 3 and 4, 1967.

Books:

Boyd, Dick, *Broadway-North Beach: The Golden Years.* San Francisco: Cape Foundation Publications, 2006.
McNally, Dennis, *A Long Strange Trip: The Inside History of the Grateful Dead.* New York: Broadway Books, 2002.
Perry, *The Haight Ashbury.*
Selvin, Joel, *Summer of Love: The Inside Story of LSD, Rock & Roll, Free Love and High Times in the Wild West.* New York: Dutton, 1994.
Tamarkin, Jeff, *Got a Revolution: The Turbulent Flight of the Jefferson Airplane.* New York: Atria Books, 2003.

3: THE WALLED CITY

Documents:

Speech by Thomas Cahill, Dec. 3, 1958, SFPL History Center files.
Program for Thomas Cahill Testimonial Dinner, June 23, 1967, SFPL History Center.

Newspapers and Magazines:

San Francisco Chronicle, Sept. 5, 1958; Apr. 11, 1964; Mar. 23, 27, 29, 30, 1967; Sept. 9, 10, 1967; Nov. 8, 1967, Feb. 28, 1968, Sept. 2, 1974.
San Francisco Examiner California Living Magazine, Apr. 30, 1967.
San Francisco News, Sept. 20, 1958.
The Irish Digest, Apr. 1960, "San Francisco's Fighting Irish Chief of Police," Lenore Archuletta.

Books:

Perry, *The Haight-Ashbury*.

4: THE FREE CITY

Interviews:

Berg, Peter
Coyote,Peter
Rosenthal, Irving

Documents:

Diggers street sheets, Hippie Collection, SFPL History Center.
Diggers papers, The Digger Archives, *www.diggers.org*.

Newspapers and Magazines:

San Francisco Chronicle, Jan. 23, May 5, 1967.

Books:

Coyote, Peter, *Sleeping Where I Fall: A Chronicle*. Berkeley, CA: Counterpoint, 1999.
Grogan, Emmett, *Ringolevio: A Life Played for Keeps*. New York: New York Review Books, 1990.
McNally, *A Long Strange Trip*.
Perry, *The Haight Ashbury*.

5: THE LOST CHILDREN OF WINDY FEET

Interviews:

Beggs, Edward.
Coyote, Peter.

Documents:

"Huckleberry House and the Summer of Love," Beggs.
Runaway children's correspondence, Huckleberry House files, SFPL History Center.

Newspapers and Magazines:

San Francisco Chronicle, Feb. 8, 1966; Apr. 19, 1966; Jan. 2, 3, 1967; Oct. 21, 1967; Dec. 12, 1968; Jan. 31, 1969.
San Francisco Examiner, Mar. 27, 1965; Apr. 28, 1966; Aug. 10, 1967.
New York Times, Feb. 5, 6, Oct. 11, 1966; Sept. 27, 1967; Apr. 9, 1968.
New York Times Magazine, May 10, 1964, "Why They Run Away from Home."
Wall Street Journal, Aug. 11, 1969.
Life, Nov. 3, 1967, "Runaway Kids."

Books:

Beggs, Edward (Larry), *Huckleberry's for Runaways.* New York, Ballantine Books, 1969.
Staller, Karen M., *Runaways: How the Sixties Counterculture Shaped Today's Practices and Policies.* New York: Columbia University Press, 2006.

6: STREET MEDICINE

Interviews:

Smith, Dr. David
Welch, Calvin

Newspapers and Magazines:

San Francisco Chronicle, October 8, 1967.
San Francisco Examiner, June 8, 1987.
San Francisco Medicine, Sept. 2009, "David Smith: Pioneering Community-Based Health Care."

Documents:

"We Built This Clinic on Rock 'n' Roll," essay by Dr. David Smith, *www.DrDave.org.*
"The Evolution of Addiction Medicine and Its San Francisco Roots," draft essay by Dr. David Smith, courtesy of the author.

Books:

Smith, David E., and Luce, John, *Love Needs Care: A History of San Francisco's Haight-Ashbury Free Medical Clinic and Its Pioneer Role in Treating Drug-Abuse Problems.* Boston: Little, Brown & Co., 1971.
Sturges, Clark S., *Dr. Dave.* Walnut Creek, CA: Devil Mountain Books, 1993.

7: MURDER ON SHAKEDOWN STREET

Interviews:

Brown, Willie   Hall, Harry
Cleary, Jack   Sullivan, Marion
Davis, Belva

Documents:

Proceedings of the coroner's hearing on the death of Charles Sullivan, Aug. 18, 1966, case number 1966–1545.

Newspapers and Magazines:

San Francisco Chronicle, Oct. 17, 21, 1963; Aug. 3, 1966; Aug. 31, 1971; July 21, 2008
San Francisco Examiner, Aug. 2, 1966
San Francisco Examiner Pictorial Living, Sept. 2, 1962, "The Man Who's Renewing the City," Jerry Adams.
San Francisco Sun-Reporter, Aug. 13, 1966.
National Journal, Sept. 18, 1971, "Herman Death Ends an Era."

Documentary Films:

The Fillmore, directed by Rick Butler, produced by KQED and PBS, 2000.

Books:

Graham, Bill, and Greenfield, Robert, *Bill Graham Presents: My Life Inside Rock and Out.* Cambridge, MA: Da Capo Press, 2004.
Hartman, Chester, *City for Sale: The Transformation of San Francisco.* Berkeley, CA: University of California Press, 2002.
Pepin, Elizabeth, and Watts, Lewis, *Harlem of the West: The San Francisco Fillmore Jazz Era.* San Francisco: Chronicle Books, 2006.

8: THE NAPOLEON OF ROCK

Interviews:

Berg, Peter	Selvin, Joel
Coyote, Peter	Smith, Dr. David
Hart, Mickey	Sullivan, David
Kantner, Paul	Stepanian, Michael
Lewis, Peter	Wenner, Jann
Miller, Jerry	Zagaris, Michael
Rohan, Brian	

Newspapers and Magazines:

San Francisco Chronicle, Oct. 28, 29, Nov. 3, 1991; Apr. 17, 1994.
San Francisco Examiner Image magazine, Dec. 8, 1991, "Raging Bill," Paul Kantner and Mickey Hart.
San Francisco Good Times, Dec. 10, 1971; July 9, 1973.

Books:

Glatt, John, *Rage & Roll: Bill Graham and the Selling of Rock.* New York: Birch Lane Press, 1993.
Graham and Greenfield, *Bill Graham Presents.*
Hertzberg, Hendrick, *Politics: Observations and Arguments, 1966–2004.* New York: Penguin Books, 2005.
McNally, *A Long Strange Trip.*
Selvin, *Summer of Love.*

9: THE DAILY CIRCUS

Interviews:

Newhall, Jon
Wenner, Jann

Oral Histories:

Newhall, Scott, the Bancroft Library, University of California at Berkeley, interviewed
    1988–1989.

Documents:

Scott Newhall files, SFPL History Center.

Newspapers and Magazines:

American Journalism Review, Jan.–Feb. 1999, "The Battle of the Bay," Cynthia Gorney.
Old Town Newhall Gazette, Jan.–Feb. 1996, "The Life and Times of Scott Newhall,"
    Ruth Waldo Newhall.
San Francisco Chronicle, Dec. 23, 2004; June 21, 2009.
Rolling Stone, July 17, 1975, "Ralph Gleason in Perspective," edited by Jann Wenner.
San Francisco magazine, July and August 1968, "My Search for Scott Newhall," two-part
    article, John Luce.

10: SAN FRANCISCO'S MORNING KISS

Interviews:

  Brown, Willie
  Caen, Christopher
  Moose, Ed

Newspapers and Magazines:

San Francisco Chronicle, Mar. 31, 1996, Feb. 3, 13, May 11, 1997; April 5, 2009.
San Francisco Chronicle, Herb Caen columns, 1967–1997.
San Francisco Examiner, Feb. 2, 1997.
Harper's Magazine, Nov. 2009, "Final Edition," Richard Rodriguez.
San Francisco City Magazine, May 14, 1975, "Herb Caen: San Francisco's All-Time
    Favorite Sweetheart," Burton Wolfe.
San Francisco Focus, Apr. 1986, "The Interview: Herb Caen, The 70-Year-Old Kid, " Ken
    Kelley.
San Francisco Focus, Dec. 1987, "The Wooing of Herb Caen," Michael Munzell.
San Francisco Focus, Dec. 1995, "Citizen Caen," Mark Powelson.
San Francisco magazine, Dec. 1978, "The World According to Caen," Wayne Warga.

Books:

Caen, Herb, *Baghdad By-the-Bay,* Garden City, NY: Doubleday & Co., 1950.
Caen, Herb, *The Best of Herb Caen, 1960–1975,* San Francisco: Chronicle Books, 1991.
Conrad, Barnaby, editor, *The World of Herb Caen: San Francisco, 1938–1997,* San Fran-
    cisco: Chronicle Books, 1997.

11: RADIO FREE AMERICA

Interviews:

  Brand, Stewart   Nisker, Wes "Scoop"
  Davis, Patti Reagan   Reagan, Ron
  Hart, Mickey   Rodriguez, Spain
  Lewis, Peter   Wenner, Jann
  Miller, Jerry

Oral Histories:

"R. Crumb in Conversation with Francoise Mouly," Oct. 31, 2010, Jewish Community
   Center, San Francisco.

Documents:

"The History of Crumb," *www.RCrumb.com*.
The Very Best of Moby Grape, Sony, 1993, liner notes by David Fricke.

Newspapers and Magazines:

Austin Chronicle, Jan. 8, 2010, "Naked if I Want To: Moby Grape Now and Then," Louis
   Black.
Time, Apr. 29, 2005, "R. Crumb Speaks," Andrew D. Arnold.

Books:

Cannon, Lou, *Governor Reagan: His Rise to Power.* New York: Public Affairs, 2003.
Davis, Patti, *The Way I See It.* New York: G.P. Putnam's Sons, 1992.
Nisker, Wes "Scoop," *The Big Bang, the Buddha, and the Baby Boom.* New York: Harp-
   erOne, 2004.
Perry, *The Haight Ashbury.*
Selvin, *Summer of Love.*

12: THE PALACE OF GOLDEN COCKS

Interviews:

Hauser, Fayette   Missabu, Rumi
Koldewyn, Richard "Scrumbly"   Rosenthal, Irving

Documents:

"Before the Castro: North Beach, a Gay Mecca," essay by Dick Boyd, *www.foundsf.org*
Kreemah Ritz papers, Cockettes files, SFPL History Center.
"Kaliflower and the Dream Continues," essay by Eric Noble, *www.foundsf.org.*
"The Cockettes," essay by Sebastian, Cockettes files, SFPL History Center.

Newspapers and Magazines:

San Francisco Chronicle, Rex Reed column, Oct. 3, 1971, Dec. 2, 1971.
New York Times, Aug. 17, 2003.
Rolling Stone, Oct. 14, 1971, "Les Cockettes de San Francisco," Maitland Zane.

Documentary Films:

The Cockettes, David Weissman and Bill Weber, co-directors, Strand Releasing Home
   Video, 2002.

Books:

Boyd, *Wide Open Town.*
Sides, *Erotic City.*
Stryker, Susan, and Van Buskirk Jim, *Gay by the Bay: A History of Queer Culture in the
   San Francisco Bay Area.* San Francisco: Chronicle Books, 1996.
Tent, Pam, *Midnight at the Palace: My Life as a Fabulous Cockette.* Los Angeles: Alyson
   Books, 2004.

PART TWO: TERROR
13: A DEATH IN THE FAMILY

Interviews:

Hauser, Fayette   Reisman, Alex
Hallinan, Terence   Stepanian, Michael

Documents:

"The People v. James Martin Gurley," crim. no. 9084, ruling by Court of Appeal of California, First Appellate District, Division One.

Books:

Caserta, Peggy, *Going Down with Janis*. New York: Dell Publishing, 1973.
Dalton, David, *Piece of My Heart: A Portrait of Janis Joplin*. New York: Da Capo, 1991.
Echols, Alice, *Scars of Sweet Paradise: The Life and Times of Janis Joplin*. New York: Holt Paperbacks, 1999.
Friedman, Myra, *Buried Alive: The Biography of Janis Joplin*. New York: Three Rivers Press, 1992.
Joplin, Laura, *Love, Janis*. New York: Harper, 2005.
Selvin, *Summer of Love*.
Sporke, Michael, *Living with the Myth of Janis Joplin: The History of Big Brother and the Holding Company, 1965–2005*, Books on Demand, Norderstedt, Germany, 2003.

14: LUCIFER RISING

Interviews:

Cleary, Jack   Smith, Dr. David
Lewis, Peter   Welch, Calvin
Rohan, Brian

Documents:

"The Green Rebellion: Notes on the Life and Times of American Hippies," essay by Dr. Louis Jolyon West and Dr. James R. Allen, University of Oklahoma digital libraries.

Newspapers and Magazines:

San Francisco Chronicle, Jan. 27, Mar. 15, June 7, Aug. 8, Aug. 17, Dec. 12, 1967.
San Francisco Examiner, Nov. 7, 1997.
Washington Post Magazine, Feb. 23, 1986, "Anton LaVey: America's Satanic Master of Devils, Magic, Music and Madness," Walt Harrington.

Books:

Atkins, Susan, *Child of Satan, Child of God*. New York: Bantam, 1978.
Emmons, Nuel, *Manson in His Own Words*. New York: Grove Press, 1986.
Hayden, Tom, *The Long Sixties: From 1960 to Barack Obama*. Boulder, CO: Paradigm Publishers, 2009.
Lee, Martin A., and Shlain, Bruce, *Acid Dreams: The Complete Social History of LSD— The CIA, the Sixties, and Beyond*. New York: Grove Weidenfeld, 1992.
Perry, *The Haight-Ashbury*.
Sanders, Ed, *The Family*. New York, Thunder's Mouth Press, 2002.
Smith and Luce, *Love Needs Care*.

15: A KNIFE DOWN YOUR THROAT

Interviews:

Brand, Stewart   Lewis, Peter
Coyote, Peter   Wenner, Jann
Hart, Mickey   Zagaris, Michael
Kantner, Paul

Newspapers and Magazines:

San Francisco Chronicle, Dec. 8, 1969.
San Francisco Examiner, Dec. 7, 1969.
Good Times, Jan. 7, Oct. 16, 1970.
Mademoiselle, Mar. 1971, "A Talk with Stephen Gaskin," Mary Cantwell and Amy Gross.
Rolling Stone, Jan. 21, 1970, "Let It Bleed," Lester Bangs et al.
San Francisco magazine, Aug. 1970, "The Rainbow Maker," Geoffrey Link.

Documentary Films:

Gimme Shelter, 1970, directed by Albert and David Maysles, Criterion Pictures.

Books:

Barger, Ralph "Sonny," *Hell's Angel: The Life and Times of Sonny Barger and the Hell's
    Angels Motorcycle Club.* New York: William Morrow, 2000.
Booth, Stanley, *The True Adventures of the Rolling Stones.* New York: Vintage Books,
    1985.
McNally, *A Long Strange Trip.*
Selvin, *Summer of Love.*
Tamarkin, *Got a Revolution.*

16: BENEVOLENT DICTATOR

Interviews:

Alioto, Angela   Roff, Hadley
Feinstein, Dianne   Welch, Calvin
Moose, Ed

Oral Histories:

Alioto, Joseph, Bancroft Library, UC-Berkeley, interviewed 1991–92

Documents:

"Mayor Alioto and the Haight," excerpt from lecture by Calvin Welch,
www.FoundSF.org.

Newspapers and Magazines:

San Francisco Chronicle, Jan. 23, Feb. 20, Mar. 9, Mar. 14, July 18, July 30, Aug. 13,
    Oct. 28, Nov. 9, Nov. 20, Nov. 26, 1968; Nov. 18, 1969; Oct. 21, 1970; Feb. 1, 1998.
San Francisco Examiner California Living, Mar. 24, 1968.
San Francisco Examiner Magazine, Mar. 17, 1996, "King of the City," Kandace Bender.
The Bay Guardian, Oct. 31, 1967, "Shelley, Alioto—It's a Deal!" Bruce Brugmann.
Look magazine, Sept. 23, 1969, "The Web That Links San Francisco's Mayor Alioto and
    the Mafia," Richard Carlson and Lance Brisson.

Books:

Alioto, Angela, *Straight to the Heart*. San Francisco: Russian Hill Press, 1997.
Hartman, *City for Sale*.
Issel, William, *For Both Cross and Flag: Catholic Action, Anti-Catholicism, and National Security Politics in World War II San Francisco*. Philadelphia: Temple University Press, 2010.
Demaris, Ovid, *The Last Mafioso: The Treacherous World of Jimmy Fratianno*. New York: Bantam Books, 1981.

17: LOVE'S LAST STAND

Interviews:

Ferguson, "Sag" Darel   McCarthy, Robert "Mouseman"
Huston, Will "Wild Bill"   Moore, Dan "Spud"
Jaffe, Dana   Serra, Tony
Kever, Steve   Welch, Calvin
Lautzker, Larry "The Hat"   Wickman, Chris

Documents:

"Communes and Housing," essay by Calvin Welch, *www.FoundSF.org*.
Goddam Independent commune newspaper and other Good Earth documents and memorabilia, courtesy of Robert McCarthy.
The Good Earth conversation thread, *www.hipforums.com*.
The People v. Steven Kever, Municipal Court of the City and County of San Francisco, Jan. 18, 1971, Minute Order Holding Person in Contempt and Commitment.

Newspapers and Magazines:

San Francisco Chronicle, Jan. 19, 27, 1971.
Good Times, Jan. 6, 1971; June 2, 1972.

18: DUNGEONS AND DRAGONS

Interviews:

Hanlon, Stuart
Serra, Tony

Documents:

"A Letter to the People," by Nancy Ling Perry and other documents from the Symbionese Liberation Army files, SFPL History Center.

Newspapers and Magazines:

The Bay Guardian, Feb. 27, 1974.
The Black Panther, Nov. 17, 1973.
Daily Californian, Feb. 9, 1974.
Montclarion, Nov. 8, 14, 24, 1973.
New York Times, Nov. 20, 1973.
Oakland Tribune, Mar. 21, 1973.

San Francisco Chronicle, Nov. 7, 9, 1973; Jan. 19, Feb. 11, Apr. 8, 1974; Nov. 28. 1979.
San Francisco Examiner, Jan. 20, 1974.
Village Voice, Feb. 28, 1974.

Books:

Headley, Lake, *Vegas P.I.: The Life and Times of America's Greatest Detective.* New York: Thunder's Mouth Press, 1993.
Jackson, George, *Blood in My Eye.* Baltimore: Black Classic Press, 1996.
Jackson, George, *Soledad Brother: The Prison Letters of George Jackson.* Chicago: Lawrence Hill Books, 1994.
Mitford, Jessica, *Kind and Usual Punishment: The Prison Business.* New York: Vintage, 1974.
Payne, Les, and Findley, Tim, *The Life and Death of the SLA.* New York: Ballantine, 1976.

19: THE REVOLUTION WILL BE TELEVISED

Interviews:

Bortin, Michael   Molinari, Jim
Hallinan, Terence   Weir, David
Hearst, Will

Documents:

Symbionese Liberation Army files, SFPL History Center.

Newspapers and Magazines:

Berkeley Barb, Feb. 14, 22, 1974.
Daily Californian, Mar. 5, 1974.
Detroit Sun, Jan. 22, 1976, "Who Ran the SLA?," Dick Russell.
Los Angeles Times, Feb. 15, Mar. 20, Apr. 7, 17, May 18, 1974.
New York Times, Feb. 15, Apr. 14, May 24, 1974.
Oakland Tribune, Feb. 23, 1974.
Ramparts, May 1974, "Terrorism and the Left."
Rolling Stone, June 20, 1974, "The Revolution Was Televised," Tim Findley.
Rolling Stone, Oct. 23, 1975, "The Inside Story," Howard Kohn and David Weir.
Rolling Stone, Apr. 22, 1976, "The Lost Year of the SLA," Kohn and Weir.
San Francisco Bay Guardian, Feb. 13, May 11, 1974.
San Francisco Chronicle, Feb.19, 23, Mar. 5, 7, 12, 26, Apr. 4, 10, 16, 17, 1974; Nov. 29, 1979.
San Francisco Examiner, Apr. 16, 1974.
Washington Post, Dec. 31, 2006.

Books:

Alexander, Shana, *Anyone's Daughter: The Times and Trials of Patty Hearst.* New York: Viking Press, 1979.
Graebner, William, *Patty's Got a Gun: Patricia Hearst in 1970s America.* Chicago: University of Chicago Press, 2008.
Hearst, Patricia Campbell, *Every Secret Thing.* New York: Doubleday & Co., 1982.
Headley, *Vegas P.I.*
Payne and Findley, *The Life and Death of the SLA.*
Spieler, Geri, *Taking Aim at the President: The Remarkable Story of the Woman Who Shot at Gerald Ford.* New York: Palgrave MacMillan, 2009.

20: BLACK AND WHITE AND RED ALL OVER

Interviews:

Agnos, Art   Coreris, Gus
Brown, Rev. Amos   Jennings, Duffy
Cleary, Jack

Oral Histories:

Alioto, Joseph, Bancroft Library UC-Berkeley

Documents:

www.thezebraproject.blogspot.com.

Newspapers and Magazines:

San Francisco Chronicle, Jan. 30, Apr. 18, May 2, July 10, 1974; Feb. 25, 2007.
People magazine, May 6, 1974, "San Francisco's Alioto: Snarled in a Zebra Dragnet."

Books:

Graysmith, Robert, *Zodiac,* Berkley, New York, 2007.
Howard, Clark, *Zebra: The True Account of the 179 Days of Terror in San Francisco.* New
    York: Richard Marek Publishers, 1979.
Sanders, Earl Prentice, and Cohen, Bennett, *The Zebra Murders: A Season of Killing,
    Racial Madness and Civil Rights.* New York: Arcade Publishing, 2006.

21: THE EMPRESS OF CHINATOWN

Interviews:

Chin, Gordon   Moose, Ed
Lee, Ed   Pak, Rose

Documents:

"Overview of Chinese American-Asian American Political Power in San Francisco,"
    essay by Gordon Chin, Oct. 14, 2008, courtesy of author.

Newspapers and Magazines:

Asian Week, July, 22, 2005.
San Francisco Chronicle, Aug. 4, 1997; Sept. 3, 2000; June 8, 2001; July 7, 2005; Dec.
    2, 2007; Sept. 19, 2010; Jan. 8, 11, 24, Feb. 21, 2011.
San Francisco Examiner, Jan. 31, 1996.

Books:

Chang, Iris, *The Chinese in America: A Narrative History.* New York: Viking, 2003.
Hartman, *City for Sale.*
Robbins, Trina, *Forbidden City: The Golden Age of Chinese Nightclubs.* Cresskill, NJ:
    Hampton Press, 2010.
Tsui, Bonnie, *American Chinatown: A People's History of Five Neighborhoods.* New York:
    Free Press, 2009.

22: SAN FRANCISCO SATYRICON

Interviews:

Alioto, Angela   St. James, Margo
Calcagno, Vince   Tower, Jeremiah
Maupin, Armistead

Documents:

"Ivory Snow Girl, R.I.P.," by Warren Hinckle, *www.counterpunch.org.*

Newspapers and Magazines:

San Francisco Chronicle, July 21 2007.
San Francisco Focus, Oct. 1992, "The Outsider: Interview with Armistead Maupin," Amy Rennert.
San Francisco magazine, Dec. 1977, "The Tale Behind Tales of the City," Nora Gallagher.
San Francisco magazine, June 1979, "The Greening of Margo St. James," Jennifer Thompson.
Smithsonian magazine, July 2007, "Mad, Stark Mad," Armistead Maupin.
Washington Post, Apr. 14, 2009.

Books:

Boyd, Nan Alamilla, *Wide Open Town.*
Hubner, John, *Bottom Feeders: From Free Love to Hard Core—The Rise and Fall of Counterculture Heroes Jim and Artie Mitchell.* New York: Doubleday, 1993.
Maupin, Armistead, *Tales of the City.* New York: Harper, 1994.
Morgan, *I Celebrate Myself.*
Shilts, Randy, *The Mayor of Castro Street: The Life and Times of Harvey Milk.* New York: St. Martin's Press, 2008.
Sides, *Erotic City.*
Tower, Jeremiah, *California Dish: What I Saw (and Cooked) at the American Culinary Revolution.* New York: Free Press 2004.

23: CIVIC WAR

Interviews:

Barbagelata, Paul   Moose, Ed
Brown, Willie   Moscone, Christopher
Burton, John   Peri, Don
Busch, Corey   Sklar, Richard
Hallinan, Terence   St. James, Margo
Maher, Bill   Stepanian, Michael
Molinari, Jim   Welch, Calvin

Documents:

Mayoral campaign literature, 1975, George Moscone files, SFPL History Center.
Personal files of John Barbagelata, courtesy of Paul Barbagelata.

Newspapers and Magazines:

City magazine, Dec. 9, 1975, "The Phenomenal John Barbagelata," Warren Hinckle and
    Marjorie Leland.
Los Angeles Times, Nov. 27. 1998.
New West magazine, Mar. 28, 1977, "The Broken Promises of Mayor Moscone," Phil
    Tracy.
Santa Barbara Independent, Dec. 11, 2008.
San Francisco Chronicle, Dec. 12, 1975; Jan. 8, 9, 1976; Jan. 8, 1977; Nov. 18, 1978;
    Nov. 26, 1998; Dec. 5, 2008.
San Francisco Examiner, May 25, Oct. 6, 24, Nov. 5, 10, Dec. 6, 7, 12, 14, 17, 18, 25,
    26, 29, 1975; Jan 9, 20, July 8, Nov. 27, 1976; Apr. 30, May 9, Aug. 3, Oct. 26, Nov.
    3, 1977; Feb. 1, Apr. 11, May 14, 1978.
San Francisco magazine, Jan. 1976, "Moscone: What's in Store for the City?" Lawrence
    Fanning.

Books:

Brown, Willie, *Basic Brown: My Life and Our Times.* New York: Simon & Schuster, 2008.
Jacobs, John, *A Rage for Justice: The Passion and Politics of Phillip Burton.* Berkeley, CA:
    University of California Press, 1997.
Richardson, James, *Willie Brown: A Biography.* Berkeley, CA: University of California
    Press, 1996.
Shilts, *The Mayor of Castro Street.*
Sides, *Erotic City.*

24: INSIDE MAN

Interviews:

Barbagelata, Paul   Jones, Jim Jr.
Buford, Terri   Reuben, David

Documents:

Personal files of John Barbagelata.
"Madman in Our Midst: Jim Jones and the California Cover Up," essay by Kathleen and
    Tom Kinsolving, *www.rickross.com.*

Newspapers and Magazines:

New York Times, Dec. 17, 1978.
San Francisco Chronicle, June 25, 1976; Jan. 20, July 31, Aug. 1, 1979; Nov. 12. 1998.
San Francisco Examiner, Jan. 21, 1979.

Books:

Klineman, George, and Butler, Sherman, *The Cult That Died: The Tragedy of Jim Jones
    and the Peoples Temple.* New York: Putnam Publishing Group, 1980.
Layton, Deborah, *Seductive Poison: A Jonestown Survivor's Story of Life and Death in the
    Peoples Temple.* New York: Anchor Books, 1998.
Reiterman, Tim, *Raven: The Untold Story of the Rev. Jim Jones and His People,* New York:
    Penguin Group, 2008.

25: SLOUCHING TOWARD SAN FRANCISCO

Interviews:

Brown, Rev. Amos	Jones, Cleve
Buford, Terri	Reuben, David
Busch, Corey	Sklar, Richard
Fortson, Hue	Williams, Rev. Cecil
Jones Jr., Jim	

Documents:

Election Special, Nov. 1979, published by Barbagelata, "Peoples Temple and Joe Freitas." Jonestown Institute files, courtesy of Fielding McGehee III, *www.jonestown.sdsu.edu*. Peoples Temple collection, California Historical Society, San Francisco.

Newspapers and Magazines:

New West, Aug. 1, 1977, "Inside Peoples Temple," Marshall Kilduff and Phil Tracy.
San Francisco Chronicle, Nov. 23, 2003.
San Francisco Examiner, Aug. 7, 1977; Nov. 20, 1978.

Documentary Films:

The Fillmore, Butler, KQED.
Jonestown: The Life and Death of Peoples Temple, "American Experience," PBS, 2006.

Books:

Klineman, *The Cult That Died*.
Layton, *Seductive Poison*.
Moore, Rebecca, ed., *Peoples Temple and Black Religion in America*, Bloomington, IN: Indiana University Press, 2004.
Reiterman, *Raven*.
Shilts, Randy, *The Mayor of Castro Street*.
Williams, Cecil, *I'm Alive: An Autobiography*, San Francisco: Harper & Row, 1980.

26: PROPHET OF DOOM

Interviews:

Barbagelata, Paul
Leach, Norman

Documents:

Personal files of John Barbagelata.

Newspapers and Magazines:

City magazine, Dec. 9, 1975, Hinckle and Leland.
San Francisco Chronicle, Jan. 12, Feb. 9, 1976; Mar. 7, July 18, Aug. 3, 4, 1977.
San Francisco Examiner, Jan. 12, 1976; Jan. 25, Mar. 3, Aug. 3, 4, 1977.
San Francisco Today, Sept. 21, 1977; Jan. 17, 1978.
San Francisco Weekly, Nov. 18, 1998.

27: EXODUS

Interviews:

  Agnos, Art   Kilduff, Marshall
  Jones Jr., Jim Reuben, David

Documents:

Internal SF District Attorney's office memo from Bob Graham to Joe Freitas and Danny Weinstein, Aug. 28, 1977.
Peoples Temple collection, California Historical Society.

Books:

Layton, *Seductive Poison.*
Reiterman, *Raven.*

28: RAPTURE IN THE JUNGLE

Interviews:

  Fortson, Hue
  McGehee III, Fielding

Documents:

"The Death Tape," Jonestown Audiotape Project, transcript prepared by McGehee, *www.jonestown.sdsu.edu.*
"Christine Miller: A Voice of Independence," essay by Michael Bellefountaine, Jonestown Institute, *www.jonestown.sdsu.edu.*

Newspapers and Magazines:

San Francisco Chronicle, Nov. 17, 1998.

Books:

Layton, *Seductive Poison.*
Reiterman, *Raven.*

29: THE RECKONING

Interviews:

  Brown, Willie Leach, Norman
  Jones Jr., Jim Reuben, David

Documents:

George Moscone files, SFPL History Center.

Newspapers and Magazines:

Lincoln (NE) Journal Star, Mar. 12, Aug. 24, 2004, "Leach Gets One Year in Assault."
San Francisco Chronicle, Nov. 17, 2008.
San Francisco Examiner, Nov. 19, 20, 1978.

30: A TALE OF TWO CITIES

Interviews:

Busch, Corey   Moscone, Christopher
Falzon, Frank   Sklar, Richard
Jones, Cleve   St. James, Margo
Kopp, Quentin

Documents:

Harvey Milk, George Moscone files, SFPL History Center.

Newspapers and Magazines:

San Francisco Chronicle, June 24, 1977; April 11, Sept. 16, 1978.
San Francisco Examiner, Nov. 28, 1978.

Books:

Shilts, *The Mayor of Castro Street*.
Weiss, Mike, *Double Play· The Hidden Passions Behind the Double Assassination of George Moscone and Harvey Milk*. San Francisco: Vince Emery Productions, 2010.

31: DAY OF THE GUN

Interviews:

Brown, Willie   Jennings, Duffy
Cleary, Jack   Jones, Cleve
Falzon, Frank   Molinari, Jim
Feinstein, Dianne   Moscone, Christopher

Documents:

Harvey Milk, George Moscone files, SFPL History Center.

Newspapers and Magazines:

Los Angeles Times, Nov. 21, 1993; Nov. 23, 1998.
San Francisco Chronicle, Nov. 10, 16, 21, 28, 29, 1978; Feb. 1, 1979; Nov. 18, 26, 2008.
San Francisco Examiner, Nov. 27, 28, 29, Dec. 2, 3, 1978; Nov. 9, 1998.
San Francisco Focus, Nov. 1988, "New Revelations About the City Hall Assassinations," edited by Amy Rennert.

Books:

Brown, *Basic Brown*.
Shilts, *The Mayor of Castro Street*.
Weiss, *Double Play.*

PART THREE: DELIVERANCE
32: FIRE BY TRIAL

Interviews:

Britt, Harry	Moscone, Christopher
Falzon, Frank	Roff, Hadley
Feinstein, Dianne	Sklar, Richard
Kopp, Quentin	Williams, Cecil
Maher, Bill	

Documents:

Dianne Feinstein files, SFPL History Center.

Newspapers and Magazines:

Los Angeles Times, July 9, 1979.
New York Times, Dec. 3, 11, 1978; Jan. 27, Feb. 10, 16, 1979.
San Francisco Chronicle, Dec. 12, 1978; Feb. 23, 1979.
San Francisco Examiner, Nov. 28, 29, Dec. 4, 5, 1978; Mar. 4, 1979.
San Francisco Examiner California Living, Apr. 29, 1984, "Bucking That White Bow Image," Carol Pogash.
Bay Views, Apr. 1981, "San Francisco's First Lady," Betsy Foster.
People, Oct. 8, 1990, "Dianne Feinstein," J.D. Reed.
San Francisco magazine, July 1975, "What Makes Feinstein Tick?," Mavis Groza.
San Francisco magazine, Dec. 1981, "Feinstein in the Middle," Jeff Gillenkirk.

Documentary Films:

Uncle Bob, 2010, directed by Robert Oppel, *www.unclebobmovie.com.*

Books:

Shilts, *The Mayor of Castro Street.*
Weiss, *Double Play.*

33: THE CENTER HOLDS

Interviews:

Britt, Harry	Molinari, Jim
Feinstein, Dianne	Nothenberg, Rudy
Fertig, Jack "Sister Boom Boom"	Pak, Rose
Hennessy, Mike	Sklar, Richard

Documents:

Dianne Feinstein files, SFPL History Center.

Newspapers and Magazines:

New York Times, May 23, 24, July 6, Sept. 5, 8, 27, Oct. 8, Nov. 1, 6, Dec. 24, 1979; June 29, July 29, Dec. 10, 1982; Sept. 9, 1984.
San Francisco Chronicle, Mar. 1, Apr. 6, May 3, 22, 23, July 9, 13, Oct. 8, 26, Dec. 10, 11, 12, 1979; Jan. 24, Mar. 13, Dec. 14, 1981.

34: STRANGE ANGELS

Interviews:

Ammiano, Tom	Hicks, Dwight
Britt, Harry	McLean, Lindsy
Dean, Fred	Policy, Carmen
DeBartolo Jr., Eddie	Seifert, George
Dickey, Glenn	Turner, Keena
Edwards, Harry	Walsh, Craig
Fahnhorst, Keith	Zagaris, Michael

Newspapers and Magazines:

San Francisco Chronicle, Sept. 2, 4, Oct. 12, 14, 15, 26, 27, Nov. 2, 10, 23, Dec. 2, 8, 23, 29, 31, 1981; Jan. 15, 18, 19, 20, 22, 1982; Apr. 22, 2008.
San Francisco Examiner, Sept. 21, Dec 27, 1981; Jan. 3, 4, 5,10, 1982.
San Francisco Examiner Image, Oct. 6, 1985, "Eddie D.," Burr Snider.

Documentary Films:

Distant Replay: Kezar Stadium, YouTube.

Books:

Barber, Phil and Zagaris, Michael, *We Were Champions: The 49ers' Dynasty in Their Own Words.* Chicago: Triumph Books, 2002.
Dickey, Glenn, *Glenn Dickey's 49ers: The Rise, Fall and Rebirth of the NFL's Greatest Dynasty.* Roseville, CA: Prima Publishing, 2000.
Harris, David, *The Genius: How Bill Walsh Reinvented Football and Created an NFL Dynasty.* New York: Random House, 2008.
Montana, Joe, and Raissman, Bob, *Audibles: My Life in Football.* New York: William Morrow & Co., 1986.
Walsh, Bill, *Building a Champion: On Football and the Making of the 49ers.* New York: St. Martin's Press, 1990.
Walsh, Bill, *The Score Takes Care of Itself: My Philosophy of Leadership.* New York: Portfolio Penguin Group, USA, 2009.

35: PLAYING AGAINST GOD

Interviews:

Bertelli, Cheryl	Hicks, Dwight
Dean,Fred	Policy, Carmen
DeBartolo Jr., Eddie	Seifert, George
Fahnhorst, Keith	Turner, Keena
Feinstein, Dianne	Zagaris, Michael

Newspapers and Magazines:

San Francisco Chronicle, Jan. 1, 2, 4, 5, 6, 7, 8, 9, 10, 11, 12, 15, 17, 18, 23, 25, 26, 1982; July 31, Aug. 9, 10, 2007.
San Francisco Examiner, Dec. 27, 1981.

Books:

Bayless, Skip, *God's Coach: The Hymns, Hype and Hypocrisy of Tom Landry's Cowboys.*
New York: Fireside, 1990.
Dickey, *Glenn Dickey's 49ers.*
Harris, *The Genius.*
Montana, *Audibles.*
Myers, Gary, *The Catch: One Play, Two Dynasties, and the Game That Changed the NFL.*
New York: Crown, 2009.
Walsh, *Building a Champion.*

36: THE CITY OF SAINT FRANCIS

Interviews:

Alioto, Angela	Jones, Cleve
Barbagelata, Paul	Maupin, Armistead
Britt, Harry	McLean, Lindsy
Calcagno, Vince	Reagan, Ron
Falzon, Frank	Selvin, Joel
Feinstein, Dianne	Volberding, Dr. Paul
Florez, Elisa	

Documentary Films:

Life Before the Lifeboat: San Francisco's Courageous Response to the AIDS Outbreak, produced and directed by Shipra Shukla, 2009.
We Were Here, directed by David Weissman and Bill Weber, Red Flag Releasing, 2011.

Newspapers and Magazines:

Los Angeles Times, Oct.22, 1985.
New York Times, May 22, Oct. 22, Dec. 14, 1985.
San Francisco Chronicle, Jan. 16, 1981; Sept. 18, 1998; July 26, 2003; June 8, 2004; Mar. 10, 2005; June 4, 2006.
San Francisco Examiner Image, June 15, 1986, "Safe Sex on the Silver Screen," David Talbot.
Mother Jones, Apr. 1985, "The AIDS Mecca of the World," Alexis Jetter; "At Risk," David Talbot and Larry Bush.
Noe Valley Voice, Feb. 2006, "Ruth Brinker: A Hero in Our Midst."
People, Nov. 4, 1985, "The Suicide of Dan White Brings a Notorious San Francisco Murder Case to a Bizarre End," David Van Biema.
Time, Oct. 24, 1983, "AIDS Dilemma."

Books:

Jones, Cleve, *Stitching a Revolution: The Making of an Activist.* San Francisco: Harper, 2000.
Shilts, Randy, *And the Band Played On: Politics, People and the AIDS Epidemic.* New York: St. Martin's Press, 1987.

INDEX

ABOUT THE AUTHOR

DAVID TALBOT is the author of the *New York Times* bestseller *Brothers: The Hidden History of the Kennedy Years*. The founder of *Salon*, he has been hailed a "pioneer of online journalism" by the *New York Times*. Talbot has worked as a senior editor for *Mother Jones* magazine and has written for numerous publications. He lives with his family in San Francisco.